Handbook of
Individual Differences,
Learning, and
Instruction

Handbook of Individual Differences, Learning, and Instruction

David H. Jonassen
Pennsylvania State University

Barbara L. Grabowski
Pennsylvania State University

IEA LAWRENCE ERLBAUM ASSOCIATES, PUBLISHERS
1993 Hillsdale, New Jersey   Hove and London

Lawrence Erlbaum Associates, Inc., Publishers
365 Broadway
Hillsdale, New Jersey 07642

Library of Congress Cataloging-in-Publication Data

Jonassen, David H., 1947-
  Handbook of individual differences, learning, and instruction /
David H. Jonassen, Barbara L. Grabowski.
      p.   cm.
  Includes bibliographical references and index.
  ISBN 0-8058-1412-4. -- ISBN 0-8058-1413-2 (pbk.)
  1. Learning, Psychology of. 2. Cognitive styles.
3. Individualized instruction. I. Grabowski, Barbara Louise
Hopkins, 1948-   . II. Title.
LB1060.J66 1993
370.15'23--dc20   93-12909
                                         CIP

Books published by Lawrence Erlbaum Associates are printed on acid-free paper, and their
bindings are chosen for strnegth and durability.

Printed in the United States of America

10 9 8 7 6 5 4

Contents

Dedication

This book is dedicated to the individuals who mean so much to us: Cristen Jonassen and Anne (Pat) Hopkins, who in their own unique ways model for us an intense passion for life and serve as a constant source of inspiration.

Acknowledgments

First, symbolically and practically, we would like to recognize two of the most important researchers in the field, Lee J. Cronbach and Richard E. Snow, for their incredible contributions to the literature, not the least of which was their biblical *Aptitudes and Instructional Methods* in 1977. Although they did not contribute directly to this work, they made significant indirect contributions by instigating our curiosity about the role of individual differences in learning and instruction.

Second, many students in many sections of many courses have contributed many ideas to this work, including Sherwood Wang, Marion J. Honemann, Judith Kemp, Jeanne Cole, Mary Ann Kersten, Jim Farris, Susan Ellis, Daisey Holt, Valerie Siml, Robert Janka, Pat Foley, Patti Skari, LaVon Honnick, Carolyn Cummings, Karen Pessler, Kathy Jones, Kelly Allmer, Earline Hill, Martin Ryder, Mark Davidson, and Eleanor Lehman.

Third, valuable and tireless research assistance digging out little known references, summarizing studies, and providing critical comment at critical moments was provided by Eileen Schroeder and Rita Schnittgrund.

Fourth, we would like to acknowledge our appreciation for the insightful comments from our anonymous reviewers and Glenn Snelbecker.

Fifth, this manuscript came to life with the invaluable writing and editorial assistance provided by Christopher Rynd.

Sixth and finally, we would like to acknowledge educators and designers everywhere who have struggled to understand the labyrinthine complexes of the learning process, who have puzzled about the role of the individual in the process and what they could do, if anything, to better understand and exploit those differences.

INTRODUCTION

Assumptions of the Book

The study of individual differences is often referred to as *differential psychology*. Differential psychology investigates the role of individual differences such as intelligence, cognitive styles, and personality on human behavior. This book is about the differential psychology of learning and instruction. It describes a range of individual differences and the ways that they impact learning and responding to instruction. Although many forms of human behavior are manifested by individuals, our concern in this book is only with learning behavior and learning processes.

In the first part of this book, we provide a model for considering the range of individual differences by describing differences in learning outcomes, differences in instructional methods, and the interactions between them. Much of the research base for these first three chapters comes from aptitude-by-treatment interaction (ATI) research. The ATI research (described in more detail in Chapter 2) investigated the effects of learner aptitudes and traits on learning outcomes from different forms of instruction. According to this research, learners with different traits will not respond similarly to each form of instruction. An outgrowth of this hypothesis, investigated in Chapter 1 and throughout the book, is that learners with different traits will be variably successful in learning any specific task or content depending on the mental operations required for the task and their own aptitudes and styles. Although both of these beliefs are intuitively obvious to any experienced educator, the research base is inconsistent. Support for these hypotheses is less than definitive. We discuss limitations, such as insufficient and poorly executed research, in Chapter 2. There are, however, some reasons for reviewing this research and using an ATI model to study individual differences:

> 1. *Individual differences play an important role in learning and instruction.* Every learner filters instruction through a set of individual difference filters or lenses. Individual difference filters may prevent the mental assimilation or accommodation of ideas by the learner. Individual difference lenses will focus the skills and content in ways that will affect how any individual learns. The effects of those differences are universal.
> 2. *Awareness of individual differences will make educators (teachers and instructional designers) more sensitive to their role in learning.* At the very least, this awareness may provide educators

with a better understanding of difficulties that arise for certain learners in relation to specific tasks.

3. *ATI research provides a descriptive model for considering the role of individual differences in learning that will be useful in directing further investigation.* More and better research may enable those descriptive theories to be translated into prescriptive theories. This book will be successful to the degree that the reader is willing to project the role of differences onto the learning process and adapt the nature of instruction or the type of learning outcomes based upon some individual differences. ATI hypotheses provide a model for instructional descriptions and prescriptions. As a model, they are useful for understanding the role of individual differences in the learning process. In this book, we make prescriptions based upon the available research, our interpretations of the literature, and more often than not, projections or conjectures about interactions that we believe may occur. It is important to note that many of our implications and predictions are *not* validated by existing research; however, they are based on reasonable inferences that may be used by the reader as hypotheses for conducting research or as metaphors or as useful heuristics for describing how to adapt instruction to individual differences.

In Parts II through VI, we review different dimensions of individual differences and how they interact with learning and instruction. Part II focuses on mental abilities--the components of intelligence. Mental abilities enable humans to interpret information and learn from it. The chapters in Part II describe three models that seek to map these components of intelligence.

Each individual, discussed later in further detail, possesses a unique pattern of mental abilities. These patterns of abilities are described by the various cognitive controls and cognitive styles reviewed in Parts III and IV of the book. These individual difference characteristics describe the ways in which humans are able to perceive and conceive interactions with their environment. The chapters in Part III describe cognitive controls, which are more similar to mental abilities than the cognitive styles in Part IV. Therefore, they affect learning more directly. The chapters in Part IV describe cognitive styles that are patterns for extracting information from the environment and for organizing and making sense of what learners acquire. Both cognitive controls and styles reflect patterns of thinking in learners, and both may be described as components of personality.

When learners interact with various modes of instruction, they develop preferred patterns for engaging the physical, mental, and emotional requirements imposed by those learning modes. These are known as learning styles and are treated in Part V of the book.

As described in Part V, an individual's personality is comprised of cognitive, emotional, and motivational components. The cognitive components are the aforementioned cognitive styles and controls. The latter two affect the individual's ability and disposition to learn. The chapters in this part of the book concern themselves with the various emotional and motivational characteristics that interact with learning and instruction.

Part VII may seem to diverge from the previous sections in that it does not deal directly with learner tendencies or propensities for learning. Rather, the two chapters attempt to characterize the effects of a learner's previously acquired knowledge on his or her ability to learn. Prior knowledge and ability can be important factors in projecting the effectiveness of specific instructional techniques.

A book is necessarily linear in sequence. It proceeds from the first to the last page. Such a linear structure is inappropriate for describing the complex interrelationships between the content in the different parts of the book. In Fig. I.1, we attempted to map these interrelationships to provide a diagram of the underlying structure of the content in this book. Mental abilities, as reflected by cognitive controls and styles, which are reflected by learning styles, enable learners to interact with instruction. Personality influences the learner's emotional stability and motivation to learn. And what an individual already knows affects his or her ability to learn from instruction. The goal of studying all of these is to better understand the individual's role in producing learning from instruction.

Geographic Metaphor

Sternberg (1990) described a number of "metaphors of mind." These metaphors have motivated theory and research on intelligence over the past few decades. Each metaphor represents a different research paradigm for thinking about and investigating the nature of intelligence. Each metaphor, needless to say, engages a different set of assumptions about the mind and intelligence.

We have chosen the geographic metaphor to describe individual differences. The geographic metaphor views individual differences as a map of the mind. A geographer of individual differences seeks to develop a topographical map of the mind of the individual. Each individual has a different terrain, as illustrated in Fig. I.2.

The study of individual differences is complex. In this book, we review theories and models of intelligence, cognitive styles, personality, learning styles, and prior knowledge. These perspectives cannot be effectively conveyed on a two-dimensional road map. A landscape metaphor for describing individual differences is far more appropriate to the complexity of the subject matter. The individual's mind can be viewed as a landscape of traits and abilities. Each individual landscape varies. Each

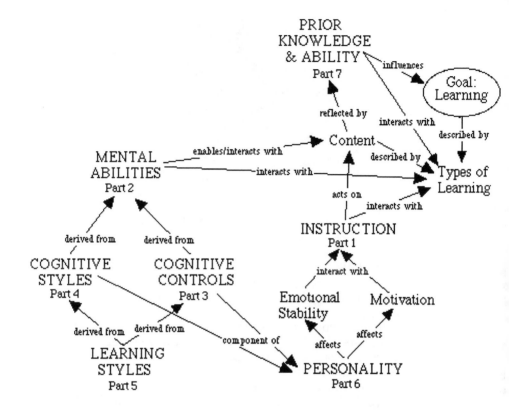

Fig. I.1. Interrelationships between parts of the book.

consists of peaks and valleys. The peaks represent trait strengths, whereas the valleys represent absences of specific learning abilities. That is, the relief on an individual's landscape treats abilities and personality variables as unipolar values. The particular combination of aptitudes and traits possessed by each individual is reflected in the individual's cognitive styles, personality, and learning styles. That is, the cognitive, personality, and learning styles described in this book reflect the individual's combination of aptitude/trait strengths and weaknesses (peaks and valleys on his or her mental landscape) Completing the geographic metaphor, we say that the study of individual differences is similar to that of a mental cartographer mapping the ranges of individual traits.

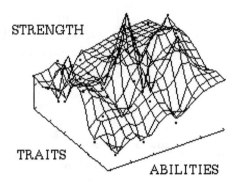

Fig. I.2. Landscape of traits and abilities.

Goals of the Book

Our goals (or objectives, if you prefer) include the following:

1. We want to make you aware, in a concise way, of the range and types of individual differences that interact with learning and instruction. Individual differences are learning filters. They mediate the process of learning in overt and subtle ways. We hope, as a result of reading these descriptions, you will be able to recognize these differences in your students or in yourself, and come closer to an understanding of the roles these differences play in the learning process.

2. We have attempted to synthesize the research, theory, and experiences about individual differences into an accessible, usable, and meaningful explanation of the range of individual differences that relate to learning and instruction. As such, we hope that it is a useful handbook. To support this goal, we use a consistent chapter structure. Most chapters are organized using a structure that consists of the following components:

> Description of the individual difference
> characteristic differences
> Related individual differences
> Instruments for measuring the individual difference
> Theoretical background
> Individual differences and learning
> > Research
> > Implications of the characteristics and research
> Individual differences and instruction
> > Research

Implications of the characteristics and research
References
Bibliography

3. We hope to stimulate additional research in aptitude-by-treatment and aptitude-by-task interactions. The research base is in need of further development. By making information on these differences accessible and by suggesting possible topics or hypotheses in our conclusions, we expect to stimulate the generation of additional research that may substantiate these conclusions or generate more useful ones.

4. We hope to provide design guidelines for accommodating individual differences in instructional design. The most thorough review of instructional design models (Andrews & Goodson, 1980) showed that although most instructional design and development models referred to individual differences or learner characteristics, their design recommendations, procedures, processes, or even principles for accommodating them were virtually nonexistent. So, in this book, we hope to at least partially fill a prominent gap in the instructional design literature by providing some *guidelines* for how to accommodate them in practice.

We have included, in each chapter, sections that detail the implications of the individual differences being discussed for learning and instruction. In those sections, we reviewed research on learning and instruction related to each individual difference. Based on that research we make recommendations about the types of interactions that have occurred or may plausibly occur. Those interactions are based upon actual research (marked with a •) or based on speculation about plausible interactions with the types of learning described in Chapter 1 or types of instruction described in Chapter 2 (marked with an *).

Uses of the Book

As indicated in the Goals section of this introduction, we hope that this book will stimulate additional research on the role of individual differences, learning, and instruction. We see this handbook as a reference tool as well as an instructional tool. The consistencies in structure that we have built into the book should facilitate that goal by providing easier access to information and by underscoring the relationships between the various individual differences and their data.

So, we hope that this book serves the following functions as outlined in Table I.1:
• *an instructional text,* the book theoretically and practically describes a range of individual differences that interact with learning outcomes and instructional methods in normal learners.

- *a reference handbook,* the book facilitates research by reviewing pre-existing descriptions of instrumentation and suggesting research hypotheses.
- *a design guide,* the book attempts to explain why learners respond as they do to different learning tasks and instructional methods and recommends learning outcomes and instructional methods that may benefit the range of learners.

Just as this book may support different functions, it can, we believe, also serve different audiences. As a textbook, it will most likely be used in advanced undergraduate and graduate courses in educational psychology. For universities that offer courses in differential psychology, this book could serve as a primary course text with, of course, the expectation that every chapter probably would not be addressed. It could also serve as a supplementary text in a variety of education and psychology courses.

Perhaps the primary function of the book is as a reference guide for graduate students and researchers in a variety of disciplines that are affected by individual differences. To support its use as a reference book, we have employed a consistent chapter structure that clearly identifies the major types of information that students or researchers would seek, such as instrumentation, research, and implications. It is the implications section that researchers may find most interesting because the implications, although not all supported by empirical research, are reasonable inferences that may serve as hypotheses for future research. Our hope is that this book may support a range of future research on individual differences.

Finally, this book may function as a design guide for educational practitioners. Teachers may use it to help them understand and explain the role of individual differences in learning. It may also assist in the development of individual student lesson plans as prescribed in such plans as Individually Guided Education (IGE), Individually Prescribed Instruction, and so on. This book may also be a tool for helping instructional designers, courseware designers, and trainers to develop adaptive instructional programs and courseware.

This book may be used in any of the ways described earlier by a variety of users. There are doubtless uses that we have not covered as well. We hope that you find it helpful whatever your need.

Concerns and Limitations

There are many compromises required in writing a book. Our major compromise is the selection of breadth over the kind of coverage that could offer a deeper analysis of each of the individual differences described. Greater depth is problematic for a number of reasons. First, the characteristics described in this book vary in their specificity and certainly in the amount of research literature describing them. Several, such as

Function	For	In	To Support As
Textbook	Upper level undergraduate and graduate students	Education, Psychology, Educational Psychology, Health Education, Instructional Design, Applied Psychology, Cognitive/Computer Science	*Primary text* in an individual differences course (doubtful every chapter addressed) *Supplementary text* in Educational Psychology, Teacher Education, Instructional Design courses
Reference Handbook	Graduate students	Educational Psychology, Applied Psychology, Instructional Design	Reviewing research on individual differences
	Researchers	Educational Psychology, Learning and Instruction, Instructional Design	Reviewing research, generating hypotheses
Design Guide	Teachers, educators, administrators	Primary, secondary schools, community colleges (especially), universities	Assessing or explaining learner differences; individually prescribed instruction, adapting instruction to learners
	Instructional designers, course and courseware designers, trainers	Business, industry, military, agencies, universities, community colleges	Developing adaptive training programs, adaptive courseware

Table I.1. Uses of the book.

cognitive flexibility, have only a few research studies that have been conducted, whereas others, such as field independence, have books written about them.

In addition to the disparity in available research literature, we are constrained by very real page restrictions. If we attempted to exhaustively represent all of the research literature and implications of every individual difference, this book would exceed a thousand pages. It would also be difficult to maintain the type of handbook orientation for which we are striving.

In trying to fulfill the various functions, for all the various audiences to perform all the various tasks described in Table I.1, we have implemented a consistent chapter structure. It is possible that the structure that we have chosen does not support all functions and purposes equally well. We hope that the structure enhances its use and regret any diminution of use caused by the structure for any purpose.

In researching the literature base for each characteristic, we analyzed and reported only those studies that relate fairly directly to intentional learning outcomes and instruction with "normal" student populations. This is a handbook for designers and teachers of non-"special" student populations. Much of the research on these differences involved special population learners. Our review of the literature in each chapter omitted research on counseling or therapy, administration, and other related fields. We also excluded research that dealt with special education. Although we believe that such research is important, we are instructional designers and learning theorists, not special educators. Clearly, we are well outside our domain of expertise in the realm of special education literature. Therefore, we make no claims about the applicability of any of these ideas to special needs populations.

In preparing these sections, we conducted retrospective literature reviews in Psychological Abstracts, Educational Resource Information Center, and Dissertation Abstracts. We attempted to summarize all of the research cited in those databases that investigated learning and instruction with normal learners. However, we did not try to represent all of the research relative to each individual difference.

The implications and inferences that we conclude about these characteristics (which may be taken as recommendations for practice or hypotheses for research) are, whenever possible, based on hard research evidence. As we pointed out earlier, many of the research inferences are flawed by a dearth of research, inconsistent results, inadequate methodology, and a lack of reliability or validity. For individual differences where little research is available or the conclusions from that research are equivocal, which is very common, we use our best professional judgment in drawing those conclusions and conjecturing about possible interactions. We want to make it clear that the implications of practice in each of these chapters are not truths. You may look at them as professional recommendations or as hypotheses for research.

We hope that you, the reader, find this collection of information and the inferences and implications that we drew useful in developing a greater sensitivity to the role of individual differences in the processes of learning and instruction. We truly hope that you will conduct research, formally or informally, about these roles.

References

Andrews, D. H., & Goodson, L. A. (1980). A comparative analysis of models of instructional design. *Journal of Instructional Development, 3* (4), 2-16.

Sternberg, R. J. (1990). *Metaphors of mind: Conceptions of the nature of intelligence.* Cambridge: Cambridge University Press.

PART I

INDIVIDUAL DIFFERENCES IN LEARNING AND INSTRUCTION

1

INDIVIDUALS, DIFFERENCES, AND LEARNING

Introduction

As educators, we often wonder why some students find it difficult to learn whereas others find it easy. Why are students better equipped to learn some skills but not others? Why can't all students learn all skills equally well? Student learning differs because student learning traits differ, and because the thinking process differs depending on what the student is trying to learn. First, student learning traits differ. Individuals vary in their aptitudes for learning, their willingness to learn, and the styles or preferences for how they learn if they choose to. These differences impact the learning process for each student. That is, these learner traits determine to some degree if and how well any individual is able to learn. Second, the nature of the thinking and learning processes varies with the task. The outcomes of learning require that students think in different ways. Third, learner traits interact with learning outcomes and the thinking requirements entailed by them. Different learners will have varying aptitudes for different learning outcomes. This first chapter briefly describes these differences in traits and learning outcomes:

We begin by defining some assumptions about individuals and how they learn. The following assumptions form the structure of this chapter and the foundation for the arguments presented in subsequent chapters.

- Individuals differ in their general skills, aptitudes, and preferences for processing information, constructing meaning from it, and applying it to new situations.
- Individuals also differ in their abilities to perform different school-based or real-world learning tasks and outcomes.
- Different school-based or real-world learning tasks and outcomes require the use of different skills, aptitudes, and preferences.
- These general abilities or preferences affect the student's ability to accomplish different learning outcomes; that is, one's learning aptitude interacts with the accomplishment of learning tasks and outcomes.

Individual Differences in Learning Traits (Aptitudes, Skills, and Preferences)

Learning is a complex process. It requires that a student is willing or motivated to learn, that a student is able to learn, that a student is in a social and academic environment that fosters learning, and that the instruction that is available is comprehensible and effective for the learner. This chapter first focuses on the learner traits that motivate and enable a student to learn. The following list of learner traits (described in subsequent chapters) represents a broad range of differences that span from specific abilities to general styles:

General mental abilities (intelligence)
      Hierarchical abilities (fluid, crystallized, and spatial)
Primary mental abilities
      Products
      Operations
      Content
Cognitive Controls
      Field dependence/independence (global vs. articulated style)
      Field articulation (cognitive flexibility)
      Cognitive tempo (reflectivity/impulsivity)
      Focal attention (scanning/focusing)
      Category width (breadth of categorizing)
      Cognitive complexity/simplicity
      Strong versus weak automatization
Cognitive styles: Information gathering
      Visual/haptic
      Visualizer/verbalizer
      Leveling/sharpening
Cognitive styles: Information organizing
      Serialist/holist
      Conceptual style
Learning styles
      Hill's cognitive style mapping
      Kolb's learning styles
      Dunn and Dunn learning styles
      Grasha-Reichman learning styles
      Gregorc learning styles
Personality: Attentional and engagement styles
      Anxiety
      Tolerance for unrealistic experiences
      Ambiguity tolerance
      Frustration tolerance
Personality: Expectancy and incentive styles

Locus of control
Introversion/extraversion
Achievement motivation
Risk taking vs. cautiousness
Prior knowledge
Prior knowledge and achievement
Structural knowledge

This list of individual differences describes the range of learner traits. These traits, described in subsequent chapters, are of several types that range from specific abilities to general styles. The first type describes intellectual aptitudes for learning. We eschew use of the term *intelligence* because it is too complex, yet too vague, and cannot be correlated with the specific learning requirements of instructional approaches. It is also inconsistent with the geographic metaphor that we use to describe individual differences. Although we all share some understanding about what it means to be intelligent, the term has different meanings for each of us. Also, the sources and causes of intelligence vary. Some people appear to be intelligent because they are experienced, others because they are fluent in language, others because they can comprehend and use abstract ideas. Because of these complexities of the concept of intelligence, we choose to describe it in terms of its constituent mental abilities, both primary and secondary.

The next types of traits are cognitive controls and cognitive styles. The particular combination of mental abilities possessed by an individual determines an individual's cognitive controls and styles. These controls and styles describe how an individual interacts with his or her environment, extracts information from it, constructs and organizes personal knowledge, and then applies that knowledge. Cognitive controls are more closely related to mental abilities, whereas cognitive styles describe more general perceptual and processing characteristics, that is, more general tendencies.

The next type of traits, learning styles, describes learner preferences for different types of learning and instructional activities. These styles are generally measured by self-report techniques that ask individuals how they think that they prefer to learn. As such, they are not tied directly to mental abilities, but rather to more general learner perceptions of their own preferences. They are, however, related to mental abilities because most of us prefer to use the mental abilities and cognitive controls and styles with which we are more skilled and familiar.

Individuals also differ in their personalities, another type of learner traits. Personality describes how an individual interacts with his or her environment and especially with other people. Some see personality as the overarching theory that subsumes all individual differences (see Introduction to part 7). Personality is a complex of mental dispositions to behave in certain ways. In this book, we describe only those personality traits that more directly affect learning. We do not intend to review the entire field of personality.

Finally, individuals differ in their kinds and levels of *prior knowledge*, an important learner trait. Prior knowledge does not describe the ability to know or one's preferred mode of coming to know--just what the individual already knows. Included in this term is prior structural knowledge (what people know and how it is organized) as well as prior achievement. Achievement describes the skills and learning abilities that individuals have previously acquired. Both types of prior knowledge are important predictors of how well an individual is able to learn new ideas and skills.

The large number of learner traits denotes the complexity of the individual learner and the learning process. It is important to note that these are traits, that is, general learner abilities and skills. Specific task-related skills call on combinations of these traits. Each of these traits is treated in greater depth later in the book.

Individual Differences in Learning Tasks and Outcomes

Individual learning varies also because of the mental processing required by the learning task. That is, learning and acquiring different skills and knowledge will demand the use of different sets of traits. A common criticism of schools is that they teach only the rote memorization of facts. In truth, students engage in many complex forms of learning. The types of learning that are required in schools and other educational settings are usually described in terms of taxonomies of learning.

A *taxonomy* is a classification scheme that orders objects or phenomena hierarchically. That is, terms at the top of the taxonomy are more general, inclusive, or complex, subsuming terms at a lower level. Taxonomies are used commonly in the natural sciences to classify animals, plants, elements, and so on. Teachers and instructional designers use taxonomies of learning outcomes to classify either the instructional objectives (or goals) to be accomplished or the test items used to evaluate these goals. Behaviors at the top levels of the taxonomy are more complex than lower level behaviors. Lower level behaviors are prerequisite to higher level behaviors. That is, any level of behavior is dependent on the capability of a learner to perform at the next lower level which is, in turn, dependent on the next lower level ability and so on.

In this section, we briefly present four different learning taxonomies (see Fig. 1.1 for a comparison) that may be used to classify learning outcomes. As you read them, focus on the similarities and differences between these taxonomies. All are presented in a sequence that describes first the easier, lower level skills, and then moves on to the more difficult, higher level outcomes.

Bloom's Taxonomy of Objectives

Bloom is best known for his Taxonomy of Cognitive Objectives (Bloom, Englehart, Furst, Hill, & Krathwohl, 1956; Furst, 1981) that described the range of cognitive behaviors--intellectual abilities or skills involving recall or use of knowledge--which are found in educational testing. Most stated educational outcomes are described by this domain. Bloom also helped to develop taxonomies of affective (interest, attitudes, and values) outcomes (Krathwohl, Bloom, & Masia, 1964) and the psychomotor domain of behaviors including physical, manipulative capabilities involving the senses of touch (kinesthetic) and balance (proprioception) and including typing, sports, and mechanics. In this book, we consider only the cognitive outcomes of learning, which are described in the following hierarchy of learning types.

Knowledge Level. Learning at the knowledge level involves only the recall of facts, terminology, methodology without understanding. Sometimes, knowledge level behavior sounds complex, but no comprehension is expected. For example:
• What is the capital of Zaire?
• State the memory requirement for operating a specific software package.
• State the procedure for discarding Class 6 toxic chemicals.

Comprehension. Comprehension involves elementary understanding and use of knowledge, such as translation, and interpretation. For example:
• Identify examples of pragmatism from the front page of the newspaper.
• Translate the directions for assembling the machine into French.
• Determine preference rankings from bar and circle graphs.

Application. Application requires the abstraction of a rule or generalization from knowledge. The learner then applies it to solve a related problem. For example:
• Determine the hypotenuse of a right triangle.
• Select the appropriate nonparametric statistic to use in analyzing survey data.
• Decide which bedding plants to use in a garden at 7,500 feet above sea level.

Analysis. Analysis involves investigating a knowledge domain, breaking it down, and identifying its component elements and the relationships between those elements. Analysis requires determining the structure or organization of a set of ideas. For example:
• Determine the logical flaw in the traffic flow plan in the downtown area.
• Based on stylistic criteria, decide which 20th century novelist wrote this passage.
• Determine the causes of contaminated reactants in a process.

TAXONOMIES OF LEARNING (Increasing Order of Complexity)			
Bloom	Gagné	Merrill	Leith
Knowledge	Verbal Information Concrete Concept	Remember Facts Concepts Rules Principles	Stimulus Discrimination Response Learning Associations Serial Learning/ Chaining
Comprehension	Defined Concept	Use Concept	Learning Set Formation Concept
Application	Rule Learning	Use Rules	Learning Concept Integration
Analysis	Higher Order Rule Learning	Use Principles	Problem Solving
Synthesis			
Evaluation	Cognitive Strategies	Find Concepts Rules Principles	Learning Schemata

Fig. 1.1. Taxonomies of learning.

Synthesis. Knowledge that has been analyzed can be reassembled into a new form of communication. Deriving a new plan from the elements of the old is synthesis. For example:
• Develop an advertising campaign that conveys stability and reliability.
• Develop a legal defense for a client based on the recent Supreme Court ruling.
• Design a needs analysis that will identify the most significant problems of the organization.

Evaluation. Evaluation is the highest level of cognitive activity. It involves making judgements about some content based on internally generated or externally provided criteria. For example:
• Evaluate an investment portfolio using the criterion of long-term growth.
• Evaluate alternative health plans for yourself and for your company.

- Select the most appropriate roofing material based on mildew resistance and durability.

Gagne's Taxonomy of Learning

Gagne (1970) identified different levels of learning for the purpose of sequencing instruction. He believed that instruction should begin with the simplest skills and proceed hierarchically to greater levels of difficulty. This later version of his taxonomy includes six levels of learning:

Verbal Information. Verbal information is similar to Bloom's knowledge level, requiring learners only to memorize and recall information without understanding or applying it. For example:
- State the amendments to the Bill of Rights.
- State the memory requirements for each piece of application software.
- Recite the building code for electrical circuits.

Concrete Concepts. Concrete concepts are based on discrimination between members and nonmembers of a concept without extensive awareness of the basis for classification. Concrete concepts are typically physical in nature. For example:
- Identify all of the shades of green on the color chart.
- Select circle shapes from a pile of assorted shapes.
- Distinguish resistors from capacitors in the bin of parts.

Defined Concepts. Defined concepts are understood through their definitions, that is, through their defining characteristics. They are the basis for most understanding. For example:
- Identify the "sports cars" at the auto show.
- Identify the previously unseen Picasso paintings in a gallery without reading the labels.
- Identify the types of deciduous trees by the shapes of their leaves and color of their bark.

Rule. Rules are the statement of relationships between two or more concepts. Most often, they indicate cause-effect relationships. Using rules implies that learners apply those statements in a new situation. For example:
- Use a city map to locate and drive to an unfamiliar location.
- Use electrolysis to convert water into oxygen and hydrogen.
- Solve the quadratic equation.

Higher Order Rule. Higher order rules are more general statements of relationships, usually referred to as principles. The use of higher order rules is similar to problem solving. It requires the learner to select, interpret, and apply appropriate rules. For example:
- Exploit loopholes in the contract to gain a competitive advantage.

- Determine the composition of a new chemical compound by selecting and using qualitative analysis.
- Develop an investment strategy to counteract the effects of a recession.

Cognitive Strategy. Cognitive strategies originate systems or techniques for solving problems or for acquiring new information. Learning how to learn is a cognitive strategy. For example:
- Design a traffic plan for downtown Denver.
- Develop a new semiconductor material that carries electric current more efficiently.
- Develop a rehearsal technique for efficiently acquiring a new language.

Merrill's Component Display Theory

Performance-Content Matrix. An underlying assumption of component display theory (CDT) is that different learning outcomes require different instructional conditions. Merrill evolved his own taxonomy of learning, over a period of years, through the analysis of school-based learning outcomes (Merrill, 1973; Reigeluth, Merrill, & Bunderson, 1978). He concluded that almost all learning activities involve facts, procedures, concepts, and principles. Whereas most taxonomies describe learning outcomes only in a single dimension, Merrill's taxonomy describes both the content (the type of information) and the performance level (the actions taken by the learner on the content). One can remember content, use content (one version distinguishes between use with an aid and use unaided), and, in later versions, find content (discover, generate, or use cognitive strategies).

Content Level. CDT classifies levels of content in terms of facts, concepts, procedures, and principles. Facts are arbitrary associations. Concepts are classes of objects or events (the same as concepts in Gagne's and Leith's taxonomies). Procedures are sequences of replicable behavior. Principles are generalized explanations that relate two or more concepts and are used to predict, explain, or infer.

Remember. Remember-level performance is similar to Gagne's verbal information category and Bloom's knowledge level. Other taxonomies tend to lump all remember-level behavior into a single category. Component display theory distinguishes the type of content being remembered. For example:

Remember Fact
- What is the population of Indianapolis?
- What is the symbol for debit in the transaction statement?
- Name the 16th president of the United States.

Remember Concept
• What is the definition of asset?
• What are the chemical characteristics of an isomer?
• List the important characteristics of metamorphic rock.

Remember Procedure
• Describe how to field strip an M16 rifle.
• State the procedures in the preflight checklist for a B-737.
• Describe how to load a 35mm camera.

Remember Rule
• State the formula for Ohm's Law.
• State the Federal Reserve Board's response to increased interest rates.
• Which solvent should be used to remove grease stains from upholstery?

Remember Principle
• Explain the effects of toxic chemicals on the circulation system.
• Describe the ways in which the parliamentary system differs from the U.S. governmental system.
• Explain how an aircraft wing provides lift.

Use. Use-level performance describes the act of applying concepts or principles in new situations. Note that facts cannot be used or found; facts can only be remembered, according to Merrill. Use level is similar to Gagne's class of intellectual skills, Bloom's comprehension and application levels of learning, and Leith's learning set and problem solving. For example:

Use Concept
• Classify this painting as baroque or impressionistic.
• Are those clouds cirrus or cumulus?
• Is this sedimentary rock?

Use Procedure
• Lower the flaps on a 1011 to take-off position.
• Close the cash register at the end of a shift.
• Start a computer program.

Use Rule
• Predict the percentage increase in the density of the negative from a one-stop exposure increase.
• Calculate the amount of equity gained from information on the P&L sheet.
• Determine the height of the outside wall necessary to provide the amount of pitch specified by code.

Use Principle
• Infer the causes of a performance problem in the personnel department.
• Predict the effects of doubling the amount of catalyst injected.
• Explain why a nuclear treaty may not contribute to world peace.

Find. The find level of performance refers to the derivation, discovery, or invention of a new concept, principle, or application. This level corresponds roughly to Gagne's cognitive strategies and Bloom's synthesis level.

Find Concept
• Develop a document classification system that accounts for all entries.
• Rearrange the inventory according to the popularity and potential sales of the items.

Find Procedure
• Develop a new overdue system that will eliminate the the overdue card.
• Write a computer program for entering and sorting the receipts.

Find Rule
• Decide which of Newton's laws to use in solving this physics problem.
• Design new parking regulations to relieve traffic congestion around the new mall.

Find Principle
• Devise and test hypotheses for eliminating sulfur dioxide emissions from this process.
• Design a simulation of the relationship between the arithmetic logic unit and CPU in the computer.

Leith's Taxonomy of Learning

Leith's taxonomy of learning (Leith, 1970, 1971) is concerned only with cognitive behaviors. Leith identified 10 levels of cognitive behavior.

Stimulus Discriminations. This lowest level of cognitive behavior entails the perception of different sounds, shapes, objects, and so forth. The learner's ability to respond in appropriate situations is predicated through his or her ability to perceive differences in situations. For example:
• Distinguish language sounds (e.g., syllables) in a new language.
• Separate resistors from transistors.
• Learn the shapes of traffic control signs.

Response Learning. New learning is usually response learning, that is, learning to make a response given a particular stimulus. Response learning is shaped by practice that is followed by reinforcement. For example:

- Make a Y sound when encountering *ll* in Spanish.
- Call a resistor a resistor, a transistor a transistor, and so forth.
- Turn a valve counterclockwise.
- Activate the on-off switch on a new computer.

Response Integration. Assembling already learned responses in particular ways, using other cues and eliminating errors, results in response integration. For example:
- Insert the charge card properly into the charge machine.
- Tie shoe laces.
- Use *i* before *e* except after *c* when spelling English words.

Associations. Associations become stable connections between stimulus and response. Association requires discriminating between stimuli and making the appropriate responses without prompting. For example:
- State the capital of North Carolina.
- Recall an associate's phone number.
- State the compensation formula for district salesmen.

Serial Learning/Chaining. Chaining associations together in a sequence results in serial learning. In serial learning, a response creates a situation that becomes a stimulus for the next response, which cues the next response, and so on. For example:
- Start your car.
- Apply the sequence of steps for copying a file from one disk to another.
- Attach a computer to a printer.

Learning Set Formations. Learning set formations involves the application of appropriate chains of behavior in solving specific problems. These problems typically have no exceptions and are performed in nearly the same way. For example:
- Subtract numbers.
- Ring credit card sales on the new cash register.
- Answer a call and direct it to the appropriate party.

Concept Learning. Concept learning requires the discrimination of examples from nonexamples, and the correct classification of new instances of concepts. For example:
- Identify cirrus clouds in the sky.
- Recognize a bull market.
- Classify, correctly, the levels of learning according to this taxonomy.

Concept Integration. Concept integration describes the learning of sets of concepts. It also entails an understanding of the relationships among concepts. Concepts may have coordinate, additive, or disjunctive relationships. For example:

- Describe the relationship between quarks and quanta.
- Classify plant life by level and class in the taxonomy.
- Describe the relationship between supply and demand.

Problem Solving. Problem solving has its roots in concept integration. It requires the learner to activate relevant concepts (and rules that are formed by concepts), make hypotheses, gather data, and draw conclusions and inferences about the hypotheses. For example:
- Prescribe a new drug for depression.
- Try a new reagent to reduce the byproduct from a chemical reaction.
- Try a new theme in window displays to increase sales.

Learning Schemata. Learning schemata include an amalgamation of concepts into networks, principles, and problem situations. Subject matter knowledge is based on schemata, which is a combination of types and levels of learning that are integrated together. For example:
- Recommend policies based on supply side economics.
- Select an offensive strategy based on Desert Storm tactics.
- Formulate a strategy for trading in futures.

Summary

When determining the most appropriate form of instruction or predicting how well learners will learn, the most important variable is the type of learning outcome. Learning outcomes, like learner's abilities, vary in complexity and form. It is important to understand the type of learning outcome because different types of learners possessing different learner traits (described earlier) will be variably able to produce different levels and types of learning. That is, learner traits interact with learner outcomes as described next.

Learning Outcome-by-Trait Interactions

In the Introduction, we stated that different school-based or real-world learning tasks require the use of different skills, aptitudes, and preferences, and that the learner's performance of these tasks is dependent on his or her preferences and abilities, that is, task requirements interact with learner traits. Individual learners find some forms of learning outcomes more difficult than others. Therefore, different learners prefer and benefit from different strategies for approaching a task. This section describes some of those interactions and a rationale for considering them.

- Fields (1985) found that cognitive ability level (expressed in Piagetian terms) and cognitive learning style (field independence/dependence) interacted with achievement. Being field independent and of a higher cognitive ability level was more indicative of achievement than being field dependent and of a higher cognitive ability level. Students of lower ability levels were more often field dependent and mastered the biology concepts infrequently.

- High-ability students, regardless of instructional treatment, performed better than less able students on a computer game and the transfer tasks (Mandinach, 1984).

Most teachers or educators will support these results. Yet the conclusion that students who are more able will learn better than those who are less able is still an inadequate one. We have pointed out repeatedly that ability is multifaceted. The form of "brightness" or ability that facilitates learning a particular skill may be of no use in learning others. This book describes, in detail, specific forms of learner ability and reviews the research on different types of learning outcomes by learning ability or style. Specific learner traits do interact with learning outcomes. For example:

- In a paired-associate transfer task, wide categorizers were shown to be slower learners than narrow categorizers, with fewer correct responses and more errors. Broad categorizers were also shown to be more susceptible to interference (Hart, 1974).

- Field independent learners were found to be more proficient in sight-word recognition, recognition of vocabulary in context, use of structural analysis in word recognition, and silent reading comprehension (Hall, 1987).

- Pritchard (1975) found that sharpeners were better at nonsequential tasks as well as sequential judgements and that both tasks required similar processing.

- In a review of 36 studies on locus of control and academic achievement (Bar-Tal & Bar-Zahor, 1977), 31 showed that internals achieved more because of internals' greater persistence and effort and better use of task-relevant information.

So as not to misrepresent the previous research, it is important to note that not all of the educational research on learner traits and learning outcomes have shown strong interactions. The tacit assumption of this research is that varying the instructional method results in the use of different processing in learners, which, in turn, leads to different learning outcomes (Tobias, 1989). According to Tobias, there is little research support for this assumption. This research also assumes that the differences in thinking processes that result from different instructional methods can be related to learner traits. Again, there is little support for this assumption (Tobias, 1989). Tobias claims that the role of prior knowledge is more important than any higher level processing strategy that learners use. Learning results from many factors, including the disposition to learn, the aptitude to learn, and the positive transfer of prior learning and knowledge to the comprehension and acquisition of new knowledge and skills.

The lack of consistent research support for these hypotheses is examined more closely in the next chapter. In summary however, there has been too little research on these issues, and it has too often been of poor methodological quality. In many cases, methodologies are simply not available or they are too insensitive to assess the types of processing required by the learning task or the effects of that processing.

Conclusion

In this chapter, we reviewed the ways in which:

- individuals differ in traits such as skills, aptitudes, and preferences for learning,
- individuals differ in their abilities to perform learning outcomes,
- different learning outcomes require the use of different processing requirements manifested through learner traits, and
- learner traits affect the the learner's ability to accomplish different learning outcomes.

That learners think, process information, and learn differently is obvious. Those differences affect the courses they take and succeed in, the careers they choose, and even the friends they select. Although the relationships between learner traits and information-processing effects, and learning outcomes is often methodologically fuzzy, the relationships are still obvious to anyone who has ever taught. Two strong rationales exist for studying learner traits. First, we hope in some small way that this book will facilitate the need for clearer, higher quality research on these issues. Second, developing even a mere awareness of how individuals differ will clarify the process of learning and the act of teaching for educators and designers in a substantial way. "Educational practitioners might usefully begin by looking to general abilities for the design of more coarse, overall programs and move to more narrowly defined abilities or aptitudes for smaller, more specific treatment design" (Carrier & McNergney, 1979). Learner traits, at the very least, are useful metaphors for describing the learning process. These metaphors make the educators more sensitive to the differences that exist among students. They also at least provide a starting point in designing instruction that is described in the next chapter.

This brief review of learner traits, learning outcomes, and the relationship between them serves as a preview for some of the primary themes of this book. Each chapter following this first section will review research on the relationships between learner traits and learning outcomes, and will project how the learner trait being studied may interact with other learning outcomes. Because of the dearth of research, most of these projections are not empirically supported. Rather, they are based upon a rational analysis of the processing entailed and may function as hypotheses for future research. This, alone, would justify all of the effort in writing this book.

References

Bar-Tal, D., & Bar-Zahor, Y. (1977). The relationship between perception of locus of control and academic achievement. *Contemporary Educational Psychology, 2,* 181-199.

Bloom, B. S., Englehart, M. D., Furst E. J., Hill, W. H., & Krathwohl, D. R. (1956). *Taxonomy of educational objectives: The classification of educational goals. Handbook 1 cognitive domain.* New York: McKay.

Carrier, C., & McNergney, R. (1979). Interaction research: Can it help individualized instruction? *Educational Technology, 19*(4), 40-45.

Fields, S.C. (1985, April 15-18). *Assessment of aptitude interactions for the most common science instructional strategies.* Paper presented at the 58th annual meeting of the National Association for Research in Science Teaching, French Lick Springs, IN.

Furst, E. J. (1981). Bloom's taxonomy of educational objectives for the cognitive domain: Philosophical and educational issues. *Review of Educational Research, 51,* 444-453.

Gagne, R. M. (1970). *The conditions of learning.* New York: Holt, Rinehart & Winston.

Hall, M. J. (1987). Relationships between reading proficiency and field dependence, field independence, and sex (Doctoral dissertation, Auburn University.) *Dissertation Abstracts International, 49,* 226.

Hart, J. J. (1974). Interference in a paired-associate transfer of training paradigm as a function of breadth of categorization. *Psychological Reports, 34,* 167-173.

Krathwohl, D. R., Bloom, B. S., & Masia, B. B. (1964). *Taxonomy of educational objectives: The classification of educational goals: Handbook 2: Affective domain.* New York: Longman.

Leith, G. O. M. (1970). The acquisition of knowledge and mental development of students. *Journal of Educational Technology, 1,* 116-128.

Leith, G. O. M. (1971). *Working papers on instructional design and evaluation II: Analysis of objectives and tasks.* Geneva: World Health Organization.

Mandinach, E. B. (1984, April). *Clarifying the "A" in CAI for learners of different abilities: Assessing the cognitive consequences of computer environments for learning (ACCCEL).* Paper presented at the

68th annual meeting of the American Educational Research Association, New Orleans.

Merrill, M. D. (1973). Content and instructional analysis for cognitive transfer tasks. *A V Communication Review, 21,*109-125.

Pritchard, D. A. (1975). Leveling-sharpening revisited. *Perceptual and Motor Skills, 40* (1), 111-117.

Reigeluth, C. M., Merrill, M. D., & Bunderson, V. (1978). The structure of subject matter content and   its instructional design implications. *Instructional Science, 7,* 107-127.

Tobias, S. (1989). Another look at research on the adaptation of instruction to student characteristics. *Educational Psychologist, 24* (3), 213-227.

Bibliography

Cronbach, L. J., & Snow, R. E. (1969). *Individual differences in learning ability as a function of instructional variables* (Final report, Contract No. OEC-4-6-061269-1217, U.S. Office of Education) Stanford, CA: School of Education, Stanford University. (ERIC Document Reproduction Service No. ED 029 001)

Cronbach, L. J., & Snow, R. E. (1977) *Aptitudes and instructional methods.* New York: Irvington.

Divesta, F. J. (1975). Trait-treatment interactions, cognitive processes and research on communication media. *AV Communication Review, 23,* 185-196.

Gagne, R. M., & Brown, L. T. (1961). Some factors in the programming of conceptual learning. *Journal of Experimental Psychology, 62,* 313-321.

Snow, R. E. (1977). Individual differences and instructional theory. *Educational Researcher, 6,* 11-15.

Snow, R. E. (1977). Research on aptitudes: A progress report. In L.S. Shulman (Ed.), *Review of Research in Education,* (Vol. 4. pp. 50-105). Itasca, IL: Peacock.

Snow, R. E. (1977). Individual differences and instructional design. *Journal of Instructional Development, 1*(1), 23-26.

Snow, R. E. (1980). Aptitude and achievement. *New Directions for Testing and Measurement, 5,* 39-59.

Snow, R. E., & Lahman, D.F. (1984). Toward a theory of cognitive aptitude for learning from instruction. *Journal of Educational Psychology, 76,* 347-376.

2

INDIVIDUAL
DIFFERENCES AND INSTRUCTION

Introduction

The major assumption of this chapter, as well as a major assumption of this book, is that it is possible and desirable to adapt the nature of instruction to accommodate differences in ability, style, or preferences among individuals to improve learning outcomes. In the previous chapter, we discussed the following assumptions that underlie this belief:

• Different learning outcomes require different skills or abilities.
• Individuals differ in their abilities to process information, construct meaning from it, or apply it to new situations.

In this chapter, we discuss the following assumptions that underlie the goal of adaptive instruction (later, we also discuss impediments to this goal):

• Learning outcomes may be fostered or taught in many ways through the use of different microlevel and macrolevel strategies.
• These different forms of instruction require different learning aptitudes, abilities, styles, or preferences. That is, individuals will respond to different forms of instruction in different ways.
• Learning outcomes are affected by the form of instruction. So, different instructional activities will differentially affect learning outcomes.

As in the previous chapter, we treat each of these variables separately. First, we look at the range of instructional strategies and tactics. Then we describe how those instructional techniques interact with learner traits. In the next chapter, we discuss macrolevel strategies for intentionally adapting those strategies to meet the needs of different learners.

Instructional Strategies and Tactics

Instruction may be accomplished in many ways; that is, as teachers or designers, there are many different strategies that we can employ to help learners acquire knowledge. Instructional strategies represent a set of decisions that result in a plan, method, or series of activities aimed at obtaining a specific goal (Jonassen, Grabinger, & Harris, 1990). This definition is derived from its historical use as a term that represents an overall plan, for instance, to win a game. In tennis, the strategy is an overall plan of action to win a match. The tactics represent specific actions that are well rehearsed and are used to enable the strategy. For example, a player may decide to rush the net to effect a strategy of keeping an opponent off guard. A strategy is like a blueprint; it shows what must be done but does not tell how to do it. Instructional strategies do not describe how to deliver instruction, but rather how to organize, sequence, and present it. An instructional strategy may recommend motivating the learner prior to instruction. This may call for tactics such as arousing learner uncertainty, asking a question, or presenting a picture. A strategy aimed at teaching a concrete concept may call for the use of tactics, such as matched example/nonexample pairs, or deriving the criterial attributes from a set of examples. Instructional strategies provide the overall plan that guides the selection of instructional tactics which facilitate learning. Tactics are those learner/teacher activities in a lesson that facilitate a variety of instructional events, such as:

• using graphic organizers to introduce a lesson
• asking learners to summarize a text passage
• informing learners of the goal of a lesson

Next, we present the taxonomy of instructional strategies and tactics (Jonassen, Grabinger, & Harris, 1990). As we reviewed in the previous chapter, a taxonomy is a classification scheme for conceptually describing a domain of objects, ideas, or organisms. Objects or ideas are grouped together based on shared characteristics. The shared characteristics or attributes form the classes that organize the domain of information. This taxonomy groups instructional strategies into four main classes: contextualizing instruction, providing learner control, organizing and cuing learning, and assessing and evaluating learning. These classes of strategies are not descriptive enough to be useful for designers. Subsumed by these classes are the actual instructional strategies. These instructional strategies have been proposed and researched by designers and educational psychologists. All are supported by research, a review of which is beyond the scope of this book. These strategies are implemented, in different instructional situations, in the form of instructional tactics. This taxonomy subsumes instructional tactics under the strategies, as specifications of those strategies.

In the following taxonomy of instructional strategies and tactics (reprinted with permission of NSPI), *classes* of strategies are presented in bold italics; **instructional strategies** are presented in bold; and tactics are in plain text style.

Contextualizing instruction
Gaining the attention of the learner
arouse learner with novelty, uncertainty, surprise
pose question to learner
ask learners to pose questions to be answered by lesson
Relate the goals of instruction to the learner's needs
explain purpose or relevance of content
present goals for learner to select
ask learners to select own goals
have learner pose questions to answer
State the outcomes of instruction
describe required performance
describe criteria for standard performance
ask learners to establish criteria for standard performance
Present advance organizers
verbal expository: establish context for content
verbal comparative: relate to content familiar to learner
oral expository: establish context for instruction
oral comparative: relate to content familiar to learner
pictorial: show maps, globes, pictures, tables
adapt context or provide a variety of contexts for explaining
content
Present structured overviews and organizers
present outlines of content: verbal
present outlines of content: oral
use graphic oganizers/overviews
Providing learner control of instruction
Elicit learner approaches
review prerequisite skills or knowledge
ask learners to select information sources
ask learners to select study methods
ask learners to estimate task difficulty and time
ask learners to monitor comprehension
ask learners to relate questions to objectives
ask learners to recall elaborations
ask learners to evaluate meaningfulness of information
Elicit recall strategies
rehearse, repeat, reread
use mnemonic strategies
use cloze reading activities
make identifications with location or room
create summaries: hierarchical titles
create summaries: prose
create summaries: diagrammatic/symbolic (math)
create summaries: mind maps

Enable learner elaborations
>create images
>infer from information
>generate analogies
>create story lines: narrative descriptions of information

Learning Organization: Structured Cues to Context

Vary lesson unit size
>large chunks
>small chunks

Preteach vocabulary
>present new terms plus definitions
>ask students to look up list of new terms
>present attributes of rule definition, concept, principle
>paraphrase definitions
>derive definitions through concept analysis
>derive definitions from synonym list

Provide examples
>provide prototypic examples
>provide matched example/nonexample pairs
>provide divergent examples
>provide close-in nonexamples
>vary the number of examples
>model appropriate behavior

Use cuing systems
>provide graphic cues: lines, colors, boxes, arrows, highlighting
>provide oral cues: oral direction
>provide auditory cues: stimulus change (e.g., music, sound effects, voice change)
>provide type-style cues: font changes, uppercase, type size, headings, numbering
>present special information in windows

Help learners integrate new knowledge
>paraphrase content
>use metaphors and learner generated metaphors
>generate examples

Enable learner elaborations
>identify key ideas
>create content outline
>categorize elements
>use pattern note techniques
>construct graphic organizers
>construct concept map

Advise learner
>advise about instructional support: number of examples, amount of practice, tools, materials, resources, strategies

Assessing Learning
>   **Provide feedback after practice**
>>   provide confirmatory, knowledge of correct response
>>   provide corrective and remedial feedback
>>   provide informative feedback
>>   provide analytical feedback
>>   provide enrichment feedback
>>   provide opportunities for self-generated feedback
>   **Provide practice**
>>   provide massed practice sessions
>>   provide distributed practice sessions
>>   provide overlearning
>>   apply in real-world or simulated situations (near transfer)
>>   change context or circumstances (far transfer)
>>   vary the number of practice items
>   **Testing learning**
>>   pretest for prior knowledge
>>   pretest for prerequisite knowledge or skills
>>   pretest for endpoint knowledge or skills
>>   embed questions throughout instruction
>>   use objective referenced performance
>>   use normative referenced performance
>>   use incidental information, not objective referenced

This list of instructional strategies is not exhaustive, but it does represent the range of instructional activities or treatments. An information-processing analysis of all of these treatments would be necessary for providing any recommendations on their specific use in facilitating instructional outcomes or meeting the needs of individual learners. Such an analysis would fill a book longer than this one. The next section describes how these treatments may interact with various learner traits. Each treatment will have different effects on different learners, or different learners will profit more from certain different strategies and tactics.

Aptitude-by-Treatment Interactions

The concept of aptitude-treatment interactions (ATI) is one of the best known in the educational research field today. It began when Cronbach (1957) used a correlational approach to relate individual differences and achievement on different experimental treatments. Cronbach and Snow (1969) laid the groundwork for contemporary ATI research by suggesting methodological and conceptual guidelines for its conduct. In essence, ATI is a research methodology that explores interactions between alternative aptitudes (Cronbach & Snow, 1969), attributes (Tobias, 1976), or traits (Berliner & Cahen, 1973) and alternative instructional methods.

Aptitudes refer to any of the personological variables (such as mental abilities, prior knowledge, personality, or cognitive styles) that were listed in chapter 1. Treatments consist of the structural and presentational properties of instructional methods such as those described previously in this chapter. Interactions occur between aptitudes and treatments when individual differences in the former predict different outcomes from alternative forms of the latter. That is, instructional treatments may either facilitate or inhibit learning depending upon the effects of their structural characteristics on different types of learners.

To understand ATIs, it is necessary to understand the rudiments of a statistics-based research methodology known as *regression analysis*. Regression analysis is a method that seeks to ascertain the predictive effects of one variable on another, for instance, the effects of intelligence on achievement. To determine whether intelligence as a general learner trait has an effect on achievement, we must first measure intelligence, say, in terms of IQ, and then measure achievement, say, a test of mathematics achievement, following instruction in which the learners were given no remedial help. Both scores for each individual are then plotted on the axis of a two-dimensional graph, such as Fig. 2.1. Each dot on Fig. 2.1 represents the intersection of an individual's scores on both tests. Move upward along the achievement line to find the student's score and then across the intelligence line to the student's IQ. Next, identify the intersection of those two points on the graph. Each dot in the figure represents an individual's combination of scores. Regression analysis identifies a regression line that minimizes the differences in the points on its regression line. In this case, the regression line has a positive slope. This indicates that as the intelligence scores increase, achievement scores also increase. We can conclude from Fig. 2.1 that intelligence has a positive effect on achievement when the learners are given no special help.

Suppose that to help the less intelligent learners achieve higher math scores we devise a primary treatment that provides practice followed by feedback (knowledge of the correct answer). Results from this treatment are then compared with those of another group of learners given the original no-help instruction. This produces two regression lines in Fig. 2.2 -- one for the practice treatment (Treatment 1) and one for the no-help group (Treatment 2). It is obvious the practice treatment helped the learners. The less intelligent learners performed better in Treatment 1 than in Treatment 2. Notice also that the more intelligent learners performed better than the less intelligent learners in both groups. In this case, because the slopes were the same, the effects of intelligence on math achievement were the same, regardless of the nature of instruction.

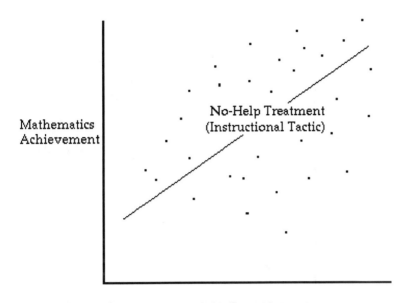

Fig. 2.1. Regression slope.

In another case, we decide to develop a superinstructional treatment, including analogies, graphic organizers, and practice with corrective and remedial feedback, to improve the achievement of the less intelligent students. We measure IQ, teach one group of students using the Super Treatment and another group with the No-Help Treatment and then measure math achievement and plot the results in Fig. 2.3. This plot shows that the treatments variably affected different learners because the slope of the regression lines are different. In the case of the No-Help Treatment, students with higher IQs performed better; however, in the Super Treatment, students with higher IQs performed more poorly (as indicated by the negative slope). We finally found a treatment that helps lower IQ students perform as well or better than higher IQ students. This situation indicates the existence of an ATI. Different instructional treatments produced varied effects on different types of learners.

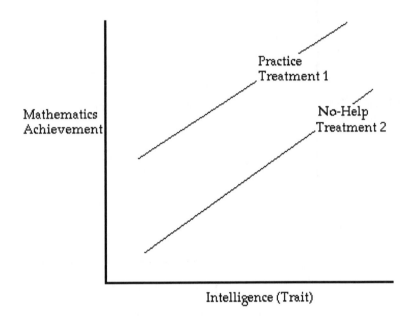

Fig. 2.2. No interaction.

The ATI in Fig. 2.3 is a disordinal interaction. This means that not only were the regression slopes different, but they also intersected. This is less common than an ordinal interaction (as shown in Fig. 2.2) where the regression slopes are different (indicating different effects of treatments) but do not cross.

There is a growing body of research on ATIs where variably designed instructional methods have produced different interactions with different types of learners. For example:

• Qualitative data (analysis of a think-aloud protocol) indicated an interaction between fear of failure and structuring of instruction. Those subjects with a high fear of failure did not learn well in an unstructured instructional condition (Kamsteeg & Bierman,1989).

• The cognitive restructuring ability of the learners interacted with levels of teacher guidance for items having continuous perceptual distracters (Cramer, 1989).

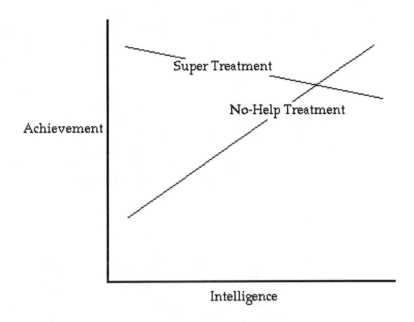

Fig. 2.3. Disordinal ATI.

- Learners with different cognitive entry behaviors (CEB) were differentially affected by mastery versus nonmastery learning strategies among third graders on comprehension achievement (Chan & Cole, 1987).

- Eight problems in drawn versus verbal versus telegraphic formats were administered to 854 students in grades three through seven. Readers of high ability chose correct operations more often than low-ability readers. The drawn format was better for low-ability readers than high-ability readers (Moyer, 1984).

- Instruction that included the use of metaphors was helpful to students with a preference for a visual format (visualizers) but not to those with a preference for a verbal format (verbalizers) (de Klerk, 1987).

- Field dependent subjects had faster response times and fewer response errors when given an explanation of their errors and strategies for correcting them, whereas field independent subjects had lower response rates and fewer errors when given only an indication that an error had been made.

These examples of ATIs from the research literature are descriptive of the variety of effects that may occur. The implications of these results for instruction are obvious. If we can identify instructional treatments that facilitate learning in different learner types, we can adapt our instruction accordingly. Indeed, there has been much interest in adapting instructional methodologies to accommodate individual learner characteristics based on aptitude-by-treatment interaction research. Individual differences identified by this field have obvious implications for the design of individualized systems of instruction. "All attempts to individualize instruction, it turns out, rest explicitly or implicitly on some kind of ATI idea" (Snow, 1977b, p. 23). Many designers have assumed that ATIs that are conceptually coherent and can be consistently generated will provide guidelines for accommodating the individual differences they assess.

Limitations of ATIs

Extensive reviews of ATI research (Berliner & Cahen, 1973; Bracht, 1970; Cronbach & Snow, 1977) found what Bond and Glaser (1979) indicated are "mostly A and T with not much I." The lack of consistent support for the ATIs has resulted from the weak conceptual grounding and deficient methodology often employed in many of the research studies. Small samples sizes, abbreviated treatments, specialized aptitude constructs or standardized tests, and a lack of conceptual or theoretical linkage between aptitudes and the information-processing requirements of the treatment further compound the inconsistencies in research findings.

ATI research is largely atheoretical. Although a major goal of ATI research has been the identification of explanatory principles concerning the nature of instruction (Salomon, 1972), most studies have focused on the predictive relationships of aptitudes to assign subjects to different treatments. Although Berliner and Cahen (1973) advised that an "understanding of the psychological processes of a specific learning task is prerequisite to the development of a theory on the interaction between traits and treatments," previous ATI research was often conceived without this understanding (p. 59). Without an adequate conceptual basis for selecting aptitude variables, researchers have often resorted to a shotgun approach. The need for a better conceptualization of treatments, which considers the information-processing requirements called on by the treatments, is one of the most persistent issues in ATI research (Fagan, 1979). Recent models have sought to overcome this problem. If ATI research is to be fruitful, DiVesta (1975) claimed that the "theory underlying ATI research must consider the cognitive processes assumed to be correlated with the traits and/or processes induced by the treatments" (p. 189). This assumption led to his search for TTPIs (trait-treatment-process interactions). One of the purposes of this book is to provide some conceptual bases for making these decisions.

ATI results lack consistency. Tobias (1981) concluded from several studies that ATI results were generally inconsistent. Significant interactions are offset by other nonsignificant treatment differences. Very few replications of ATI research have yielded significant interactions. In fact, many replications have reversed the findings of the previous study or were followed by non-significant differences. Tobias has also found that different researchers evaluating the same aptitudes or treatments produced dissimilar results. When ATIs do occur, most are not strong; that is, they are not disordinal and therefore are not useful for differential assignment. Results are often isolated and full of artifacts. When meaningful conceptually based aptitudes and treatments are employed, however, replications may occur (Peterson, Janicki, & Swing, 1980).

ATI results lack generality. In addition to the lack of consistency, most ATI results cannot be generalized to similar populations across time. They lack what researchers call external validity. Many ATI studies are not classroom-based. When they are, class effects often interact with treatments or aptitudes. The social context of the classroom plays an important role in learning, although it adds another order to the interactions. The interactions both among and between aptitude variables and instructional conditions are so complex as to render generalization impossible (Snow, 1977a). It is impossible "to store up generalizations and constructs for ultimate assembly into a network" (Cronbach, 1975, p. 123). A generalizable theory of aptitude-treatment interactions may not be possible. Learning may be too context-specific. At best we can hope to develop local instructional theories related to local instructional situations concerned with small portions of the curriculum and small segments of the population (Snow, 1977a). Snow concludes that it is possible, through continuous, systematic, formative evaluations of ATIs over time in a given place, to generate a dynamic instructional theory for that place alone.

ATIs also do not generalize over time. Long-term, realistic studies suggested by Cronbach and Snow (1977) are capable of producing some interactions. For instance, Hickey (1980) found in a semester-long study that internal, high-general reasoners benefitted from low-instructional support. Unfortunately, this type of longer term interaction is subject to instability over time. For instance, over a sequence of four units, Burns (1980) found that crystallized intelligence (see chapter 4) was consistently correlated to performance, yet all other aptitudes fluctuated over time. Treatment effects may also change over longer periods of time, suggesting what Cronbach (1975) referred to as Decade X Treatment interactions. It seems that ATI effects can only be generalized to individual classes in a specific locale during a finite period in history.

ATIs also interact with task and content. ATIs also interact with processing requirements of the learning task to produce complex performance differences (Rhetts, 1974). Rhetts found that error rates were higher but response latencies were shorter for impulsive learners (see chapter 9), with opposite results for reflectives. Aptitude-by-treatment-by-subject (task relevant) interactions were also reported by Tallmadge, Shearer, and Greenberg (1968). In fact, Rhetts (1972) and DiVesta (1975) recommended that designers first concentrate on the task characteristics (e.g., demands on memory, as described in chapter 1) and then identify the individual difference variables that may be related to those characteristics. This additional level of interaction is not surprising. It simply adds complexity and ambiguity to an already uncertain process. The major issue here is how designers or teachers can be expected to effectively adapt instruction to aptitude x, treatment x, class x, time x, and context x task interactions in designing instruction for each objective.

Conclusion

The ultimate purposes of ATI research are (a) to better understand learning processes and the role of individual differences in those processes, and (b) to make prescriptions about which instructional activities will best bring about those processes. Chapter 1 briefly described the range of learner traits and the differences in processing required by different learning outcomes. It also described how these learner traits can interact with learning outcomes. This chapter reviewed a range of instructional treatments that can be used to facilitate the accomplishment of those outcomes and how the instructional variables can interact with learner traits. Knowing how learner traits interact with *outcomes* will help us to determine the degree of assistance that learners require to accomplish them. Knowing how learner traits interact with *instructional treatments* will help us to determine the types of instruction that are most productive for individual learners. The purpose of this knowledge is to adapt instruction to learners' needs. The models and methods for those prescriptions are described in the next chapter.

The limitations of ATI research described earlier affect the prescriptions about adapting learning outcomes to learner traits as well as adapting instructional treatments to learner traits. Both types of prescriptions have been limited by the lack of clarity of instructional treatments and the lack of clarity of learner traits. Without clear descriptions of learner traits and replicable forms of instruction, we cannot develop meaningful and replicable prescriptions for adapting instruction. A major purpose of this book is to clarify learner traits and describe how they may interact with different learning outcomes and different forms of instruction. In nearly every chapter, we review research on the interactions between the learner trait being described in that chapter and learning outcomes. We also review the research on interactions between the learner trait being described in the chapter and various instructional treatments. In both cases there is rarely enough quality research to make replicable predictions about how to adapt instruction or learning outcomes. Based upon the available research and a rational analysis of the learner trait being described, we offer predictions about these interactions that have a probable relationship. These prescriptions may provide hypotheses for research and some guidelines for the teacher or designer to begin thinking about how to adapt instruction. Even a simple awareness of learner traits and the possible interactions with learning and instruction will improve our understanding of those processes and the quality of our educational efforts.

References

Berliner, D. C., & Cahen, L. S. (1973). Trait-treatment interaction and learning. In F.N. Kerlinger (Ed.), *Review of research in education*, Vol. 1, pp. 58-94. Itasca. IL: Peacock.

Bond, L., & Glaser, R. (1979). ATI but mostly A and T with not much I. *Applied Psychological Measurement, 3*, 137-140.

Bracht, G. E. (1970). Experimental factors related to aptitude-treatment interactions. *Review of Educational Research, 40*, 627-646.

Burns, R. B. (1980). Relation of aptitudes to learning at different points in time during instruction. *Journal of Educational Psychology, 72*, 785-795.

Chan, K. S., & Cole, P. G. (1987). An aptitude-treatment interaction in a mastery learning model of instruction. *Journal of Experimental Education, 55*, 189-200.

Cramer, K. A. (1989). Cognitive restructuring ability, teacher guidance, and perceptual distracter tasks: An aptitude-treatment interaction study. *Journal for Research in Mathematics Education, 20*, 103-110.

Cronbach, L. J. (1957). The two disciplines of scientific psychology. *American Psychologist, 12*, 621-684.

Cronbach, L. J. (1975). Beyond the two disciplines of scientific psychology. *American Psychologist, 30*, 116-127.

Cronbach, L. J., & Snow, R. E. (1969). *Individual differences in learning ability as a function of instructional variables.* (Final report, Contract No. OEC-4-6-061269-1217) Stanford: Stanford University, School of Education. (U.S. Office of Education, ERIC Document Reproduction Service No. ED 029 001)

Cronbach, L. J., & Snow, R. E. (1977). *Aptitudes and instructional methods.* New York: Irvington.

de Klerk, L. F. W. (1987, April 20-24). *The role of prior experience in learning from instruction.* Paper presented at the annual meeting of the American Educational Research Association, Washington, DC.

Divesta, F. J. (1975). Trait-treatment interactions, cognitive processes and research on communication media. *AV Communication Review, 23,* 185-196.

Fagan, R. (1979). *A functional approach to analyzing treatments in ATI research.* Paper presented at the annual meeting of the American Educational Research Association, San Francisco.

Hickey, P. S. (1980). A long-range test of the aptitude treatment interaction hypothesis in college level instruction (Doctoral dissertation, University of Texas at Austin, 1980). *Dissertation Abstracts International, 41,* 1452A.

Jonassen, D. H., Grabinger, R. S., & Harris, N. D. C. (1990). Analyzing instructional strategies and tactics. *Performance and Instruction Quarterly, 3* (2), 29-45.

Kamsteeg, P. A., & Bierman, D. J. (1989, March 25-30). *Cognitive ATI research: A simulated laboratory environment in (PCE-) Prolog.* Paper presented at the Annual Meeting of the American Educational Research Association, San Francisco.

Moyer, J. C. (1984). Story problem formats: Drawn versus verbal versus telegraphic. *Journal for Research in Mathematics Education, 15,* 342-351.

Peterson, P. L., Janicki, T. C., & Swing, S. R. (1980). Aptitude-treatment interaction effects of three social studies teaching approaches. *American Educational Research Journal, 17,* 339-360.

Rhetts, J. E. (1972). Aptitude-treatment interactions and individualized instruction. In L. Sperry (Ed.), *Learning performance and individual differences* (pp. 269-285). Glenview, IL: Scott, Foresman.

Rhetts, J. E. (1974). Task, learner, and treatment variables. *Journal of Educational Psychology, 66,* 339-347.

Salomon, G. (1972). Heuristic models for the generation of aptitude-treatment interaction hypotheses. *Review of Educational Research, 42,* 327-343.

Snow, R. E. (1977a). Individual differences and instructional theory. *Educational Researcher, 6,* 11-15.

Snow, R. E. (1977b). Individual differences and instructional design. *Journal of Instructional Development, 1*(1), 23-26.

Tallmadge, G. K., Shearer, J. W., & Greenberg, A. M. (1968). *Study of training equipment and individual differences: The effects of subject matter variables* (Tech. Rep. NAVTRADENCEN 67-C-0114-1) Palo Alto, CA.: American Institutes for Research in the Behavioral Sciences.

Tobias, S. (1976). Achievement-treatment interactions. *Review of Educational Research, 46,* 61-74.

Tobias, S. (1981). Adapting instruction to individual differences among students. *Educational Psychologist, 16,* 111-120.

Bibliography

Cahen, L. S., & Linn, R. L. (1971). Regions of significant criterion differences in aptitude treatment interaction research. *American Educational Research Journal, 8,* 521-530.

Carrier, C., & McNergney, R. (1979). Interaction research: Can it help individualized instruction? *Educational Technology, 19*(4), 40-45.

Cronbach, L. J., & Gleser, G. C. (1965). *Psychological tests and personal decisions.* Urbana, IL: University of Illinois Press.

Driscoll, M. P. (1987, February 26-March 1). *Aptitude-treatment interaction research revisited.* Paper presented at the Annual Convention of the Association for Educational Communications and Technology, Atlanta, GA.

Gay, G. (1985, March 31-April 4). *Interaction of learner control and prior conceptual understanding in computer-assisted video instruction.* Paper presented at the Annual Meeting of the American Educational Research Association, Chicago, IL.

Hedberg, J. G., & McNamara, S. E. (1985, March 31-April 4). *Matching feedback and cognitive style in visual CAI tasks.* Paper presented at the Annual Meeting of the American Educational Research Association, Chicago, IL.

Holtan, B. (1982). Attribute-treatment-interaction research in mathematics education. *School Science and Mathematics, 82,* 593-602.

Pothoff, R. F. (1964). On the Johnson-Neyman technique and some extensions thereof. *Psychometrika, 29,* 241-256.

Salomon, G. (1976). Cognitive approach to media. *Educational Technology, 16*(5), 25-28.

Salomon, G. (1979). *Interaction of media, cognition, and learning.* San Francisco: Jossey-Bass.

Snow, R. E. (1978). Theory and method for research on aptitude processes. *Intelligence, 2,* 225-278.

Snow, R. E. (1980). Aptitude and achievement. *New Directions for Testing and Measurement, 5,* 39-59.

Snow, R. E. (1980). Aptitude, learner control, and adaptive instruction. *Educational Psychologist, 15,* 151-158.

Snow, R. E., & Salomon, G. (1968). Aptitudes and instructional media. *AV Communication Review, 16,* 341-357.

Tobias, S. (1977). Anxiety-treatment interactions: A review of the research. In J. Sieber, H.F. O'Neil, & S. Tobias (Eds.), *Anxiety, learning, and instruction* (pp. 86-116). Hillsdale, NJ: Lawrence Erlbaum Associates.

3

ADAPTING INSTRUCTION
TO INDIVIDUAL DIFFERENCES
AND LEARNING OUTCOMES

Introduction

Adaptive instruction prescribes the methods for changing the form of instruction to suit the needs or desires of individuals. This assumes that all learners will not perform equally given a single form of instruction. The idea also entails the assumption that the nature of instruction *should* be adapted, and that we make available to the learners more than one form.

Probably the most important yet least-considered issue related to adaptive instruction is identifying *what* we are trying to accomplish. Shuell (1980) specified three mutually exclusive ends: academic equality, the elimination of individual differences, or the maximization of all learners' outputs. For instance, the latter goal expands the differences between individuals, thereby reducing academic equality. Can we afford the social ramifications of reducing academic equality? On the other hand, should we provide unequal opportunity by matching instruction only to the needs and requirements of a few?

Adaptive instruction is premised on aptitude-by-learning outcome research (see chapter 1) and aptitude-by-treatment interaction research (see chapter 2). This research documents differences in learning as a function of learner traits and instructional methods. The obvious implications of ATI research is the adaptation of instruction to learners' traits to maximize learning outcomes. Snow (1977a) suggested the matching of instruction to traits at two levels: macroadaptations, which match treatments to fit different classes of students, and microadaptations of treatments on a lesson-by-lesson, student-by-student basis. Macroadaptation implies a multiple method approach to individualization, the design of alternate treatments that engage different groups of students through different forms of information processing, whereas microadaptations focus on treatments to adapt the tasks and forms of instruction to meet more specific learner needs and abilities (Carrier & McNergney, 1979).

Matching Instruction to Learner Traits

Most ATI-based adaptive instructional designs employ one of three types of matches: remediation of learner deficiencies, compensation for deficiencies by modeling cognitive behavior, and capitalizing on learner strengths (Salomon, 1972). Although these were intended only as heuristics for generating ATI hypotheses, they have formed the basis for the matching model of instruction. Additional methods for matching methods to learners, based on individual differences and the existence of aptitude-by-treatment interactions, include combination matches (the aforementioned combinations) and challenge matches. The latter are mismatches that challenge the learner to acquire necessary but currently deficient mental skills (Messick, 1976).

Preferential Match: Capitalizing on Learner Strengths or Preferences

The most common approach to adaptive instruction is the preferential match. Learners are taught using instructional methods that call on traits or processing skills which the learners already possess. Preferential matching teaches to the learners' strengths. An example of this is the use of illustrations to teach learners who have been classified as visualizers rather than verbalizers (see chapter 15). Because these learners are more adept with visuals and prefer to learn through visual media, the illustration of concepts will capitalize on their strengths. Preferential match is the most common of the three types because the maximization of content learning is a frequent goal of educators. An approach that teaches to a learner's most effective traits will allow that learner to more freely consider and assimilate the content of the lesson without a lot of cognitive effort. Because this approach teaches to a learner's preferred processing mode, achievement will presumably improve.

Remediation Match: Eliminating Deficiencies in Learner Traits

The next most common type of instructional match is the remediation match. Remedial instruction is a prevalent classroom technique where content instruction is fortified with instruction on how to learn using specific methods or skills that the learners lack. Providing strong verbalizers with instruction on how to interpret visuals is an example of a remediation match. Remedial instruction seeks not only to maximize content learning, but also to enable learners to acquire generalizable learning skills as well. These general skills help to maximize overall learning in a way that preferential match does not. However, when remedial instruction is presented to skilled learners, performance often diminishes because of the repetitive and even boring nature of the instruction.

Compensatory Match: Supplanting Skills or Learner Traits

The compensatory or supplantation match is the most difficult to understand. Essentially, supplanting a learner trait involves an instructional method that is, itself, a model of the deficient skill. The instructional method replaces the deficient ability in the learner. For example, narrow scanners (see chapter 10) focus on only a limited amount of a visual display, thereby missing important information. Teaching content with film/video that pans systematically back and forth across the whole visual display would supplant the learner's lack of tendency to scan. Research by Salomon showed that not only will learners acquire the content, but also they will tend to imitate the information-seeking behavior modeled by the instruction (Salomon, 1974, 1976).

    Ausburn and Ausburn (1978) proposed an approach to the supplantation instructional design model that compensatorily matches instruction to differences in learners' cognitive styles. The first step, task analysis, determines the stimulus-transformation requirements of the task. The second step determines, based on an assessment of learning styles, the group of learners for whom treatment will need to supplant (compensate) the required cognitive process. Finally, designers then determine how to structure the treatment so that it will supplant that ability, that is, take the learner in Step 2 to the goal stated in Step 1.

Challenging Learner Skills

Messick (1976) suggested that it may not be appropriate to always accommodate learners' preferences or weaknesses, but rather to challenge the learner to learn using methods that are not preferred or more efficient. He argued that as learners acquire more educational experiences, they are required to adapt to a variety of instructional methods and styles. They acquire the ability to develop new information-seeking and organizing strategies that facilitate different forms of instruction. For example, providing verbalizers with only visual forms of instruction forces them to develop and use visual skills. The purpose of challenge matching is to require the learner to adapt to the instruction rather than having the instruction adapted to the learner. Challenge-match proponents argue that adapting to different instructional styles prepares the learner with important life skills.

Limitations of Matching Instruction

There are at least two problems with trying to implement these adaptive instructional design models, especially those based on ATI research, regardless of whether the model is intended to adapt instructional treatments or to match learner characteristics.

1. In the previous chapter, we discussed some of the conceptual and methodological problems in ATI research that have produced inconsistent and ungeneralizable results. Generalizing procedures from weak data may only produce weak designs. Better research, perhaps beginning with some of the hypotheses suggested in this book, may improve the research base enough to strengthen these results and, therefore, the recommendations.

2. Perhaps the major limitation of a matching model of instruction is its feasibility. Accommodating individual differences resulting from ATI may not be feasible in most educational settings. The logical implication of ATI research is to provide for individualized programs of instruction. When you consider all of the possible individual differences that could be matched by instruction and the number of alternative treatment methods available and then project them for all of the goals and objectives, even in a single course, the number of required instructional alternatives appears endless. That is, developing separate instructional treatments to accommodate each learner trait/instructional outcome match in a course would require thousands of different "lessons." This problem could be alleviated by finding the most powerful predictor variables and matching only to those. Likewise, educators could identify the most problematic learning outcomes, that is, the goals that are most difficult for learners, and adapt only to those. There is no assumption in adaptive learning theory that numerous alternative forms of instruction should be developed for each and every learning outcome.

There are alternative uses of the information in this book to matching instruction to the specific needs of each individual. The major purpose of adaptive instruction should be correction, not adaptation. The implicit assumption of adaptive design models is that research results should be interpreted so that instruction may be adapted to individual learner needs. Rather than fitting treatments to learners or learners to treatments as suggested by a matching model, educators should progressively modify instructional designs so that they are less vulnerable to learner aptitudes (Gehlbach, 1979). This correction approach would seek to flatten out the regression lines described in chapter 2, using ATI research to help identify weak designs.

Adaptive instruction is problematic in that it requires extensive resources and a very sensitive instructional team for implementation. Very few educational agencies, with the exception, perhaps, of large corporate training departments, have the capacity for these types of adaptations. Yet, individualized programs or individually guided education plans have often been used for special education students. The availability of computers makes the organization and administration of these programs much more feasible.

Matching Instruction to Differences in Learning Outcomes

Rather than adapting instruction to learner traits for each learning outcome, an alternative approach is to adapt instruction for all learners to meet the requirements of the task. That is, if we teach each outcome in a manner that supports the knowledge or skill acquisition required by that goal, then our compensating is not based on learner traits but rather on task requirements. Jonassen (1982) referred to these as content-by-treatment interactions (CTIs). CTIs entail some important assumptions.

Assumptions of Content-Treatment Adaptations

1. One assumption of CTI is that subject matter structures provide an important basis for how to sequence and synthesize instruction (Reigeluth, Merrill, & Bunderson, 1978). Additionally, task analysis can be used to describe the optimal mental processes for completing a task or acquiring specific knowledge. To do this, designers should develop instructional treatments (sequences, codes) that simulate those processes. Just as ATI assumes that no treatment is appropriate for all learners, CTI assumes that no particular treatment method is appropriate for all content. In chapter 1, we described how different types of content (facts, concepts, principles, problems) call on different mental processes. If that is the case, then instructional treatments can be coded or sequenced to simulate those processes to maximize learning for all learners. In a number of studies Salomon (1972, 1974, 1979) found that instructional treatments that model the internal-processing requirements of the task result in superior learning. Burns (1980) concluded that different forms of intelligence were related to content and methodology. Fluid-spatial forms of intelligence (see chapter 4) tend to interact more with content differences, whereas crystallized forms tend to transcend them. So a CTI approach focuses on supplanting fluid intellectual processes.

2. Learners should be assigned to the treatment that best simulates the content processing requirements that result in the most efficient learning. The most obvious initial criticism of such an approach is that individuals do not process information alike. Why instruct them alike? Three reasons exist.

- First, content process analysis indicated that a certain sequence of operations is necessary for learning a specific type of content, and that a particular sequence, as represented by the treatment, is the most efficient combination of processes.
- Second, human learners are very capable of adapting to specific task requirements. Although distinctive, individual learning styles do exist (Rhetts, 1972).
- Third, entry level learners deficient in certain mental operations will, through appropriately structured lessons, acquire those skills.

Rationale for Content-Treatment Adaptations

Perhaps the most significant rationale for considering CTIs in instructional design is feasibility. For most cognitive objectives, such an approach would suggest "one best method." Rather than attempting to adapt instructional methods, it seems preferable to progressively modify instructional designs so they are more uniformly effective (Gehlbach, 1979).

Designing instruction that can teach a content objective as well as the mental skills required for its performance is preferable to the production of a potentially infinite number of treatments to teach different learner types. This approach at least addresses the feasibility issue. Shaping the processing of individuals may be accomplished. Of course, such designs would not be completely impervious to individual differences or contextual differences as suggested by Snow (1977a).

CTIs are based on the idea that cognitive task analysis of content would identify task-treatment interactions that would provide the basis for recommending treatment strategies. Less elaborate decision models would be required to determine the treatment characteristics.

Another rationale for CTIs is that content differences account for a larger portion of performance variance than aptitude differences, so that differential assignment to treatments that accommodate content differences would flatten performance regressions.

Conclusion

There are alternative ways of using the interpretations of learner differences and the descriptions of learning outcomes for different instructional methods that are outlined by this book. Instructional treatments may be adapted to meet the needs or preferences of individual learners, or they may be adapted to the requirements of the learning tasks. In most of the chapters of this book, we provide recommendations about some adaptations that have been or may be tried. These recommendations are based on research, and on interpretations of the literature where no research is available. The underlying assumptions are that instruction need not be identical for all learners, and that by adapting the forms of instruction that we use, we help individuals to become more effective learners and cause learning to improve. These assumptions rest on an understanding of the ways that learners differ. This topic is addressed in the remainder of this book.

References

Ausburn, L. J., & Ausburn, F. B. (1978). Cognitive styles: Some information and implications for instructional design. *Educational Communications and Technology Journal, 26*, 337-354.

Burns, R. B. (1980). Relation of aptitudes to learning at different points in time during instruction. *Journal of Educational Psychology, 72*, 785-795.

Carrier, C., & McNergney, R. (1979). Interaction research: Can it help individualized instruction. *Educational Technology, 19*(4), 40-45.

Gehlbach, R. D. (1979). Individual differences: Implications for instructional theory, research, and innovation. *Educational Researcher, 8*(4), 8-14.

Jonassen, D. H. (1982). Aptitude- versus Content-treatment interactions: Implications for instructional design. *Journal of Instructional Development, 5*(4), 15-27.

Messick, S. (1976). Personal styles and educational options. In S. Messick & Associates (Eds.), *Individuality in learning* (pp. 327-368). San Francisco: Jossey Bass.

Reigeluth, C. M., Merrill, M. D., & Bunderson, V. (1978). The structure of subject matter content and its instructional design implications. *Instructional Science, 7*, 107-127.

Rhetts, J. E. (1972). Aptitude-treatment interactions and individualized instruction. In L. Sperry (Ed.), *Learning performance and individual differences* (pp. 269-285). Glenview, IL: Scott, Foresman.

Salomon, G. (1972). Heuristic models for the generation of aptitude-treatment interaction hypotheses. *Review of Educational Research, 42*, 327-343.

Salomon, G. (1974). Internalization of filmic schematic operations in interaction with learners' aptitudes. *Journal of Educational Psychology, 66*, 513-518.

Salomon, G. (1976). Cognitive approach to media. *Educational Technology, 16*(5), 25-28.

Salomon, G. (1979). *Interaction of media, cognition, and learning.* San Francisco: Jossey-Bass.

Shuell, T. J. (1980). Learning theory, instructional theory, and adaption. In R. E. Snow, P. Federico, & W. E. Montague (Eds.), *Aptitude, learning, and instruction* (Vol. 2, pp. 277-302). Hillsdale, NJ: Lawrence Erlbaum Associates.

Snow, R. E. (1977a). Individual differences and instructional theory. *Educational Researcher, 6*, 11-15.

Snow, R. E. (1977b). Research on aptitudes: A progress report. In L.S. Shulman (Ed.), *Review of Research in Education* (Vol. 4, pp. 50-105). Itasca, IL: Peacock.

Snow, R. E. (1977c). Individual differences and instructional design. *Journal of Instructional Development, 1*(1), 23-26.

Bibliography

Anderson, R. C., & Faust, C. W. (1973). *Educational psychology: The science of instruction and learning.* New York: Dodd Mead.

Evans, J. L., Homme, L. E., & Glaser, R. (1962). RULEG system for constructing programmed verbal learning sequences. *Journal of Educational Research, 55,* 513-518.

McCombs, B. L., & McDaniel, M. A. (1981). On the design of adaptive treatments for individualized instructional systems. *Educational Psychologist, 16,* 11-22.

Rhetts, J. E. (1974). Task, learner, and treatment variables. *Journal of Educational Psychology, 66,* 339-347.

Salomon, G. (1977). *The language of media and the cultivation of mental skills.* Report submitted to the Spencer Foundation. Jerusalem, Israel: Hebrew University. (ERIC Document Reproduction Service No. ED 145 808)

Schmitt, J. B. (1980). The interactive effects of selected personality variables and a fixed treatment in two content areas on an analytical reasoning task (Doctoral dissertation, University of Southern California). *Dissertation Abstracts International, 1980, 41,* 1555-156A.

Snow, R. E. (1978). Theory and method for research on aptitude processes. *Intelligence, 2,* 225-278.

Snow, R. E. (1980). Aptitude and achievement. *New Directions for Testing and Measurement, 5,* 39-59.

Snow, R. E. (1980). Aptitude, learner control, and adaptive instruction. *Educational Psychologist, 15,* 151-158.

Snow, R. E., & Salomon, G. (1968). Aptitudes and instructional media. *AV Communication Review, 16,* 341-357.

Worthen, B. R. (1968). Discovery and expository task presentation in elementary matehmatics. *Journal of Educational Psychology, Monograph Supplement, 58* (1, Pt. 2).

PART II

INTELLIGENCE:
Mapping Mental Abilities

Introduction

The concept of intelligence is one of the most enigmatic in learning psychology. Although we all share a fundamental understanding of what it means to be intelligent, our interpretations are diverse. When asked to define intelligence, students frequently struggle by associating concepts such as "thinking," "memory," "problem solving," and "mental ability," often resorting to the tautology of "what it means to be an intelligent person." Even psychologists admit that "intelligence does not exist except as a resemblance to a prototype, but that the concept of an intelligent person is based on fact" (Neisser, 1979, p. 225). That is, we do not understand what intelligence is, but we know what intelligent people are. Whatever it is, intelligence plays a crucial role in learning and instruction and so is important to the definition and description of individual differences. Intelligence forms the foundation for most cognitive and many other personality differences described throughout this book.

In this introduction, we will briefly describe a range of theoretical models for describing intelligence. We will focus on a particular type of model, psychometric, as the most appropriate for discerning and describing individual differences and their implications for learning and instruction.

Fig. 4.1 illustrates a hierarchy of types of theoretical models of intelligence: complexity, psychometric, and information processing. The complexity models consist of theoretical descriptions of the multiple types of intelligence, including brief descriptions of Gardner's "multiple intelligences" and Sternberg's "metaphors of mind." These models provide a good introduction to individual differences and a conceptual basis for studying intelligence. Psychometric models are those that have evolved from empirical research on mental abilities. The next three chapters describe three of these psychometric models in greater detail. Psychometric models, we argue later, are the most consistent with the overall approach of this book. Information-processing models are based on the analyses of the component processes that are entailed by putatively intelligent behavior, such as problem solving and analogical reasoning. They are similar to psychometric outcomes in that they seek to isolate components of intelligent behavior, but they do it in a much different way. We note that there are other classes of intelligence models that are described by other authors. For this book, however, these three types are adequate.

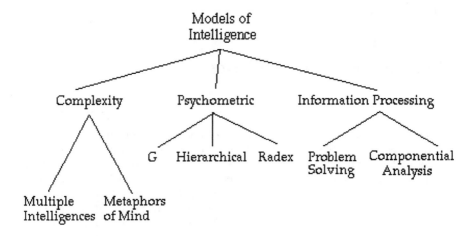

Fig. 4.1. Models of intelligence.

Complexity Models

In this section, we briefly describe two models or metaphorical conceptions of intelligence. We refer to these as complexity models, because their primary intent is to convey the complexity of the concept of intelligence. Both models describe the variety of types of intelligence, concluding that intelligence is a complex of abilities.

Multiple Intelligences

Intelligence is a complex of abilities and skills that are differentially present in individuals. To define the different types of intelligences, Gardner and his colleagues examined the literatures in cognitive capacities in normal individuals, pathological breakdowns in humans, and cognitive processing in special populations. The resulting theory of multiple intelligences (Gardner, 1983; Gardner & Hatch, 1989) synthesized that literature by describing seven intelligences.

Logico-mathematical--discerning and using logical and numerical patterns; deductive reasoning; activities of mathematicians, scientists, logicians.

Linguistic--sensitivity to sounds and meanings of words and how they are assembled; language abilities; activities of a writer, literature teacher.

Musical--uses of rhythm, pitch, melody; appreciating musical expressions; activities of a musician.

Spatial--visuospatial capabilities; spatial memory; manipulating and transforming perceptions of visual objects; activities of artist, architect.

Bodily-kinesthetic--control of body movements; proprioceptive abilities; activities of an athlete, skilled artist.

Interpersonal--understanding and dealing with moods, temperaments, motivations, behaviors of other people; activities of a counselor, social worker, salesperson.

Intrapersonal--understanding of one's own feelings, motivations, needs; knowledge of one's own strengths and weaknesses; guiding one's own behavior.

These multiple intelligences are pervasive in our lives. The differences in these abilities predict and explain how well we learn different skills, why we select different career paths, enjoy different types of entertainment, and choose to relate to different individuals. Gardner's theory of multiple intelligences is a very useful model for thinking about the individual differences that are described in this book.

Metaphors of Mind

Whereas Gardner conceived of each individual as possessing different forms of intelligence, Sternberg reviewed different interpretations of intelligent behavior in each individual. Because Sternberg (1990) believed that models of intelligence are inconsistent, he suggested a comprehensive list of the metaphors that underlie these theories.

Geographic--a mapping of the mind, components or factors of intelligence, sources of individual differences, predictors of achievement.

Computational--mind as a computing device, information processing routines or components underlying intelligence.

Biological--electrophysiological and biochemical functions of the brain and central nervous system, not well understood or very predictable, neural model.

Epistemological--theory of genetic epistemology, focusing on equilibration for knowledge acquisition and developmental periods of growth, structure of knowledge (see chapter 33).

Anthropological--intelligence as a cultural intervention, adapting to cultural influences, culturally dependent intelligence.

Sociological--Vygotsky influence, internalization of social observations, zone of proximal development.

Systems--interaction of multiple intelligences, combination of different
metaphors.

As we pointed out in the Introduction to the book, the metaphor that is
most useful for our purposes is the geographic metaphor. In this section,
we highlight three psychometric theories that clearly attempt to map the
components of intelligence in a geographic fashion. Because these component capabilities interact with different learning outcomes and instructional methods, the psychometric models are the best predictors of performance on learning tasks and interactions with instructional treatments.

Psychometric Models

Psychometric models of intelligence are derived from empirical, psychological research on individual differences. This research has employed statistical analysis of a variety of tests to inductively develop theories of intelligence. Typically, researchers have administered tests and then analyzed
the underlying structure of the responses. Perhaps the most universal
conception of intelligence is the ability to perform well on intelligence
tests. Although tests are allegedly objective measures of a concept as complex as intelligence, we must, as Terman (1921, p. 131) suggested, "guard
against defining intelligence solely in terms of ability to pass the tests of a
given intelligence scale." Otherwise, psychometric definitions of intelligence, as Neisser (1979) suggested, are nothing more than self-fulfilling
prophecies. Yet we have learned a great deal from psychometric research
about the nature of intelligence. Psychometric models of intelligence describe a variety of landscapes of human ability.

Hierarchical (Factor Analytic) Models

According to different psychometric approaches, there are three types of
intelligence or intellectual abilities: general, secondary, and primary abilities. The relationship between these abilities is often thought to be a hierarchical one. Snow (1978), for instance, suggested that intelligence constitutes a hierarchy of abilities, with the broadest, most general conception
(G) at the top, which is comprised of secondary abilities such as fluid and
crystallized intelligence, which in turn are comprised of primary abilities
(see Fig. 4.2). This hierarchical relationship has been derived from the statistical relationships between the different factors and variables.

General Mental Ability (G)

In the early part of the 20th century, psychologists and researchers sought
to describe the general nature of human intelligence (Binet & Simon, 1916;

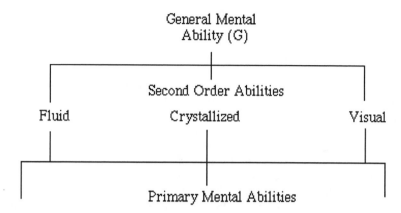

Fig. 4.2. Primary and secondary mental abilities.

Spearman, 1927; Terman, 1916). These researchers sought practical defini-
Much of the early research focused on identifying the single factor that tied
together performance on different mental tests and could be used to predict other forms of performance. The intent was to develop tests based on
this research (for example, the Stanford-Binet) that could be used to measure this single factor. The rationale for researching and using a G is that
it is parsimonious to think about a single factor which impacts on all types
of performance rather than multiple ones (Detterman, 1982). Its most
common form of expression is IQ. IQ describes a single measure of intelligence. For the purposes of this book, we assume that there is no such
thing as G, that describing someone as intelligent is not descriptive of any
specific ability or prescriptive of the ability to perform any given task.
Rather, intelligence is best described as an aggregate of mental abilities that
interact with different learning outcomes and modes of instruction.

Primary Mental Abilities

Research on primary mental abilities started with a different set of assumptions about intelligence. Rather than searching for a general ability,
these researchers believed that intelligence could be best understood by resolving some constituent factors or primary mental abilities that comprise
intelligent behavior. Thurstone (1938) led a research group in analyzing
the constituent processes of intelligent behavior. He helped to initiate factor analysis, now a fairly common psychometric tool, as a technique to
support some of this early research. Factor analysis looks for the underlying structure among intercorrelations between variables. Chapter 5 describes Thurstone's work and the seven primary mental abilities that he
found. Guilford (1967) expanded on the concept of primary abilities, breaking primary mental factors such as Thurstone's into more specific abilities.
He describes, theoretically, as many as 150 different mental abilities. An

account of Guilford's "structure of intellect" theory is presented in Chapter 6.

Secondary Mental Abilities

Cattell (1971) observed that the primary factors, identified by research in primary mental abilities, were intercorrelated, suggesting that there were higher order or secondary factors. He proposed that many of the factors identified by the primary mental abilities research were actually measuring the same thing. He sought to identify secondary factors that described the overlapping primary factors. Chapter 4 describes the major second-order factors that Cattell discovered--fluid and crystallized intelligence and later, visual intelligence. This description indicated that second order abilities are comprised of primary abilities. However, chronologically, second-order factors such as Cattell's were identified by analyzing primary abilities. That is, secondary abilities were derived from primary abilities, yet, hierarchically, they are more general and inclusive than primary abilities. This is why secondary abilities are described after the primary ones in this introduction, whereas the chapter describing them precedes the one on primary abilities in this book. An analysis of general intelligence for its few types also reveals these secondary abilities.

Radex Models

Radex models are another psychometric approach to showing the complexity and organization of intelligence. These models were developed by Guttman (1954) as methods for analyzing intercorrelations among ability tests without factor analysis (Marshalek, Lohman, & Snow, 1983). Using multidimensional scaling to represent test scores as points in space, the radex model relates test scores within a content domain with tests of similar complexity from different content domains to produce a two- or three-dimensional representation of the similarity and structure of different test scores. The statistical model produced by this method corresponds well with the aforementioned hierarchical model of factor-analytic data (Snow, 1978). That is, there are theoretical and empirical parallels between hierarchical and radex models of intelligence (Marshalek et al., 1983). Because of the confirmatory nature of this research and the complexity of its methodology, it does not provide any additional support for the landscape metaphor of intelligence.

Conclusion

Psychometric models of intelligence, especially those of primary and secondary abilities, provide useful models of mental abilities and have numerous implications for learning and instruction. First, they form the basis for many of the individual differences described in this book.

Combinations of mental abilities comprise cognitive controls. These, in turn, define cognitive styles at a more general level, which define learning styles at the most general level.

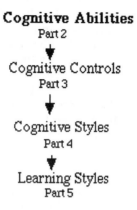

Cognitive Abilities
Part 2
↓
Cognitive Controls
Part 3
↓
Cognitive Styles
Part 4
↓
Learning Styles
Part 5

Second, the ability factors also form the basis for most types of achievement and aptitude testing. For instance, reading tests often isolate primary mental abilities that are directly related to reading. According to Wagner and Sternberg (1987), psychometric abilities also help educators to state learning outcomes, test for initial competence (entry level behavior), accommodate to different learning styles, and develop models for assessing initial competence. To provide more consistent results, research on the interactions between instructional methods and individual aptitudes (described in Part I) has begun to focus more on the identification of their common underlying information processes. Primary and secondary abilities that have been identified by psychometric models provide some metrics for conducting this type of research. A comprehensive review of intelligence is beyond the scope of this volume, so we have chosen the models of intelligence that are more closely related to the purpose of this book and that best describe the geography of mental abilities.

Information-Processing Models

Information-processing models of intelligence rely on the computational metaphor of mind (Sternberg, 1990). They are based on information-processing theories that describe intelligent behavior as a series of computations or processes that can be isolated and structured. There are at least two types of information-processing approaches--problem solving and componential analysis.

Problem Solving

Newell and Simon (1972) conducted extensive research on the nature of human problem solving. Their theory of problem solving consisted of production systems that perform system-regulated operations. These operations were stated in terms of IF-THEN decisions--if certain conditions are met, then process information in a certain way. The operations that are performed comprise a production system. Each production system possesses an executive control device that seeks to satisfy a certain set of conditions. Their theory of problem solving conceives of intelligent activity as a set of production systems that process information and make decisions. Their technique, like Sternberg's (see next section) was to isolate the decisions and actions that comprised intelligent operations.

Componential Analysis

Componential analysis (Sternberg, 1977, 1979) is a process that decomposes a domain of tasks (such as analogical reasoning, deductive reasoning, problem solving, or memory) into its components and constructs tests to measure each component. It consists of a series of intensive task analyses. A task is modeled, and the model is verified with learners working on real-world tasks. For example, analogical reasoning consists of steps such as encoding the terms, inferring the relationship between the first two terms, mapping the first term onto the fourth, applying the third term to the answer options, and making a response (Sternberg, 1977). Componential analysis, like some of the psychometric models of intelligence, is hierarchical in that it predicts that the isolated components in task completion are controlled by metacomponents that regulate the processes. It has become a useful tool for describing a myriad of mental abilities. With its deconstructive approach, it is not an appropriate method for deriving global theories of intelligence.

Conclusion

In the context of this book, we believe that intelligence is the aggregate of the mental abilities that an individual possesses and can use in accomplishing learning outcomes and interacting with instruction. These mental abilities are the most specific and fundamental of human cognitive differences. That is, they are the foundation of cognitive controls, which form the foundation for cognitive styles and so on.

One of the purposes of this book is to map individual differences onto learning and instruction. This presupposes that we have a map of mental abilities. Consistent with a geographic metaphor of human abilities and individual differences, the specific mental abilities that an individual possesses, their relative strengths, and their relationships to each other form an intellectual landscape for the individual. Each individual landscape has different peaks and valleys. A particular combination of peaks and valleys (mental abilities) manifests a certain combination of cognitive controls and cognitive styles that an individual uses to interact with his or her environment. Each individual's mental ability landscape is somewhat different, so that his or her landscape of cognitive controls and styles will differ as well.

Mapping individual differences in mental abilities (intelligence) enables us to better understand how each individual takes in information, thinks, organizes, solves problems, and so on. Mapping mental abilities, therefore, enables us to predict the cognitive controls and styles that an individual will use. Predicting these cognitive controls and styles enables us to predict the types of learning outcomes that each individual will prefer and achieve, as well as the types of instruction that will result in the greatest learning. A road map to the mind will help each of us better understand the learning and instruction processes.

References

Binet, A., & Simon, T. (1916). *The development of intelligence in children.* Baltimore: Williams & Wilkins.

Cattell, R. B. (1971). *Abilities: Their structure, growth, and action.* Boston: Houghton Mifflin.

Detterman, D. K. (1982). Does "g" exist? *Intelligence, 6,* 99-108.

Gardner, H. (1983). *Frames of mind.* New York: Basic.

Gardner, H., & Hatch, T. (1989). Multiple intelligences go to school: Educational implications of the theory of multiple intelligence. *Educational Researcher, 18* (11), 4-10.

Guilford, J. P. (1967). *The nature of human intelligence.* New York: McGraw-Hill.

Guttman, L. A. (1954). A new approach to factor analysis: The radex. In P.F. Lazersfeld (Ed.), *Mathemeatical thinking in the social sciences* (pp. 416-438). Glencoe, IL: Free Press.

Marshalek, B., Lohman, D. F., & Snow, R. E. (1983). The complexity continuum in the radex and hierarchical models of intelligence. *Intelligence, 7,* 107-127.

Neisser, U. (1979). The concept of intelligence. *Intelligence, 3,* 217-227.

Newell, A., & Simon, H.A. (1972). *Human problem solving.* Englewood Cliffs, NJ: Prentice-Hall.

Snow, R. E. (1978). Theory and method for research on aptitude processes. *Intelligence, 2,* 225-278.

Spearman, C. E. (1927). *The abilities of man: Their nature and measurement.* New York: Macmillan.

Sternberg, R. J. (1977). *Intelligence, information processing and analogical reasoning.* Hillsdale, NJ: Lawrence Erlbaum Associates.

Sternberg, R. J. (1979). The nature of mental abilities. *American Psychologist, 34,* 214-230.

Sternberg, R. J. (1990). *Metaphors of mind: Conceptions of the nature of intelligence.* Cambridge: Cambridge University Press.

Terman, L. M. (1916). *The measurement of intelligence.* Boston: Houghton-Mifflin.

Terman, L. M. (1921). Intelligence and its measurement. *Journal of Educational Psychology, 12,* 127-133.

Thurstone, L. L. (1938). *Primary mental abilities.* Chicago: University of Chicago Press.

Wagner, R. K., & Sternberg, R. J. (1987). Alternative conceptions of intelligence and their implications for education. *Review of Educational Research, 54,* 179-223.

4

SECOND-ORDER MENTAL ABILITIES: Cattell's Crystallized/Fluid Intelligence

Description of Fluid and Crystallized Intelligence

During the early part of the 20th century, researchers sought to describe intelligence as a singular, general mental ability--G. During the 1930s and 1940s, researchers rejected the idea of a single intellectual ability in favor of primary mental abilities (see chapters 5 and 6 that describe two separate conceptions of these abilities). Raymond Cattell (1940, 1941, 1945) called into question both approaches. He believed that research would reject the idea of a unitary structure defining intelligence, but he also believed that the numerous primary mental abilities identified by the factor-analytic studies could be combined into more comprehensive structures. The results of his factor analysis of the primary mental abilities produced the theory of fluid and crystallized intelligence (Cattell, 1957, 1963; Horn & Cattell, 1966, 1967), which contends that, rather than being organized into a single general ability, primary mental abilities are organized into two principal classes of abilities and achievements.

Fluid intelligence (Gf) describes adaptive mental behavior in unfamiliar situations. Gf represents different forms of reasoning including abstracting, forming and using concepts (classification), perceiving and using relations, identifying correlates, maintaining awareness in reasoning, and abstracting ideas, especially from figural and nonverbal, symbolic and semantic content. According to Cattell, Gf is independent of content, that is, culture free. It is also independent of previous learning experiences. Gf represents general reasoning ability and is often related to general intelligence.

Fluid intelligence is more influenced by biological factors, such as heredity and central nervous system growth and maintenance, which is consistent with other culture-free aspects of the construct. For instance, Cattell (1963) noted that generalized brain damage has a greater affect on fluid abilities, whereas localized damage more directly affects crystallized skills. Cattell (1980) later conducted research that showed fluid intelligence to be more heritable than crystallized intelligence.

Crystallized intelligence (Gc) consists of those cognitive performances that have been habituated or crystallized (hence its name) as a result of previous learning experiences. That is, Gc describes cognitive behavior that is patterned by earlier learning experiences. Examples of Gc include verbal and numerical skills and other achievement-related activities. Crystallized intelligence includes the awareness of concepts and ideas pertaining to a topic, so it is more culture bound. Development of crystallized intelligence, therefore, is more influenced, according to the theory, by an individual's experiences, education, and acculturation.

Characteristic Differences in Fluid and Crystallized Intelligence

Fluid and crystallized intelligence represent two distinct and separate general abilities and are not simply poles on a single characteristic (as are so many other characteristics described in this book). Therefore, they are described separately as unipolar abilities.

Individuals high in fluid intelligence exhibit greater ability in:
• classification by inductive reasoning
• abstracting and inducing the meaning of concepts (classification)
• perceiving and using relations
• maintaining awareness in reasoning
• figural and spatial reasoning

Individuals high in crystallized intelligence exhibit greater ability in:
• verbal ability
• numerical ability
• serial reasoning
• low levels of excitability
• low levels of independence
• high levels of achievement on information tests

Individual Differences
Related to Fluid and Crystallized Intelligence

General Intelligence--Undheim and Gustafsson (1987) used a linear structural relations technique to show that fluid intelligence is equivalent to general intelligence.

Information Processing--The information-processing skill of information reduction was related to Gc whereas information generation was related to Gf (Hussy & Scheller, 1977).

Creative Thinking--Crawford (1974) found that creative thinking was positively related to Gc but unrelated to Gf.

Instruments for Measuring Secondary Mental Abilities

We describe two sets of instruments--those that are intended to measure fluid intelligence and those that are intended to measure crystallized intelligence. Common methods for assessing Gf include manipulation of matrices, concept classification, and induction of concepts or rules. Gc is most often assessed by general vocabulary tests (or general information tests that measure knowledge of science, literature, etc.), vocabulary comprehension tests, and similarities tests.

Tests of Fluid Intelligence

IPAT Culture Fair Intelligence Test (Cattell, 1965)

This is a revised version of the Culture-Free Intelligence Test that Cattell and his colleagues produced in the 1940s. There are three scales: young children, older children, and average adults, and a scale for superior adults. The latter two scales consist of four subtests, including:

series--requires the completion of a series of four drawings by selecting the appropriate one from five options.
classifications--requires the selection of one of five drawings that is different from the others.
matrices--requires the selection of a drawing to complete a matrix.
conditions--requires the selection from five drawings of overlapping geometric figures the one in which one or two dots could be placed to fit the specification of the model.

These are primarily figural reasoning tasks. The scales have been validated in a series of studies employing thousands of students. Consistency over items is .87, over parts is .80, and over time is .84. Validity was determined by comparing it to general intelligence tests ($r=.77$). Test scores, however, are independent of school achievement.
    A number of studies, including Nenty's (1986), showed, despite its intentions, a substantial portion of the Culture Fair Test is culturally biased when used with cultures from different continents.

Raven's Progressive Matrices Test (Raven, 1985)

The Progressive Matrices Test has three scales: the Standard Progressive Matrices test, the Coloured Progressive Matrices test, and the Advanced Progressive Matrices test. The Standard test consists of 60 items in which the subject selects from multiple options the design or design part that best fits the stimulus figure. For instance, items may require the completion of a pattern, a visual analogy, an alteration of the pattern, permutations, or resolving figures into parts. The score is the number of items correctly identified. The test requires up to 60 minutes to complete. Reliability is generally good, although the scales have been revised so often that consistent findings are difficult.

Necessary Arithmetic Operations Test (French, Ekstrom, & Price, 1963)

The Necessary Arithmetic Operations Test is a test of the general reasoning factor from the Kit of Factor-Reference Cognitive Tests. Cattell (1971) believed that this factor was a first-order perception of Gf. The test consists of 30 multiple-choice questions, in two parts, which require the test taker to determine what numerical operations are required to solve arithmetic problems without actually having to carry out the calculations.

Tests of Crystallized Intelligence

While most traditional intelligence tests, for example the Wechsler Adult Intelligence Scale (WAIS) or the Wechsler Intelligence Scale for Children (WISC), are considered useful measures of crystallized intelligence, the following specific tests have been used in the research to test it.

Peabody Picture Vocabulary Test (PPVT)

The PPVT is designed to provide assessment of verbal intelligence. It is an untimed individual test that usually requires less than fifteen minutes and consists of 150 test items. Each item contains a stimulus word and four numbered pictures. The examiner reads the stimulus word, and the subject identifies the picture that is associated with the stimulus word. The items are arranged in ascending order of difficulty. The subject continues to respond until he or she misses six of any eight. Reliabilities range from .67 to .84, increasing with the age of the norm group. It has a high (.88) test-retest reliability. The test is simple to complete and to administer, but should not be used as a measure of general intelligence.

Vocabulary Subtest: WAIS (Wechsler, 1958)

The WAIS is among the most popular intelligence tests. It produces numerous scores, including verbal (information, comprehension, arithmetic, similarities, digit span, vocabulary) and performance (digit symbol, picture completion, block design, picture arrangement, object assembly). The vocabulary subscale consists of 40 items with a range of difficulty. Because vocabulary is a measure of learning ability, Wechsler (1958) believed it to be an index of general intelligence, and not merely an index of schooling.

Theoretical Background

Cattell's discovery of two general mental abilities was built upon much of the factor-analytic work reported in the next two chapters, especially that of Thurstone (see chapter 5). Most of the early intelligence research sought to identify what a general mental ability looks like. Researchers like Thurstone, on the other hand, sought to describe primary mental abilities, which are the constituent abilities that comprise intelligence. Cattell (1971) observed that during the late 1930s and early 1940s, research on various perceptual tests was showing that increases in many of these perceptual abilities flattened out at an earlier age than did performance on tests of numerical ability, vocabulary, and synonyms, indicating two distinct intellectual development processes. This observation was supported by Thurstone (1938), who factor-analyzed the primary ability factors that he had found in earlier research. Rather than finding the single general intelligence factor, Thurstone found more than one general factor, causing Cattell (1941) to develop his *two general factor theory* of intelligence. To test this theory, he developed and tested the Culture Fair Intelligence Test (Cattell, 1940; Cattell, Feingold, & Sarason, 1941).

The theory evolved over the years. Later research with the theory (Horn & Cattell, 1966) claimed that Gf and Gc are only two (albeit the two most prominent) among several forms of general ability. Other general abilities include:

General visualization (Gv)--This involves visual acuity, light sensitivity, visual field, and depth perception, which are used in orienting to and visualizing movements and transformations of visual objects in space.

General fluency (Gf)--This involves recalling and recognizing names for cultural concepts.

General speediness (Gs)--This describes the quickness with which intellectual tasks are performed, especially in simple perceptual tasks, yet independent of these other general abilities.

Subsequent research (Cattell, 1963; Horn & Cattell, 1966) used factor analysis to analyze primary factors and personality factors to confirm the existence of Gf and Gc. Additional research (Lansman, Donaldson, Hunt, & Yantis, 1982) used confirmatory factor analysis to confirm the independence of Gc, Gf, Gv, and perceptual speed. Rubin, Brown, and Priddle (1978) found that the Gf and Gc factors did not show up as independent factors until the third grade.

Other researchers, however, had different points of view. Humphreys (1970) concluded from an analysis of Cattell and Horn's research that the model was very tentative. Guilford criticized the methodology of Cattell and Horn's research and the consistency of their findings.

He claimed that fluid and crystallized intelligence were "fanciful concepts" that do not represent valid constructs, and are better accounted for by his own Structure-of-Intellect model (see chapter 6).

Fluid/Crystallized Intelligence and Learning

Research

- Gc and level of aspiration correlated significantly with performance on five school-based tests but Gf was not related (Eno, 1978).

- Trial-and-error problem solving was more highly related to fluid intelligence than to crystallized, and Gf and Gc were more correlated among well-educated individuals than among poorly educated ones (Schroth, 1983).

Implications of the Characteristics and Research

Implications which are drawn from research are noted with a •; those drawn logically from descriptive information regarding the trait are noted by an *. Based on the very little bit of learning research and the descriptions of Gf and Gc, we conclude that *fluid* learners are more likely to excel at learning tasks such as:

- problem-solving and far transfer reasoning tasks
- identifying or forming new concepts
- determining relationships between ideas

and acquire and use effectively learning strategies such as:

* gauging task difficulty and estimating time and effort
* predicting outcomes, inferring causes, and evaluating implications
* testing personal skills

Based upon the very little bit of research and the descriptions of Gf and Gc, we conclude that *crystallized* learners are more likely to excel at learning tasks such as:

- verbal tasks, such as reading and comprehending information
- numerical skills
- awareness of concepts and ideas pertaining to a topic
- general vocabulary ability
- general information or world knowledge
- identifying similarities between items

and acquire and use effectively learning strategies such as:

* concentrating on information
* reviewing and paraphrasing materials

Fluid/Crystallized Intelligence and Instruction

Research

• A cognitive training program designed to enhance the figural relations aspect of Gf did enhance performance on three different fluid reasoning tests (Plemons, Willis, & Baltes, 1978).

• Physical fatigue affected Gf more than it did Gc (Nirmal, 1982).

• Contrary to the hypothesis, Federico (1984) found that learners higher in fluid ability did not adapt and perform better in an unconventional educational environment than able learners who were better skilled in traditional learning situations.

• Fluid intelligence did not interact with a discovery versus expository treatment in either near or far transfer tasks, although the discovery approach produced better far transfer regardless of the Gf level of the learners (Sugrue & Thomas, 1989).

Implications of the Characteristics and Research

Implications which are drawn from research are noted with a •; those drawn logically from descriptive information regarding the trait are noted by an *. Based on the descriptions of Gf and Gc and the very little bit of research, we recommend considering the following instructional approaches.

Instructional conditions that capitalize on the preferences of the *fluid* student include:

• requiring learners to abstract or induce and then use concepts
• requiring learners to perceive and use relations or correlations
• using figural and nonverbal instructional materials
* analyzing key ideas
* sequencing instruction inductively

Instructional conditions that capitalize on the preferences of the *crystallized* student include:

• using traditional, reading and lecture-based instruction
* creating summaries
* using deductive instructional sequence
* stating outcomes of instruction
* presenting vocabulary or requiring students to look it up and then paraphrase it
* providing various examples
* asking learners to paraphrase content

References

Cattell, R. B. (1940). A culture-free intelligence test. *Journal of Educational Psychology, 31*, 161-179.

Cattell, R. B. (1941). Some theoretical issues in adult intelligence testing. *Psychological Bulletin, 38*, 592.

Cattell, R. B. (1945). Personality traits associated with abilities. 1. With intelligence and drawing ability. *Educational & Psychological Measurement, 5*, 131-146.

Cattell, R. B. (1957). *Personality and motivation structure and measurement.* New York: World Book.

Cattell, R. B. (1963). Theory of fluid and crystallized intelligence: A critical experiment. *Journal of Educational Psychology, 54*, 1-22.

Cattell, R. B. (1965). *The IPAT Culture Fair Intelligence Scales 1, 2 and 3* (3rd ed.). Champaign, IL: Institute for Personality and Ability Testing.

Cattell, R. B. (1971). *Abilities: Their structure, growth, and action.* Boston: Houghton Mifflin.

Cattell, R. B. (1980). The heritability of fluid, Gf, and crystallized, Gc, intelligence, estimated by a least squares use of the MAVA method. *British Journal of Educational Psychology, 50*, 253-265.

Cattell, R. B., Feingold, S., & Sarason, S. (1941). A culture-free intelligence test. 2. Evaluation of cultural influence on test performance. *Journal of Educational Psychology, 32*, 81-100.

Crawford, C. B. (1974). Fluid and crystallized intelligence, creativity, and achievement in elementary school. *Journal of Behavioral Science, 2* (2), 43-48.

Eno, L. (1978). Predicting achievement and the theory of fluid and crystallized intelligence. *Psychological Reports, 43* (3, Pt. 1), 847-852.

Federico, P. A. (1986). Crystallized and fluid intelligence in a "New" instructional situation. *Contemporary Educational Psychology, 11*, 33-53.

French, J. W., Ekstrom, R. B., & Price, L. A. (1963). *Kit of reference tests for cognitive skills.* Princeton: Educational Testing Service.

Horn, J. L., & Cattell, R. B. (1966). Age differences in in fluid and crystallized intelligence. *Acta Psychologica, 26,* 107-129.

Horn, J. L., & Cattell, R. B. (1967). Refinement and test of the theory of fluid and crystallized intelligence. *Journal of Educational Psychology, 57,* 253-270.

Humphreys, L. G. (1970). A skeptical look at the factor pure test. In C. E. Lunneborg (Ed.), *Current problems and techniques in multivariate psychology* (pp. 23-32). Seattle: University of Washington.

Hussy, W., & Scheller, R. (1977). Human information processing and intelligence. *Acta Psychologica, 41,* 373-380.

Lansman, M., Donaldson, G., Hunt, E., & Yantis, S. (1982). Ability factors and cognitive processes. *Intelligence, 6,* 347-386.

Nenty, H. J. (1986). Cross-culture bias analysis of Cattell Culture-Fair Intelligence Test. *Perspectives in Psychological Researches, 9* (1), 1-16.

Nirmal, B. S. (1982). The effect of physical fatigue on measures of crystalized and fluid intelligence of school children. *Personality Study and Group Behavior, 2,* 20-27.

Plemons, J. K., Willis, S. L., & Baltes, P. B. (1978). Modifiability of fluid intelligence in aging: A short-term longitudinal training approach. *Journal of Gerontology, 33,* 224-231.

Raven, C. (1985). *Raven progressive matrices.* Western Psychological Services, Los Angeles.

Rubin, K. H., Brown, I. D., & Priddle, R. L. (1978). The relationships between measures of fluid, crystallized, and "Piagetian" intelligence in elementary school children. *The Journal of Genetic Psychology, 132,* 29-36.

Schroth, M. L. (1983). A study of aging, intelligence, and problem solving. *Psychological Reports, 53,* 1271-1279.

Sugrue, B. M., & Thomas, R. A. (1989, March 27-31). *Effects of discovery and expository instruction on recall and transfer of procedural knowledge: Interactions with learner aptitude.* Paper presented at the annual meeting of the American Educational Research Association, San Francisco. (ERIC Document Reproduction Service No. ED 308 218)

Thurstone, L. L. (1938). *Primary mental abilities.* Chicago: University of Chicago Press.

Undheim, J. O., & Gustafsson, J. E. (1987). The hierarchical organization of cognitive abilities: Restoring general intelligence through the use of linear structural relations (LISREL). *Multivariate Behavioral Research, 22,* 149-171.

Wechsler, D. (1958). *The measurement and appraisal of adult intelligence* (4th ed.). Baltimore: Williams & Wilkins.

Bibliography

Cattell, R. B. (1943). The measurement of adult intelligence. *Psychological Bulletin, 40,* 153-193.

Cattell, R. B. (1946). *The description and measurement of personality.* New York: World Book.

Cattell, R. B. (1951). Classical and standard IQ score standardization of the IPAT Culture-Free Intelligence Scale 2. *Journal of Consulting Psychology, 15,* 154-159.

Guilford, J. P. (1980). Fluid and crystallized intelligences: Two fanciful concepts. *Psychological Bulletin, 88,* 406-412.

Stankov, L., Horn, J. L., & Roy, T. (1980). On the relationship between Gf/Gc and Jensen's Level I/Level II theory. *Journal of Educational Psychology, 72,* 796-809.

5

THURSTONE'S
PRIMARY MENTAL ABILITIES

Description of Primary Mental Abilities

Thurstone (1938) believed that intelligence could only be defined in terms of a domain of essential mental abilities. He used empirical, experimental methods to identify the domain of skills that comprise intellectual behavior. Primary mental abilities represent these component skills of intelligence. Primary abilities may be combined to define larger intellectual components, such as those described by Cattell (see chapter 4), which in turn may be combined to define the concept of intelligence. Primary mental abilities are the cognitive skills that enable individuals to learn, think, and reason. These abilities are called on in the performance of real-world tasks. Differences in primary abilities account for differences in individual cognitive performances.

These primary mental abilities are rather stable throughout life until around 55 years of age, at which time small decreases in most abilities begin to appear (Hertzog & Schale, 1988). After 60, these decrements, especially those in reasoning ability, become more pronounced (Schale & Hertzog, 1983).

Classes of Abilities

The original studies (Thurstone, 1938, 1940; Thurstone & Thurstone, 1941) identified and confirmed seven primary mental abilities.

Perceptual Speed--The mental ability indicated by this factor relates to quickness in identifying objects that are perceived, that is, a perceptual set. This is a generalized skill that relates to conceptual, as well as visual information. It involves discriminating between competing stimuli and identifying those with similarities. It also involves grouping objects into meaningful sequences. Rearranging disordered words into sentences, for instance, requires moving words around until they are perceived as being in proper sequence.

Numerical--This mental ability obviously describes the mental manipulation of numbers. The more complex the manipulation, the more integral the operation is to the skill.

Word Fluency--This mental skill has been referred to as ideational fluency or divergent production. The learner generates as many ideas as possible from a set of arbitrary rules, such as "all of the things that you can think of that are red and round."

Verbal Comprehension--This ability is more concerned with semantic interpretation, that is, the comprehension of word combinations such as interpreting quotes or proverbs, or generating antonyms, synonyms, or analogies.

Spatial--This factor represents visual skills, spatial manipulation, similarity of visuals, and imagining how visuals might appear in other orientations.

Memory--This ability describes the capacity to store and retrieve information without additional processing. That is, there is no emphasis on the semantic interpretation or manipulation of the information, only on the ability to memorize and recall it. Memory is usually tested using paired-associate tasks.

Inductive Reasoning--This is the ability that is most often associated with general intelligence because it involves reasoning skills. It is often equated with fluid intelligence (see Chapter 4), another construct closely associated with general intelligence. This ability involves reasoning tasks such as inference, extrapolation, interpolation, and so on.

Instruments for Measuring Primary Mental Abilities

Primary Mental Abilities Test **(PMA)** (SRA, 1962)

The PMA Test consists of five scores: verbal meaning, perceptual speed, number facility, spatial relations, and total. The primary mental abilities were statistically analyzed through oblique rotation in order to select the most reliable combination of factors for these subtests. There are four versions of the test: kindergarten-grade 1, grades 2-4, grades 4-6, grades 6-9, and grades 9-12. Previous editions contained a motor subtest for the lower levels and a verbal fluency subtest for the higher levels. Test-retest reliability coefficients vary by subtest and grade level: .73-.93 for the verbal subtest, .51-.81 for the perceptual speed, and .84-.94 for total scores.

Tests Supporting Original Factors

In a series of studies, Thurstone (1938, 1947) used factor analysis techniques to isolate the seven *primary* (essential, most important, basic) mental abilities described in an earlier section. He administered a battery of 56 tests representing the broadest range of mental abilities possible to 240 volunteers at the University of Chicago. Thurstone and Thurstone (1941) then administered 60 tests to another 1,154 subjects. In both of these studies, Thurstone factor-analyzed the subjects' scores on each of the tests, looking for commonalities in performance. The first study isolated seven significant and reliable factors, whereas the second study verified them. Each isolated factor represents a skill or primary mental ability defined by the tests that "load" significantly onto it. That is, the skills assessed by those tests, themselves, significantly describe or predict that type of ability.

Thurstone and Thurstone (1941) administered the top three tests that loaded onto each of the seven factors from the previous studies to another 437 eighth graders. In this follow-up study, perceptual speed was not strongly supported and was subsequently dropped from the measures of the PMA. Thurstone identified the following tests to measure these primary mental abilities:

Instruments for Measuring Perceptual Speed (P) (Thurstone, 1938; Thurstone & Thurstone, 1941)

Verbal Classification--This 70-item test consists of two columns of words that belong to the same classes (e.g., animals, furniture) and a third column in which the words belong to both. Subjects classify each of the words in the third column.

Word Grouping--This is a test of 71 items, each containing five words, four of which are examples of the same concept. The student must identify the one word that is not a member (e.g., carrot, radish, beet, book, turnip).

Disarranged Sentences--In this test of 81 items, subjects determine the truth of sentences that must be unscrambled (e.g., blue is sky the sometimes is true).

Identical Forms--This is a timed test of 60 items that show a stimulus figure and five other figures. The student is required to identify the one that is identical to the stimulus.

Faces--This timed test of 54 items consists of three line drawings of faces that require the student to identify the one that is different.

Instruments for Measuring Numerical Ability (N)

Number Code--In this test, the subject is asked to perform multiplication tasks using codes for numbers from 1-20.

Addition--In this test, the subject must add seven two-digit numbers.

Subtraction--In this test, the student is asked to perform subtraction tasks using four-digit numbers.

Multiplication--The student must multiply six-digit numbers by a single-digit number.

Division--This test requires the student to divide seven-digit numbers by a single-digit number.

Instruments for Measuring Word Fluency (W)

Disarranged Words--This test consists of 72 disarranged items (e.g., odg) from which words are to be made.

Anagrams--Subjects are required to make as many words as possible from the letters in a word (e.g., generation).

Spelling--This is a true-false test of 100 spelling words.

Grammar--The student corrects each incorrect sentence by changing a single word.

First Letters--This timed test requires the student to write as many words as possible that begin with a *P*.

Four-Letter Words--In this timed test students are directed to write as many words as possible that begin with a *B* and have four letters.

Instruments for Measuring Verbal Comprehension (V)

Reading Quotations--This test consists of 25 items that ask for an interpretation of short quotations, such as "In calamity any rumor is considered worth listening to."

Reading Proverbs--This test contains 24 items that ask for an interpretation of short proverbs, such as "Tall oaks from little acorns grow."

Word Grouping--This is a test of 71 items, each containing five words, four of which are examples of the same concept. The student must identify the one word that is not a member (e.g., carrot, radish, beet, <u>book</u>, turnip).

Inventive Synonyms--In this test of 30 items, the student is asked to produce two synonyms for each word (e.g., <u>aid: help</u> and <u>assist)</u>.

Inventive Opposites--In this test of 30 items, the student is asked to produce two opposites for each word (e.g., <u>large: little</u> and <u>small</u>).

Verbal Analogies--In this test, students are asked to complete 56 analogies (e.g., foot:shoe::hand:<u>glove</u>).

Instruments for Measuring Spatial Ability (S)

Cubes--In this test, there are 32 timed problems asking students to determine if two cubes showing three faces could be the same cube.

Lozenges--This test was designed to assess kinesthetic imagery in a paper-pencil test. Subjects are shown a parallelogram with a circle in one corner and one edge painted dark. They are required to imagine how it would appear if it were picked up, turned over, and placed face down.

Flags--This is a test of 48 items consisting of two American flags rotated into various positions, requiring the subject to determine if they are opposite sides.

Surface Development--The learner is shown pictures of six objects made of cardboard that are to be unfolded with dotted lines representing the folds, similar to paper-folding scales in many intelligence tests.

Pursuit--This test depicts eight diagrams, each consisting of 10 irregular and overlapping lines going from one side of the diagram to the other. Subjects must trace the lines across the diagram and mark the position of the line on the opposite side.

Instruments for Measuring Memory (M)

Word-Number--This is a paired-associate test consisting of word and number pairs. The student is asked to recall the number given the word.

Initials--This is another paired-associate test of 25 name-initial pairs. Students are asked to recall the initials given the names.

Number-Number--This test presents paired associates consisting of pairs of two-digit numbers. Given one number, the student must recall its pair.

Instruments for Measuring Inductive Reasoning (R)

Tabular Completion--This test consists of four incomplete tables of numbers with row and column headings. Students are required to calculate and fill in the missing items.

Number Series--This test consists of 22 series of numbers with items missing (e.g., 8 11 14 __ 20 __). Students must fill in the missing numbers.

Theoretical Background

Thurstone (1931) was among the first researchers to employ factor analysis to overcome arbitrary general definitions of intelligence or personality by empirically isolating primary mental abilities. With the goal of proving the assumption that there is no such entity as general intelligence, his research agenda proposed to find and describe those component skills. Indeed, his results yielded no such general factor. Rather, intelligence was found to be a complex of constituent abilities. Thurstone also introduced the idea of "simple structure," which holds that any given test should load onto, or be affected by, only one or two factors.

The factor analysis techniques that Thurstone worked on have been extended and expanded by several researchers subsequent to Thurstone's work. French, Ekstrom, and Price (1963) set out to differentiate Thurstone's primary abilities into smaller, more distinct abilities. This work led to the development of the Kit of Factor Referenced Cognitive Tests, which consists of a number of separate skills and factors. Pawlik (1966) differentiated 19 primary abilities (separate skills or factors) including:

- perceptual speed--speed of comparing visual perceptions
- spatial visualization--imaging spatial manipulations
- spatial relations--recognizing objects from different perspectives
- spatial orientation--spatial relations from different body orientations
- speed of closure--relating perceptions into Gestalt wholes
- flexibility of closure--abstracting an object from a more complex visual field
- verbal comprehension--meanings of words and phrases
- numerical facility--performing arithmetic operations
- word fluency--generating words with syntactic or structural similarities
- ideational fluency--generating ideas with given specifications
- associational fluency--generating specific words to meet certain requirements
- expressional fluency--generating appropriate verbal expressions
- deduction--reasoning from general to specific

- induction--reasoning from specific to general
- general reasoning--problem-solving or arithmetic reasoning
- associative memory--paired-associate memory
- meaningful memory--memory for semantically meaningful material
- visual memory--memory for visual objects
- memory span--memory of time elements

Thurstone's major contribution to research was the discrimination of specific abilities or factors of intelligence, rather than the reliance on the arbitrary definitions of intelligence developed by previous researchers. The next chapter examines research by Guilford (1972) that conceptually identified as many as 120 different mental abilities.

Primary Mental Abilities and Learning

Research

The implications of Thurstone's research on the components of intelligence for school learning were to be worked out by other researchers. Because of the age of his research, little if any secondary research has been reported that examined the interactions of primary mental abilities and learning outcomes.

Implications of the Characteristics and Research

Implications which are drawn from research are noted with a •; those drawn logically from descriptive information regarding the trait are noted by an *. We reason from the descriptions of primary mental abilities that learners with high *perceptual speed* are more likely to excel at learning tasks such as:

- comparing and contrasting objects to classify them into groups
- disambiguating or organizing irregular information displays, that is, identifying the important information in a display
- evaluating and arranging objects according to some criteria such as height

and acquire and use effectively learning strategies such as:

* searching for, or evaluating, information
* analyzing key ideas
* judging utility or value of ideas

We reason from the descriptions of primary mental abilities that learners with high levels of *numerical* abilities are more likely to excel at learning tasks such as:

• solving well-formulated math problems
• mathematic calculations

We reason from the descriptions of primary mental abilities that learners with high levels of *word fluency* are more likely to excel at learning tasks such as:

• brainstorming and generating new ideas
* editing text and manuscripts for spelling and grammar errors

and acquire and use effectively learning strategies such as:

• using mnemonics to remember content

We reason from the descriptions of primary mental abilities that learners with high levels of *verbal comprehension* are more likely to excel at learning tasks such as:

• reading text for comprehension
• interpreting passages, quotes, proverbs

and acquire and use effectively learning strategies such as:

* outlining content
* paraphrasing or summarizing content
* comparing new information with existing knowledge or beliefs
• generating metaphors and analogies

We reason from the descriptions of primary mental abilities that learners with high levels of *spatial* abilities are more likely to excel at learning tasks such as:

• imagining outcomes or changes in visual ideas
• design tasks, such as those in mechanical drawing or architecture
• visual-tracking tasks required by computer games and fighter pilots

and acquire and use effectively learning strategies such as:

* concept mapping and semantic networking

We reason from the descriptions of primary mental abilities that learners with high levels of *memory* are more likely to excel at learning tasks and strategies such as:

• repeating or rehearsing material to be recalled
* mnemonics

We reason from the descriptions of primary mental abilities that learners with high levels of *inductive reasoning* are more likely to excel at learning tasks such as:

• solving complex or novel problems
• drawing conclusions, generating implications, extrapolations, or interpolations

and acquire and use effectively learning strategies such as:

* predicting outcomes, inferring causes, explaining implications
* generating metaphors and analogies

Primary Mental Abilities and Instruction

The focus of Thurstone's research was never on the effects of instruction as a function of primary mental abilities. Rather, he was interested only in isolating the components of intelligence. The implications of the primary mental abilities was to be worked out by other researchers. No research has been reported, to our knowledge, that has examined the interactions of instruction with primary mental abilities.

The primary mental abilities, however, form the basis for many of the cognitive controls and styles that are described later in this book. There are significant bodies of research that have examined the interactions of those abilities and instructional treatments.

References

French, J. W., Ekstrom, R. B., & Price, L. A. (1963). *Kit of reference tests for cognitive skills.* Princeton: Educational Testing Service.
Guilford, J. P. (1972). Thurstone's Primary Mental Abilities and Structure of the Intellect. *Psychological Bulletin, 77* (2), 129-143.
Hertzog, C., & Schale, K. W. (1988). Stability and change in adult intelligence: 2. Simultaneous analysis of longitudinal means and covariance structures. *Psychology and Aging, 3,* 122-130.

Pawlik, K. (1966). Concepts and calculations in human cognitive abilities. In R. B. Cattell (Ed.), *Handbook of multivariate experimental psychology* (pp. 535-562). Chicago: Rand McNally.

Schale, K. W., & Hertzog, C. (1983). Fourteen-year-cohort-sequential analysis of adult intellectual development. *Developmental Psychology, 19,* 531-543.

SRA. (1962). *Manual for the Primary Mental Abilities Test.* Chicago: Science Research Associates.

Thurstone, L. L. (1931). Multiple factor analysis. *Psychological Review, 38,* 406-427.

Thurstone, L. L. (1938). Primary mental abilities. *Psychometric Monographs,* No. 1.

Thurstone, L. L. (1940). An experimental study of simple structure. *Psychometrika, 5,* 153-168.

Thurstone, L. L. (1947). *Multiple factor analysis.* Chicago: University of Chicago Press.

Thurstone, L. L., & Thurstone, T. G. (1941). Factorial studies of intelligence. *Psychometric Monographs,* No. 2.

6

GUILFORD'S
STRUCTURE OF THE INTELLECT

Description of Structure-of-Intellect

The Structure-of-Intellect (SOI) model, described most completely by J. P. Guilford (1967), is the most comprehensive of the factor-analytic models of intelligence. Prior to its introduction, numerous factor-analytic studies of intelligence were capable of identifying only 40 separate factorial abilities. In less than 10 years of work, however, researchers at the Aptitudes Research Project at the University of Southern California identified over 100 abilities (Guilford, 1988). The SOI is a morphological model of intelligence that organized the large number of factors that was generated by this research during the 1950s and 1960s along with those that was derived by Thurstone (see Chapter 5) and other previous researchers.

The SOI model originally conceived of 120 different mental abilities in three different dimensions: operations, content, and products (see Fig. 6.1). Later, one of the operations and one of the contents were divided, adding 60 more abilities to the model. Every mental ability is defined in terms of the mental *operation* on a specific form of *content* of a specific type of intellectual *product*. For example, the shaded block in Fig. 6.1 identifies a specific mental ability--cognition of figural units.

Characteristic Differences in Structure-of-Intellect

Operations

Operations in the SOI represent the mental activities or processes that individuals perform on the objects of content and product. Operations are the the mental manipulations required for processing information. Operations include:

Cognition (C)--This is the awareness, recognition, comprehension, or elementary understanding of information. Cognition is essential to all other mental operations; that is, information cannot be manipulated until it is comprehended.

STRUCTURE OF INTELLECT

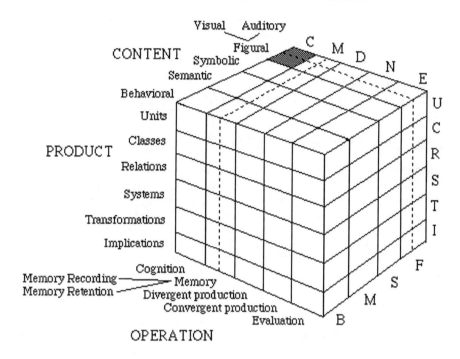

Note: Dotted lines represent changes in the model made by Guilford (1977, 1988).

Fig. 6.1. Guilford's structure of the intellect (SOI) model of intelligence.

Memory (M)--This is the storage and retention of information for later re-trieval. In his last published paper, Guilford (1988) separated memory into two operations, memory recording and memory retention. *Memory recording* is the process of encoding information into memory, and is more concerned with short-term memory. *Memory retention*, on the other hand, is concerned with processing required for longer term reten-tion of content.

Divergent production (D)--This involves producing or generating alterna-tive forms of information; producing a variety (quantity) of relevant an-swers; transfer of learning, especially in creativity; and fluency of idea generation.

Convergent production (N)--This involves producing the unique or best possible answer or conclusion from given information that may entail rule using or problem solving.

Evaluation (E)--This involves making judgements or making decisions about the correctness, suitability, appropriateness, identity, adequacy, or consistency of information based on criteria that may be given or generated by the individual.

Contents

Contents represent the format of the information that is mentally manipulated by the individual. Contents include:

Figural (F)--Information takes concrete, visual, spatial, or imaginal form, such as shapes or concrete objects. Guilford (1977) separated figural content into visual and auditory content. Visual and auditory content were originally combined because of the limited number of identifiable auditory abilities. Later research reported additional auditory abilities, allowing them greater autonomy in the model. *Visual* includes spatial, figural, or imaginal information, whereas *auditory* includes aural, sounds, or other auditory stimuli.

Symbolic (S)--This represents information in the form of arbitrary signs or sign systems that have no meaning in themselves (e.g., letters, numbers, musical notation, codes).

Semantic (M)--This entails information about mental constructs that convey meaning to words, objects, or pictures; the mental associations that are stimulated by objects, words and so forth.

Behavioral (B)--This involves information about human behavior and interactions including attitudes, moods, desires, intentions, perceptions; the human responses that are evoked by stimuli. These behavioral contents are not as well instantiated as the other content types.

Products

Products represent the type of information that is acted on or processed by the individual. They are the result or the perceivable outcome of the operation. Products include:

Units (U)--These are individual items or entities of information; a single object or item.

Classes (C)--These are concepts that define objects based on their shared attributes or characteristics.

Relations (R)--these are connections between classes or items of information.

Systems (S)--These are organized or structured accumulations of objects, their interrelated and interacting parts, and the relations between all of the objects.

Transformations (T)--These are changes in the form or nature of information such as transitions, translations, or changes in the form or structure of information.

Implications (I)--These are circumstantial or causal connections between items of information such as those involved in abstract ability or anticipating consequences.

General Differences

It is noteworthy that each of these three dimensions (operations, content, and products) are arranged in roughly hierarchical order, that is, in ascending levels of difficulty or complexity. Systems, for example, are more difficult mental products than relations or classes. Like all taxonomies; higher level operations, content, or products rely on the cumulative abilities of all lower level operations, and so forth. An individual cannot produce systems without understanding the relations between its components, which in turn depend on understanding the classes of objects that make up those relations, and so on.

As previously mentioned, each cell in the SOI model in Fig. 6.1 represents a distinct mental ability that involves the operation on content of a product. For example:

> Creating an analogy (father is to son as mother is to _____) is an example of NMR (convergent production of semantic relations).

> An ideational fluency task (listing all of the things that you can think of that are red and round) is an example of DMU (divergent production of semantic units).

> A recall task (naming the capital of Tennessee) is an example of MMU (memory for semantic units).

> Playing a piano from sheet music is an example of CST (convergent production of symbolic transformations).

It is also important to point out that each cell does not necessarily define a unitary form of behavior or outcome. Each cell describes a particular mental ability; however, most of those mental abilities can describe a combination of different mental activities. Some of these different mental activities were identified in the factor-analytic research of Guilford and the Educational Testing Service (ETS) (French, Ekstrom, & Price, 1963). For example:

> Cognition of figural transformations (CFT) can be measured by the Form Board Test, the Paper Folding Test, or the Surface Development Test from ETS.

> Memory for symbolic implications (MSI) can be measured by the Addition Test, the Division Test, and the Subtraction and Multiplication Tests from ETS.

> Divergent production of semantic units (DMU) can be measured by the Topics Test, Theme Test, and the Thing Categories Test from ETS.

Finally, it is also important to note that although the SOI model originally defined 120 different mental abilities only 98 of them were manifested in practice (Guilford & Hoepfner, 1971). Years of factor-analytic studies with hundreds of subjects were unable to isolate any tasks that assessed memory for behavioral products, convergent production of behavioral products, or evaluation of behavioral products (effectively eliminating 18 of the hypothesized intelligence factors). Additionally, Guilford was not able to isolate divergent production of figural relations or convergent production of figural units or systems. He was able to identify instances of each of the other factors. These gaps were not as serious as might be indicated by their numbers because they did not define any common conceptions of intelligence or commonly occurring learning tasks.

Individual Differences Related to Structure-of-Intellect

The SOI model extended the number of mental abilities using the same techniques and approaches that Thurstone employed in his work. Although most of Guilford's abilities were found to be independent of Thurstone's, Guilford (1972) found some overlap between them. For example:

Thurstone's "verbal" ability is consistent with Guilford's CMU.
Thurstone's "space" ability is consistent with Guilford's CFT.
Thurstone's "perception" ability is consistent with Guilford's EFU.
Thurstone's "word fluency" ability is consistent with Guilford's EFU.

Thurstone's "letter series" ability is consistent with Guilford's CSS.
Thurstone's "letter-grouping" ability is consistent with Guilford's CSC.
Thurstone's "perception" ability is consistent with Guilford's EFU.
Thurstone's "number" ability is consistent with Guilford's MSI and NSI.

Field dependence/independence--Guilford (1980) claims that the disembedding of hidden figures that is assessed in field independence (see chapter 7) essentially involves convergent production of visual transformations (NVT).

Instruments for Measuring Structure-of-Intellect Abilities

Structure-of-Intellect Learning Abilities Test (SOI-LA) (Meeker, Meeker, & Roid, 1985)

The SOI-LA was designed to measure 28 of Guilford's factors, including CFU, CFC, CFR, CFS, CFT, CSR, CSS, CMU, CMR, CMS, MFU, MSU-Visual, MSS-Visual, MSU-Auditory, MSS-Auditory, MSI-Visual, MSI-Auditory, EFU, EFC, ESC, ESS, NFU, NSS, NST, NSI, DFU, DMU, and DSR. These factors were measured in seven forms: Basic Form A, Basic Form B, Gifted Screening Form, Arithmetic-Math Form, Reading Form, Primary Form, and Reading Readiness Form. The first two forms are comprehensive combinations of all 28 tests, whereas the others represent a selection of subtests that best predict the function specified by their name.

The authors conducted extensive standardization studies with primary students, finding test-retest reliabilities of .58 to .77 for figural, symbolic, and semantic scores and reliabilities of .81 to .94 for total scores. They also conducted many studies showing that the SOI-LA had good criterion and predictive validity and that the subtests had good concurrent validity based on comparison with other tests. Maxwell (1984) found that the SOI-LA is capable of distinguishing SOI abilities at a very fine level of analysis, corroborating the Guilford model. Lagagnoux, Michael, Hocevar, and Maxwell (1990) found that the test was very susceptible to retest effect (improved scores on retesting over a two to four week period), especially for younger children and lower ability children. Retest gains were also greater when the identical form, rather than the equivalent form, was used.

Theoretical Background

The Structure-of-Intellect model (Guilford, 1967) is a psychometric theory of intelligence (derived from testing rather than theory) that was built on the work of Thurstone. The model resulted from the multiyear Aptitudes

Research Project (ARP) in which Guilford and his colleagues used factor-analytic techniques on large samples of students and military service personnel to isolate the factors of intelligence rather than accept the one general mental ability theory. The early stages of ARP were spent trying to verify Thurstone's factors. Guilford's findings were closely related to Thurstone's except that the SOI further separates factors (or mental processes) and content that were combined in Thurstone's research (Meeker et. al., 1985).

Guilford began by identifying the types of mental processes involved in intelligence including memory, comprehension, and fluency of ideas. Guilford revolutionized conceptions of intelligence by classifying, additionally, the form of the information on which those mental activities are applied. These included figural, symbolic, semantic, and behavioral categories. It took Guilford a few years to identify the structures (or types) of information items, including classes, relations, systems, and so on. These three dimensions were combined to form the morphological model shown in Fig. 6.1. Rather than beginning with a theory about intelligence, Guilford applied factor analysis to the discovery of the underlying factors and dimensions of intelligence.

Structure-of-Intellect and Learning

Research

- SOI abilities increased in importance as concept learning progressed (Durham, Guilford, & Hoepfner, 1967). During learning, memory seems to be the most important operation, with convergent production becoming more important later.

- Forming new associative connections involved constructing new implications (Guilford, 1985).

- Student achievement in an accounting course was found to be a function of memory for symbolic implications, convergent production of semantic classes, and convergent production of semantic systems (Gorham, 1980).

Implications of the Characteristics and Research

Very few studies relating SOI to instructional outcomes have been conducted; therefore, it is difficult to develop implications. The great number of factors, and subsequent interactions between those factors, required to complete specific learning tasks make it difficult to speculate about the range of them.

Structure-of-Intellect and Instruction

Research

Most research on the SOI has been concerned with the effects of training SOI intellectual skills on the academic performance of students.

• SOI trained teachers performed significantly better on divergent production outcomes (Burr, 1982).

• Training of SOI abilities did not contribute to increased academic performance with elementary students (Stubbs, 1983).

Meeker et al. (1985) described a number of unpublished studies that were collected by the SOI Institute:

• Training in SOI divergent production skills significantly increased creativity scores when compared with the control group receiving convergent production training (Manning, 1974).

• Training gifted students in divergent thinking skills resulted in greater increases in creativity as measured by divergent thinking subtests rather than in training convergent thinking tasks (Meeker, 1979).

• Friedberg (1979) showed that after 6 months of training, forth through sixth graders significantly improved their performance on divergent production, semantic, relations, transformations, and implications activities.

• Prescriptive SOI training resulted in significant gains in grades 2-6 on the CMR, CMS, and NST subtests and increases as some grade levels on DMU, MSU, MSS, and NSI (Jones, 1980).

• SOI instruction in figural skills (CFS and CFT) improved performance on both tests (Ring, 1981).

• Goodloe-Kaplan (1982) showed significant gains on all memory subtests as a result of SOI training in normal classrooms.

• SOI instruction over a 3-week period dramatically improved MSU, MSS, DFU, DMU, and DMR, indicating an increase in creativity and giftedness (Patton, Goodloe-Kaplan, & Shore, 1982).

Implications of the Characteristics and Research

Implications that are drawn from research are noted with a •; those drawn logically from descriptive information regarding the trait are noted by an *.

• It appears that the abilities that are most trainable are the divergent production skills. This is probably because of the lack of practice or instruction of that skill in public schools, which seem to focus more on convergent production outcomes.

• For the same reason, students should receive instruction on the higher order productions, such as semantic, relations, transformations, and implications.

• Because teachers who are more skilled in the higher order operations and products are more likely to affect their students in a similar manner, training should be provided to them as well.

References

Burr, L. G. (1982). Comparison of structure of intellect divergent production measures for three groups of teachers (Doctoral dissertation, Texas Woman's University). *Dissertation Abstracts International,* *43*, 1117.

Durham, J. L., Guilford, J. P., & Hoepfner, R. (1967). Multivariate approaches to the discovering of the intellectual components of concept learning. *Psychological Review, 75*, 206-221.

French, J. W., Ekstrom, R. B., & Price, L. A. (1963). *Kit of reference tests for cognitive skills.* Princeton: Educational Testing Service.

Friedberg, D. (1979). *Training in memory and cognition: St. Joseph study.* St. Joseph, MO: St. Joseph School District.

Goodloe-Kaplan, B. (1982). *SOI training with various cultures and ability levels.* Unpublished manuscript.

Gorham, J. P. (1980). The relationship between selected structure-of-intellect abilities and achievement in an urban community college introductory accounting. (Doctoral dissertation, New York University) *Dissertation Abstracts International, 41*, 2896.

Guilford, J. P. (1967). *The nature of human intelligence.* New York: McGraw-Hill.

Guilford, J. P. (1972). Thurstone's primary mental abilities and structure-of-intellect abilities. *Psychological Bulletin, 77*, 129-143.

Guilford, J. P. (1977). *Way beyond the IQ: Guide to improving intelligence and creativity.* Buffalo, NY: Barely Limited.

Guilford, J. P. (1980). Cognitive styles: What are they? *Educational and Psychological Measurement, 40,* 715-735.

Guilford, J. P. (1985). The structure-of-intellect model. In B.B. Wolman (Ed.), *Handbook of intelligence* (pp. 225-266). New York: Wiley.

Guilford, J. P. (1988). Some changes in the structure-of-intellect model. *Educational and Psychological Measurement, 48,* 1-4.

Guilford, J. P., & Hoepfner, R. (1971). *The analysis of intelligence.* New York: McGraw-Hill.

Jones, B. (1982). *SOI instruction for gifted in arithmetic and reading.* Ft. Bragg, NC. Unpublished manuscript.

Lagagnoux, G., Michael, W. B., Hocevar, D., & Maxwell, V. (1990). Retest effects on standardized structure-of-intellect ability measures. *Educational and Psychological Measurement, 50,* 475-492.

Manning, E. (1974). *Training creativity.* Whittier, CA: Whittier Public Schools.

Maxwell, V. L. (1984). Sex differences in memory ability: A structure of intellect analysis (Doctoral dissertation, University of Southern California). *Dissertation Abstracts International, 45,* 791.

Meeker, R. (1979, September). Can creativity be be developed in gifted. *Roeper Review,* 17-18.

Meeker, M., Meeker, R., & Roid, G. H. (1985). *Structure of intellect learning abilities test (SOI-LA).* Los Angeles: Western Psychological Services.

Patton, S., Goodloe-Kaplan, B., & Shore, B. (1982). *Intense program for gifted using SOI.* Montreal: Montreal Public Schools.

Ring, A. (1981). *Figural training for gifted students.* Montreal: McGill University.

Stubbs, C. A. (1983). An investigation of the effect of structure-of-intellect training on academic achievement with low-achieving primary students (Doctoral dissertation, University of Tennessee). *Dissertation Abstracts International, 45,* 136.

Bibliography

Durham, J. L., Guilford, J. P., & Hoepfner, R. (1969). Cognition, production and memory of class concepts. *Educational and Psychological Measurements, 29,* 515-538.

Guilford, J. P. (1956). The structure of intellect. *Psychological Bulletin, 52,* 267-293.

Guilford, J. P. (1980). Fluid and crystallized intelligence: Two fanciful concepts. *Psychological Bulletin, 88,* 406-412.

Meeker, M. N. (1969). *The structure of intellect: Its interpretation and use.* Columbus: Charles Merrill.

PART III

COGNITIVE CONTROLS

Introduction

The seven chapters in Part III review the most direct descendants of mental abilities, cognitive controls. Whether you ascribe to 7 or 70 distinct mental abilities, they form patterns of thinking or reasoning in human individuals. Cognitive controls derive directly from these varied arrangements. They represent patterns of thinking that control the ways that individuals process and reason about information. Each cognitive control represents a separate landscape or pattern of thinking.

Cognitive control theory is often equated with cognitive style theory (see Parts IV and V) because they emerged at about the same time. Cognitive controls, however, are the psychoanalytic entities that regulate perception. They have different theories, methods, and assumptions than cognitive styles (Klein & Schlesinger, 1949). Cognitive styles define learner traits, whereas cognitive controls "have the status of intervening variables that define principles by which motoric behavior, perception, memory and other basic quantitative forms of cognitive functioning are organized as an individual coordinates himself with his environment" (Santostefano, 1978, p. 100). The cognitive controls described in the next seven chapters influence and control an individual's perception of environmental stimuli, whereas the styles described in Parts IV and V reflect an individual's perceptual habits.

Jonassen (1978) listed the following characteristics of cognitive controls:

- Cognitive dimension: The theory differentiates multiple cognitive dimensions of individual differences.
- Inference: The theory identifies situational requirements that activate each control.
- Theoretical base: Cognitive controls are based on the assumptions and propositions of psychoanalytic theory.
- Distinguishing goal: Cognitive control theory seeks to identify how cognitive mechanisms manage, regulate, and adapt to environmental information, needs, and motives.

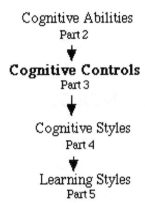

Cognitive controls, therefore, define a level of individual differences that falls between mental abilities and cognitive styles. They share some characteristics with both categories. Messick (1984) distinguished cognitive styles from mental abilities as noted in Table 7.1.

Cognitive Abilities	Cognitive Controls	Cognitive Styles
Content/Level	x	
Manner/Form		
Competencies	x	
Propensities		
Maximal	x	Typical
Unipolar	x	Bipolar
Value Directional	x	Value Differentiated
Domain/Function	x	
Specific		
Pervasive/Organizing		
Enabling	x	Controlling

Table 7.1. Differences and shared factors.

Mental abilities, such as those described in Part II of this book, refer to the content and level of cognitive activity, whereas styles refer to the manner and form of learning. Abilities specify the competencies, the mental operations, and the kind of information being processed, whereas styles are stated in terms of propensities. Abilities are stated in terms of maximal performance, whereas styles are expressed in terms of typical performance.

Abilities are unipolar measures (less ability ... more ability), whereas styles are bipolar (visual ... verbal); and abilities are value directional (having more is better than having less), whereas styles are value differentiated (neither pole is necessarily better). Cognitive abilities are affected by the content domain or the nature of the task, whereas styles are generalizable tendencies that cut across content. Finally, abilities enable learners to perform tasks, whereas styles control the way in which the task is performed.

Cognitive controls are closely derived from the mental abilities described in Part II, but maintain significant aspects of styles. That is, controls do not represent true abilities. They are stylelike in that they are concerned with the manner and form of learning. They refer to propensities and are stated in terms of typical behavior. They reflect information-processing techniques, as do cognitive styles, and they are seen as controlling rather than enabling. Controls diverge from cognitive styles, however, in their tendency to be unipolar. For instance, being a reflective processor of information (see Chapter 9) is good, but impulsive processing is generally regarded as a deficiency. Because controls may be unipolar, they are not value neutral. For example, there are numerous reflectivity training programs but no impulsive training programs.

Cognitive controls, according to Messick, are specific to or affected by different content domains and tasks. This is an important distinction, and addresses the age-old question of "which is better?" That is, although cognitive controls may be unipolar and value directional (as with cognitive abilities), unipolarity and value may, in some cases, be *context sensitive*. Using the same example, where reflective processing is a strength for deep thinking and problem solving, quicker, impulsive processing may be of greater value for surface level thinking and timed tasks. This is also the case with field dependence/independence. Although analytic, detailed, and independent thinking may be valued in one context, holistic, social thinking is more worthwhile for other tasks or in other environments.

Due to these important differences from cognitive abilities and cognitive styles, we felt, as did Messick, that they should be treated as a unique category and separate section in this book.

References

Jonassen, D. H. (1978). Cognitive styles/controls and media. *Educational Technology, 18*(6), 28-32.

Klein, G. S., & Schlesinger, H. J. (1949). Where is the perceiver in perceptual theory? *Journal of Personality, 18,* 32-47.

Messick, S. (1984). The nature of cognitive styles: Problems and promise in educational practice. *Educational Psychologist, 19,* 59-74.

Santostefano, S. (1978). *A biodevlopmental approach to clinical child psychology.* New York: Wiley.

7

FIELD DEPENDENCE
AND FIELD INDEPENDENCE
(Global vs. Articulated Style)

Description of Field Dependence/Independence

Field dependence/independence (FD/I) is the most extensively researched cognitive control. Research on FD/I began over 40 years ago, and it remains among the most prescriptive of learning and instructional outcomes. FD/I describes the extent to which:
- the surrounding framework dominates the perception of items within it,
- the surrounding organized field influences a person's perception of items within it,
- a person perceives part of the field as a discrete form,
- the organization of the prevailing field determines the perception of its components, or
- a person perceives analytically.

FD/I describes the degree to which a learner's perception or comprehension of information is affected by the surrounding perceptual or contextual field, that is, "the extent to which the organization of the prevailing field dominates perception of any of its parts" (Witkin, Oltman, Raskin, & Karp, 1971, p. 7). When field dependents interact with stimuli, they find it difficult to locate the information they are seeking because other information tends to mask what they are looking for. Field independents, on the other hand, find it easier to disambiguate information, that is, to recognize and select the important information from its surrounding field.

Individuals also vary in the amount of structure they tend to impose on an otherwise ambiguous field of experience or perception. Field independents are more likely to reorganize, restructure, or represent information to suit their own need, conceptions, or perceptions. Field dependents are more likely to accept and encode the information in their own memories as it is presented without reorganization, restructuring, or revision.

FD/I is also referred to as global versus articulated cognitive style. Those with a global cognitive preference are highly influenced by the entire perceptual field. They see the forest rather than the trees. They are content to experience a new concept within the presented format and context. FDs have a global cognitive style because they more readily allow the external cues of an experience to point the way to understanding. Field independents, on the other hand, are internally oriented and may ignore or even distrust external cues. FIs have an articulated cognitive style because they prefer to create their own models in an attempt to understand the perceived field. They are better at articulating their knowledge because they more readily impose their own structures on it. Most of us fall somewhere between these two extremes, exhibiting a moderate bias toward one style or the other, but sharing aspects of both across a range of different contexts.

FD/I appears to change over the human life span. Children are generally field dependent, but their field independence increases as they become adults. Adults (especially adult learners) are more field independent (Gurley, 1984). After that time, field independence gradually decreases throughout the remainder of life, with older people tending to be more field dependent than their younger cohorts (Witkin et al., 1971). Field independence also seems to increase with the amount of formal education.

Characteristic Differences in Field Dependence/Independence

Field Dependent	Field Independent
global	analytic
accepts structure	generates structure
externally directed	internally directed
attentive to social information	inattentive to social cues
conflict resolvers	philosophical, cognitive
sociable and gregarious	individualistic
affiliation oriented	distant in social relations
interpersonal	intrapersonal
needs friendship	reserved, aloof
conventional, traditional	experimental
influenced by the salient features	generates own hypotheses
factually oriented	conceptually oriented
acquires unrelated facts	acquires information to fit conceptual scheme
accepts ideas as presented	represents concepts through analysis
influenced by format/structure	less affected by format/structure
gets feelings/decisions from others	impersonal orientation
sensitive to others	insensitive to social undercurrents
affected by stress	ignores external stress

Individual Differences
Related to Field Dependence/Independence

The field dependence/independence cognitive control is closely associated with other cognitive styles and controls:

Analytical Reasoning--Goodenough and Karp (1961) showed that FD/I loaded heavily on the analytical factor that was represented in the Wechsler Intelligence Test, including Block Design, Object Assembly, and Picture Completion tasks, which require individuals to separate items from their context.

Introversion/extroversion--Field independents are driven from internal motivations; they are more introverted (see chapter 29). Field dependents are more sensitive to others, so they tend to be more extroverted (Riding & Dyer, 1983).

Ambiguity Tolerance--There is a negative correlation between FI and ambiguity tolerance, especially under stress (Williams, 1980). Field independents are less affected by ambiguity (see chapter 26) and uncertainty in the learning environment because they are more likely to impose their own structure. Field dependents are uncomfortable with the unconventional.

Leveling/Sharpening--FIs ignore details that do not support their conceptualization, so they may tend to be levelers (see chapter 16). Field dependents are more attentive to detail and may tend to be sharpeners.

Risk Taking/Cautiousness--FIs may welcome nonstandard approaches; they should be greater risk takers. Field dependents often rely on standard approaches and are less likely to take risks (see chapter 31).

Dogmatism--FI was negatively correlated with dogmatism (Forisha-Thiel, 1983).

Formal Operational Reasoning--Students classified as formal operational (based on Piaget's classification of formal, abstract logic) were more field independent than independent (Wilborn, 1981).

Hemispheric Laterality--Neurological theories hold that the right and left sides of the cerebrum specialize in different cognitive functioning. Neurologically based research has tied FD/I to hemispheric laterality (O'Conner & Shaw, 1978). For instance, handedness and ear preference (highly lateralized functioning) are related to FD/I (Pizzamiglio, 1974). Eye dominance (also neurologically lateralized) is also related to FD/I (Oltman & Capobianco, 1967).

Instruments for Measuring Field Independence/Dependence

Embedded Figures Test (EFT) (Witkin et al., 1971)

The Embedded Figures Test (Forms A and B) is an individually administered, timed (3-minute limit), 12-item test divided into two parts. The test
consists of two sets of 12 cards with complex figures and a set of eight cards
with simple figures. Reliabilities range from . 61 to .92 depending on age
and gender. Numerous studies have verified the concept of FD/I and the
construct validity of the EFT.

Children's Embedded Figures Test (CEFT) (Witkin et al., 1971)

The CEFT is a 25-item, individually administered test consisting of simple
forms, incomplete pictures, and a test series of 11 complex figures with the
simple forms (tent or house) embedded in them. The test was normed
with children from 5-12 years of age with reliability ratios of .84 to .90 and
validity coefficients of .7 for 9-10-year-olds and .85 for 11-12-year-olds.

Group Embedded Figures Test (GEFT) (Witkin et al., 1971)

The GEFT is a group-administered, 25-item test administered in three
timed sections (2, 2, and 5 minutes each). The form of the test is very similar to the EFT. The individual must trace one of eight simple figures embedded in figures of greater complexity. The test is reliable ($r = .82$) and is
highly correlated to the EFT ($r = .63 - .82$) on the two forms.

Hidden Figures Test (HFT) (French, Ekstrom, & Price, 1963)

The Hidden Figures Test is one scale from the Kit of Factor-Referenced
Cognitive Tests from the Educational Testing Service. It is a timed, 32-
item, self-administered test in two parts that requires the individual to tell
which five simple figures are embedded in more complex patterns (see Fig
7.1). It has been used extensively in research and has high reliability with
good construct validity because, according to Witkin, it correlates highly
($r = .67 - .88$) with the Group Embedded Figures Test.

Closure Flexibility Test (Concealed Figures) (Baehr, 1965)

Part of a series to measure primary mental abilities, this test measures the
"second closure factor" (Thurstone, 1944), that is, the ability to hold a figure in mind in spite of distraction. It is a timed test consisting of 49 items
where the subject is given a figure that is embedded in a larger, more
complex diagram. Based on the Gottschaldt Figures (Gottschaldt, 1926), it

was not designed to measure FD/I; however, it calls on the same mental ability and may be used as an alternative to the other tests.

Auditory Embedded Figures Test (White, 1954)

An attempt to generalize Witkin's finding from visual to auditory perception, these tests measure two closure factors. The first consists of 40 tape-recorded, spoken words from which various consonant sounds have been dropped. Subjects are required to identify the complete word and write it. It also includes 50 recorded words from which the low-frequency sounds were filtered, resulting in a tinny sound. Subjects are required to identify and write the words. The second test, Hidden Tunes, requires the subject to identify simple melodies embedded in more complex ones. Also, subjects are required to identify words played against a distracting background noise. Reliability of the auditory items ranged from .65 to .83.

Tactile Embedded Figures Test (Axelrod & Cohen, 1961)

This test consists of 14 enlarged test pairs from the Gottschaldt figures constructed of balsa wood on plywood. In the test, the subject's left index finger is guided over the sample. He or she is then required to trace out the simple figure that is embedded in the more complex figure of each pair using both hands. Performance on the tactile test correlated highly (.78) with performance on the visual embedded figures task.

Theoretical Background

Social psychologist Herman Witkin is credited with the definition of this cognitive control. Witkin was influenced by the works of Muzafer Sharif and Solomon Asch, who had studied the effects of external (primarily social) influences on individual perception and judgment. Working with Asch (Witkin & Asch, 1948a, 1948b), Witkin studied how individuals orient themselves in space. Using the Body Adjustment Test and the Rod-and-Frame Test, he measured a subject's perception of the upright as influenced by a surrounding field. The former required an individual sitting in a tilted chair, set within a tilted room, to adjust his or her body to upright. In the Rod-and-Frame Test, the subject, seated within a totally darkened room, was asked to view a tilted luminous rod centered within a tilted luminous frame. The subject was then instructed to adjust the rod until it was in a totally upright position disregarding the tilted frame that surrounded it. Witkin's research focused on the relationship between a person's visual and kinesthetic cues. This dependence on visual cues from the surrounding field led to the constructs of field dependence and field independence.

A test created by Gottschaldt (1926) asked a subject to find a simple figure embedded within a more complex drawing. Witkin and his colleagues found a positive (.54) correlation between a version of Gottschaldt's test and the Rod-and-Frame Test. Field independent subjects could easily identify the embedded figures. As a result, Witkin began to investigate whether or not his ideas would transfer to situations that did not require perception of the upright. He devised the Embedded Figures Test (Witkin, 1950a) which provided a simpler method for measuring the ability to disembed a visual item from a more complex visual field. He found that performance on the Embedded Figures Test correlated well with the bodily oriented tests described previously, in that, those who were distracted by the visual field found it difficult to find the figure within that visual field. To Witkin, the effect of the contextual field on the ability to locate a simpler figure was a fundamental perceptual style that described general analytical ability. His future research focused on transferring the findings to a variety of social and learning contexts.

Witkin integrated the various dimensions of social and intellectual behavior into a Theory of Psychological Differentiation (Witkin, Dyk, Faterson, Goodenough, & Karp, 1962), which includes four dimensions: global-articulate, articulation of body concept, sense of identity, and defense structures. The most obvious implications for learning come from the third dimension, which separates self from nonself. Two sub-dimensions spin off from this self/nonself dichotomy--autonomy of interpersonal relations and cognitive restructuring (Witkin & Goodenough, 1976a). These two dimensions most often describe the social and intellectual characteristics that impact on learning and instruction. The first describes the interpersonal relations that one develops and uses as referents. FDs rely on external referents for psychological functioning, whereas FIs rely on themselves as their primary referents. The second dimension describes the ability to analyze and structure disorganized fields of information, a skill that is essential to problem solving. FIs are adept at imposing their own cognitive structure on situations (because they use internal referents), and FDs rely more readily on structure or organization that is provided by the environment or by others. The most important aspect of Witkin's theory is his belief that these are stable traits that predict cognitive and social functioning across environments.

Field Dependence/Independence and Learning

Research

A great deal of research on the effects of FD/I on learning outcomes has been conducted. A representative sampling of that research is presented here.

- Males were generally more field independent than females (Witkin, 1954; Witkin, Dyk, Faterson, Goodenough, & Karp, 1962).

- FIs are more efficient hypothesis testers than FDs while learning and solving set problems (Davis & Haueisen, 1976).

- Representations of the psychological structures of FIs more closely resemble the content structure in social studies instruction (Stasz, Shavelson, Cox, & Moore, 1976). The psychological structures of FDs were less differentiated than FIs.

- Goodenough (1976) concluded from research that FDs are dominated by salient cues in concept-learning tasks, FDs use a "spectator" approach to learning, FDs are more affected by negative reinforcement, and FDs are better at incidental learning of social information.

- Field independence predicted higher proficiency in learning Spanish, especially for FI females because of the ability to cognitively restructure information (Hansen, 1980).

- Passing students were more FI, whereas failing students and students who dropped out of nursing courses were more FD (Goodfellow, 1980).

- FI was the strongest predictor of divergent tasks in a course, including media skills and development of a teaching module (Jonassen, 1980).

- FDs had more difficulty in abstracting relevant information from instruction supporting more difficult learning tasks (Canelos, Taylor, & Gates, 1980).

- Across grades, FI was correlated with higher mathematics achievement, especially for concepts and application (Vaidya & Chansky, 1980).

- FIs were better at transferring rules to new contexts as well as generating rules to solve novel problems (Maloney, 1981).

- FI is important in analyzing and categorizing visual stimuli (Wise, 1981). This represents not only a perceptual disembedding skill but also an analytical approach to problems.

- Wyatt (1982) showed a tendency for FI males to be overly analytical in solving objective test items and read irrelevant information into the solutions.

- FIs were significantly better at perceiving ambiguity in language and re-structuring that ambiguity to produce multiple interpretations (Newsome, 1982).

- FIs were better at operational thinking and recalling details in a prose passage (Riding & Dyer, 1983).

- FIs scored better on a music reading task than FDs (King, 1983).

- FIs recalled significantly more from mathematical/scientific passages whereas FDs recalled more from socially oriented passages (Phifer, 1983). Also, field dependents tended to use a single strategy for comprehending passages, whereas independents flexibly used different strategies.

- FIs process text in an analytical manner by imposing order when neces-sary, so they score higher than FDs (Hansen, 1983).

- FIs were more likely to solve problems than FDs (Heller, 1982; Ronning, McCurdy, & Ballinger, 1984).

- FIs were better at performing outlining tasks, which improved compre-hension (Lipsky, 1984).

- FIs were found to be more proficient in sight word recognition, recogni-tion of vocabulary in context, use of structural analysis in word recogni-tion, and silent reading comprehension (Hall, 1987).

- FIs recalled more structural and functional information (organization and functions of equipment parts) than FDs (Skaggs, Rocklin, Dansereau, & Hall, 1990).

Implications of the Characteristics and Research

Implications that are drawn from research are noted with a •; those drawn logically from descriptive information regarding the trait are noted by an *. Based on the extensive amount of research on FD/I (samples of which are represented in this chapter), we conclude that *field dependent* learners are more likely to excel at learning tasks such as:

- group-oriented and collaborative work situations where individuals need to be sensitive to social cues from others
- situations where participants must follow a standardized pattern of per-formance
- tests requiring learners to recall information in the form or structure that it was presented

and acquire and use effectively learning strategies such as:

* concentration on information
* repetition or rehearsal of information to be recalled

Based on the extensive amount of research on FD/I (samples of which are represented in this chapter), we conclude that *field independent* learners are more likely to excel at learning tasks such as:

• problem solving, especially in mathematics
• situations in which learners must figure out the underlying organization of ideas in the domain, such as concept mapping or outlining
• language learning, especially disambiguating syntax and structural rules
• identifying the salient or important aspects of any body of information, especially when the information is ambiguous or poorly organized
• transfer tasks where operation must be transferred to novel situations

and acquire and use effectively learning strategies such as:

* selecting information sources
* searching for and validating information
* transferring knowledge (predicting outcomes, inferring causes, or evaluating implications)
* generating metaphors and analogies
* evaluating knowledge (test personal skills or judge utility or value of knowledge)
* analyzing information structurally

Field Dependence/Independence and Instruction

Research

• FIs learned the most in math lessons when given minimum guidance and maximum opportunity for discovery, whereas FDs profited most from maximum guidance (Adams & McLeod, 1979; McLeod, 1978).

• Advanced organizers were most effective with FDs when they were used with specific reference to their properties (Satterly & Telfer, 1979).

• FD students taught by FI teachers achieved more than FD students taught by FD teachers (Jolly, 1980). All students learned more from FI teachers.

- FIs performed better than FDs after receiving loosely structured pre-instruction, whereas FDs performed as well after receiving well-structured, integrated instruction (Lambert, 1981).

- FIs learned more from an individualized, self-paced course than FDs (Wilborn, 1981).

- FDs achieved higher scores on a nutrition test after using highly structured materials (presented in a logical order using a deductive sequence requiring written answers to convergent questions), whereas FIs achieved more from the low-structured treatment materials (Tannenbaum, 1982).

- When collaborative pairs of learners consisted of two FIs, they performed much better than two FDs (Frank & Davis, 1982). One of each produced intermediate results.

- FIs were more efficient at taking notes in outline format than FDs, which improves their performance over FDs (Frank, 1984). Frank found that some combination of teacher-supplied organizational structure and training in notetaking will maximize the learning of FDs.

- Prequestions facilitated incidental and total retention for FDs but not for FIs. FIs scored better than FDs on all outcomes under the no question treatment (Chobot, 1984).

- Supervisors taught in a more analytical style with FI students and a more probing style with FD students (Rosenberg, 1985). FD students more readily accepted feedback from FD teachers.

- In a computer-based lesson, FDs had faster response times and fewer errors when their errors were explained and they were given strategies for correcting them, whereas FIs had faster times and fewer errors when given no explanation (only told that an error had occurred) (Hedberg & McNamara, 1985).

- FIs were more likely to participate in correspondence study (Thompson & Knox, 1987).

- Text passages with headings improved scores for field dependent students, whereas FIs scored better in passages without headings (Thompson, 1987).

Implications of the Characteristics and Research

Implications that are drawn from research are noted with a •; those drawn logically from descriptive information regarding the trait are noted by an *. Instructional conditions that capitalize on the preferences of the *field dependent* student and challenge the *field independent* student include:

- • providing a synergogic (social) learning environment
- • offering deliberate structural support with salient cues, especially organizational cues such as advanced organizers
- • providing clear, explicit directions and the maximum amount of guidance
- • including orienting strategies before instruction
- • providing extensive feedback (especially informative)
- * presenting advance organizers (verbal, oral, or pictorial)
- * presenting outlines or graphic organizers of content
- * providing prototypic examples
- * advising learner of instructional support needed (examples, practice items, tools, resources)
- * providing graphic, oral or auditory cues
- * embedding questions throughout learning
- * providing deductive or procedural instructional sequence

Instructional conditions that remediate or compensate for the deficiencies of the *field dependent* student include:

- • providing well-organized, well-structured material
- • insuring that salient features of materials match key objectives
- • pairing the FD student up to work with an FI student or an FI teacher
- • providing abundant feedback, both positive and negative
- • limiting stress to moderately low levels
- • offering a model of structure for a given field; encouraging the student to emulate the model in a related field
- • beginning exercises with clear structure, abundant cues, consistent feedback; as the student progresses, take away structure, then cues, finally feedback.
- * asking learners to select their own goals
- * asking learners to evaluate the meaningfulness of information
- * paraphrasing content
- * providing analytic feedback
- * providing matched example/nonexample pairs

Instructional conditions that capitalize on the preferences of the *field independent* student and challenge the *field dependent* student include:

- providing an independent learning environment
- utilizing inquiry and discovery teaching methods
- providing abundant content resources and reference material to sort through
- providing independent, contract-based self-instruction
- providing minimal guidance and direction
* asking the learner to pose questions to be answered
* using inductive instructional sequence
* creating outlines, pattern notes, concept maps, etc.
* using theoretical elaboration sequences

    Instructional conditions that remediate or compensate for the deficiencies of the *field independent* student include:

- pairing the FI student up to work with an FD student or an FD teacher
- offering guidance, but not imposing structure; moving aside and allowing student-directed learning
- insuring the accessibility of supporting resources
- requiring learners to explicitly filter out materials which are not relevant to the task
- presenting a task in which the most successful outcome always involves reliance upon external structure and support
- providing team building exercises and demonstrating the power of synergy

References

Adams, V. M., & McLeod, D. B. (1979). The interaction of field independence with discovery learning in mathematics. *Journal of Experimental Education, 48*, 32-35.

Axelrod, S., & Cohen, D. L. (1961). Senescence and embedded figures performance in vision and touch. *Perceptual and Motor Skills, 12*, 283-288.

Baehr, M. E. (1965). *Manual: Closure Flexibility Test.* Park Ridge, IL: London House.

Canelos, J., Taylor, W. D., & Gates, R. B. (1980). The effects of three levels of visual stimulus complexity on the information processing of field-dependents and field-independents when acquiring information for performance on three types of instructional objectives. *Journal of Instructional Psychology, 7*, 65-70.

Chobot, M. C. (1984). The interactive effects of field dependence and adjunct questions on learning from prose by library/information science students. (Doctoral dissertation, Catholic University of America), *Dissertation Abstracts International, 45*, 2036.

Davis, J. K., & Haueisen, W. C. (1976). Field independence and hypothesis testing. *Perceptual and Motor Skills, 43,* 763-769.

Forisha-Thiel, A. (1983). The relationship of selected personality and cognitive factors to critical thinking among graduate students in educational psychology (Doctoral dissertation, University of Southern California), *Dissertation Abstracts International, 44,* 3325.

Frank, B. M. (1984). Effect of field independence-dependence and study technique on learning from lecture. *American Educational Research Journal, 21,* 669-678.

Frank, B. M., & Davis, J. K. (1982). Effect of field-independence match or mismatch on a communication task. *Journal of Educational Psychology, 74,* 23-31.

French, J. W., Ekstrom, R. B., & Price, L. A. (1963). *Kit of reference tests for cognitive skills.* Princeton: Educational Testing Service.

Goodenough, D. R. (1976). The role of individual differences in field dependence as a factor in learning and memory. *Psychological Bulletin, 83,* 675-694.

Goodenough, D. R., & Karp, S. A. (1961). Field dependence and intellectual functioning. *Journal of Abnormal and Social Psychology, 63,* 241-246.

Goodfellow, D. H. (1980). Relationships between field independence-dependence and student and faculty performance in a baccalaureate nursing program (Doctoral dissertation, Vanderbilt University), *Dissertation Abstracts International, 41,* 3951.

Gottschaldt, F. (1926). Uber den Einfluss der Erfahrung asuf die Wahruehmung von Figuren I; Uber den Einfluss gehaufter Einpragung von Figuren auf ihre Sichtbarkeit in unfassendem Konfigurationen. *Psychol. Forsch., 8,* 261-317.

Gurley, M. P. (1984). Characteristics of motivation, field independence, personality type, learning style, and teaching preference of the adult learner as compared with traditional-age college students (Doctoral dissertation, Catholic University of America), *Dissertation Abstracts International, 45,* 1268.

Hall, M. J. (1987). Relationships between reading proficiency and field-dependence, field independence, and sex. (Doctoral dissertation, Auburn University), *Dissertation Abstracts International, 49,* 226.

Hansen, J. (1980). Field dependent-independent cognitive styles and foreign language proficiency among college students in an introductory Spanish course (Doctoral dissertation, University of Colorado), *Dissertation Abstracts International, 41,* 3460.

Hansen, R. (1983). The effects of varied text conditions on field independent and field dependent readers' formation of inferences in expository text (Doctoral dissertation, University of Wisconsin), *Dissertation Abstracts International, 44,* 2722.

Hedberg, J. G., & McNamara, S. E. (1985, March 31-April 4). *Matching feedback and cognitive style in a visual CAI task.* Paper presented at the annual meeting of the American Educational Research Association, Chicago. (ERIC Document Reproduction Service No. ED 260 105)

Heller, L. C. (1982). An exploration of the effect of structure variables on mathematical word problem-solving achievement (Doctoral dissertation, Rutgers University), *Dissertation Abstracts International, 44,* 416.

Jolly, P. J. E. (1980). Student achievement in biology in terms of cognitive styles of students and teachers (Doctoral dissertation, Louisiana State University), *Dissertation Abstracts International, 41,* 3403.

Jonassen, D. H. (1980, April 21-24). *Cognitive style predictors of performance.* Paper presented at the annual meeting of the Association for Educational Communications and Technology, Denver. (ERIC Document Reproduction Service No. ED 194 072)

King, D. W. (1983). Field-dependence/field-independence and achievement in music reading (Doctoral dissertation, University of Wisconsin), *Dissertation Abstracts International, 44,* 1320.

Lambert, T. (1981). Effects of structure in preinstructional strategies on memory for sentences in field dependent individuals (Doctoral dissertation, University of Southern California), *Dissertation Abstracts International, 42 ,* 1063.

Lipsky, S. A. (1984). Effect of cognitive style on the success of two textbook note-taking techniques (Doctoral dissertation, University of Pittsburgh), *Dissertation Abstracts International, 45,* 1703.

Maloney, T. J. (1981). The relation between field-independence and rule-transfer (Doctoral dissertation, University of Toledo), *Dissertation Abstracts International, 442,* 2575.

McLeod, D. B., Carpenter, T. P., McCornack, R. L., & Romualdas, S. (1978). Cognitive style and mathematics learning: The interaction of field independence and instructional treatment in numeration systems. *Journal for Research in Mathematics Education, 9,* 163-174.

Newsome, V. J. (1982). Field independent cognitive style and sentential disambiguation performance: Some relations between them (Doctoral dissertation, University of Maryland), *Dissertation Abstracts International, 43,* 3802.

O'Conner, K. P., & Shaw, J. C. (1978). Field independence, laterality, and the EEG. *Biological Psychology, 6,* 93-109.

Oltman, P. K., & Capobianco, F. (1967). Field dependence and eye dominance. *Perceptual and Motor Skills, 25,* 645-646.

Phifer, J. (1983). Effects of individual cognitive style and processing differences on metacognitive reading strategies (Doctoral dissertation, University of Nebraska), *Dissertation Abstracts International, 44,* 2420.

Pizzamiglio, L. (1974). Handedness, rear preference and field dependence. *Perceptual and Motor Skills, 38,* 700-702.

Riding, R. J., & Dyer, V. (1983). Extraversion, field independence and performance on cognitive tasks in twelve-year-old children. *Research in Education, 29,* 1-9.

Ronning, McCurdy, & Ballinger (1984, January). Individual differences: A third component in problem-solving instruction. *Journal of Research in Science Teaching, 21,* 1, 71-82.

Rosenberg, B. L. (1985). Cognitive style as a mediator in the the quality of interaction between supervisors and counselor trainees in a practice setting (Doctoral dissertation, Fordham University), *Dissertation Abstracts International, 46,* 656.

Satterly, D. J., & Telfer, I. G. (1979). Cognitive style and advance organizers in learning and retention. *British Journal of Educational Psychology, 49,* 169-178.

Skaggs, L. P., Rocklin, T., Dansereau, D., & Hall, R. H. (1990). Dyadic learning of technical material: Individual differences, social interaction, and recall. *Contemporary Educational Psychology, 15,* 47-63.

Stasz, C., Shavelson, R. J., Cox, D. L., & Moore, C. (1976). Field independence and the structuring of knowledge in a social studies minicourse. *Journal of Educational Psychology, 68,* 550-558.

Tannenbaum, R. K. (1982). An investigation of the relationship(s) between selected instructional techniques and identified field dependent and field independent cognitive styles as evidenced among high school students enrolled in studies of nutrition (Doctoral dissertation, St. John's University), *Dissertation Abstracts International, 43,* 68.

Thompson, G., & Knox, A. B. (1987). Designing for diversity: Are field dependent learners less suited to distance education programs of instruction? *Contemporary Educational Psychology, 12,* 17-29.

Thompson, M. E., & Thompson, G. (1987, March 26-April 1). *Field dependence-independence and learning from instructional text.* Paper presented at the annual meeting of the Association for Education Communications and Technology, Atlanta. (ERIC Document Reproduction Service No. ED 285 563)

Thurstone, L. L. (1944). A factorial study of perception. Chicago, IL: University of Chicago press.

Vaidya, S., & Chansky, N. M. (1980). Cognitive development and cognitive style as factors in mathematics achievement. *Journal of Educational Psychology, 72,* 326-330.

White, B. W. (1954). Visual and auditory closure. *Journal of Experimental Psychology, 48,* 234-240.

Wilborn, M. R. (1981). An investigation of the relationships among proportional reasoning, field-dependence/independence, sex, and grades in science of eighth grade ISCS students (Doctoral dissertation, Georgia State University), *Dissertation Abstracts International, 42,* 92.

Williams, R. A. (1980). The relationship of field independence, tolerance of ambiguity and stress in undergraduate nursing students (Doctoral dissertation, University of Washington), *Dissertation Abstracts International, 41,* 3121.

Wise, R. E. (1980). The differential employment of cognitive skills as a function of increasing iconic stimulus complexity (Doctoral dissertation, Pennsylvania State University), *Dissertation Abstracts International, 41,* 3963.

Witkin, H. A. (1949). Perception of body position and the position of the visual field, *Psychological Monographs, 63,* 1-46.

Witkin, H. A. (1950a). Individual differences in the ease of perception of embedded figures. *Journal of Personality, 19,* 1-15.

Witkin, H. A. (1950b). Perception of the upright when the direction of the force acting on the body is changed. *Journal of Experimental Psychology, 40,* 93-106.

Witkin, H. A. (1954). *Personality through perception: An experimental and clinical study.* New York: Harper.

Witkin, H. A. (1959). Perception of the upright. *Scientific American, 200,* 50-56.

Witkin, H. A., & Asch, S. E. (1948a). Studies in space orientation, III. Perception of the upright in the absence of visual field. *Journal of Experimental Psychology, 38,* 603-614.

Witkin, H. A., & Asch, S. E. (1948b). Studies in space orientation, IV. Further experiments on perception of the upright with displaced visual field. *Journal of Experimental Psychology, 38,* 762-782.

Witkin, H. A., Dyk, R. B., Faterson, H. F., Goodenough, D. R., & Karp, S. A. (1962). *Psychological differentiation.* New York: Wiley.

Witkin, H. A., & Goodenough, D. R. (1976a). *Field dependence and interpersonal behavior,* (RB 76-12). Princeton: Educational Testing Service.

Witkin, H. A., & Goodenough, D. R. (1976b). *Field dependence revisited,* (RB 76-39). Princeton: Educational Testing Service.

Witkin, H. A., & Goodenough, D. R. (1981). *Cognitive styles: Essence and origins: Field dependence and field independence.* New York: International Universities Press.

Witkin, H., Moore, C., Goodenough, D., & Cox, P. (1977). Field dependent and field independent cognitive styles and their educational implications. *Review of Educational Research, 47,* 1-64.

Witkin, H., Oltman, P., Raskin, E., & Karp, S. (1971). *A Manual for the Embedded Figures Test.* Palo Alto, CA: Consulting Psychologists Press.

Wyatt, C. J. (1982). The relationship of field independence-dependence to the ability to utilize varying degrees of structure in solving verbal problems (Doctoral dissertation, Washington State University), *Dissertation Abstracts International, 43,* 2944.

Bibliography

Crow, L., & Piper, M. (1985).*The effects of instructional aids on the achievement of community college students enrolled in a geology course.* (ERIC Document Reproduction Service No. ED 256 566)

DeLeeuw, L. (1983). Teaching problem solving: an ATI study of the effects of teaching algorithmic and heuristic solution methods. *Instructional Science, 12,* 1-48.

Doebler, L. K., & Eike, F. J. (1979). Effects of teacher awareness of the educational implications of field-dependence/field-independent cognitive style on selected classroom variables. *Journal of Educational Psychology, 71,* 226-231.

Douglass, C. B. (1978). The effects of instructional sequence and cognitive style on the achievement of high school biology students. *Journal of Research in Science Teaching, 15,* 407-412.

Hart, R. (1984). *An effective strategy to design mediated instruction for female adults--compositional syntactic placement.* Paper presented at the National Adult Education Conference. (ERIC Document Reproduction Service No. ED 249 369)

Peterson, D., & Eden, D. (1981). Cognitive style and the older learner. *Educational Gerontology, 7,* 57-66.

8

COGNITIVE FLEXIBILITY
(Constricted vs. Flexible Control)

Description of Cognitive Flexibility

Constricted/flexible control is a measure of the ability to ignore distractions to focus on relevant stimuli (Klein, 1954). This control also measures the ability to inhibit incorrect verbal responses. The flexible individual is not as easily distracted as a constricted processor and therefore is better able to inhibit irrelevant responses. Constricted processors are also more susceptible to distraction when completing tasks with conflicting cues. The flexible individual tends to concentrate more completely on the task at hand (Gardner, Holzman, Klein, Linton, & Spence, 1959). Constricted/flexible control is sometimes referred to as rigidity/flexibility, which is defined as one's readiness (or lack thereof) to review and change one's judgment of a proposed solution to a problem.

Cognitive flexibility is sometimes included in the more general construct, *field articulation*, a term applied to situations of perceived incongruity. Field articulation is a composite of the constricted/flexible control and field dependence/independence. Constricted/dependent individuals have a tendency to organize and order incongruities in information along the simplest possible lines, responding to only the most compelling incongruous elements and usually ignoring the other elements. Flexible/independent individuals, on the other hand, are able to articulate incongruities by focusing attention on those areas designated by instruction. They are able to ignore or actively resist responding to irrelevant contradictory cues (Gardner et al., 1959).

Characteristic Differences in Cognitive Flexibility

Constricted Processors	Flexible Processors
distracted	focused
global	analytic
resistant to change	open to change
avoid emotions as information	use feelings as information
overgeneralize cognitive set cue	use all available cues

Individual Differences Related to Cognitive Flexibility

The constricted/flexible cognitive control is closely associated with other cognitive styles and controls:

Focusing-scanning--describes how attention/concentration is systemically deployed or distributed when objects are being compared (see chapter 10). Constricted processors will tend to be focusers; flexible processors will tend to be scanners.

Field-dependence/independence (or field articulation)--the ability and approach used by individuals to articulate or separate relevant and irrelevant stimuli in an information field (see chapter 7). Guilford (1980) considered the nature of field independence to be representative of flexibility, which is a readiness to make changes in information, and an ability or an inclination (or both) to effect transformations. The lack of flexibility is evident in the field-dependent individual's difficulty in re-organizing problems and using information in new ways for problem-solving.

Ambiguity tolerance--describes an individual's readiness to accept perceptions in opposition to convention or those deviating from the ordinary (see chapter 26). Constricted processors should have a lower tolerance for ambiguity, whereas flexible processors should have a higher tolerance.

Instruments for Measuring Cognitive Flexibility

Gestalt Completion Test (Street, 1931)

The Street Gestalt Completion Test is a measure of the ability to perceive discrete pieces as a whole figure or as a pattern. The test includes 2 sample cards and 13 test cards containing fragmented black or white background shapes that are to be mentally integrated into complete, meaningful pictures (Gaines, 1975). This task requires flexibility (rather than rigidity) and general (rather than concrete) percepts. Persons scoring above the mean tend to be socially outgoing, confident and optimistic, energetic and impulsive, but not logical or theoretical (Tyler, 1984). Tyler also suggested that reliability as reported in three studies is not adequate (.68, .70, and .67).

Color-Word Test (Stroop, 1935; Golden, 1978)

The Stroop Color-Word Test consists of three parts that yield three basic scores. Each score is the number of items completed in 45 seconds. Part I is a "warm-up" exercise reading color names that are in random order and printed in black. This provides the Word Score. Part 2 is the Color Score and consists of items written as XXXX printed in either red, green, or blue ink which are to be named by color. Part 3, the Color-Word Score, consists of the words in part 1 printed in the colors of part 2. The task is to name the color of the ink that the words are printed in rather than reading the color words themselves. The automatic word-reading response must be suppressed through volitional control. The basic abilities measured by this instrument are cognitive flexibility and selective attention. Reliability is consistent across studies (.69-.89), although it is low for the third subtest (.69-.73) (Evans, 1987).

Fruit Distraction Test (Santostefano & Paley, 1964)

In this test, the subject is asked to name the colors of fruit items on card 1. Card 2 contains the same colored fruit items as well as black-and-white food and nonfood objects inserted as distractions or interfering stimuli. The subject is again requested to name the colors in which the fruits are depicted. The flexible individual is able to selectively withhold his or her attention from the intrusive or interfering stimuli and focus on what is considered "central" to task completion.

Theoretical Background

The cognitive control, cognitive flexibility, evolved from clinical research by Gardner and Klein and their colleagues at the Menninger Clinic. For years they were involved with major studies aimed at defining the concept of cognitive control and analyzing how cognitive structures modulate and control human drives. They postulated that a number of controls coexist within the personality. These controls regulate motivations and drives. What is distinct about their theoretical orientation is the putative role that personality plays in determining cognitive styles. Klein described the combination of controls that are moderately determined by personality as cognitive styles. He considered cognitive styles to be not only cognitive but also comprised of emotional, motivational, and affective elements. The relationship between personality functioning and cognitive control, according to this conception, is fairly strong (Ludwig & Lazarus, 1983).

Cognitive Flexibility and Learning

Research

Most of the research on cognitive flexibility has focused on personality issues or diagnosing neurological problems. For instance:

• Immam and Karachi (1974) confirmed earlier research that showed an increase in rigidity with age.

• Gaines (1975) suggested that artists are more flexible and therefore less likely to be rigid in their perceptions of the environment. They demonstrated an ability to perceive a meaningful whole on the Gestalt Test and thus were not deterred by the fragmented appearance of the pictures. The nature of being an artist requires the ability to resist pressure to conform to the standards of the majority; in addition, perceptual accuracy and cultural independence may be a requirement for creativity.

Implications of the Characteristics and Research

Implications which are drawn from research are noted with a •; those drawn logically from descriptive information regarding the trait are noted by an *. Based on the few research studies and the descriptions of cognitive flexibility, we conclude that *flexible* learners are more likely to excel at learning tasks such as:

• divergent production tasks
• creative and interpretive outcomes
• argumentation, including articulation of arguments and especially the presentation and rejoindering of arguments
* simultaneous processing tasks, where numerous judgements are required or time is limited
* complex problem solving in ill-structured knowledge domains

and acquire and use effectively learning strategies such as:

• selecting information sources
* estimating time and/or effort
* comparing new knowledge with existing ideas, beliefs
* analyzing of key ideas
* predicting outcomes and inferring causes
* judging utility or value of knowledge

Based on the few research studies and the descriptions of cognitive flexibility, we conclude that *constricted* learners are more likely to excel at learning tasks such as:

* convergent production tasks
* reproductive tasks, such as recall
* well-defined and structured tasks, with explicit parameters
* social interaction skills

and acquire and use effectively learning strategies such as:

* rehearsing and reviewing material
* regulating environment

Cognitive Flexibility and Instruction

Research

• Ludwig and Lazarus (1983) found that individuals with certain personality traits, such as shyness, were "high distractors." A shy individual reduces the number of accessible perceptual cues and indicates high distractability/susceptibility to competing stimuli. This reduced-cue utilization is related to maintaining a perceptual set long after its appropriateness or effectiveness ends.

• Saracho (1984) found that constricted subjects are more resistant to cognitive style modifications than are flexible individuals. Flexible learners are more willing to use a variety of techniques. They also notice when a specific strategy is effective or ineffective.

Implications of the Characteristics and Research

Implications which are drawn from research are noted with a •; those drawn logically from descriptive information regarding the trait are noted by an *. Instructional conditions that capitalize on the preferences of the flexible student and challenge the constricted student include:

* high learner control (more learner self-regulation)
* self-instructional learning environments
* use of inductive teaching methods (requiring the student to organize, hypothesize, manipulate symbolic meaning)

Instructional conditions that remediate or compensate for the deficiencies of the flexible student include:

* mixed-ability groupings in cooperative learning situations (i.e., constricted with flexible)
* self-monitoring or self-evaluation checks with criteria developed by the teacher
* advance organizers presenting different points of view or perspectives

Instructional conditions that capitalize on the preferences of the constricted student and challenge the flexible student include:

* high instructional mediation
* direct instruction in large group or small mixed ability groupings
* teacher monitoring and encouragement for insecure, anxious learners
* attention-directing procedures, such as advance organizers
* procedures eliciting active participation
* reduction of impulsivity, self-directed verbal commands
* treatments forcing students to be attentive to and differentiate among details

Instructional conditions that remediate or compensate for the deficiencies of the constricted student include:

* advising about instructional decisions
* on-line help that presented an alternative but supportive point of view
• presenting a rich set of examples of similar hypotheses or solutions

References

Evans, J. R. (1987). Review of Stroop Color Word Test. In O. K. Buros (Ed.), *Seventh Mental Measurements Yearbook* (pp. 1483-1485). Highland Park, NJ: Gryphon.

Gaines, R. (1975). Developmental perception and cognitive styles: From young children to master artists. *Perceptual and Motor Skills, 40,* 983-998.

Gardner, R. W., Holzman, P. S., Klein, G. S., Linton, H. B., & Spence, D. P. (1959). *Cognitive control: a study of individual consistencies in cognitive behavior.* New York: International Universities Press.

Golden, C. (1978). *Stroop Color and Word Test: a manual for clinical and experimental uses.* Wood Dale, IL: Stoelting Company.

Guilford, J. P. (1980). Cognitive styles: What are they? *Educational and Psychological Measurement, 40,* 715-735.

Immam, A., & Karachi, P. (1974). Rigidity-flexibility and incidental learning. *Pakistan Journal of Educational Psychology, 7* (1-2), 3-17.

Klein, G. S. (1954). *Need and Regulation in Nebraska Symposium on Motivation.* Lincoln, NB: University Press.

Ludwig, R. P., & Lazarus, P. J. (1983). Relationship between shyness in children and constricted control as measured by the Stroop Color-Word Test. *Journal of Consulting and Clinical Psychology, 51*(3), 386-389.

Santostefano, S., & Paley, E. (1964). Development of cognitive controls in children. *Child Development, 35,* 939-949.

Saracho, O. N. (1984). *Cognitive style and children's learning: Individual variation in cognitive processes*. Washington DC: National Institute of Education.

Street, R. F. (1931). *A Gestalt completion test*. New York: Teacher's College.

Stroop, J. R. (1935). Studies of interference in serial verbal reactions. *Journal of Experimental Psychology, 18,* 643-662.

Tyler, L. E. (1984). Review of Gestalt Completion Test. In O. K. Buros (Ed.), *Sixth Mental Measurements Yearbook* (pp. 850-851). Highland Park, NJ: Gryphon.

Bibliography

Hopkins, J., Perlman, T., Hechtman, L., & Weiss, G. (1979). Cognitive style in adults originally diagnosed as hyperactives. *Journal of Child Psychology and Psychiatry, 20,* 209-216.

Messick, S. (1984). The nature of cognitive styles: Problems and promise in educational practice. *Educational Psychologist, 19,* 59-74.

9

IMPULSIVITY/REFLECTIVITY
(Cognitive Tempo)

Description of Impulsivity/Reflectivity

Impulsivity/reflectivity (I/R), also referred to as *cognitive tempo* or *conceptual tempo*, defines an information-processing continuum that is most prominent in children. Essentially, it measures a person's tendency to inhibit initial responses and to reflect on the accuracy of an answer rather than the tendency to respond impulsively. Individuals display this tendency with most tasks, especially when the tasks contain uncertainty (Kagan, Rosman, Day, Albert, & Phillips, 1964). *Impulsives* respond faster and commit more performance errors, whereas *reflectives* have longer response times and commit fewer performance errors (Kagan, 1965a, 1966).

There are two separate dimensions to I/R--response latency and performance errors. Response latency describes the amount of time that a subject waits before making a response. Impulsives tend to respond quicker than reflectives respond. Performance errors describe the accuracy of the performance that results from those responses. Typically, reflectives tend to commit fewer errors in their performances. These two variables are obviously highly related. The faster a student responds, the more likely he or she is to commit performance errors. As a result of fewer performance errors, reflective children tend to be higher achievers, whereas impulsive children tend to be less correct in their responses. I/R, therefore, is really a unipolar dimension that reflects the presence or absence of the processing skill or style, reflectivity. Whereas reflective processors reflect on and evaluate their responses before making them, those deficient in this skill (impulsives) exhibit a failure to stop, think, and listen.

Differences between impulsive and reflective children appear to stem from differences in their concern for minimizing error. To avoid error, reflectives take longer to consider alternative solutions. In contrast, impulsives do not (Gullo, 1988). When compared with reflectives, impulsives were rated as being more anxious and lacking in self-confidence. Block, Block, and Harrington (1974) claimed that these characteristics predispose the impulsive children to fast responding because stress is induced by the uncertain and ambiguous nature of the situation. Impulsive children are anxious because they fear they will be judged incompetent if their response is slow.

I/R is related to problem solving in children and adults. That is, I/R describes not only a delay in response speed accompanied by greater accuracy but also the way in which an individual's problem-solving activities might differ. "The reflection-impulsivity dimension describes the degree to which a subject reflects on the differential validity of alternative solution hypotheses in situations where many response possibilities are available simultaneously" (Kagan, 1966, p. 119). Therefore, reflective children gather information more systematically and evaluate it more thoroughly than impulsive children (Drake, 1970).

Cognitive tempo is developmental in nature (Carroll, 1980; Fischer, 1979); however, it remains fairly stable over time (Kagan et al., 1964). Kagan and Kogan (1970) reported that Matching Familiar Figures test errors decreased and response times increased markedly from ages 5-11. Cairns (1978) noted a nonsignificant increase in response time over ages 5-13, but a statistically significant decrease in errors.

Characteristic Differences in Impulsivity/Reflectivity

Impulsives	Reflectives
active	reflective
anxious	contemplative
haptic	verbal
global	analytic
dissipated	focused
excitable	calm
lower achievers	higher achievers
reward sensitive	unaffected by rewards
future oriented	present oriented

Individual Differences Related to Impulsivity/Reflectivity

Scanning-focusing--Impulsives (see chapter 10) do not scan all of the options on the Matching Familiar Figures Test before making a response (Drake, 1970). Instruction in scanning strategies may increase response time and decrease errors (Heider, 1971).

Verbal ability--Reflectives score higher on verbal ability tests (Cormicle, 1983; Simpkins, 1981); however, these deficits for impulsives can usually be reduced through training.

Field dependence/independence (FD/I)--Leitgeb, Bolocofsky, and Obrutz (1986) found that field dependence/independence (see chapter 7) was related to cognitive tempo, with independents being more reflective and dependents being more impulsive. FD/I and I/R involve similar modes of information processing, so they are highly related with that relationship becoming stronger with age (Haynes & Miller, 1987).

Intelligence--Lajoie and Shore (1987) found no relationship between I/R and intelligence. Other researchers believed that I/R might be related to performance on some aspects of intelligence tests. A study by Brannigan, Ash, and Margolis (1980) using the Wechsler Intelligence Scale for Children (WISC-R) indicated that "normal" reflective children scored significantly higher than "normal" impulsive children on the Attention-Concentration (Arithmetic and Digit Span) and Visual Organization (Block Design, Object Assembly, and Picture Completion) factors, but not on the Verbal Comprehension factors. In another study, reflective fourth graders outperformed impulsives on all WISC scales except Vocabulary (Walker, 1985). The middle-SES reflectives outperformed the middle-SES impulsives on all tests.

Instruments for Measuring Impulsivity/Reflectivity

Matching Familiar Figures Test (MFFT) (Kagen, Rosman, Day, Albert, & Phillips, 1964)

The MFFT is the most commonly used measure of I/R. The test for adolescents and adults consists of a booklet of 12 standard pictures, each with eight alternatives. Only one of the alternatives is identical to the standard. The other alternatives differ slightly from the standard. In this experimenter-controlled test, subjects are required to point at the matching picture. Messer (1976) found internal consistency coefficients of .89 for response time, but only .5 for errors, and test-retest coefficients of .56-.78. A computer-administered version of the MFFT is available (van Merrienboer & Jelsma, 1988). It correlates highly to the MFFT (reflectivity indices of .58-.83) and has high test-retest coefficients (.87 for errors and .76 for time) (van Merrienboer, Jelsma, Timmermans, & Sikken, 1989).

Kansas Reflection-Impulsivity Scale for Preschoolers **(KRISP)** (Wright, 1971)

The KRISP is a standardized version of the MFFT adapted for use with preschoolers. The goal in this test is to match the one drawing that is identical to the prototype in 15 questions--5 practice and 10 criterion. Reliability information was not available.

Theoretical Background

Kagan believed that cognitive styles have implications for a child's behavior in the classroom. His early research (Kagan, 1966) focused on the effects of impulsivity on academic failure in "normal" and emotionally disturbed children. This research focused especially on reading performance. Reading difficulties, for some children, are brought on by restlessness, inattentiveness, and fidgeting (Harris & Sipay, 1975). The beginning reader deals with the mechanical processes of letter recognition, sight word retention, and words by sight, shape, phonics, context clues, and unusual word characteristics. The speed and accuracy of word identification have strong implications to the future success of the child's reading ability. Tests have shown that reflective children do better in word recognition skills than impulsive children do.

Some research has also focused on the personality attributes associated with I/R. Impulsive children are not only less analytical than reflective children, but they also show signs of being more restless, less able to recognize and adhere to rules, and less able to control movements on request (Bucky & Banta, 1972).

Although children have been the focus of reflectivity and impulsivity research, some research is being conducted in the workplace. Schon (1983) stated that reflection is characterized by concentration and careful consideration. Reflective practice is the mindful consideration of one's actions, specifically, one's professional actions. Most learning theorists believe that learning cannot take place without reflection. Reflective practice, then, is viewed as a professional development technique that enhances organizational, as well as individual, performance (Osterman, 1990).

Impulsivity/Reflectivity and Learning

Research

There is a considerable body of research on the effects of I/R on academic performance, most begun by Kagan and his colleagues.

- Impulsives consistently performed poorer than reflectives performed on problem-solving tasks where the answer was not known (Kagan, 1965, 1966).

- Younger Japanese children made fewer errors than American or Israeli children made, whereas latency for Japanese children peaked two years before American or Israeli children (Salkind, Kojima, & Zelniker, 1978).

- Response latency was positively correlated with composition length and amount of time spent writing compositions (Fischer, 1979).

- Reflectives used fewer redundant actions and made fewer errors solving a fault diagnosis problem (Rouse & Rouse, 1982).

- Use of strategies and metamemory were higher for reflectives than for impulsives during transfer situations (new learning) but not during acquisition (Borkowski, Peck, Reid, & Kurtz, 1983).

- Reflectiveness was associated with increased fluency in writing and intelligence, and reflectiveness significantly predicted several types of learning outcomes (Parry, 1984).

- Reflectives recalled more stated actions from reading a script, regardless of how many times these actions appeared (Swanson & Schumaker, 1986).

- On a stimulus recognition task, reflectives adopted a more conservative response bias than impulsives, so they performed more accurately (Friedrich, 1986). On difficult tasks, impulsives also adopted a more conservative response bias.

- Reflectives scored higher on reading comprehension than impulsives scored because they allowed themselves more time to solve problems (Joffe, 1987). The same effect was not found for word identification.

- Reflective children had more incidental recall than impulsive children (Haynes & Miller, 1987) and fewer errors in serial recall tasks (Thompson, Teare, & Elliot, 1983).

- Reflective children appeared to outperform impulsive children on paper-pencil tests (Gullo, 1988).

Implications of the Characteristics and Research

Implications which are drawn from research are noted with a •; those drawn logically from descriptive information regarding the trait are noted by an *.

Based upon the research and the descriptions of impulsivity/reflectivity, we conclude that it is a unipolar construct, so impulsives are less skilled than reflectives, and therefore they will probably not excel at any tasks. At least, there is no research to support any advantages for impulsives.

Based on the research and the descriptions of impulsivity/reflectivity, we conclude that reflective learners are more likely to excel at learning tasks such as:

• recall of structured information
• reading comprehension and interpretation of text
• problem-solving and decision-making tasks

and acquire and use effectively learning strategies such as:

* setting own learning goals
* concentrating on information
* comparing new knowledge with existing knowledge or beliefs
* metacognitive strategies, such as regulating mood or testing personal skills

Impulsivity/Reflectivity and Instruction

Research

Again, a fairly extensive amount of research focused on the effects of instruction on impulsives and reflectives, and most was begun by Kagan and his colleagues.

• Threats of failure introduced into learning situations created more anxiety in reflectives and caused them to commit more errors on a serial learning task (Kagan, 1966).

• Students became more reflective after observing reflective, as opposed to impulsive adult models. Reflective teachers fostered reflectivity, whereas impulsive teachers had little impact on students' tempo (Denney, 1972; Yando & Kagan, 1968).

• Four main types of intervention have been successful in modifying impulsive cognitive styles. These are: (1) forced delay, (2) reinforcement for increasing response time or decreasing errors, (3) the teaching of scanning strategies directly, and (4) modeling (Messer, 1976).

• Reinforcement for correct responding produced increases in accuracy but not latency. Reinforcement for increased latency in responding did not produce accompanying improvements in accuracy (Williams & Lahey, 1977).

- Reflectives performed better in science in a low-control condition, while impulsives did better in a high-control teaching situation (Thumann, 1982).

- A structured, computer-assisted instruction program in math increased the achievement of impulsives (who normally achieve less) more than open-learning experiences achieved with Logo (Forte, 1984).

- Akerstrom (1984) found that rather than behaving predictably as reflectives or impulsives in a problem-solving task, seventh graders used a repertoire of behaviors containing both kinds of behaviors. Specific behaviors were differentially elicited by variables such as problem type, content, difficulty, expertise, stability of conceptual models, anxiety, social understanding, and investment in the problem.

- Reflectives were generally unaffected by rewards. Rewarded impulsives, however, increased their response latencies (Maldonado, 1984). Impulsivity scores decreased under reward and increased without reward.

- Through a supplantive effect, haptic training significantly reduced impulsivity (Ciotti, 1984).

- Explicit teaching of reflective test strategies enhanced recall test performance of impulsives (Huey-You, 1985).

- Impulsives were deficient in metacognitive skills, such as awareness of task objectives, planning and evaluating strategies, and ability to monitor progress, which caused inefficiencies in problem solving (Stober, 1985).

- The use of verbal labeling procedures to support nonverbal inductive reasoning tasks increased accuracy and latency for both reflectives and impulsives. These procedures disrupted reflectives' performances, however, by causing them to process like impulsives when required to perform a concurrent verbal task (Welsh, 1987).

- Positive effects of practicing a cursor-movement task under a random practice schedule decreased for reflectives and forced impulsives to behave like reflectives, thus improving their retention (Jelsma & van Merrienboer, 1989).

There is a cognitive behavior modification technique known as Verbal Self-Instruction (VSI) that can be used as a procedure for increasing reflective thought. The VSI technique trains children to talk to themselves and use language mediation to control their behavior. First, the children observe a self-verbalization model on a task. Second, the children follow the same task using the verbal instruction model. Third, the children model the task while verbalizing the steps aloud. Finally, the children perform the task while using an inner silent verbalization. The following research describes the effects of VSI training on the reflectivity of children.

- Vocabulary, reading comprehension, and reflectivity improved following training on delaying responses and using more efficient scanning and search strategies (Learner & Richman, 1984).

- VSI modified only self-control and not impulsivity (Hoover, 1985).

Implications of the Characteristic and Research

Implications which are drawn from research are noted with a •; those drawn logically from descriptive information regarding the trait are noted by an *. Instructional conditions that capitalize on the preferences of the impulsive student and challenge the reflective student include:

- highly structured lessons that control the processing of the learner
* small lesson chunks
* algorithmic instructional sequence

Instructional conditions that remediate or compensate for the deficiencies of the impulsive student include:

- reducing the uncertainty in tasks; providing directions and outcomes
- explicit teaching of reflective test strategies
- haptic training
- verbal mediation strategies, such as labeling new information
- forcing delays in processing to enable the learner to reflect on material
- reinforcing learners for increasing their response time and decreasing errors
- modeling reflective performance
* describing the required performance and the criteria of evaluation
* asking the student to look up list of new vocabulary
* advising learner of instructional support needed (e.g., number of examples, practice items)
* asking learners to relate questions to objectives
* providing corrective and remedial feedback

Instructional conditions that capitalize on the preferences of the reflective student and challenge the impulsive student include:
- low structure
- treatments that provide for more learner control and decision making

Instructional conditions that remediate or compensate for the deficiencies of the reflective student are not needed because of the processing advantages that reflectivity provides them.

References

Akerstrom, S. (1984). Individual differences and group problem solving: A study of the cognitive style reflection-impulsivity (Doctoral dissertation, Northwestern University). *Dissertation Abstracts International, 45*, 454.

Block, J., Block, J. H., & Harrington, D. (1974). Some misgivings about the Matching Familiar Figures Test as a measure of reflection-impulsivity. *Developmental Psychology, 10*, 611-632.

Borkowski, J. G., Peck, V. A., Reid, M. K., & Kurtz, B. E. (1983). Impulsivity and strategy transfer: Metamemory as mediator. *Child Development, 54*, 459-473.

Brannigan, G., Ash, G., and Margolis, H. (1980). Impulsivity-reflectivity and children's intellectual performance. *Journal of Personality Assessment, 44*, 41-43.

Bucky, S. F., & Banta, T. J. (1972). Racial factors in test performance. *Developmental Psychology, 6*, 7-13.

Cairns, E. (1978). Age and conceptual tempo. *Journal of Genetic Psychology, 133*, 13-18.

Carroll, J. A. (1980). The effects of cognitive tempo on cue selection Strategies of kindergarten, first, and second grade children (Doctoral dissertation, University of Kansas). *Dissertation Abstracts International, 41*, 2925.

Ciotti, J. E. (1984). The effects of impulsivity attentuation through training of haptic differentiation and matching strategies on locus of control and risk taking (Doctoral dissertation, University of Hawaii). *Dissertation Abstracts International, 46*, 1707.

Cormicle, D. W. (1983). Effects of self-verbalization and cognitive tempo upon logical abilities of children (Doctoral dissertation, University of Maryland). *Dissertation Abstracts International, 45*, 143.

Denney, D. R. (1972). Modeling effects upon conceptual style and cognitive tempo. *Child Development, 43*, 105-119.

Drake, D. M. (1970). Perceptual correlates of impulsive and reflective behavior. *Developmental Psychology, 2*, 202-214.

Fischer, C. A. (1979). The relationship between the reflection-impulsivity dimension of cognitive style and selected temporal aspects of time bound, first draft, expository transcribing (Doctoral dissertation, Vanderbilt University). *Dissertation Abstracts International, 42*, 583.

Forte, M. M. (1984). The effect of 'Logo' computer program versus a 'mathematics' computer program on reflection-impulsivity, perceived competence, motivational orientation, and academic achievement (Doctoral dissertation, Rutgers University). *Dissertation Abstracts International, 45,* 2803.

Friedrich, M. A. (1986). Cognitive tempo as a response strategy in children (Doctoral dissertation, University of South Florida). *Dissertation Abstracts International, 47,* 1754.

Gullo, D. (1988). An investigation of cognitive tempo and its effects on evaluating kindergarten childen's academic and social competencies. *Early Child Development and Care, 34,* 201-215.

Harris, A. J., & Sipay, E. R. (1975). *Readings on reading and instruction,* (2nd ed.). New York: David McKay.

Haynes, V. F., & Miller, P. H. (1987). The relationship between cognitive style, memory, and attention in preschoolers. *Child Study Journal, 17,* 21-33.

Heider, E. (1971). Information processing and the modification of an impulsive conceptual tempo. *Child Development, 42,* 1276-1281.

Hoover, V. L. (1985). The effect of verbal self-instruction training on the cognitive styles of impulsive elementary school students (Doctoral dissertation, Oklahoma State University). *Dissertation Abstracts International, 47,* 836.

Huey-You, P. A. (1985). A comparison of two cognitive behavior modification strategies designed to increase reflective test response of mildly language-impaired first graders (Doctoral dissertation, Southern Illinois University). *Dissertation Abstracts International, 46,* 2996.

Jelsma, O., & van Merrienboer, J. J. (1989). Contextual interference: Interactions with reflection-impulsivity. *Perceptual and Motor Skills, 68* (3, Pt. 2), 1055-1064.

Joffe, R. T. (1987). Reflection-impulsivity and field independence as factors in the reading achievement of children with reading difficulties (Doctoral dissertation, Temple University). *Dissertation Abstracts International, 48,* 867.

Kagan, J. (1965a). Impulsive and reflective children: significance of conceptual tempo. In J. Krumboltz (Ed.), *Learning and the educational process.* (pp. 133-161). Chicago: Rand McNally.

Kagan, J. (1965b). Individual differences in in the resolution of response uncertainty. *Journal of Personality and Social Psychology, 2,* 154-160.

Kagan, J. (1965c). Reflection-impulsivity and reading development in primary grade children. *Child development, 36,* 609-628.

Kagan, J. (1966). Developmental studies in reflection and analysis. In A.H. Kidd & J.L. Rivoire (Eds.), *Perceptual development in children* (pp. 487-522). New York: International University Press.

Kagan, J., & Kogan, N. (1970). Individuality and cognitive performance. In P. Mussen (Ed.), *Carmichael's manual of child psychology, 1.* (pp. 77-86). New York: Wiley.

Kagan, J., Rosman, B. L., Day, D., Albert, J., & Philips, W. (1964). Information processing in the child: Significance of analytic and reflective attitudes. *Psychological Monographs, 78* (1, Whole No. 578).

Lajoie, S. P., & Shore, B. M. (1987). Impulsivity, reflectivity, and high IQ. *Gifted Education International, 4*(3), 139-141.

Learner, K. M., & Richman, C. L. (1984). The effect of modifying the cognitive tempo of reading-disabled children on reading comprehension. *Contemporary Educational Psychology, 9*(2), 122-134.

Leitgeb, J. L., Bolocofsky, D. N., & Obrutz, J. E. (1986). The relationship of cognitive tempo to psychological differentiation and locus of control. *Journal of Psychology, 120*, 353-361.

Maldonado, J. L. (1984). The relationship of English oral proficiency, impulsivity, elementary school children (Doctoral dissertation, Oklahoma State University). *Dissertation Abstracts International, 46*, 1413.

Messer, S. B. (1976). Reflection-impulsivity: A review. *Psychological Bulletin, 83*, 1026-1052.

Osterman, K. (1990). Reflective practice: A new agenda for education. *Education and Urban Society, 22*, 133-153.

Parry, T. S. (1984). The relationship of selected dimensions of learner cognitive style, aptitude, and general intelligence factors to selected foreign language proficiency tasks of second-year students of Spanish at the secondary level (Doctoral dissertation, Ohio State University). *Dissertation Abstracts International, 45*, 2425.

Rouse, S. H., & Rouse, W. B. (1982). Cognitive style as a correlate of human problem-solving performance in fault diagnosis tasks. *IEEE Transactions on Systems, Man and Cybernetics, 12* (5), 649-652.

Salkind, N. J., Kojima, H., & Zelniker, T. (1978). Cognitive tempo in American, Japanese, and Israeli children. *Child Develpment, 49*, 1024-1027.

Schon, D. (1983). *The reflective practitioner: How professionals think in action.* New York: Basic.

Simpkins, L. J. L. (1981). Effects of adjusted teaching strategies on reading achievement of impulsive third-grade students (Doctoral dissertation, Virginia Tech University). *Dissertation Abstracts International, 42*, 2594.

Stober, S. F. (1985). The relationship between conceptual tempo and metacognition (Doctoral dissertation, University of Toronto). *Dissertation Abstracts International, 46*, 2637.

Swanson H., & Schumaker, G. (1986). Reflection-impulsivity and script-action recall. *Bulletin of the Psychonomic Science, 24*, 28-309.

Thompson, R. W., Teare, J. F., & Elliot, S. N. (1983). Impulsivity: From theoretical constructs to applied interventions. *Journal of Special Education, 17*, 157-168.

Thumann, E. H. (1982). Interactions between two methods of teaching science and two cognitive styles (Doctoral dissertation, University of

California, Los Angeles). *Dissertation Abstracts International, 43,* 2227.

van Merrienboer, J. G., & Jelsma, O. (1988). Computer versus experimenter controlled administration? *Educational and Psychological Measurement, 48,* 161-164.

van Merrienboer, J. G., Jelsma, O., Timmermans, J. H., & Sikken, J. (1989). Computer versus experimenter controlled administration of the MFFT: Mean test scores and reliabilities. *Educational and Psychological Measurement, 49,* 883-892.

Walker, N. W. (1985). Interactional effects of socioeconomic status and cognitive tempo on WISC-R performance. *Measurement and Evaluation in Education, 18* (2), 58-63.

Welsh, M. (1987). Verbal mediation underlying inductive reasoning: Cognitive tempo differences. *Cognitive Development, 2*(1), 37-57.

Williams, M., & Lahey, B. B. (1977). The functional independence of response latency and accuracy: Implications for the concept of conceptual tempo. *Journal of Abnormal Psychology,* 371-378.

Wright, J. C. (1971). *The Kansas-Reflection-Impulsivity scale for preschoolers (KRISP).* St. Ann, MO: Cemrel.

Yando, R. M., & Kagan, J. (1968). The effect of the teacher tempo on the child. *Child Development, 39,* 27-34.

Bibliography

Argyris, C., & Schon, D. A. (1974). *Theory in practice: Increasing professional effectiveness.* San Francisco: Jossey-Bass.

Ault, R. L. (1973). Problem-solving strategies of reflective, impulsive, fast-accurate, and slow-inaccurate children. *Child Development, 44,* 259-266.

Finch, A. J., Spirito, A., & Brophy, C. J. (1982). Reflection-impulsivity and WISC-R performance in behavior-problem children. *Journal of Educational Psychology. 111,* 217-221.

Graybill, D., Jamison, M., & Swerdlik, M. E. (1984). Remediation of impulsivity in learning disabled children by special education resource teachers using verbal self-instruction. *Psychology in the Schools, 21,* 252-253.

Herman, B. P., Passmore, L., & Horne, A. (1982). *Treating cognitively impulsive children using academic materials and peer models.* (ERIC Document Reproduction Service No. ED 260 105)

Walczyk, J. J., & Hall, V. C. (1989). Is the failure to monitor comprehension an instance of cognitive impulsivity? *Journal of Educational Psychology, 81* (3), 294-298.

Weithorn, C. J., Kagan, E., & Marcus, M. (1983). The relationship of activity level ratings and cognitive impulsivity to task performance and academic achievement. *Child Psychology and Psychiatry,* 587-602.

10

FOCAL ATTENTION
(Scanning vs. Focusing)

Description of Focal Attention

The cognitive control, *focal attention*, (also referred to as *scanning/focusing*) describes individual differences in the processing of stimulus fields. When learners scan a field, they cognitively record and compare both visual and verbal properties from the available information. Differences occur in the *intensity* and *extensiveness* of their attention (Santostefano, 1978).

Intensity is the *level of control* the learner exerts over the stimulus field and the scanning activity. On one end of the continuum are individuals who direct their attention passively by scanning or making contact with only a few elements of the informational field. The other end of the continuum is represented by individuals who direct their attention actively (i.e., focusing). Passive scanning is marked by a tendency to track a moving target or piece of information with visual attention. The information moves, and attention passively follows. In contrast, active scanning (focusing) is demonstrated by visually seeking out, exploring, and registering the elements of a display of information (Santostefano & Paley, 1964). Extensiveness refers to the *breadth* of scanning. A narrow breadth of scanning is characterized by individuals who limit their attention to a small segment of the field, versus those who scan a broad area.

This continuum is represented by two types of scanners: extensive and extreme. These are characterized at one end by individuals who direct their attention actively and freely to all parts of the field, and, at the other end, by individuals who are more passive in directing their attention to relatively narrow aspects of the field. Extensive scanning is associated with active concern for detail, and a sharp, yet wide-ranging focus of attention. These individuals are meticulous and intense, noticing even incidental facets of their surroundings. They have an obsessive, almost paranoid, regard for accuracy and exactness. Extreme scanning, or focusing, on the other hand is associated with a narrow focus of attention and a restricted attention to fewer facets of the surroundings (Messick, 1976; Tiedemann, 1989; Wolitzky & Wachtel, 1973).

Scanners will tend to assimilate large amounts of information before making a response to stimuli. Therefore, scanners are less susceptible to making quick first impressions. Focusers, on the other hand, will react to smaller amounts of stimuli and might tend to "jump to conclusions." Scanners are also more likely to be paranoid schizophrenics because of their cautious, uncertain, and distrustful approach to the world (Santostefano, 1978).

Characteristic Differences in Focal Attention

Focusers	Scanners
passive scanning	active scanning
narrow scanning	broad scanning
developmentally early	developmentally advanced
global	differentiated
attracted by visuals	visually self-controlled
restricted attention	sharp, wide range of focus
diffused	integrated
deploy attention unsystematically	deploy attention systematically
inefficient surveyor	efficient surveyor

Individual Differences Related to Focal Attention

Focal attention is related to other cognitive styles and controls, including:

Constricted/Flexible Control--(See chapter 8) Based on the characteristics of both types of control, focusers will tend to be constricted processors, whereas scanners tend to be flexible processors.

Cognitive Tempo--(See chapter 9) Focusers tend to be similar to impulsives, who do not scan all of the options before making a response, whereas scanners have a more reflective cognitive tempo (Drake, 1970).

Leveling/Sharpening--This cognitive style describes how individuals perceive and memorize images (See chapter 16). Scanners will tend to be levelers, whereas focusers will tend to be sharpeners. However, no research supports this theory.

Instruments for Measuring Focal Attention

The tests for the cognitive control of focal attention deal with comparative-size estimations as indicators of attention deployment (Buss & Polety,

1976). An individual's preferred method of sampling or registering a field of information will reflect his or her functioning level of focal attention.

Circles Test of Focal Attention (Santostefano, 1978)

This test, originally developed by Santostefano and Paley in 1964, and revised by Santostefano in 1978, is designed to assess the intensity and extensiveness of one's attention. Respondents who scan items broadly and actively show better performance on this instrument. The test is administered in an individual setting. The examiner shows the student two circles, one larger than the other, separated on a page. Those who distribute their attention extensively and equally between the circles make more accurate size estimations. This 33-item test is designed for adolescents and children ages 5-15.

Scattered Scanning Test (SST) (Santostefano, 1978)

The SST is a 50-item, group-administered test that takes about one hour to complete. The test is designed to measure the speed and breadth (active/passive and broad/narrow dimensions of focal attention) of marking specific shapes. Adolescents and children ages 3-15 are given 30 seconds to scan and mark the circles and crosses on a sheet containing geometric shapes. There are two forms to this test, which differ only in the number of items on the sheet. Form 1 contains 50 shapes, whereas form 2 contains 200 shapes. Two scores are generated by the test: the active-passive score as measured by the total number of figures marked during the 30-second period, and the breadth score as measured by the size of the perimeter of the area scanned by connecting the outermost figures that were crossed with line segments. Active, extensive scanners mark more items than focusers and spread their marks over the entire page.

Because motor ability may affect the scores on the SST, Santostefano (1978) developed the Motor Tempo Test to be administered as a preliminary measure. It addresses attention control, psychomotor skills, and visual discrimination.

Continuous Performance Test of Attention (Santostefano, 1978)

This individually administered test is designed to measure continuous attention as well as the degree of activity and breadth of visual scanning. The individual is scored by the number of squares and crosses detected among rows of geometric shapes that are continuously displayed on a memory drum. The test is also designed for adolescents and children ages 3-15 and should be administered in an individual setting. The measurements taken relate to visual perception using visual stimuli.

Size Estimation Test (Gardner, Holzman, Klein, Linton, & Spence, 1959)

The Size Estimation Test is similar to the aforementioned Circles Test. For this test, adult subjects are given three disks in four test periods. For each one, they are given a disk to hold and are shown one projected on a screen. They are then asked to adjust the size of the projected disc to match the size of the one in their hand. Three scores result from this test: total judgement time, the number of stops, and the average error of over-estimation. Scanners are those individuals who score lower on the average error of overestimation. Focusers overestimate to a greater degree. The key factor, attention deployment, is not confounded in this test by other distractors such as those found in the geometric shapes of the SST (Wolitzky & Wachtel, 1973). Corrected odd-even reliability coefficients were .95 for men and .92 for women.

This test was converted by Gardner in 1964 to a pencil-and-paper version to be administered to children.

Picture Sorting Test (Gardner, Holzman, Klein, Linton, & Spence, 1959)

In this test, adult subjects are shown 60 sexual, aggressive, and neutral pictures of varying content, emotive value, and artistic quality. They are asked to separate the images into affective or indifferent categories. Focusers are less likely to commit themselves, either because they may not wish to express their feelings or are slow in assessment, and therefore do not have any true emotional response (Gardner et al., 1959, p. 47).

Theoretical Background

This factor has developed through a series of conflicting definitions. The term *focal attention* has evolved from the work of Schlesinger (1954), who termed it *focusing* and identified two main attributes. Gardner et al. (1959) described these attributes as (a) "a tendency to narrow awareness and to keep experiences discrete, and (b) a tendency to separate affect from idea" (p. 46). From these tendencies Wolitzky and Wachtel (1973) traced the construct back to work by Freud, who researched attributes of isolation and the effect of concentration, Rorschach, who researched the relation to isolation-scanning links, and Piaget and his centration hypothesis, which dealt with attentional field. Piaget's work led to Gardner's (1959) reinterpretation of the attributes of the two terms. This interpretation switched their meaning and shifted the emphasis from focal attention to "scanning." As a result of this reattribution, Gardner and Long conducted a series of studies from 1959 to 1962 (Wolitzky & Wachtel, 1973). Finally, Santostefano and Paley (1964) preferred the term *focal attention* which embraces "breadth of scanning" and is used currently.

It is important to note that there has been disagreement about the nature of broad and narrow attention and how to assess and interpret the results. Because of the conflicting perception of the construct, several different tests were developed to reflect the various attributes. These attributes included the two originally defined by Schlesinger (1954), narrow awareness and separate affect, and the more recently accepted attributes of intensity and extensiveness of selected attention.

Another noteworthy area of research is that of the developmental nature of scanning in infants (Cohen & Ivry, 1989; Kagan & Kogan, 1970). These studies showed that the young child typically scans information slowly and directs attention to only narrow segments of the available field. With age, the child scans more actively and sweeps attention across larger segments.

Focal Attention and Learning

Research

It seems that most of the research relating focal attention to learning has been conducted in two areas; reading and pictures presented with words, and learning of abnormal learners. Noted later, this research has conflicting results.

- Focal attention has been found to be noncritical to reading, although further testing in this area might be beneficial (Santostefano & Paley, 1964).

- A study by Santostefano and Rutledge (1965) concluded that reading-disabled children are not handicapped in terms of breadth of scanning. These results are consistent with studies by Gibson (1965).

- Samuels (1967, 1970) and Singer, Samuels, and Spiroff (1974) testing their "focal attention hypothesis" found that during acquisition trials, pictures served as prompts and facilitated correct responses. However, on test trials, when pictures were withdrawn, pupils who had learned sight words with pictures scored significantly lower than pupils who learned words alone. This research supported the value of extensive scanning (a more deliberate, nondistracted approach) for learning.

- Arlin, Scott, and Webster (1978) and Arlin (1980) disproved the focal attention hypothesis in a study of kindergarten children who were taught words with or without pictures. Providing pictures with the words facilitated rather than hindered learning.

- Psychiatrically hospitalized children representing high- or low-aggression groups were tested for focal attention (Santostefano & Rieder, 1984).

The highly aggressive children scanned in a very narrow field when observing aggressive stimuli.

• Morrison (1988) studied college students and found that focusers and field independent students were superior fault diagnosticians. Verbal training was more effective for field independents. Little difference from training, however, was found along the focuser/scanner dimension.

Implications of the Characteristics and Research

Because of the limited amount and conflicting results of the research, we have based our recommendations on the theoretical descriptions of focal attention. Implications which are drawn from research are noted with a •; those drawn logically from descriptive information regarding the trait are noted by an *. We conclude that *focusers* are more likely to excel at learning tasks such as:

* convergent production tasks
* reproductive tasks, such as tracing or copying
* well-defined and structured tasks, with explicit parameters
• diagnosing faults

and acquire and use effectively learning strategies such as:

* preparing environment
* rehearsing and review material
* regulating environment

Based on the limited amount of research and on descriptions of focal attention, we conclude that *scanners* are more likely to excel at learning tasks such as:

* recalling structured information
• reading comprehension and interpretation of text
• problem-solving and decision-making tasks

and acquire and use effectively learning strategies such as:

• setting own learning goals
• concentration
• comparing new knowledge with existing knowledge or beliefs
• metacognitive strategies, such as regulating mood or testing personal skills
• analyzing key ideas

Focal Attention and Instruction

Research

Because focal attention does not seem to be critical to reading and very little research is available on normal learners, some extrapolation is necessary.

- Focal attention was subject to developmental factors. Immature individuals tended to direct their attention passively and narrowly and then move toward active and broad attention as they matured (Santostefano & Paley, 1964).

- Focal attention has been found to be non-critical to reading (Santostefano & Rutledge, 1965), though its effects on perception of visual or bimodal presentations are untested. Scanners can be reasonably expected to more efficiently survey a wide stimulus field such as multimedia presentations (Jonassen, 1978, 1979).

Implications of the Characteristic and Research

Implications which are drawn from research are noted with a •; those drawn logically from descriptive information regarding the trait are noted by an *. Instructional conditions that capitalize on the preferences of focusers and challenge the scanners include:

* keeping the field of information simple, don't mix information
* using a fairly small field to allow for the narrow scanning of focusers
* using simple pictures and graphics that allows the focuser a simple field to study
* presenting one topic at a time
* presenting a relatively small area over which information is distributed to allowing the focuser a narrow field of information
* presenting information without details using only central themes
* presenting information in an organized fashion with little complexity
* using relatively quick movements through a field

Instructional conditions that remediate or compensate for the deficiencies of the focusers include:

* introducing, under controlled conditions, broader and more active scanning activities
* using tracking techniques, such as tachistoscopes that can vary speed and field of vision, to build an individual's ability to actively scan a field
* using highlighting, motion, and animation techniques

* using progressive disclosure, in which a picture is assembled one section at a time
* using matched examples/nonexamples and highlight differences

    Instructional conditions that capitalize on the preferences of the scanners and challenge the focusers include:

* using multi-image presentations that require active attention to a broad information field (i.e., visual mobility)
* using a field of information that contains different stimuli that are scattered over the field
* using pictures and graphics with many types of information spread out over a large field
* presenting information with many details
* using learner-recalled elaborations

    Instructional conditions that remediate or compensate for the deficiencies of scanners include:

* using summaries and paraphrases
* using global images to illustrate main ideas

References

Arlin, M. (1980). A commentary on a previous critique by Harry Singer of a focal attention study. *Reading Research Quarterly, 15,* 550-558.

Arlin, M., Scott, M., & Webster, J. (1978). The effects of pictures on rate of learning sight words: A critique of the focal attention hypothesis. *Reading Research Quarterly, 14,* 645-660.

Buss, A. R., & Polety, W. (1976). *Individual differences: Traits and factors.* New York: Gardner Press.

Cohen, A., & Ivry, R. (1989). Illusory conjunctions inside and outside the focus of attention. *Journal of Experimental Psychology Human Perception and Performance, 15*(4), 650-663.

Drake, D. M. (1970). Perceptual correlates of impulsive and reflective behavior. *Developmental Psychology, 2,* 202-214. '

Gardner, R. W. (1959). Cognitive control principles and perceptual behavior. *Bulletin Menniger Clinic, 23,* 241-248.

Gardner, R., Holzman, P. S., Klein, G. S., Linton, H. B., & Spence, D. (1959). Cognitive control: A study of individual consistencies in cognitive behavior. *Psychological Issues 1, 4,* 1-185.

Gibson, E. (1965). Learning to read. *Science, 148,* 1066-1072.

Jonassen, D. H. (1978). Implications of multi-image for concept acquisition. *Educational Communications & Technology Journal, 27,* 291-302.

Jonassen, D. H. (1979). Cognitive styles/controls and media. *Educational Technology, 19,* 28-32.

Kagan, J., & Kogan, N. (1970). Individual variation in cognitive processes. In P. H. Mussen (Ed.), *Carmichael's manual of child psychology (Vol. 1, pp. 1273-1365).* New York: Wiley.

Messick, S. (1976). Personality consistencies in cognition and creativity. In S. Messick (Ed.), *Individuality in Learning* (pp. 4-22). San Francisco: Jossey-Bass.

Morrison, D. L. (1988). Predicting diagnosis performance with measures of cognitive style. *Current Psychology Research and Reviews, 7*(2), 136-156.

Samuels, S. J. (1967). Attentional processes in reading: The effect of pictures in the acquisition of reading responses. *Journal of Educational Psychology, 58,* 337-342.

Samuels, S. J. (1970). Effects of pictures on learning to read, comprehension and attitudes. *Review of Educational Research, 40,* 397-407.

Santostefano, S. (1978). *A biodevelopmental approach to clinical child psychology.* New York: Wiley.

Santostefano, S., & Paley, E. (1964). Development of cognitive controls in children. *Child Development, 35,* 939-949.

Santostefano, S., & Rieder, J. (1984). Cognitive controls and aggression in children: The concept of cognitive-affective balance. *Journal of Consulting and Clinical Psychology, 52,* 46-56.

Santostefano, S., & Rutledge, L. (1965). Cognitive styles and reading disabilities. *Psychology in Schools, 2,* 57-62.

Schlesinger, H. L. (1954). Cognitive attitudes in relation to susceptibility to interference. *Journal of Personality, 22,* 354-374.

Singer, H., Samuels, J. J., & Spiroff, J. (1974). The effect of pictures and contextual conditions on learning responses to printed words. *Reading Research Quarterly, 9*(4), 555-567.

Tiedemann, J. (1989). Measures of cognitive styles: A critical review. *Educational Psychologist, 24*(3), 261-275.

Wolitzky, D. L., & Wachtel, P. L. (1973). Personality and perception. In B. B. Wolman (Ed.), *Handbook of general psychology* (pp. 826-857). Englewood Cliffs, NJ: Prentice Hall.

Bibliography

The ETS Test Collection Catalog, Volume 4: Cognitive Aptitude and Intelligence Tests. Phoenix: Oryx Press.

Gardner, R. W. (1953). Cognitive styles in categorizing behavior. *Journal of Personality, 22,* 214-233.

Gardner, R. W. (1961). Cognitive controls of attention deployment as de-
    terminants of visual illusions. *Journal of Abnormal and Social
    Psychology. 62*, 120-129.
Santostefano, S. (1985). *Cognitive control therapy with children and ado-
    lescents.* New York: Permagon Press.
Wachtel, P. L. (1967). Conceptions of broad and narrow attention.
    Psychological Bulletin. 68, 417-429.

11

CATEGORY WIDTH
(Breadth of Categorizing)

Description of Category Width

Category width (also known as *breadth of categorization, band width,* or *equivalence width*) is a measure of "the range of instances included in a cognitive category" (Pettigrew, 1958). For example, given a particular group of ideas and asked to apply some form of categorical description, an individual will respond along a continuum of inclusion to exclusion for instances within a categorical class. Narrow categorizers are typically conservative, excluding items and forming narrow classes. When measuring cognitive categories, narrow categorizers prefer to exclude possibly inappropriate instances through overdiscrimination and limiting the scope of their category ranges. Broad/wide categorizers, on the other hand, prefer to risk the inclusion of possibly inappropriate instances by expanding the scope of their category ranges and over-generalizing (Pettigrew, 1958). In other words, narrow categorization usually implies a willingness to risk the exclusion of positive categorical items, whereas wide categorizers are more willing to risk the inclusion of negative categorical items.

An individual's category width (CW) is fairly consistent regardless of content types; however, CW is affected by the level of task difficulty. As the depth of processing increases, CW narrows with the individual's rise in concern for accuracy. Wide categorizers will segment confusing content into subcategories if uncertainty exists among conceptual items, enabling them to create less ambiguous or more clearly defined categories. Wide categorizers more easily adapt to the strategies of a narrow categorizer. Wide categorizers may alter their responses on subsequent tasks as a result of performances on previous tasks (Phares & Davis, 1966).

Some research suggests that CW may measure openness to attitude change. Narrow categorizers tend to be more willing to alter their attitudes than wide categorizers. This may be due to the narrow categorizer's desire for conformity among differing points of view because of the tendency to resolve inconsistencies and discrepancies to reduce dissonance (Eagly & Telaak, 1972).

Category width, like most cognitive styles, remains relatively stable over an individual's lifetime. For the most part, CW has not been shown to be a measure of intelligence, authoritarianism, or dogmatism. Since its inception, CW has been used to predict problem-solving abilities, generalization abilities, quantitative skills, and so on.

Women are generally narrow categorizers. Men tend to be wide categorizers and have a propensity to make wider estimations than females. Also, whereas women tend to remain narrower, some men tend to be more bipolar or extreme in their responses (Parsons, 1973).

Contextual changes also affect responses. For example, a child may perceive a group of other children as friendly in a familiar playground situation, yet the same group may take on hostile connotations on the street. The reward on the playground may be new friendships; the consequences of the street group may be hostilities. These rewards and consequences may alter the amount of risk taking, which, in turn, may alter CW. Generally, narrow categorizers are affected more by changes in the environment.

Strong correlations have been shown between maturation and CW. Pettigrew (1958) suggested that societal pressures early in life may direct personal growth, particularly between the sexes. It is also possible that older individuals may move toward narrow CW, particularly when content is evaluative. Finally, risk taking decreases with age and may cause a move toward narrow CW, although a consensus has not been reached as to how risk taking affects which type of categorizer.

Characteristic Differences in Category Width

Narrow	Wide
introvert	extrovert
conformist	nonconformist
overdiscriminate	overgeneralize
microlevel preference	macrolevel preference
fear of change, narrow outlook	openness, novelty
limited risk taking	enjoys risk taking
traditional	change-oriented
searches for differences (exclusion)	searches for similarities (inclusion)
narrow self-concept span	wide self-concept span
nonquantitative	quantitative
older	younger
low tolerance for cognitive dissonance	high tolerance for cognitive dissonance
reacts to environmental change	unaffected by environmental change
intolerant of ambiguity	tolerant of ambiguity
ambivalent	obsessive, anxious doubters
likes detailed, analytic tasks	likes general and global strategies

Individual Differences Related to Category Width

Leveling/sharpening--Narrow categorizers tend to be sharpeners (see chapter 16), and wide categorizers are obviously levellers (Bieri, 1969).

Field dependent/independent--CW may also be thought of as "active analysis versus global acceptance" (Messick & Fritzky, 1962). Narrow categorizers should be more analytic given their efforts to make fine discriminations (see chapter 7). Using an eye-movement paradigm, Huang and Byrne (1978) concluded that narrow categorizers make greater use of the left hemisphere and are therefore more analytic. Broad categorizers, however, tend to be more field independent (Parsons, 1970). It is likely that field independence and CW assess different dimensions of thinking, so the relationship is not reliable.

Ambiguity tolerance--Narrow categorizers obviously have less ambiguity tolerance (see chapter 26), while wide categorizers have more ambiguity tolerance (Gardner, 1953).

Intelligence--Bruner and Tajfel (1961) found a relationship between IQ and CW scores. Wide categorizers were less intelligent than narrow categorizers.

Risk taking--Narrow categorizers seem to be less willing to take risks because they make finer discriminations before classification. These discriminations reduce uncertainty. "Inclusion implies greater certainty of class membership than does exclusion" (Kogan & Wallach, 1964). Hence, a lesser degree of risk. Kogan and Wallach suggested that wide categorization actually represents a *reduction* in risk taking (see chapter 31) because a reduced judgmental confidence reduces uncertainty. Narrow categorizers, they surmised, take greater risks by segmenting. Harris (1970) found that wide categorizers were actually more conservative in nonpay-off conditions than narrow categorizers.

Instruments for Measuring Category Width

Category Width Estimation Questionnaire (Pettigrew, 1958)

Pettigrew developed a 20-item Estimation Questionnaire that tests an individual's tendency toward the extreme in estimation. Each item gives an average number for a particular variable. Two multiple choice questions are then presented asking the individual to identify the largest and smallest possible instances of the variable. Each choice is assigned a number depending on its distance from the mean of the category (e.g., +3, +2,

+1 and 0). For example, "It has been estimated that the average width of windows is 34 inches. (A) What do you think is the width of the widest window: 1,363 inches, 341 inches, 48 inches, or 81 inches? (B) What is the width of the narrowest window: 3 inches, 11 inches, 18 inches, or 81 inches?" In this example, the widest categorizer would choose 1,363 inches for (A) and 3 inches for (B) because they represent the widest possible range of instances. This measures the individual's range of estimations--how much or how little the individual will include in a particular class. Test-retest reliability was .72 and internal consistency ratings ranged from .86 to .93. Criterion validity was high.

Object Sorting (Gardner, 1953; Gardner, Holzman, Klein, Linton, & Spence, 1959)

An object-sorting task consists of 73 common objects arranged randomly "in a way that seems most natural, most logical, and most comfortable" (Gardner et al., 1959). The score for this test is the number of groups into which the subject categorizes the objects. Narrow categorizers will form more groups, whereas wide categorizers will form fewer groups.

Neophilia Scale (Walker & Gibbins, 1989)

This test measuring neophilia (openness to change and novel ideas) was used by Walker and Gibbins to show correlations between neophilia and Pettigrew's Category Width Estimation Questionnaire. It is a 50-item test rated on a 5-point Likert Scale of agreement. The test was shortened to a 38-item scale after items with low-item correlation were eliminated. Alpha reliability was .85. Given its strong correlation to CW, Neophilia Scale scores may be used to make inferences about an individual's categorical width.

Knowledge Scale (Piskorz, 1989)

Piskorz hypothesized that knowledge of conceptual content may effect CW. This scale was developed to measure cognitive category width in varying domains of knowledge. It is a 55-item test containing five subscales measuring specific types of knowledge. The scale was designed specifically for Piskorz's experiment, but it is easily adaptable.

Theoretical Background

Much of the research on category width began during the 1950s in an attempt to define cognitive preferences among individuals for over- or under-generalization. Early work began with Gardner, who developed an object-sorting task in an attempt to measure consistencies in estimates of equivalence range. In 1956, Bruner and Rodriguez found consistencies among estimations of individual CW (Rogers, 1973). Pettigrew (1958) and Fillenbaum (1959) followed with scales to measure CW. Pettigrew's Category Width Scale has been the most widely used among researchers.

Category width researchers have yet to provide consistent, empirically supported generalizations about individual differences, yet significant correlations have been made between CW and cognitive processes. Pettigrew found strong correlations between widths of individual category selections and risk taking, quantitative ability, and inclusion/exclusion. The question of whether CW is independent of content, however, remains unresolved. Some recent research has supported Pettigrew's claim of independence, except in cases where the individual's knowledge of the content is self-referent. Others question the independence of the variable beyond the quantitative categories as measured by Pettigrew's instruments. This same research considered the effect of content importance on CW. When content requires qualitative, evaluative judgments on the part of the individual, CW may again be affected. This results in a "richer conceptual structure" (Piskorz, 1989) and, possibly, a narrower CW. To avoid such measurement bias, it is suggested that content remain descriptive rather than evaluative.

Category Width and Learning

Research

- Messick & Kogan (1963) showed that narrow categorizers created a greater number of smaller categories, which correlated highly with vocabulary fluency.

- In a "memory of faces" test, narrow categorizers outperformed their counterparts, probably because of an inherent attention to detail which enables finer distinctions. Narrow categorizers possess superior spatial skills (Messick & Damarin, 1964).

- Narrow categorizers were superior in recalling disagreements with colleagues. Due, most likely, to dissonance-reduction efforts (feeling they had to produce data to support their opinion), they weighed the differences more heavily (Steiner & Johnson, 1965).

- Phares and Davis (1966) found that wide categorizers generalize between seemingly unrelated tasks. Performance on one task caused wide categorizers to alter their response on a subsequent task.

- In a multiattribute learning task, wide categorizers recalled twice as many attributes as narrow categorizers, displaying a greater "degree of versatility and imagination" as opposed to the "rote" approach of the narrow categorizers (Parsons, 1973).

- In decision-making behavior, wider categorizing males committed more Type I errors (deciding positive when it should have been negative) but made better decisions (Rogers, 1973).

- Wide categorizers recalled more items on a free-recall test (Strassberg-Rosenberg & Schuell, 1974).

- In a paired-associate transfer task, wide categorizers were shown to be slower learners than narrow categorizers with fewer correct responses and more errors (Hart, 1974). Broad categorizers were also shown to be more susceptible to interference.

- Wider categorizers were less adept in assessing uncertainties. Category width may be useful in understanding overconfidence in probability assessment (Hession & McCarthy, 1975).

- Narrow categorizers searched for differences in determining classification and wide categorizers searched for similarities (Huang, 1981); that is, broad categorizers remembered more common features of designs, whereas narrow categorizers recalled more variable features. Narrow categorizers used more differentiated semantic categories.

- In a course on FORTRAN programming, male narrow categorizers realized greater achievement early on, but cognitive styles had little effect on females until the end of the course. The study showed correlations between narrow CW and analytic tasks. (Kagan & Douthat, 1984).

- In detecting fraud, narrow categorizers were more confident about their correct decisions and more aware of clues that fraud might exist (Pincus, 1984).

- Carroll and Simington (1986) found that after performing paired-associate tasks, wide categorizers realized a greater "feeling of knowing."

Implications of the Characteristics and Research

Implications which are drawn from research are noted with a •; those drawn logically from descriptive information regarding the trait are noted by an *. Based on the research and the descriptions of category width, we conclude that *wide (broad) categorizers* are more likely to excel at learning tasks such as:

- generalizing concepts; that is, including all members in a class

- recalling information that is organized in multiple dimensions
- decision making and rule using
- recalling attributes of a multiattribute learning task

and acquire and use effectively learning strategies such as:

* generating metaphors and analogies

Based on the research and the descriptions of category width, we conclude that *narrow categorizers* are more likely to excel at learning tasks such as:

- discriminating between members of a class and examples that are not members
- following directions and applying procedures
- recalling detailed information
- spatial recognition tasks
- resolving ambiguities and evaluating or assessing incomplete information

and acquire and use effectively learning strategies such as:

* selecting information sources
* evaluating current information
* analyzing key ideas and outlining

Category Width and Instruction

Research

- Wide categorizers altered their responses on subsequent tasks as a result of their performances on the previous tasks, whereas narrow categorizers did not (Phares & Davis, 1966).

- When considering stimuli in groups or individually, the same respondents made wider categorizations from the synergistic group environment, whereas more narrow estimations were made from stimuli on an individual basis (Widman, 1974).

- Subjects tended to answer with narrow categories to questions that were self-referent, whereas external referents were subject to broader categorization (Nosal & Piskorz, 1989).

Implications of the Characteristics and Research

Implications which are drawn from research are noted with a •; those drawn logically from descriptive information regarding the trait are noted by an *. Instructional conditions that capitalize on the preferences of the wide categorizer and challenge the narrow categorizer include:

• providing general statements, summaries, and holistic data only
• requiring the learner to extrapolate similarities between groups of stimuli
* presenting the lesson in large chunks
* presenting the lesson in a deductive sequence

   Instructional conditions that remediate or compensate for the deficiencies of the wide categorizer include:

• providing tasks that require detailed analysis or differentiation among stimuli
• providing outlines, such as topical headings
• providing compare/contrast tables
* presenting advance organizers, especially expository, or graphic organizers and outlines
* presenting matched example/nonexample pairs of information
* providing graphic cues or clues about organization
* creating content outlines, concept maps, or graphic organizers
* providing exclusionary VENN diagrams

   Instructional conditions that capitalize on the preferences of the narrow categorizer and challenge the wide categorizer include:

• requiring a detailed inventory of critical attributes between two complex concepts
• presenting information in narrow or small chunks
* presenting the lesson in inductive sequence

   Instructional conditions that remediate or compensate for the deficiencies of the narrow categorizer include:

• providing specific details and asking the learner to make generalizations from this information
• providing instructions on the use of cognitive strategies for narrow categorizers
• providing tasks that require holistic analysis or ambiguous environments
* requiring learners to generate analogies and metaphors

References

Bieri, J. (1969). Category width as a measure of discrimination. *Journal of Personality, 37,* 513-521.

Bruner, J. S., & Tajfel, H. (1961). Cognitive risk and environmental change. *Journal of Abnormal and Social Psychology, 62,* 231-241.

Carroll, M., & Simington, A. (1986). The effects of degree of learning, meaning, and individual differences on the feeling-of-knowing. *Acta-Psychologica, 61,* 3-16.

Eagly, A. H., & Telaak, K. (1972). Width of the latitude of acceptance as a determinant of attitude change. *Journal of Personality and Social Psychology, 23,* 388-397.

Fillenbaum, S. (1959). *Some stylistic aspects of categorizing behavior* (Project # D77-94-35-55). Ottowa, Ontario: Defence Research Board of Canada.

Gardner, R. W. (1953). Cognitive styles in categorizing behavior. *Journal of Personality, 22,* 214-233.

Gardner, R. W., Holzman, P. S., Klein, G. S., Linton, H. B., & Spence, D. (1959). Cognitive control: A study of individual consistencies in cognitive behavior. *Psychological Issues, 1,* 1-185.

Harris, B. (1970). *Individual differences in information demanded prior to making risky decisions.* New York: City University of New York, Division of Teacher Education.

Hart, J. J. (1974). Interference in a paired-associate transfer of training paradigm as a function of breadth of categorization. *Psychological Reports, 34,* 167-173.

Hession, E., & McCarthy, E. (1975). Human performance in assigning subjective probability distributions. *Irish Journal of Psychology, 3,* 31-46.

Huang, M. S. (1981). Category width and differentiation in semantic categories: Narrow categorizers possess greater differentiation abilities. *British Journal of Psychology, 72,* 339-352.

Huang, M. S., & Byrne, B. (1978). Cognitive style and lateral eye movements. *British Journal of Psychology, 69,* 85-90.

Kagan, D. M., & Douthat, J. M. (1984). Writing style, category width and introductory FORTRAN. *Journal of Research and Development in Education, 18,* 7-11.

Kogan, N. & Wallach, M.A. (1964). *Risk taking; A study in cognition and personality.* New York: Holt, Rinehart & Winston.

Messick, S., & Damarin, F. (1964). Cognitive styles and memory for faces. *Journal of Abnormal and Social Psychology, 69,* 313-318.

Messick, S., & Fritzky, F. J. (1962). *Dimensions of analytic attitude in cognition and personality* (Research Grant M-4186) National Institute of Mental Health, United States Public Health Service. Rockville, MD.

Messick, S., & Kogan, N. (1963). Differentiation and compartmentalization in object-sorting measures of categorizing style. *Perceptual and Motor Skills, 16,* 47-51.

Nosal, C., & Piskorz, Z. (1989). Category width and self-reference in answering questionnaire items--toward a cognitive model. *Polish Psychological Bulletin*, 18(4), 277-285.

Parsons, R. J. (1970). *Male-female differences in width of cognitive categorization: A developmental and perceptual study*, (Final Report ED042218). Washington, DC: U.S. Office of Education.

Parsons, R. J. (1973). Category width and the learning multi-attribute paired associates. *The Journal of General Psychology*, 89, 133-140.

Pettigrew, T. F. (1958). The measurement and correlates of category width as a cognitive variable. *Journal of Personality*, 26, 532-544.

Phares, E. J., & Davis, W. L. (1966). Breadth of categorization and the generalization of expectancies. *Journal of Personality and Social Psychology*, 4, 461-464.

Pincus, K. V. (1984). Fraud detection ability: Individual differences and their relationship to cognitive style differences (Doctoral dissertation, University of Maryland). *Dissertation Abstracts International*, 46, 746.

Piskorz, Z. (1989). Conceptual category width and content of categorization judgments. *Polish Psychological Bulletin*, 20, 25-32.

Rogers, R. L. (1973). Category width and decision making in perception. *Perceptual and Motor Skills*, 37, 647-652.

Steiner, I. D., & Johnson, H. H. (1965). Category width and responses to interpersonal disagreements. *Journal of Personality and Social Psychology*, 2, 290-292.

Strassberg-Rosenberg, B., & Shuell, T. J. (1974, April 15-19). *Organization, breadth of categorization, and free-recall learning in children.* Paper presented at the annual meeting of the American Educational Research Association, Chicago, IL. (ERIC Document Reproduction Service No. ED 092 881)

Walker, I., & Gibbins, K. (1989). Expecting the unexpected: An explanation of category width? *Perceptual and Motor Skills*, 68, 715-724.

Widman, N. (1974). Effects of group discussion on category width judgments. *Journal of Personality and Social Psychology*, 29, 187-195.

Bibliography

Huang, M. S. (1981). Category width and individual differences in information processing strategies. *Journal of Psychology*, 108, 73-79.

Huckabee, M. W. (1976). Category width, confidence, expectancies, and perceptual accuracy. *Bulletin of the Psychonomic Society 8*, 19-21.

Knutson, G. G. (1984). Estimates of category width by students in regular and special education. *Perceptual and Motor Skills*, 59, 458.

Light, C. S., & Zax, M. (1965). Relationships of age, sex, and intelligence level to extreme response style. *Journal of Personality and Social Psychology*, 2, 907-909.

Nosal, Z. S. (1985). Category width, cognitive preferences and data processing: A theoretical analysis. *Polish Psychological Bulletin, 4,* 235-244.

Pal, A., & Ram, A. L. (1978). Script evaluation as a function of category width and risk-taking behavior. *Psycho-Lingua, 8,* 101-108.

Poole, M. E. (1982). Social class-sex constraints in patterns of cognitive style; a cross-cultural replication. *Psychological Reports, 50,* 19-26.

Scanlon, R. L. (1973). The perceptual press of classroom constraints. *Irish Journal of Education, 7,* 29-39.

Taylor, R. L., & Levitt, E. E. (1967). Category breadth and the search for variety of experience. *The Psychological Record, 17,* 349-352.

Touhey, J. C. (1972). Relationship of flexibility and category width to risk-taking strategy. *Journal of Experimental Research in Personality, 6,* 259-263.

Touhey, J. C. (1973). Category width and expectancies: Risk conservatism or generalization. *Journal of Research in Personality, 7,* 173-178.

Upshaw, H. S. (1970). The effect of unit size on the range of the reference scale. *Journal of Experimental Social Psychology, 6,* 129-139.

Vaught, G. M. (1970). Sex differences in category width (factor I) correlates. *Perceptual and Motor Skills, 31,* 632.

12

COGNITIVE COMPLEXITY/SIMPLICITY

Description of Cognitive Complexity/Simplicity

Cognitive complexity/simplicity describes an individual's discriminating perception of his or her environment or social behavior. This perception describes the way an individual understands, anticipates, and predicts events. Complex and simple individuals also differ in terms of their (a) degree of differentiation (the number of distinct constructs used to describe an idea), (b) degree of articulation (the number of discriminations within those constructs), and (c) flexibility of integration (the complexity of the organization and interrelationships among constructs) (Tiedemann, 1989).

Cognitively complex individuals develop complex, multi-dimensional descriptions of constructs. High-complexity individuals are conceptually oriented and either ignore or integrate facts (Sustik & Brown, 1979); that is, a complex individual has a more versatile system for perceiving the behavior of others. High-complexity individuals accept diversity and conflict, and more easily process conflicting information. Schneider and Giambra (1971) explained that highly integrative individuals have more schemata or ways of organizing observations for forming new hierarchies. This allows for greater flexibility and greater adaptability to unexpected events, greater creativity, less polarization in judgment, and less dependence on social cues (Harvey cited in Sobel, 1970). However, Schneider and Giambra (1971) also noted that high-complexity individuals may generate so many alternatives as to prove inefficient in problem-solving situations.

Low-complexity individuals, on the other hand, develop single dimensional, less complex representations of constructs. Cognitively simple subjects tend to view the world along bipolar dimensions (e.g., good vs. bad, strong vs. weak). They often do not differentiate between self and the external world, which often leads to unwarranted assumptions of similarity between self and others. This lack of discriminatory aptitude reduces their predictive abilities (Bieri, 1955). These individuals collect facts but do not readily recognize interrelationships among those facts (Sustik & Brown, 1979). They prefer consistency and regularity, and so are better able to reconcile similar experiences. Schneider and Giambra (1971) noted that individuals with low integrative structure tend to jump to conclusions, filtering out some aspects of the environment. This leads to either-or thinking.

Many regard cognitive complexity/simplicity as a bipolar cognitive control. Bieri (1966) suggested that cognitive complexity is not necessarily better than cognitive simplicity, because a more complex person might be less accurate in examining the elements of a simpler stimulus.

There is considerable debate as to the stability of cognitive complexity throughout an individual's lifetime or to its consistency across domains. Wicker (1969) claimed that cognitive complexity evolves through experience in a specific domain. The development of cognitive complexity is not easily traced developmentally because of the lack of good measurement tools for testing children. However, within the framework of Piagetian theory, cognitive complexity could be viewed as part of the progressive development of the individual. The individual develops a greater ability to differentiate stimuli and integrate constructs as he or she develops mentally (Bieri, 1966; Hale, 1980). As children are increasingly able to articulate constructs already existing in their repertoire, they are adding new constructs (Kogan, 1971). Bieri (1966) suggested that social background may play a role in the development of cognitive complexity. because children from a lower class background are expected at an earlier age to fill certain social roles (e.g., wage earner, parent substitute), they accelerate their differentiation of social dimensions.

Characteristic Differences in Cognitive Complexity/Simplicity

Cognitively Complex Individuals	Cognitively Simple Individuals
multidimensional	unidimensional
discriminating	nondiscriminating
diversity/conflict	similarity/consistency
conceptually oriented	factually oriented
abstract	concrete
intuitive	relies on senses
perceives	judges
abstract	concrete
prefers conceptual content	prefers factual content
flexible	rigid
relativistic	categorical
older	younger

Individual Differences
Related to Cognitive Complexity/Simplicity

Dogmatism--Bieri (1955) reported positive correlations between cognitive simplicity and the Dogmatism Scale, a measure of the organization of belief systems, which includes notions about the adequacy of the self, certainty of the future, and judgments on the friendliness of the world. This finding was substantiated by Gardner and Schoen (1962) who found a strong relationship between simplicity and a construct related to dogmatism, narrow-mindedness.

Research has not provided additional evidence relating cognitive complexity to any other cognitive style or construct (Goldstein & Blackman, 1978). However, descriptions of cognitive complexity/simplicity suggest some possible relationships. These have not been substantiated.

Intelligence--Although correlations have not been evident between complexity scores and verbal fluency, some researchers speculate that such a correlation would be found in a sample containing a broad range of intelligence (Kogan, 1971). Goldstein and Blackman (1978) concluded from a comprehensive review of the literature that cognitive complexity is independent of intelligence.

Field independence--Complexity appears to be positively related to field independence (see chapter 7).

Cognitive flexibility--Complexity appears to be positively related to higher levels of cognitive flexibility (see chapter 8).

Instruments for Measuring Cognitive Complexity/Simplicity

Role Construct Repertory Test **(Rep Test)** (Kelly, 1955)

The Rep Test measures how much subjects discriminate similarities and differences among stimuli. Subjects are given a list of roles (mother, favorite teacher, best friend) and are asked to attach a particular name to each role and then explain how those individuals are alike or different. Cognitive complexity is measured by the number of constructs used to define these individuals. The test is administered in grid form, and in its adapted versions often uses a pattern of checkmarks. Scoring is complex and time consuming. The test is not easily adapted to children. Reliability coefficients of .76 to .86 have been documented, depending on whether the constructs were given (Tripodi & Bieri, 1963, 1964).

Rep Test Modifications

Bieri (1955, 1966) modified the Rep Test, creating a version that requires less time to administer. Messick and Kogan (1966), Harvey, Hunt, and Schroder (1961), and Bannister and Mair (1968) also developed simplified versions of the Rep Test by providing constructs that individuals respond to, rather than formulate. Although subjects prefer to develop their own constructs, research showed that measurements with constructs provided take less time and may offer a greater range of cognitive complexity scores (Goldstein & Blackman, 1978). Later modifications included generalization to other stimuli such as artworks, nations, inanimate objects, and social issues. Arguments about the generalizability of cognitive complexity/simplicity beyond a particular stimulus proved inconclusive (Kogan, 1971). In another modification of Kelly's Rep Test (Vacc & Vacc, 1973), role titles and constructs are reworded to be more appropriate for children at the third-grade reading level. This provides some evidence for a developmental theory of cognitive complexity.

Sentence Completion Test (Schroder & Streufert, 1962)

Subjects are given a number of sentence stems ("When I am in doubt...," "When I am criticized...,") and are asked to complete each sentence as well as provide two similar sentences. Completed sentences are judged by the complexity of their underlying structure and content within three areas: (a) those implying the presence of alternatives, (b) those implying the imposition of external standards, and (c) those implying interpersonal conflict. This test is used primarily to assess integrative complexity rather than social role complexity. Correlations between this test and the Rep Test are consistently low and negative.

Two-Peer Description Task (Crockett, 1965)

This test is sometimes used for testing children. Subjects describe two individuals their own age, one whom they know and like, and one whom they know and dislike. The number of constructs produced by the individual is used to measure complexity level (Hale, 1980).

This-I-Believe Test **(TIB)** (Harvey, 1966)

In this test, the subject is given the phrase "This I believe about _____ " and is asked to complete the thought with two or three sentences. In the blank space are a variety of referents such as friendship, guilt, myself, the American way of life, majority opinion, people, and compromise. The evaluator examines the structure and content through such concepts as "absolutism of his expressed beliefs...dependency on external authorities (especially God and/or religion), frequency of trite and normative statements, degree of ethnocentrism, acceptance of socially approved modes of behavior, concern with interpersonal relationships, and the apparent simplicity/complexity of the interpretations of the world" (Harvey, 1971, p. 47). This test measures integrative complexity, requires lengthy training for judges (Kogan, 1971), and has low test-retest reliability (Goldstein & Blackman, 1978). [No longer in print.]

Paragraph Completion Test **(PCT)** (Schroder, Driver, & Struefert, 1967)

In this test, the subject is given five sentence stems and is asked to write three sentences for each stem. The more abstract the ensuing paragraph, the greater the cognitive differentiation, and the more complex the individual's system of integration (Goldstein & Blackman, 1978). The evaluation focuses on the complexity of structure. The test evaluates integrative complexity and has low test-retest reliability. Kogan (1971) stated that in the Paragraph Completion Test training of judges is a lengthy process.

Educational Set Scale **(ESS)** (Siegel & Siegel, 1965)

This test consists of 31 triads of typical topics studied in college (e.g., learning the Latin names of animal species, learning factors affecting heredity, etc.). Each topic is carefully chosen and weighted to represent varying levels of concreteness or abstractness. The weightings are distributed along a continuum from 1.0 (straightforward factual learning) to 4.99 (very high degree of conceptualization). Subjects are asked to consider each set of three topics and rank them according to which topics seem the most interesting to study. A person consistently choosing more conceptual topics would be considered more cognitively complex. Reliability coefficients were not available.

Comment. Tiedemann (1989) expressed the viewpoint that cognitive complexity is difficult to assess and that correlations among the various measurements remain at a moderate level. Even as early as 1966, Bieri noted that agreement was lacking among different measures of the construct. There is continuing disagreement among researchers concerning the meaning and measurement of cognitive complexity. Research is too often inconclusive, not systematic, or nongeneralizable.

Theoretical Background

Two streams of thought converged to form the cognitive complexity/simplicity construct. One stream evolved from the work of Bartlett, Piaget, and Lewin. Lewin discussed differentiation as a cognitive variable by which individuals categorize their world into progressively more specific units. Cognitive complexity/simplicity incorporates the idea of differentiation but adds another dimension by discussing the degrees of fineness used to describe each area of differentiation. The assumption based on this stream is that a person has cognitive structures (schemas, controls, or styles) through which he or she views the world and events that occur. The cognition of these events is mediated by the cognitive structures that the person has in place. The second stream of thought is based on the versatility of behavior employed by people trying to cope with their often complex environment. This view of complexity/simplicity stresses the stimulating nature of external stimuli.

Research on personal constructs arose out of post-World War II concern about individuals' tendencies toward authoritarianism. Kelly (1955) devised the Role Construct Repertory Test (Rep Test) as a tool for measuring personal constructs and intended it to be primarily for clinical use. Kelly was a clinician who was interested in understanding the client's behavior through his or her perspective. Kelly believed that, rather than being reactive organisms, individuals take an active role in representing and organizing their environment. This active role, rather than merely responding to environmental stimuli, drives their behavior. Individuals revise or replace their representations or constructs to correspond to their interpretation of a particular environment. This is known as constructive alternativism.

Although there are many modifications to Kelly's notion of personal constructs, Harvey et al. (1961) brought a major shift in theoretical development when they developed the notion of concrete versus abstract abilities. In this theory, the abstract individual is seen as being high in differentiating and integrating ability. The construct of cognitive complexity was redefined as an interaction between an individual's differentiating and integrating ability (integrative complexity) and the informational complexity of his environment. Whereas some researchers (Green, 1985; Kogan, 1971; Tiedemann, 1989) discussed integrative complexity as an extension of cognitive complexity, others (Goldstein & Blackman, 1978; Ragan, 1979) appeared to view integrative complexity as a separate construct because measures of integrative complexity do not relate significantly to the Rep Test commonly used for measuring cognitive complexity.

Although many hypotheses have been postulated, beginning with Kelly's conceptualizations, about cognitive complexity as developing with an individual's maturity and greater experience (Ragan, 1979), there is no concrete statistical evidence to that end. The closest substantiation of that notion is in the Harvey et al. (1961) work with integrative complexity. Harvey's four levels of cognitive functioning contribute to the development of integrative complexity:

System I--derived from authoritarian, restrictive environment--individual characteristics include concreteness, absolutist viewpoint, bias, identification with authority, ethnocentrism, and dependency on external environment

System II--derived from ambiguous environment--individual characteristics include less concrete, disassociation between self and environment leading to uncertainty, distrust, and rebellion against authority

System III--derived from over-protective, over-indulgent background--individual characteristics include more abstractness, little exploration of physical and social world, autonomy, apathy, less rebellion, but a tendency to demonstrate dependency by manipulating others

System IV--derived from childhood freedom to explore social and physical environment--individual characteristics include most abstract conceptualization, most cognitively complex, ability to solve problems with an open mind, positive internal standards, and integrated cognitive structure based on experience and thought

Thus, cognitive complexity really assesses at least two constructs--social complexity and integrative complexity. Although these are theoretically related, research has found them to be somewhat independent.

Cognitive Complexity/Simplicity and Learning

Research

- Contradicting the results of other researchers, Lundy and Berkowitz (1957) showed that high-complexity individuals are more easily swayed by the opinions of authority or their peers than low-complexity individuals.

- Low-cognitive complexity subjects showed a dramatic shift in thought when presented with conflicting information, whereas high-complexity individuals displayed ambiguity in their descriptions (Mayo & Crockett, 1964).

- Complex individuals were found to be superior to low-complexity individuals at recognizing relevant differences among listeners and were better able to adapt their messages to the requirements of their different listeners (Crockett, 1965).

- Crockett (1965) and Supnick (1964) showed that cognitively simple individuals tended to use either positive or negative attributes when describing a stimulus, whereas cognitively complex individuals tended to use both.

- Tripodi and Bieri (1963) found that cognitively complex individuals displayed greater confidence when defending their judgments of inconsistent information.

- Ware and Harvey (1967) found that low-complexity individuals tended to form generalized opinions without collecting sufficient information.

- Kogan (1971) suggested that the humanities and social studies offer greater incongruity, conflict, and contradiction and may be more conducive to the highly complex individual. The more concrete fields of mathematics, engineering, and foreign language may be better for the low-complexity individual.

- Zimring (1971) showed that the more complex the individual, the longer the reaction time on a word association task.

- Epting, Wilkins, and Margulis (1972) found that cognitively complex individuals tended to use more abstract labels for their constructs on the Rep Test than did cognitively simple individuals.

- Complex individuals took more time and considered more alternatives before they came to a decision (Stewin & Anderson, 1974).

- Low-complexity individuals functioned more efficiently than high-complexity individuals in situations where the task was very complex and where no prior experience occurred (Schneider & Giambra, 1971).

- A student's written ability to interpret literature was positively correlated with high levels of complexity and a high tolerance for ambiguity (Peters & Blues, 1978).

- Hale (1980) found a positive relationship between cognitive complexity and the ability to adapt messages to the needs of listeners. To be an effective communicator, an individual must be able to perceive and understand the other's perspective.

- In computer system analysis and design tasks, complex individuals tended to produce workable but simple solutions, whereas cognitively simple people tended to produce complex and often unworkable solutions (Clark, 1982; 1983).

- There was significant growth in complexity when college seniors' scores were compared with their freshman scores (Khalili & Hood, 1983).

- Ortega, Deems, and Weinstein (1988) observed the tendency of cognitively simple individuals to miss subtle differences among stimuli, to make decisions without careful consideration of all available information, and to feel threatened by ambiguity.

- Khalil and Clark (1989) hypothesized that a computer programmer must be able to differentiate stimuli to decompose a program into statements and be able to integrate complex information to understand or modify the program. When subjects were grouped according to differentiation or integration abilities, the high-differentiation group did not perform significantly better in either comprehension or modification of programs but did perform significantly better in modifying a relatively complex program. Modifying a computer program is apparently a processing-intensive domain, necessitating high integrative ability.

Implications of the Characteristics and Research

Implications which are drawn from research are noted with a •; those drawn logically from descriptive information regarding the trait are noted by an *. Based on the research and the descriptions of cognitive complexity/simplicity we conclude that *complex* learners are more likely to excel at learning tasks such as:

- communication tasks, especially those requiring adaptation of messages to the needs of listeners
- decision making, especially in situations with high degrees of ambiguity and inconsistent information, or where time is irrelevant
- trouble shooting tasks in which individuals must separate and control variables and consider more alternatives before coming to a decision
- tasks requiring differentiation of individual differences or needs, as in career counseling or personnel managing
- courses in the humanities and social studies that provide more incongruity, conflict, and contradiction
- debate, in which learners are required to defend their positions
- interpretation of literature
- computer systems analysis and design tasks

and acquire and use effectively learning strategies such as:

* setting or selecting own learning goals
* selecting information sources
* comparing new information with existing knowledge or beliefs

* analysis of key ideas
* generating metaphors and analogies
* predicting outcomes or inferring implications

    Based on the small amount of research and the descriptions of cognitive complexity/simplicity, we conclude that *simple* learners are more likely to excel at learning tasks such as:

• forming opinions or making decisions quickly without adequate time for data collection
• categorizing/classifying tasks, especially using existing criteria
• word association and memory tasks that require quick responses
• concrete learning such as mathematics, engineering, and foreign language

and acquire and use effectively learning strategies such as:

* concentrating on information
* using mnemonics
* paraphrasing or summarizing

Cognitive Complexity/Simplicity and Instruction

Research

• As the amount of available information increased, less complex individuals tended to improve their predictions at a greater rate than did complex individuals (Leventhal, 1957).

• Signell (1966) found that subjects, when judging individuals, showed an increase in cognitive complexity through greater articulation rather than through the addition of new constructs. When subjects were asked to judge nations, however, complexity increased only through the addition of new constructs that differentiated nations. Signell drew a distinction between experiential learning, where the child needs efficient constructs to enable him or her to adapt to the social environment, and didactic learning, where no personal security is at stake.

• Bodden and James (1976) found cognitive complexity to decrease after training in self-awareness, sensitivity, and understanding of others.

• Sustik and Brown (1979) found problem-solving performance to be enhanced by a rule-example format for low-complexity individuals. High-complexity individuals did not appear to be affected by the rule-example order.

• Less complex students performed poorly when forced to respond in a highly structured manner after receiving low-structured instructions. Complex students profited from structured problem-solving training followed by unstructured problems (Sustik & Brown, 1979).

• High-complexity teachers were more likely to encourage the use of higher mental processes, instead of mere recall, than were their lower complexity counterparts (Peters & Amburgey, 1982).

• In a research methods course taught under low-structure conditions, cognitively simple students demanded greater structure than did their complex counterparts (Harris & Ross, 1984).

• Both high- and low-complexity individuals perform equally well in highly structured tasks, whereas complex individuals perform significantly better in less structured tasks (Amernico & Beechy, 1984).

• In a study conducted on high school students, it was found that high levels of arousal induced by loud noise acted to reduce subjects' ability to function at higher levels of complexity. High arousal led to increased use of the "like-dislike" dimension (Paulhus, 1985).

Implications of the Characteristics and Research

Implications which are drawn from research are noted with a •; those drawn logically from descriptive information regarding the trait are noted by an *. Instructional conditions that capitalize on the preferences of the complex student and challenge the cognitively simple student include:

• providing low-structured instructional sequences
• relying on presentation of didactic information
• encouraging analytical thinking and synthesis of ideas
• using multistimulus, multiviewpoint concepts, possibly of a philosophical or theoretical nature
* presenting sensory-rich stimuli and complex concepts that require higher order thinking skills
* using inductive instructional sequence
* analyzing key ideas
* structuring instruction in conceptual or theoretical elaboration sequences

Instructional conditions that remediate or compensate for the deficiencies of the complex student include:

* using narrative sequence
* changing context or circumstances
* providing descriptions of social cues

Instructional conditions that capitalize on the preferences of the simple student and challenge the complex student include:

• personalizing instruction or using personal referents
• providing highly structured instructional sequence
• using a rule-example sequence
* providing expository organizers and outlines
* using prototypic examples or matched example/nonexample pairs

Instructional conditions that remediate or compensate for the deficiencies of the cognitively simple student include:

• using attention-directing devices such as labels, arrows, or circles to pinpoint specific steps or parts of a whole
* using pictures and diagrams to illustrate relationships
* providing transitions and verbal connectors among ideas
* showing interrelationships among ideas or stimuli that the learner finds difficult on his own
* avoiding ambiguous or conflicting concepts
* using explicitly deductive instructional sequence
* using graphic organizers/structured overviews
* providing numerous analogies
* providing easy-to-difficult instructional sequence
* providing tables or concept maps showing differences among constructs

References

Amernico, H., & Beechy, T. H. (1984). Accounting students' performance and cognitive complexity: Some empirical evidence. *Accounting Review, 119,* 820-829.

Banister, D., & Mair, J. M. M. (1968). *The evaluation of personal constructs.* New York: Academic.

Bieri, J. (1955). Cognitive complexity/simplicity and predictive behavior. *Journal of Abnormal Psychology, 51*(2), 263-68.

Bieri, J. (1966). Cognitive complexity and personality development. In O. J. Harvey (Ed.), *Experience, Structure, and Adaptability* (pp. 13-37). New York: Springer.

Bodden, J. L., & James, L. E. (1976). Influence of occupational information giving on cognitive complexity. *Journal of Counseling Education, 23,* 28-282.

Clark, J. D. (1982). A psychometric evaluation of Yourdan's structured design methodology. *SIGCHI Bulletin, 14,* 9-12.

Clark, J. D. (1983). A psychometric evaluation of the use of data flow diagrams. *SIGCHI Bulletin, 15,* 3-6.

Crockett, W. H. (1965). Cognitive complexity and impression formation. In B. A. Mahler (Ed.), *Progress in in experimental personality research* (Vol. 2, pp. 47-90). New York: Academic.

Epting, F. R., Wilkins, G., & Margulis, S. T. (1972). Relationship between cognitive differentiation and level of abstraction. *Psychological Reports, 31,* 367-370.

Gardner, R. W., & Schoen, R. A. (1962). Differentiation and abstraction in concept formation. *Psychological Monographs, 76* (Whole no. 560).

Goldstein, K. M., & Blackman, S. (1978). *Cognitive Style.* New York: Wiley.

Green, K. E. (1985). *Cognitive style: A review of the literature* (Tech. Report No. 1). Chicago: Johnson O'Connor Research Foundation.

Hale, C. L. (1980). Cognitive complexity-simplicity as a determinant of communication effectiveness. *Communication Monographs, 47,* 304-311.

Harris, R. M., & Ross, C. L. (1984). Teaching research methods: Students' cognitive complexity and demand for structure. *Journal of Education for Librarianship, 24,* 189-98.

Harvey, O. J. (1966). System structure, flexibility and creativity. In O. J. Harvey (Ed.), *Experience Structure and Adaptability* (pp. 39-65). New York: Springer.

Harvey, O. J. (1971). *Final Technical Report of Contract No. 1147(07).* Springfield, VA: National Technical Information Service.

Harvey, O. J., Hunt, D. E., & Schroder, H. M. (1961). *Conceptual systems and personality organization.* New York: Wiley.

Kelly, G. A. (1955). *The psychology of personal constructs.* New York: Norton.

Khalil, O. E. M., & Clark, J. D. (1989). The influence of programmers' cognitive complexity on program comprehension and modification. *Journal of Man-Machine Studies, 31,* 219-236.

Khalili, H., & Hood, A. (1983, September). A longitudinal study of change in conceptual level in college. *Journal of College Student Personnel, 24(5),* 389-394.

Kogan, N. (1971). Educational implication of cognitive styles. In G. S. Lesser (Ed.), *Psychology and Educational Practice* (pp. 271-281). Glenview, IL: Scott Foresman.

Leventhal, H. (1957). Cognitive processes and interpersonal predictions. *Journal of Abnormal Psychology, 55,* 176-180.

Lundy, R. M., & Berkowitz, L. (1957). Cognitive complexity and assimilative projection in attitude change. *Journal of Abnormal and Social Psychology, 55*, 34-37.

Mayo, C. W., & Crockett, W. H. (1964). Cognitive complexity and primacy-recency effects in impression formation. *Journal of Abnormal and Social Psychology, 68*, 335-338.

Messick, S., & Kogan, N. (1966). *Individuality and learning*. San Francisco: Jossey-Bass.

Ortega, M., Deems, F., & Weinstein, K. (1988). Cognitive simplicity in the Type A 'Coronary-Prone' pattern. *Cognitive Therapy and Research, 12(1)*, 81-87.

Paulhus, D. L. (1985, August 23-27). *The effects of arousal on cognitive complexity*. Paper presented at the 93rd Annual Convention of the American Psychological Association, Los Angeles. (ERIC Document Reproduction Service No. ED 263 474)

Peters, W. H., & Amburgey, B. S. (1982). Teacher intellectusl dispositon and cognitive classroom verbal reactions. *Journal of Educational Research, 76(2)*, 94-99.

Peters, W. H., & Blues, A. G. (1978). Teacher intellectual disposition as it relates to student openness in written response to literature. *Research in the Teaching of English, 12(2)*, 127-136.

Ragan, T. J. (1979). *Cognitive styles: A review of the literature* (Tech. Report No. AFHRL-TR-78-90(1)). Denver: Lowry Air Force Base Technical Training Division,

Schneider, G. A., & Giambra, L. M. (1971). Performance in concept identification as a function of cognitive complexity. *Journal of Personality and Social Psychology, 19(3)*, 261-73.

Schroder, H. M., Driver, M. J., & Struefert, S. (1967). *Human information processing*. New York: Holt, Rinehart & Winston.

Schroder, H. M., & Struefert, S. (1962). *The measurement of four systems of personality structure varying in level of abstractness (Sentence Completion Method)* (Tech. Rep. No. 11, ONR). Princeton: Princeton University.

Siegel, L., & Siegel, L. C. (1965). Educational set: A determinant of acquisition. *Journal of Educational Psychology, 1*, 1-12.

Signell, K. S. (1966). Cognitive complexity in person perception and nation percerption: A developmental approach. *Journal of Personality, 34*, 517-537.

Sobel, R. (1970). *A study of cognitive change resulting from participation in human relations laboratory training*. New York: Yeshiva University, 1970.

Stewin, L., & Anderson, C. (1974). Cognitive complexity as a determinant of information processing. *Alberta Journal of Educational Research, 20(3)*, 233-243.

Supnick, J. J. (1964). *An examination of the change in categorization of others following a college course in personality development.* Unpublished master's thesis, Clark University, Worcester, MA.

Sustik, J. M., & Brown, B. R. (1979). *Interaction between conceptual level and training method in computer based problem solving.* Iowa City: University of Iowa Computing Center.

Tiedemann, J. (1989). Measures of cognitive styles: A critical review. *Educational Psychologist, 24*(3), 261-275.

Tripodi, T., & Bieri, J. (1963). Cognitive complexity as a function of own and provided constructs. *Psychological Reports, 13*, 26.

Tripodi, T., & Bieri, J. (1964). Information transmission in clinical judgments as a function of stimulus dimensionality and cognitive complexity. *Journal of Personality, 32*, 119-137.

Tripodi, T., & Bieri, J. (1966). Cognitive complexity, perceived conflict, and certainty. *Journal of Personality, 34*, 144-153.

Vacc, N. A., & Vacc, N. E. (1973). An adaptation for children in the modified Role Repertory Test: A measure of cognitive complexity. *Psychological Reports, 33*, 771-776.

Ware, R., & Harvey, O. J. (1967). A cognitive determinant of impression formation. *Journal of Personality and Social Psychology, 5*, 38-44.

Wicker, A. (1969). Cognitive complexity, school size, and participation in school behavior settings: A test of the frequency of interaction hypotheses. *Journal of Educational Psychology, 60*, 200-203.

Zimring, F. M. (1971). Cognitive simplicity-complexity: Evidence for disparate processes. *Journal of Personality, 39*, 1-9.

13

AUTOMATIZATION
(Strong vs. Weak Automatization)

Description of Automatization

Automatization refers to one's "ability to understand and respond without an inordinate amount of time to formulate a[n action]...without undue groping, hesitation, or pauses" (Gatbonton & Segalowitz, 1988, p. 474). In other words, it refers to one's capacity to perform simple, repetitive tasks that have been so highly practiced that they require a minimum of conscious effort for efficient execution. According to Eakin and Douglas (1971), examples of these tasks included many everyday activities such as walking, talking, reading, writing, and maintaining perceptual constancies. Automatization occurs as the individual becomes more "adept at the attention, encoding, evaluation and control processes associated with a class of tasks" (Aster & Clark, 1985). When a task is automatized, the relevant cognitive processes function quickly, without interference from other cognitive processes that can draw attentional resources away (Gatbonton & Segalowitz, 1988).

When a task becomes automatized, differences in ability are evident. The automatization cognitive style, therefore, is an intra-individual difference in one's ability to perform simple, repetitive tasks faster or slower than the expected norm (Broverman, 1964). With a strong level of automatization one can perform simple tasks quickly, without a high level of attention, and without a great number of errors. Studies have shown that these types of individuals perform quickly and with relatively few errors even in distracting situations. Weak automatizers, on the other hand, perform tasks more slowly, with more errors, and with a greater number of errors under distracting situations.

It is important to note that these differences are only evident after a task has become automatized. Tasks that are not automatized are irrelevant. Other cognitive style differences, however, are evident prior to becoming automatized. Broverman (1960a, 1960b) found the differences in automatization ability remained the same for both conceptual and perceptual tasks.

Broverman (1960a) indicated that this cognitive style is similar to Klein's (1954) reference to constricted versus flexible control because it is a measure of the ability to ignore distractions and perform a task.

Characteristic Differences in Automatization

Strong Automatizers   Weak Automatizers

faster at simple repetitive tasks_____ slower at repetitive tasks
faster at naming familiar objects_____slower at naming familiar objects
faster at psychomotor tasks_____slower at psychomotor tasks
less distracted on simple tasks_____distracted on simple tasks
good oral reading_____poor oral reading
shallow processing_____deep processing
focus on the obvious_____ignore the obvious
not able to disembed_____able to disembed

These differences were suggested by Broverman (1960a, 1960b, 1964), Broverman, Broverman, Vogel, Palmer, and Klaiber (1964), Eakin and Douglas (1971), and Tiedemann (1989).

Individual Differences Related to Automatization

Cognitive Flexibility--This is the ability to ignore distractions while performing a task (see chapter 8). Individuals with a flexible control were considered strong automatizers, whereas those who are more distracted (constricted control) were weak automatizers (Broverman, 1960a; Klein, 1954; Loomis & Moskowitz, 1958).

Instruments for Measuring Automatization

The Stroop Word Color Interference Test (WCIT) (Stroop, 1935; Golden, 1978)

This test is used primarily to assess constricted versus flexible control; however, Broverman used it to compare individuals' speeds in making serial responses of color names to their speeds in making such responses to color hues. There are three parts to this test, yielding three basic scores. The first consists of a list of randomly ordered color names, red, green, or blue, typed in black ink. The second consists of color patches of the same three colors. The last consists of the names of the same three colors, each typed in a color other than its own. The scores from each part are then combined to determine the level of automaticity. The scores include the speed of reading the list, the speed of naming the color patches, and the speed of naming the colors of the inks. The level of automaticity is determined by subtracting "the score predicted by the regression equation of the [speed of reading the colors] onto the [speed of naming the color patches] from the speed of naming the colors" (Broverman 1960a, p. 172). Strong automatizers score less (take less time) than predicted, whereas weak automatizers score higher (take longer) than predicted. Reliability is consistent across studies (.69-.89), although it is lower for the third subtest (.69-.73) (Evans, 1987).

Theoretical Background

It is not clear whether automatization is unipolar or bipolar. The only empirical evidence of this cognitive style as a bipolar factor was found by Broverman et al. (1964). This factor is defined, at the positive pole, by typical automatization indicators (speed of naming repeated objects), and at the negative pole, by restructuring tasks. A person with strong automatization skills is able to ignore distractions and focus only on the task at hand.

Broverman (1960a,b) noted that the effect indicated by differences in automatization ability are only evident once a task moves beyond the conscious state. At this time, an "individual's limit of learning" will be approached (Broverman, 1960a). These tasks are simple, repetitive tasks that do not require concentrated effort and can be either perceptual or conceptual. Performance of those tasks that require more attention because of complexity would not be affected by one's automaticity level.

Automatization of basic skills is generally considered essential to gaining proficiency in conceptual-processing skills (such as verbal and mathematical skills), as well as perceptual-motor skills (such as typing and playing music). The creation of new skills or thought patterns requires "voluntary-effortful concentration" (Rapaport, 1951). As a person uses these skills or thought patterns continuously, automatization occurs. Because a limit exists on the availability of resources such as working memory, information-holding capacity, and processing time that can be expended in a particular task, automatizing certain aspects of performance is important. Automatization frees up attentional resources, allowing performers to allocate their limited capacities to other aspects of a task (Gatbonton & Segalowitz, 1988). Automatization can also occur from chunking the steps in a problem-solving procedure to increase efficiency. Increasing expertise in memorizing, processing, and control of learning in a content area results in greater speed and fluency of performance (Aster & Clark, 1985).

Logan (1985) believed that automatization may be more related to skill than to conceptual style. He hypothesized that although a skilled performance by experts in any field may appear effortless, as though they are using fewer resources than novices, it may be that as a skill is acquired or practiced, there is a shift in the kind of resources used. That is, experts become more specialized in the use of resources.

Strong/Weak Automatization and Learning

Research

• On simple conceptual tasks (simple addition) and perceptual-motor tasks (tracing a straight line) performed under distractions, strong automatizers were less distracted than the weak automatizers. When more complicated concentration-demanding conceptual- and perceptual-motor tasks were performed with distractions, there were no significant differences between strong and weak automatizers (Broverman, 1960a).

• Broverman (1964) found that subjects who performed above the norm levels of performance on automatization tasks (strong automatizers) tended to give below-par performances on "restructuring" tasks; the reverse pattern of abilities was found for weak automatizers.

• Proficiency in arithmetic and reading relied heavily on "automatic" behavior and overlearned computational habits (Eakin & Douglas, 1971).

• Eakin and Douglas (1971), in a study to determine the effect of automatization on oral reading, found that the poor oral readers scored significantly lower on all automatization tasks but did significantly better on the restructuring tasks. These children, who showed marked impairment in oral reading, had no apparent impairment in their ability to comprehend.

• Garnett and Fleischner (1983), in their study of learning-disabled and nondisabled children between 8 and 13 years of age, verified the theory that learning-disabled children are weak automatizers. They hypothesized that the learning-disabled children's lack of proficiency in basic skills may be partly due to this fact.

Implications of the Characteristics and Research

Implications which are drawn from research are noted with a •; those drawn logically from descriptive information regarding the trait are noted by an *. Based on the limited amount of research and the descriptions of strong/weak automatization, we conclude that strong automatizers are more likely to excel at learning tasks such as:

• timed tests or tasks (strong automatizers are faster)
• repetitive tasks that can be performed without "thinking"
• basic skills that have become automatic
• oral reading
• typing, or any simple automatic psychomotor skill
* anagrams such as forming three-letter words

* games, with competition
* memorization of rote activity
* psychomotor activities such as drumming or tapping
* verbal and mathematics basic skills

and acquire and use effectively learning strategies such as:

* chunking
* repeating material to be recalled
* rehearsing material to be recalled

Based on the limited amount of research and the descriptions of strong/weak automatization, we conclude that weak automatizers are more likely to excel at learning tasks such as:

• untimed tests or tasks
• perceptual discrimination tasks
• focusing on details
• problems that require novel solutions

and acquire and use effectively learning strategies such as:

* analyzing key ideas
* searching for information
* concentration

Strong/Weak Automatization and Instruction

Research

• Eakin and Douglas (1971) found that students who are weak automatizers of reading or arithmetic skills require intensive drills to overlearn basic sight vocabulary and simple arithmetic computations, or they must make use of their more dominant reasoning and conceptual abilities.

Implications of the Characteristics and Research

Implications which are drawn from research are noted with a •; those drawn logically from descriptive information regarding the trait are noted by an *. Instructional conditions that capitalize on the preferences of the strong automatizer and challenge the weak automatizer include:

* breaking learning tasks down into subprocesses and allowing rehearsal by the student

* providing for self-evaluation and repetition
* rehearsing/repeating/rereading
* overlearning

Instructional conditions that remediate or compensate for the deficiencies of the strong automatizers include:

* using attention-directing functions such as underlining, blinking, and arrows

Instructional conditions that capitalize on the preferences of the weak automatizer and challenge the strong automatizers include:

* providing detailed lists or menus of alternative strategies for approaching problems

Instructional conditions that remediate or compensate for the deficiencies of the weak automatizer include:

* ready-made chunking strategies to enhance memory
* reducing stress on the learner as much as possible

References

Aster, D. J., & Clark, R. E. (1985). Instructional software for users who differ in prior knowledge. *Performance and Instruction Journal, 24*, 13-15.

Broverman, D. M. (1960a). Dimensions of cognitive style. *Journal of Personality, 28*, 167-185.

Broverman, D. M. (1960b). Cognitive style and intraindividual variation in abilities. *Journal of Personality, 28*, 240-256.

Broverman, D. M. (1964). Generality and behavioral correlates of cognitive styles. *Journal of Consulting Psychology, 28*, 487-500.

Broverman, D. M., Broverman, I. K., Vogel, W., Palmer, R. D., & Klaiber, E. L. (1964). The automatization cognitive style and physical development. *Child Development, 35*, 1343-1359.

Eakin, S. M., & Douglas, V. I. (1971). "Automatization" and oral reading problems in children. *Journal of Learning Disabilities, 4*, 31-38.

Evans, C. S. (1987). Use of readability formulas in selecting American History textbooks. *The Social Studies, 78(3)*, 127-30.

Garnett, K., & Fleischner, J. E. (1983). Automatization and basic fact performance of normal and learning disabled children. *Learning Disability Quarterly, 6*, 223-230.

Gatbonton, E., & Segalowitz, N. (1988). Creative automatization: Principles for promoting fluency within a communicative framework. *TESOL Quarterly, 22*, 473-492.

Golden, C. (1978). *Stroop Color and Word Test: A manual for clinical and experimental uses.* Wood Dale, IL: Stoetling Co.

Klein, G. S. (1954). Need and regulation. In M.R. Jones (Ed.), *Nebraska Symposium on Motivation* (pp. 224-274). Lincoln: University of Nebraska Press,.

Logan, G. D. (1985). Skill and automaticity: Relations, implications, and future directions. *Canadian Journal of Psychology, 39*(2), 367-386.

Loomis, H. K., & Moskowitz, S. (1958). Cognitive style and stimulus ambiguity. *Journal of Personality, 26,* 349-364.

Rapaport, D. (1951). *Organization and pathology of thought.* New York: Columbia University Press.

Stroop, J. R. (1935). Studies of interference in serial verbal reactions. *Journal of Experimental Psychology, 18,* 643-672.

Tiedemann, J. (1989). Measures of cognitive styles: A critical review. *Educational Psychologist, 24*(3), 261-275.

PART IV
COGNITIVE STYLES

Introduction

Messick (1984) defined cognitive styles as "characteristic self-consistencies in information processing that develop in congenial ways around underlying personality trends" (p. 61). Cognitive styles reflect the ways in which learners process information to make sense out of their world. Cognitive styles are related to personality as well. The ways in which we interact with information is reflective of the ways in which we interact with each other through our personality.

Our primary belief in this book is that cognitive styles represent stable traits that learners employ in perceiving information and stimuli while interacting with their environment. Cognitive styles refer to "psychological dimensions that represent the consistencies in an individual's manner of acquiring and processing information" (Ausburn & Ausburn, 1978, p. 338). Cognitive styles describe characteristic approaches of individuals in acquiring and organizing information. We all differ in how we interact with our environment, extract and perceive information from it, and reflect and organize the knowledge that we have acquired. Some of us are linear and systematic, whereas others are random and simultaneous. The chapters in Part IV describe some of the better known cognitive styles that reflect those stylistic differences.

How do cognitive styles emerge? They are derived from cognitive controls and mental abilities. As we pointed out in the Introduction to the book, the landscape of mental abilities possessed by each individual produces a unique combination of characteristics. Similarities in mental abilities among individuals define tendencies to process information in certain ways. These tendencies are cognitive styles.

But cognitive styles are not the same as mental abilities or cognitive controls (see Introduction to Part III for a discussion of cognitive controls). They differ in terms of their generalities, their roles, and the values placed on them (Messick, 1984).

Cognitive abilities, as were described in Part II of this book, refer to the content and level of cognitive activity where styles refer to the manner and form of learning. Abilities specify the competencies, the mental operations, and the kind of information being processed, whereas styles are stated in terms of propensities. Abilities are stated in terms of maximal

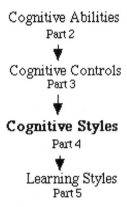

Cognitive Abilities
Part 2

Cognitive Controls
Part 3

Cognitive Styles
Part 4

Learning Styles
Part 5

performance, whereas stylistic propensities are described in terms of typical performance. Therefore, abilities are unipolar measures (less ability ... more ability), whereas styles are bipolar (visual ... verbal), and abilities are value directional (having more is better than having less), whereas styles are value differentiated (neither pole is necessarily better). Cognitive abilities are affected by the content domain or the nature of the task, whereas styles are generalizable tendencies that cut across content. Finally, abilities enable learners to perform tasks, whereas styles control the ways in which the tasks are performed.

Cognitive Abilities	Cognitive Controls	Cognitive Styles
Content/Level	x	Manner/Form
Competencies	x	Propensities
Maximal	x	Typical
Unipolar	x	Bipolar
Value Directional	x	Value Differentiated
Domain/Function Specific	x	Pervasive/Organizing
Enabling	x	Controlling

Table 14.1. Differences and shared factors.

One of the predominant attributes of cognitive styles is their consistency or stability. That is, learners develop these traits and maintain them over time and across tasks. Styles are generalizable processing tendencies regardless of information content. Cognitive styles are also stable over time. An individual's styles typically do not change significantly. Although many cognitive style characteristics do tend to strengthen with age, an individual's style relative to those of their peers tends to remain stable over time.

Cognitive styles play different roles in determining how individuals interact with their environment. There are two different kinds of cognitive styles, information-gathering cognitive styles and information-organizing cognitive styles. The former includes visual/haptic, visualizer/verbalizer, leveling/sharpening, and serialist/holist styles and are reviewed in the next four chapters. These styles describe how learners interact with and extract information from the environment. Information organizing cognitive styles, such as conceptual style, refer to the way this information is organized and encoded; that is, they describe how learners make sense out of what they have acquired. They complete Part IV of this book.

References

Ausburn, L. J., & Ausburn, F. B. (1978). Cognitive styles; Some information and implications for instructional design. *Educational Communications and Technology Journal, 26*, 337-354.

Messick, S. (1984). The nature of cognitive styles: Problems and promise in educational practice. *Educational Psychologist, 19*, 59-74.

14

VISUAL/HAPTIC

Description of Visual/Haptic

The visual/haptic cognitive style dimension describes individual preferences for visual versus tactile information processing. That is, some individuals prefer to process information through visual and spatial manipulation, whereas others, especially younger children, learn more about objects through tactile interaction with them (i.e., touching or holding them). Among adults, the most dominant perceptual style is visual, with the haptic style being second (Cherry, 1981).

Visually oriented individuals acquaint themselves with the environment through their vision. The broad scope of visual perception includes five components: *spatial relations, visual discrimination, figure-ground discrimination, visual closure,* and *object recognition*. Spatial relations refers to one's perception of the position of objects in space. In reading, for instance, words must be seen as separate entities surrounded by space. Visual discrimination refers to one's ability to differentiate one object from another. The ability to visually discriminate letters and words is essential in learning to read. Another visual characteristic, figure-ground discrimination, refers to one's ability to distinguish an object from the background surrounding it. A child with a deficit in this area cannot distinguish the item in question apart from the visual background. Visual closure is described by a task in which a subject is asked to recognize or identify an object, despite the fact that the total stimulus is not presented. For example, reading a line of print with the top half cut off requires visual closure. Finally, object recognition refers to one's ability to recognize the nature of viewed objects, including geometric shapes, animals, letters, and numbers.

The individual with haptic tendencies is more concerned with body sensations experienced through a tactile and/or kinesthetic mode. Tactile refers to the sense of touch. Kinesthetic means to experience sensation through the reactions and movement of muscles, tendons, and joints. Both dimensions of haptic perception play important roles in learning most early school tasks (Chalfant & Scheffelin, 1969).

Visual and haptic learning styles are, theoretically, at opposite ends of a continuum of perceptual organization of the external environment. Most people fall between the two extremes. The visually oriented person finds it difficult to adapt him or herself to a situation by means of touch and kinesthetic functions. An extremely haptic person can be normally sighted, but will use his or her vision for orientation only when forced to do so.

The relative importance of visual and haptic perception changes with age. There are the developmental effects, with individuals becoming more visual as they get older. The haptic perceptual style becomes less important in older adults relative to other perceptual styles, especially visual (James & Galbraith, 1984).

Characteristic Differences in Visual/Haptic

Visual	Haptic
visual oriented	body oriented
spectator	actor
sees whole and integrates parts	sees parts and **may** synthesize whole
translates tactile to visual	translates visual to tactile
field independent	field dependent
reflective	impulsive
realistic	imaginative
external	internal

Individual Differences Related to Visual/Haptic

Field dependence/independence--Ausburn (1975) found that visual learners were better able to discriminate visual detail and reacted impersonally; that is, they were field independent (see chapter 7). Haptic learners were unable to discriminate visual detail and were more field dependent, so they probably react more emotionally. However, Rouse (1965) found no correlation between visual/haptic and field dependence/field-independence.

Reflective/impulsive--Visuals tended to be more reflective, rather than impulsive on a visual test of perceptual tempo (see chapter 9), whereas haptics tended to make more errors; that is, they tended to be more impulsive (Ausburn, 1975).

Concrete/formal--In a study of university students, Butzow and Schlenker (1978) found that there was a relationship between the visual/haptic continuum and the Piagetian concrete/formal continuum. As with intellectual development, age was related to perceptual style in a curvilinear manner. Some very formal individuals negate the linear relationship between the concrete/formal and the visual/haptic; very abstract thinkers tended to be haptic.

Instruments for Measuring Visual/Haptic

Lowenfeld's Visual/Haptic Tests (Lowenfeld, 1949)

Lowenfeld's tests consisted of the following five subscales:

Test of integration of successive impressions. This test uses 10 sets of five curved and five angular symbols each. Each symbol is shown separately. The symbols are drawn on a card that is placed behind a horizontal slot so that only segments of the symbol can be seen at a given time. After the whole symbol has passed behind the slot, the student is instructed to recognize the correct symbol out of each set of five similar figures. The final score shows how much the student is able to integrate the partial impressions into a whole image; greater integration indicates a visual type.

Test of subjective impressions. This paper-and-pencil test is also known as the Table Test or Think-of-a-Building Test. For the Table Test, the subject is asked to think of an object, such as a table or a building, and draw it. The instructions are as follows: "When you are supposed to draw something, remember that this is a psychological test and that it does not depend on your drawing ability. A primitive drawing will give the same insight as a perfect one. Just draw it as you would do it if nobody asked you to. Draw a table with a glass on top. Draw a table with a chessboard on top." Haptics would represent the table according to the meaning the glass or chessboard had for them. The table with the glass would be drawn in side view, and the table with the chessboard would be drawn in top view, because those views are the most distinctive manner of drawing those items. The visually minded person would draw both the glass and chessboard in the same table view because they do not change their impression of the table according to the thing which is on it.

In the paper-and-pencil Think-of-a-Building Test, the subjects are instructed to think of a familiar building (their own home, school, or office building). They are asked, "How many floors has the building? When you thought of the number of floors, did you think of (a) how many floors you have to climb? (b) Did you count the floors singly? (c) Did you think of the whole building as it appears from the outside?" Visual types chose (c), the whole building as it appears from the outside, whereas haptics chose (a), how many floors you have to climb. Choice (a) is a haptic response because haptics picture themselves as actors in the environment.

Test of visual versus haptic word association. The subject is given a series of 20 stimulus words (greeting, walking, climbing, pulling), which produce either visual or haptic associations. The subject is instructed to write down a word indicating his or her immediate reaction. The test is scored by adding up the visual responses (reactions to environment, e. g., climbing--mountain) and then the haptic (reactions to the bodily self as indicated in actions, e. g., climbing--hard). Twelve answers in one direction shows either a visual or haptic style. Less than 12 answers in one direction, indicates an "indefinite" style.

Test for visualization of kinesthetic experience. This test is designed to determine how much a person has the ability to visualize kinesthetic experiences. Different geometric figures are cut out of cardboard or plywood. The same figures are drawn to scale on paper. The subjects are blindfolded and asked to pass their fingers around the edge of a cut-out cardboard figure or pattern. Afterward, with the blindfold removed, subjects must identify this pattern among five similar figures all somewhat different from it. Lowenfeld determined that if a score of at least 12 out of 20 was reached, the subject was considered visual. An "indefinite" will score below 12. A haptic, theoretically, will remain satisfied with a haptic exploration.

Test for tactile impressions. This test determines whether or not a person can recognize figures perceived through tactile experience. The geometric shapes from the Visualization of Kinesthetic Experience Test are placed singly in a bag. The drawings of the same five figures are placed before the subject. Only the hand may be used in exploring the figures in the bag. The subject is then asked to match the figure in the bag with the figure on the paper. This is scored like the previous test, but a haptic score will be revealed.

Haptic Letter Recognition Test (Wold, 1970)

The child is asked to give an oral response for identifying random letters of the alphabet from touch only. If oral responses are incorrect (b for d) the child is asked to write the letter on paper just as it feels to him or her.

MKM Visual Letter Recognition Test (Wold, 1970)

This test determines how children relate the things they see to the things they say. The conversion of visual symbols into their speech sounds is vital to the reading process. Children can often write the letters of the alphabet but are unable to state the sound the letters represent when they are presented visually. This test is similar to the one previously mentioned except that the child sees a random letter and is asked to make the speech sound it represents.

Learning Channel Preference Test (O'Brien, 1989)

This is a questionnaire designed to develop students' awareness of their learning styles: auditory, visual, or haptic. A student receives a score, from 10 to 30, for each learning style. The highest score indicates the preferred learning style. The visual/haptic style is the most predominant in the student population. Flat scores in the high 20s indicate that the student has developed all three learning channels. Flat scores below 20 indicate that the student has not yet developed a strong learning channel preference.

Mesa Independent Perceptual Screening Assessment

This test is used to measure higher levels of tactual feeling and direction following. The test consists of four exercises that involve asking an individual to reach through two armholes in a screen and perform manipulative tasks by following a set of posted diagrams. Exercise 1 consists of putting nine rods into nine holes. In exercise 2, the individual places the objects shown over one rod. Exercise 3 consists of placing the parts over a post in the specified manner shown. A different hole is used for the last exercise and the individual can be assisted in finding its location. When exercise 4 has been completed it is evaluated and scored. The entire test takes from 15 to 20 minutes. If the individual has not begun exercise 4 after 12 minutes, the test can be stopped.

Haptic Visual Matching Test (Kagan, 1965; Kagan, Rosman, Day, Albert, & Philips, 1964)

This test was designed for children, who first explore 20 wooden forms (approximately 3 inches square) with their fingers for as long as desired. Following this exploration, the children are shown a visual display of five figures, one of which corresponds with the figure that was explored haptically. The test produces three scores: errors, response time, and palpation time (the total time spent in haptic exploration). Research conducted by Kagan showed decreased errors and increased response latencies with age.

Perceptual Learning Style Inventory (PLSI) (Galbraith & James, 1985)

The PLSI is a learning style preference inventory that assesses elements that define an individual's learning style: print, aural, interactive, visual, haptic, kinesthetic, and olfactory. Galbraith and James defined visuals as people who prefer to learn by observation and visual stimuli, such as pictures, graphs, and so on. Haptics are people who learn best through touch (i.e., a hands on approach. There are no norms for the instrument; however, results are in line with Lowenfeld's regarding the visual and haptic dimensions (Roundtree-Wyly, Frusher, & Ficklin, 1988).

Theoretical Background

The initial work in discovering these two different styles was done by Viktor Lowenfeld in 1939. Lowenfeld discovered that some partially blind individuals would use their limited sight to examine an object or to express themselves in clay modeling. At the same time, other partially blind individuals would not use their eyes, but were content to use their sense of touch. He later discovered similar tendencies in normally sighted individuals. In 1945, he tested 1,128 normally sighted individuals through a succession of five tests. His results indicated that 47% had visual tendencies, 23% were haptic, and 30% received a score that placed them in between both. The study concluded that slightly less than one out of every four individuals are more haptically oriented.

Lowenfeld believed that perception in infancy is at first haptic and that visual perception becomes superimposed on it, gradually taking a dominant position for most people, excluding the totally and partly blind. Haptic perception is predominant in the early years of childhood, and visual perception displaces it before the age of puberty when reality demands and interests displace and exclude the fantasy interests of childhood. According to Lowenfeld, this accounts, to some extent, for the difficulty that some children have in successfully continuing their studies of art after adolescence (the age at which vision takes over for the majority). Visual modes of perception are assumed to be dominant, and visual methods are relied on in art teaching. Lowenfeld's research was aimed at making art teachers aware of these perceptual differences.

From a neuropsychological perspective, perceptual integration is supposed to occur in the parieto-occipital area of the cortex. McCarron and Horn (1979) showed significant associations between the importance of this area for organizing sensory data and intellectual functioning.

Visual/Haptic and Learning

Research

Research supports Lowenfeld's percentages of visuals, haptics, and indefinites in the general population. Research also supports his observations of visual and haptic perceptual organization.

- In a study of the relationship between haptic perception and literary creativity in children, Peddie (1952) found that the mean poetic ability of the haptic group was higher than that of the visual group. He concluded that haptic perception is slightly more related to literary creative work than is visual perception.

- In a study of university students, Butzow and Schlenker (1978) found a relationship between the visual/haptic continuum and the Piagetian concrete-formal continuum. Age was related to both perceptual aptitude (Lowenfeld) and intellectual level (Piaget) in a curvilinear manner. Males were generally more visually oriented than females. Some very formal individuals negated the linear relationship between the concrete/formal and the visual/haptic. Very abstract thinkers tended to be haptic.

- Appelle, Gravetter, and Davidson (1980) studied visual and haptic perception of proportion. Contrary to the previous literature on haptics, proportion was neither a directly nor a spontaneously perceived attribute of form.

- In a study that related haptic, auditory, and visual modalities to the mathematics achievement of third graders, a significant relationship was found among matching abilities involving the haptic modality and mathematics achievement (Sawada, 1982).

- Newman and Hall (1987) found that in sighted college students the visual modality was superior over the visual/haptic or the haptic in the learning of Braille symbols. This study supported the modality adeptness hypothesis (i.e., learners recode items in the modality that is more appropriate for the task).

Implications of the Characteristics and Research

Implications which are drawn from research are noted with a •; those drawn logically from descriptive information regarding the trait are noted by an *. Based on the research and the description of the visual/haptic continuum, we conclude that visual types are more likely to excel at learning tasks such as:

* reading-oriented tasks
* spatial interpretation tasks such as interpreting graphs, charts, or pictures
* mechanical drawing, measuring, and estimating visual distance or relationships

and acquire and use effectively learning strategies such as:

* searching for information
* concept mapping and semantic networking
* imaging

Based on the research and the description of the visual/haptic continuum, we conclude that haptic types are more likely to excel at learning tasks such as:

- comparison-contrast tasks in which abstract thinking is required
- some mathematics skills
- poetic/creative tasks
* psychomotor skills and physical education

and acquire and use effectively learning strategies such as:

* drawing relationships through the physical manipulation of data

Visual/Haptic and Instruction

Research

- Charuk (1973) exposed a group of disabled fourth-grade readers to three experimental conditions: visual/haptic, haptic/visual, and control. He found that the remediation of reading disabilities was enhanced when it was associated with a multisensory training approach.

- Three and 5-year-old children were studied for the existence of communication between visual and haptic senses. Only visual/haptic training improved performance on the haptic identification test. There appeared to be no transfer across sense modalities (Jessen & Kaess, 1973).

- Children responded better to visual-object presentation than to haptic-object or aural labeling. These results indicated that visual imagery was better for storage of concrete information (Davis & Kee, 1978).

- The addition of haptic cues did not improve performance on simple and complex visual discrimination problems for kindergartners (Etaugh, Kelliher, Osborne, & Rose, 1981).

- Visual presentation of objects was superior to haptic presentation or aural labeling of objects in a paired-associate learning task for second graders (Kee & Davis, 1979).

- In testing cross-modality matching, college students who were informed of a mismatch between instructional method and preferred learning modality showed better performance in the haptic/visual condition, whereas uninformed learners did better in the visual/haptic condition, indicating that learners had to develop processing strategies (Milewski & Iaccino, 1982).

- When vision and touch were used simultaneously to perform a puzzle-assembly task, vision dominated touch. In independent conditions, however, learners used haptic information more than visual or verbal information (Locher, 1982).

- Haptics performed better on a spatial task after using an interactive version of a video game. Visuals performed better from simply viewing a video of the interactions (Gagnon, 1986).

- Visuals and haptics did not differ in spatial performance after using a linear image or multi-image computer presentation (Ledbetter, 1985).

- Manfredo (1987), in a study to determine prediction and maximization of trainability in organization, asked subjects to perform a haptic task in which the method of instruction was varied. Manfredo found that there was no relationship between perceptual mode and cognitive style or method of instruction.

Implications of the Characteristics and Research

Implications which are drawn from research are noted with a •; those drawn logically from descriptive information regarding the trait are noted by an *. Instructional conditions that capitalize on the preferences of the visual student and challenge the haptic student include:

- imaginal (generating mental images) instructional sequence
- deductive (general-to-detailed) sequencing
* verbal advance organizers

Instructional conditions that remediate or compensate for the deficiencies of the visual student include:

- multisensory training, including tactile activities
- concrete to abstract instructional sequence
* self-generated feedback
* problem solving, rather than rule using
* affective exercises such as journal writing

Instructional conditions that capitalize on the preferences of the haptic student and challenge the visual student include:

* active touching for the haptic learner such as touch screens on the computer
* using a mouse with the computer
* electroboards, learning circles, task cards
* concrete to abstract instructional sequence

Instructional conditions that remediate or compensate for the deficiencies of the haptic student include:

• multisensory training, including visual manipulation activities
• simultaneous presentation of visual images (compensatory supplantation)
* using small, sequentially administered units of information
* using visual memory supports
* inferring from information
* lecturing and inserted testlike events
* using graphic organizers, visual overviews
* asking the student to look up and paraphrase new vocabulary
* highlighting material (underlining, boldface, graphic cues)

References

Appelle, S., Gravetter, J., & Davidson, P. (1980). Proportion judgments in haptic and visual form perception. *Canadian Journal of Psychology,* 161-174.

Ausburn. L. J. (1975, April 14-17). *The relationship of perceptual type to perceptual style and tempo in college students.* Paper presented at the annual meeting of the Association for Educational Communications and Technology, Dallas. (ERIC Document Reproduction Service No. ED 101 726)

Butzow, J. W., & Schlenker, R. M. (1978, March 31- April 3). *A study of possible relationship between Lowenfeld's Visual/Haptic Theory and Piaget's Developmental Theory.* Paper presented at the National Association for Research in Science Teaching Convention, Toronto. (ERIC Document Reproduction Service No. ED 152 705)

Chalfant, J. C., & Scheffelin, M. A. (1969). *Central processing dysfunctions in children: A review of research.* Urbana, IL: Institute of Research for Exceptional Children. (ERIC Document Reproduction Service No. ED 040 546)

Charuk, J. M. (1973). The effects of visual/haptic training on reading achievement. (Doctoral dissertation, University of South Carolina). *Dissertation Abstracts International, 34(9),* 5707.

Cherry, C. E. (1981). The measurement of adult learning styles: Perceptual modality (Doctoral dissertation, University of Tennessee). *Dissertation Abstracts International, 42,* 3852.

Davis, B. R., & Kee, D. W. (1978, March 27-31). *Children's recognition memory: An analysis of haptic, visual and verbal presentation effects.* Paper presented at the annual meeting of the American Educational Research Association, Toronto. (ERIC Document Reproduction Service No. ED 155 663)

Etaugh, C., Kelliher, R., Osborne, B., & Rose, M. (1981). The role of visual and haptic cues in children's discrimination learning. *Journal of Genetic Psychology, 138,* 75-79.

Gagnon, D. M. (1986). *Interactive Television: The influence of user control and interactive structure.* Paper presented at the International Television Studies Conference, London, England. (ERIC Document Reproduction Service No. ED 283 510)

Galbraith, M., & James, W. (1985). *Perceptual learning styles: Implications and techniques for the practitioner.* Washington, DC: American Association for Adult and Continuing Education.

James, W. B., & Galbraith, M. W. (1984). Perceptual learning styles of older adults. *Journal of Applied Gerontology, 3(2),* 214-218.

Jessen, B. L., & Kaess, D. W. (1973). Effects of training on intersensory communication by 3- and 5-year-olds. *Journal of Genetic Psychology, 123,* 115-122.

Kagan, J. (1965). Impulsive and reflective children: Significance of conceptual tempo. In J. D. Krumholtz (Ed.), *Learning and the educational process* (pp. 133-161). Chicago: Rand McNally.

Kagan J., Rosman, B. L., Day, D., Albert, J., & Phillips, W. (1964). Information processing in the child: Significance of analytic and reflective attitudes. *Psychological Monographs, 78,* No. 1 (Whole No. 578).

Kee, D. W., & Davis, B. R. (1979). Analysis of haptic, visual, and verbal presentation mode effects in children's paired-associate learning. *Bulletin of the Psychonomic Society, 14,* 230-232.

Ledbetter, C. A. (1985). An ATI investigation of the relationship between haptic and visual perceptual style and linear versus multiple image presentation on a microcomputer game with moving graphics (Doctoral dissertation, University of Texas). *Dissertation Abstracts International, 46,* 3606.

Locher, P. (1982). Influence of vision on haptic encoding process. *Perceptual and Motor Skills, 55,* 59-74.

Lowenfeld, V. (1949). *Creative and mental growth.* New York: Macmillan.

Manfredo, P. (1987). *Dimensions of cognitive style: Their interrelationships and use in maximizing trainability.* New Orleans: Tulane University. (ERIC Document Reproduction Service No. ED 307 522)

McCarron, L. M., & Horn, P. (1979). Haptic visual discrimination and intelligence. *Journal of Clinical Psychology, 35,* 117-120.

Milewski, A. E., & Iaccino, J. (1982). Strategies in cross-modality matching. *Perception and Psychophysics, 31,* 273-275.

Newman, S. E., & Hall, A. (1987). Braille learning: Relative importance of seven variables. *Journal of Applied Cognitive Psychology, 1(2),* 133-141.

O'Brien, L. (1989). Learning Styles: Make the student aware. *NASSP, 73,* 85-89.

Peddie, R. (1952). The relation of haptic perception to literary creative
    work. *Quarterly Bulletin of British Psychology, 3,* 19-21.
Roundtree-Wyly, J., Frusher, S., & Ficklin, T. (1988). *A comparison of
    learning styles in traditional and nontraditional students.* (ERIC
    Document Reproduction Service No. ED 310 671)
Rouse, M.J. (1965). *Development and validation of descriptive scale for
    measurement of art products.* Bloomington: Indiana University.
    (ERIC Document Reproduction Service No. ED 003 078)
Sawada, D. (1982). Multisensory information matching ability and math-
    ematics learning. *Journal for Research in Mathematics Education,
    14,* 390-394.
Wold, R. (1970). *Screening Tests to be Used by the Classroom Teacher* (pp.
    25-28). Reston, VA: National Association of Secondary School
    Principals.

Bibliography

Butter, E. (1979). Visual and haptic training and cross-modal transfer of re-
    flectivity. *Journal of American Psychology, 71,* 212-219.
Davidson, P., Pine, R., Kettenmann, M., & Appelle, S. (March, 1979).
    *Haptic-Visual matching of shape by mentally retarded children:
    Effects of stimulus and haptic exploratory activity.* Paper presented
    at the Biennial Meeting of the Society for Research in Child
    Development, San Francisco. (ERIC Document Reproduction
    Service No. ED 171 392)
Erickson, R. C. (1969). Visual-Haptic Aptitude: Effect on Student
    Achievement in Reading, *Journal of Learning Disabilities 5,* 256-
    260.
Gagnon, D. M. (1986). Interactive versus observational media: The influ-
    ence of user control and cognitive styles on spatial learning
    (Doctoral dissertation, Harvard University). *Dissertation Abstracts
    International, 47,* 1657.
Gibson, E. J. (1969). *Principles of perceptual learning and development.*
    New York: Appleton-Century-Crofts.
Gibson, J. J. (1966). *The senses considered as perceptual systems.* Boston:
    Houghton Mifflin Company.
Kennedy, J. M., & Fox, N. (1977). Pictures to see and pictures to touch. In D.
    Perkins and B. Leondar (Eds.), *The Arts and Cognition* (pp. 118-135).
    Baltimore: Johns Hopkins University Press.
Kidd, A. H., & Rivoire, J. L. (Eds.). (1966). *Perceptual development in chil-
    dren.* New York: International Universities Press.
Lerner, J. (1971). *Children with learning disabilities, theories, diagnosis,
    and teaching strategies.* Boston: Houghton Mifflin.
Lowenfeld, V. (1970). *Creative and Mental Growth.* New York: Macmillan.

Lowenfeld, V., & Brittain, W. (1982). *Creative and mental growth.* New York: Macmillan.

Matkin, M. W. (1983). *Perception.* Needham Heights, MA: Allyn & Bacon.

Raskin, L. (1975). Tactual and visual integration in the learning processes. *Journal of Learning Disabilities, 8,* 51-55.

Ross, C. (1982). Haptic learning. *Man/Society/Technology, 42,* 23-25.

Schaiper, L., & Flores, J. (1985, March 1985). *Perceptual learning style differences among Mexican American high school and university students.* Paper presented at the Annual Conference of the National Association for Bilingual Education, San Francisco. (ERIC Document Reproduction Service No. ED 314 226)

Schlenker, R. M. (1977). *Visual/haptic abilities in lowenfeld's adult sample as measured by 6 instruments: An evaluation of the sample size and an overview of how others have interpreted it.* Orono: University of Maine. (ERIC Document Reproduction Service No. ED 143 703)

Yarnall, G. D., & Carlton, G. R. (1981). *Guidelines and manual of tests for educators interested in the assessment of handicapped children.* International Research Institute, Austin, TX. (ERIC Document Reproduction Service No. ED 209 788)

15

VISUALIZER/VERBALIZER

Description of Visualizer/Verbalizer

The visualizer/verbalizer cognitive style describes individual preferences for attending to and processing visual versus verbal information. Some individuals prefer to process information by seeing, through the use of graphics, diagrams, or illustrations. Others prefer to process information in words, through reading or listening (Kirby, Moore, & Schofield, 1988).

The visual dimension described by the visual/haptic cognitive style (see chapter 14) is characterized by five qualities: spatial relations, visual discrimination, figure-ground discrimination, visual closure, and object recognition. The visualizer/verbal style presented in this chapter deals with a much simpler dimension--that of an individual's preference to learn via pictures or words. Visualizers tend to think more concretely, use imagery, and personalize information. When learning, they prefer graphs, diagrams, or pictures added to text-based material. Verbalizers prefer to process information from words, either by reading or listening, rather than through images (Kirby et al., 1988). They are also much more objective about the information they are learning. Finally, some students are equally comfortable using either visual or verbal information for learning. In fact, the differences between the visualizer and verbalizer are often not as vast as researchers have found with other cognitive styles.

Alternative classifications have been described along the dimension of high- and low-imagery. Although visualizers in these classifications have been contrasted with highly verbal learners, they possess characteristics similar to those described by the visual dimension of the visual/haptic style as described in the previous chapter. Those with high-imagery ability are visualizers in that they process information via images, whereas those with low-imagery ability tend to be verbalizers and process information via language symbols (Hollenberg, 1970; Stewart, 1965). A factor-analytic study revealed that those subjects who were classified as verbal demonstrated capabilities in verbal associations, labels and conceptualizations, and the ability to employ and transform these symbols. Visual learners also possess strengths in imaginal characteristics as defined by their ability to hold a percept in memory, rotate, unfold and transform it (DiVesta, Ingersol, & Sunshine, 1971).

Characteristic Differences of Visualizer/Verbalizer

Visualizer   Verbalizer

image oriented_____word oriented
fluency with illustrations_____fluency with words
has vivid dreams_____seldom dreams
prefers to have someone show them _____prefers to read about the idea
enjoys jigsaw puzzles_____enjoys word games
subjective self-orientation_____objective task orientation
left eye movement _____right eye movement
understands visuals_____understands semantic complexity
manipulates and transforms images_manipulates and transforms symbols

Individual Differences Related to Visualizer/Verbalizer

Field Dependence/Independence--This describes the ability to disambiguate or separate relevant and irrelevant stimuli in an information field (see chapter 7). It is predicted that visualizers are more field dependent, whereas verbalizers are more field independent (Kirby et al., 1988).

Holist/Serialist--This is a measure of global versus detailed processing styles (see chapter 17). It is expected that visualizers are more holistic, and verbalizers more serialistic (Kirby et al., 1988).

Hemisphericity--This is a measure of the dominance of the right or left brain to control certain psychological functions. Richardson (1977) predicted the relationship of right brain dominance with visualizers and left brain dominance with verbalizers.

Introversion-Extraversion--This is a measure of the inwardness or outwardness of thinking and behavior (see chapter 29). Visualizers are more introverted, whereas verbalizers are more extroverted (Riding & Burt, 1982).

Mental Ability--Kirby et al. (1988) found that verbal style correlated with verbal ability as measured by vocabulary, verbal similarities, verbal reasoning, and verbal analogy problem solving (see chapters 4 & 5). The visual style correlated positively with spatial visualization, which requires complex transformations of complex figures.

Instruments for Measuring Visualizer/Verbalizer

Visualizer/Verbalizer Questionnaire (VVQ)

The VVQ is the primary instrument used to measure the differences between the two learning preferences. This 15-item test, which contrasts a visual and verbal approach to learning, was developed based on correlations between subject responses on Paivio's (1971) Way of Thinking Questionnaire and the results of lateral eye movements. An example question that indicates verbalization is: "I enjoy doing work that requires the use of words." A typical question for visualizers is "My daydreams are sometimes so vivid, I feel as though I actually experience the scene." Seven of the test questions assess verbal preferences or skills, and the remaining eight assess visual preferences or skills. Of the eight visual questions, three relate to the formation of mental images. The remaining five questions relate to dreams or imagination. Test-retest reliability of this questionnaire have been reported to range from .48 to .91 (Richardson, 1977; Warren & Good, 1979). Richardson (1977), and Spoltore and Smock (1983) rated the instrument as adequately reliable for research purposes. However, when Edwards and Wilkins (1981) compared the VVQ to several other scales, the VVQ failed to discriminate. They suggested that imagery and verbal processes were independent and parallel; therefore, the test may be inappropriate for measuring these modes with this instrument.

Verbal and Visual Learning Styles Questionnaire (Richardson, 1977)

This instrument includes three parts, each with 10 items, and is designed to test verbal preferences, visual preferences, and dream vividness. The third part, using dream items, was shown not to affect results. Examples of verbal items include "I enjoy learning new words; I spend little time attempting to increase my vocabulary; I dislike word games like crossword puzzles." Content validity was obtained through principal components analysis of the 30 items and through correlation results with two spatial abilities measures; the Card Rotation Test (S-1) and the Surface Development Test (VZ-3) by Ekstrom, French, Harman, and Dermen (1976), and through one verbal ability measure, the ACER Higher Test, Form ML produced by the Australian Council for Educational Research (1981). Moderate positive correlations were found between verbal preferences and verbal ability, and between visual preferences and spatial visualization only.

Swassing-Barbe Perceptual Modality Instrument (Swassing & Barbe, 1979)

The Swassing-Barbe Perceptual Modality Instrument differentiates visual, verbal, and kinesthetic learners. Subjects are shown nine sequences of shapes for the visual test, each one getting progressively longer (from one to nine items.) For the auditory portion, subjects are read the names of the shapes. In the kinesthetic test, the subjects feel the shapes without seeing them. Examples of the sequences are "square, triangle, circle, heart; square, heart, triangle, circle, heart, heart, square." Immediately after being presented with each sequence, subjects are asked to reproduce the shapes. The number correct for each modality constitutes the score. Strengths are determined by the percentage of each subscore relative to the individual's total score on the three subtests. There has been no reliability or validity data reported on the use of this test.

Edmonds Learning Style Identification Exercise (ELSIE) (Reinert, 1976)

This exercise uses a self-reporting strategy to differentiate among four learning modalities: visual, verbal, auditory, and activity. The subjects are presented with 50 words and are asked to record the modes in which they spontaneously responded. Examples of these words are "pool, baby, long, five, law, think, warm, happy." They are scored, and profiles are drawn in comparison to a pilot group (Keefe, 1987). The assumption behind the profiles is reading the distance from the mean for each category. Those who score at the extremes can be considered to be dominant or weak in that area. No reliability data are available for this test.

Space Relations Test of the Differential Aptitude Test Battery (Bennett, Seashore, & Wesman, 1963)

This test, one of nine measures of differential aptitude, gauges a subject's ability to visually rotate objects in three-dimensional space. This 60 item test has been designed for subjects from grades 8 to 12, and adults. Little information was provided on the subscale itself; however, Bouchard (1978) reported that the entire test has little differential validity because of the intercorrelations of the scores with each other. This should not be a problem when using just one subscale.

Flag--A Test of Space Thinking (Thurstone & Jeffery, 1959)

This is a 21-item assessment that measures one's ability to manipulate visual information. The subjects are given a picture of a flag on the left. They must then compare this flag to six others that are provided on the right, decide if it is the same or opposite side, and mark an S or an O below each flag. Subjects are given 5 minutes to complete as many as they can. No data on reliability or validity were available from the authors, but Smith (1965) perceived that a verification of the test yields satisfactory results.

Theoretical Background

Prompted by Paivio's (1971) work, which defined the role of visual and verbal processes in learning, Richardson (1977) attempted to further delineate this cognitive style. He traced the development of the construct to *experiential* evidence reported by Griffiths (1927), who found differences between concrete, visual types and auditory, verbal types, and Roe (1951), who found differences in learning preferences by profession; *physiological* differences relating breathing patterns and lateral eye movements to visual/verbal preferences (Bogen, 1969; Golla & Antonovitch, 1929); and finally, *behavioral* evidence investigating perceptual and memory processes and verbal/visual habits (Bartlett, 1932). Behavior patterns distinguished verbalizers as those who reported a general class of objects and problem-solving strategies with no imaging, while maintaining an "objective task orientation," and visualizers as those who mentioned more personal and concrete objects, using a "subjective, self-orientation" (cited in Richardson, 1977 p. 111).

A significant contribution to Richardson's definition of this construct, however, was the physiological differences found in the recent research on hemisphericity and lateral eye movements. He correlated lateral eye movements with responses on Paivio's *Ways of Thinking Questionnaire* to select items that discriminated between left (visualizers) and right eye movers (verbalizers). Richardson then interpreted this research to distinguish differences between visualizers and verbalizers using a bipolar scale--the existence of strength in visualizing is interpreted as a deficiency in verbalizing. Because those who scored high on imagery vividness were also left eye movers, Richardson captured visualizing preferences by measuring conscious mental imagery and dream vividness. The verbal end of the continuum included preferences and skills with words.

Questioning the nature of Richardson's conception of this cognitive style, Kirby et al. (1988) performed a factor analysis that supported a verbal preference factor but no visual preference factor. They found that only verbal ability correlated with the verbal preference scores. They then redefined the construct through three separate, nonpolar factors, including mental imagery, verbal preference, and dream vividness as measured by a revised questionnaire. Alpha coefficients were .70 for verbal, .59 for visual, and .73 for dreams. Unlike Richardson's bipolar scale which measured preferences for one skill over another, this instrument shows the existence of individual preferences for each of the dimensions. To determine whether or not these preferences related to abilities, the scores were correlated with verbal ability and spatial ability (spatial relations and spatial visualization). They found that verbal learning preferences significantly and positively correlated with verbal ability, whereas visual ability correlated significantly with a moderate positive result with spatial visualization only. Dream vividness had a significantly low, positive correlation with spatial relations. From their studies, they concluded that visual/verbal styles do exist and can be measured but should not include the dream dimension.

Visualizer/Verbalizer and Learning

Research

- Undergraduate visualizers recalled more high-imagery adjectives from a passage than verbalizers but did slightly worse than verbalizers on low-imagery adjectives (Hiscock, 1976).

- For 11-year-olds, the verbal imagery test differentiated between the individual's recall of material differing in amount of semantic complexity and visual description (Riding & Calvey, 1981).

- Cielecki (1983) showed that the similarity attraction relationship was strongest for undergraduate visualizers, and the positive similarity attraction relationship was more pronounced in subjects who were instructed to think in words.

- Young males who could see an image on a screen after the image was gone evoked voluntary thought images more vividly, were habitual visualizers, and generally were absorbed into the imagination, fantasy, and sensory experiences (Matsuoka, 1989).

Implications of the Characteristics and Research

Implications which are drawn from research are noted with a •; those drawn logically from descriptive information regarding the trait are noted by an *. Based on the limited amount of research and descriptions of the visualizer/verbalizer style, we conclude that *visual* learners are more likely to excel at learning tasks such as:

• spatial interpretation tasks such as interpreting graphs, charts, or pictures
* mechanical drawing, measuring, and estimating visual distances or relationships

and acquire and use effectively learning strategies such as:

* searching for information
* using mnemonics
* generating metaphors
• imaging
* concept mapping and semantic networking

Based on the limited amount of research and descriptions of the visualizer/verbalizer style, we conclude that *verbal* learners are more likely to excel at learning tasks such as:

* reading
* sequential learning tasks

and acquire and use effectively learning strategies such as:

* analysis of key ideas
* outlining
* repeating information to be recalled

Visualizer/Verbalizer and Instruction

Research

- Boekaerts (1982) found that high school students had different degrees of success at retrieving visuo-spatial and verbatim information. They suggested adapting the teaching/learning process to accommodate various coding strategies.

- Riding and Burt (1982) found that when children's preferred mode of learning matched the listening task, recall was superior following listening when the details were simple but best after reading when the material was complex. For the nonpreferred mode the results were reversed.

Implications of the Characteristics and Research

Implications which are drawn from research are noted with a •; those drawn logically from descriptive information regarding the trait are noted by an *. Instructional conditions that capitalize on the preferences of the visual student and challenge the verbal student include:

- using images, pictures, graphs, or charts
- using high-imagery materials
- using graphic organizers
* using video games

Instructional conditions that remediate or compensate for the deficiencies of the visual student include:

* using multisensory training
* using concrete to abstract sequencing
* presenting word images

* presenting special text in windows, or boxes
* underlining, visual cueing in text

Instructional conditions that capitalize on the preferences of the verbal student and challenge the visual student include:

• using verbal presentations such as lecture, tapes, nonillustrated texts
* using textual outlines
* using abstract to concrete sequencing

Instructional conditions that remediate or compensate for the deficiencies of the verbal student include:

* using multisensory training
* using graphic cues, lines, boxes with text, arrows, highlighting on images

References

Australian Council for Educational Research. (1981). *Higher Test, Form ML.* Hawthorn, Australia: ACER.

Bartlett, F. C. (1932). *Remembering.* Cambridge: Cambridge University Press.

Bennett, G. K., Seashore, H. G., & Wesman, A. G. (1963). *Differential aptitude tests.* (Grades 8-13 and adults). New York: Psychological Corporation.

Boekaerts, M. (1982). Individual differences in the use of visual and verbal mediators. *Research in Education, 27,* 49-62.

Bogen, J. E. (1969). The other side of the brain: An oppositional mind. *Bulletin of the Los Angeles Neurological Society, 34,* 135-162.

Bouchard, T. J. (1978). Differential Aptitude Test: Review. In O. K. Buros, (Ed.), *8th Book of Mental Measurements* (pp. 655-665). Highland Park, NJ: Gryphon.

Cielecki, M. (1983). Perceptual imagery and verbal-conceptual determinants of the similarity attraction relationship. *Cahiers de Psychologie Cognitive, 3*(2), 159-174.

DiVesta, F. J., Ingersol, G., & Sunshine, P. (1971). A factor analysis of imagery tests. *Journal of Verbal Learning and Verbal Behavior, 10,* 471-479.

Edwards, J. E., & Wilkins, W. (1981). Verbalizer-Visualizer Questionnaire: Relationship with imagery and verbal-visual ability. *Journal of Mental Imagery, 5*(2), 137-142.

Ekstrom, R. B., French, J. W., Harman, H., & Dermen, D. (1976). *Kit of factor-referenced cognitive tests.* Princeton: Educational Testing Service.

Golla, F. L., & Antonovitch, S. (1929). The respiratory rhythm in its relation to the mechanism of thought. *Brain, 52,* 491-509.

Griffiths, C. H. (1927). Individual differences in imagery. *Psychological Monographs, 37.* (Whole No. 172).

Hiscock, M. (1976). Effects of adjective imagery on recall from prose. *Journal of General Psychology, 94*(4), 295-299.

Hollenberg, C. K. (1970). Functions of visual imagery in the learning and concept formation of children. *Child Development, 41,* 1003-1015.

Keefe, J. (1987). *Learning style: Theory and practice.* Reston, VA: National Association of Secondary School Principals.

Kirby, J., Moore, P., & Shofield, N. (1988). Verbal and visual learning styles, *Contemporary Educational Psychology 13,* 169-184.

Matsuoka, K. (1989). Imagery vividness, verbalizer-visualizer, and fantasy proneness in young adults. *Tohoku Psychologica Folia. 458* (1-4), 25-32.

Paivio, A. (1971). *Imagery and verbal processes.* New York: Holt, Rinehart & Winston.

Reinert, H. (1976). One picture is worth a thousand words? Not necessarily! *Modern Language Journal, 60,* 160-168.

Richardson, A. (1977). Verbalizer-visualizer: A cognitive style dimension. *Journal of Mental Imagery, 1,* 109-126.

Riding, R. J., & Burt, J. M. (1982). Reading versus listening in children: the effects of extraversion and coding complexity. *Educational Psychology, 2,* 47-58.

Riding, R. J., & Calvey, I. (1981). The assessment of verbal-imagery learning styles and their effect on the recall of concrete and abstract prose passages by 11-year-old children. *British Journal of Psychology, 72*(1), 59-64.

Roe, A. (1951). A study of imagery in research scientists. *Journal of Personality, 19,* 459-470.

Smith, M. (1965). Flags: A test of space thinking. In O. K. Buros (Ed.), *8th Book of Mental Measurements.* (p. 2245). Highland Park, NJ: Gryphon.

Spoltore, J. D., & Smock, D. J. (1983). The verbalizer-visualizer questionnaire: Additional normative data. *Perceptual and Motor Skills, 56,* 382.

Stewart, J. C. (1965). *An experimental investigation of imagery.* Unpublished doctoral dissertation, University of Toronto.

Swassing, R., & Barbe, W. (1979). *The Swassing-Barbe Modality Index.* Columbus, OH: Zaner-Bloser.

Thurstone L. L., & Jeffery, T. G. (1959). *Space Thinking (flags).* Chicago: Education-Industry Service.

Warren, R., & Good, G. (1979). The Verbalizer-Visualizer Questionnaire: Further normative data. *Perceptual and Motor Skills, 48,* 372.

16

LEVELING/SHARPENING

Description of Leveling/Sharpening

The cognitive style, leveling/sharpening, describes how individuals perceive and memorize images. *Leveling* and *sharpening* are terms that label differences or variations in memory processing, specifically, the ability to retain discrete images of sequential, experience-based stimuli and make distinctions between them. These stimuli may be verbal, as in a story, or visual, as in a film.

Levelers more frequently miss changes or inconsistencies in sequentially presented stimuli. As a result, they tend to condense story elements and simplify the stories (or sequence of stimuli) during recall. They merge new impressions and experiences with previous, older ones. That is, they integrate information more readily into memory. Their memory impressions, therefore, are more undifferentiated and blurred. Strong levelers would not notice if information had changed subtly because global images of past information are indistinguishable from those of the present. As a result, levelers are likely to overgeneralize events, objects, or ideas.

At the other end of this cognitive style continuum, strong sharpeners tend to retain discrete and clearly differentiated images and the small differences among them. Sharpeners retain in detail the original structure of a story (Holzman & Gardner, 1960). They rely more heavily than levelers on rote memory and recall because their memories are more distinct and different. They are able to separate memories of prior experiences more easily from current ones, so sharpeners are likely to overdiscriminate (Santostefano, 1978, p. 126).

During maturation or development, individuals generally change from leveling to sharpening. There are two separate transitions that occur during development.

fluid --> *stable*	
modify memory images	don't modify memory images

global -->*articulated*	
undifferentiated fusing	differentiation between past memory
of past & present	images and present

Characteristic Differences in Leveling/Sharpening

Levelers	Sharpeners
global	articulated
diffuse	differentiated
undifferentiated attention	attend to details/nuances
prefer generalities	prefer details
abstract reasoning	concrete reasoning
images unstable	images held stable over time
present confused with past	clear perception of chronology
overgeneralized perception	overdiscriminated perception
blur memories--confuse associated concepts	rely heavily on visual (rote) memory

Individual Differences Related to Leveling/Sharpening

Field dependence/independence (or field articulation)--This style describes the ability and approach used by individuals to articulate or separate relevant and irrelevant stimuli in an information field (see chapter 7). Levelers should tend to be field dependent, whereas sharpeners should tend to be field independent, although no research supports this.

Focusing-scanning--This cognitive control describes how attention/concentration is systemically deployed or distributed when objects are being compared (see chapter 10). Sharpeners tend to be scanners and levelers tend to be focusers.

Instruments for Measuring Leveling/Sharpening

Schematizing Squares Test (Holzman & Klein, 1954)

The Schematizing Squares Test was developed to test hypotheses regarding differences among individuals in assimilation effects. In the test, 150 squares are shown in sets of five. Squares range from 1 inch to 14 inches when projected on a screen. In each successive set, the smallest square drops out and the next largest is added. Subjects are asked to judge the size of each square. Accuracy in rank size is important. The less affected the subject is by the memory of past sets of squares, the more he or she is a sharpener. The test may be fatiguing for subjects because many of the squares are so close in size that the differences are difficult to discern, and it is a very long test. Reliability data were not evident.

Leveling/Sharpening Circles Test (Santostefano, 1964)

In this test, 60 circles are shown that gradually increase in size. Subjects push a button on a memory drum when they see a circle larger than the previous circle. The less affected the subject is by the past sets of circles, the more he or she is a sharpener. This test is easier for subjects to take than the Squares Test, but it is still difficult. It requires less time. Reliability data were not evident.

Leveling/Sharpening Wagon Test (Santostefano, 1964)

In this test, 60 simple line drawings of a child's wagon are shown. Subjects push a button on a memory drum when the wagon "looked different or changed." Parts of the picture drop out throughout the 60 drawings; once a part drops out, it stays out of the picture. Subjects who report changes early, report many changes, or report changes immediately are considered to be sharpeners, whereas levelers are just the opposite. This is an easier test for subjects to take because it is an object and not a geometric shape; however, the test is too simple to hold the attention of older children or adults.

Leveling/Sharpening House Test (Santostefano, 1964)

This test is the same as the wagon test except that it contains 60 pictures of a simple line drawing of a house and its setting (tree, sun, fence, and sidewalk). It is individually administered. The test administrator holds up and displays each picture for 5 seconds, which makes it somewhat prone to error. This is a good test for 3-year-olds to adults. A microcomputer version of this test has been developed (Burroway, 1984).

Leveling/Sharpening Parachute Test (Guthrie, 1967)

This test is similar to the House Test except that a picture of a parachutist is shown in one of two ways: (a) in free flight (no open parachute) or (b) with parachute open. Details drop out throughout the test. This assessment is used in testing parachutists.

Leveling/Sharpening Hospital Test (Guthrie, 1967)

Similar to the House and Parachute tests, this test uses a picture of a doctor in a hospital from which details drop out. The Hospital Test is used in testing presurgery patients.

Theoretical Background

The terms *leveling* and *sharpening* have been used since the 1920s, when Wulf applied the term *sharpening* to the remembering of details in a story. In the 1930s, Lauenstein used the terms to describe two ends of a continuum concerning the degree of assimilation between perceptual processes and memory traces. The Schematizing Squares Test was first employed in 1954 by Holzman. It was used to validate and expand on the work previously done by Lauenstein in the 1930s. Gardner, Holzman, Klein, Linton, and Spence (1959) did a more extensive study in which "differentiation in memory organization was a function of the extent to which successive stimuli assimilate to each other."

In normal learning situations, leveling/sharpening remains fairly stable. However, an individual's leveling/sharpening style may change when confronted with an unusual or unexpected situation. Depending on the amount of control the individual feels during a highly stressful situation, he or she may move to either end of the continuum. The more control an individual feels in a situation, the more likely it is that he or she will process information in a distinct and differentiated manner. Guthrie (1967) believed that memory functioning "reorganizes toward sharpening when the environment requires, and this allows the individual to make active use of information in management of stress."

Leveling/Sharpening and Learning

Research

- Gardner et al. (1959) conducted an extensive study in which they found a relationship between memory differentiation and the similarity of successive stimuli.

- Lohrenz and Gardner (1973) found little or no relationship between leveling/sharpening and recall of thematic material, and no relationship to recall of sequentially presented, similar designs.

- Pritchard (1975) found that sharpeners were better at nonsequential tasks as well as sequential judgments, and that both tasks required similar processing.

- Santostefano (1978) found that novice parachutists, when presented with a stressful situation (prejump, at the airport), moved toward sharpening; they processed information in a more stable and differentiated manner.

- Hospitalized presurgical patients (under stress) were prone to leveling because of the passive nature of their situation (Santostefano, 1978, p. 383).

- Satterly (1979) found that leveling/sharpening was independent of intelligence and field independence.

- Sampsel (1981) found that sharpening correlated with performance on class inclusion problems, suggesting that class inclusion entails differentiation.

- Ludwig and Lazarus (1983) found that individuals with certain personality traits, such as shyness, were found to be "high distractors." Shy individuals reduced the number of accessible perceptual cues and indicated high distractability/susceptibility to competing stimuli. This reduced cue utilization is related to maintaining a perceptual set long after its appropriateness or effectiveness ends.

Implications of the Characteristics and Research

Implications which are drawn from research are noted with a •; those drawn logically from descriptive information regarding the trait are noted by an *. Based on the small amount of research and the descriptions of leveling/sharpening, we conclude that *levelers* are more likely to excel at learning tasks such as:

* determining the gist of a story; summarizing and selecting main ideas
* developing, interpreting, or using prototypes

and acquire and use effectively learning strategies such as:

* evaluating current information
* paraphrasing/summarizing

    Based on the small amount of research and the descriptions of leveling/sharpening, we conclude that *sharpeners* are more likely to excel at learning tasks such as:

- concept classification tasks, especially using a comparison-contrast strategy
- recalling sequences or lists of objects or events
- problem solving

and acquire and use effectively learning strategies such as:

* searching for information

* repeating material to be recalled
* rehearsing material to be recalled

Leveling/Sharpening and Instruction

Research

Very little research on this cognitive style has been completed with normal learners.

• Cotungno (1983) found that leveling deficiencies can be more effectively remediated with structure-based instruction than with skill-based instruction, which had no significant effect.

Implications of the Characteristic and Research

Implications which are drawn from research are noted with a •; those drawn logically from descriptive information regarding the trait are noted by an *. Instructional conditions that capitalize on the preferences of the leveler and challenge the sharpener student include:

* presenting information without details, using only central themes
* presenting information in an organized fashion with little complexity
* presenting large chunks of information
* using prototypic examples
* creating summaries
* paraphrasing content

Instructional conditions that remediate or compensate for the deficiencies of levelers include:

* highlighting details on a computer screen
* using mnemonic systems such as acronyms
* describing criteria for standard performance
* using graphic organizers or overviews
* using matched example/nonexample pairs with close-in nonexamples
* providing graphic cues: lines, colors, boxes, arrows, highlighting
* using inductive sequence

Instructional conditions that capitalize on the preferences of the sharpeners and challenge the levelers include:

* presenting information with many details in a sequential order, focusing on details not themes
* using flowcharts

* presenting small chunks of information
* asking learners to recall elaboration
* rehearsing, repeating, rereading
* categorizing elements

   Instructional conditions that remediate or compensate for the deficiencies of the sharpeners include:

* presenting information in an organized way, gradually increasing complexity and randomness
* presenting new information in such a way that students are made to recall previously introduced information
* paraphrasing definitions, using synonyms

References

Burroway, R. L. (1984, January 20-24). *Testing and measurement potentials of microcomputers for cognitive style research and individualized instruction*. Paper presented at the annual meeting of the Association for Educational Communications and Technology, Dallas. (ERIC Document Reproduction Service No. ED 243 415)

Cotugno, A. J. (1983). Cognitive controls: A test of their modifiability and structural arrangement. *Psychology-in-the-Schools, 20*, 351-362.

Gardner, R. W., Holzman, P. S., Klein, G. S., Linton, H. B., & Spence, D. P. (1959). Cognitive control: A study of individual consistencies in cognitive behavior. *Psychological Issues*. New York: International Universities Press.

Guthrie, G. D. (1967). Changes in cognitive functioning under stress: A study of plasticity in cognitive controls (Doctoral dissertation, Clark University, Worcester, MA. *Dissertation Abstracts International, 28*, 212-513.

Holzman, P. S., & Gardner, R. W. (1960). Leveling/sharpening and memory organization. *Journal of Abnormal and Social Psychology, 61*, 176-180.

Holzman, P. S., & Klein, G. S. (1954). Cognitive system-principles of leveling and sharpening: Individual differences in assimilation effects in visual time error. *Journal of Psychology, 37*, 105-122.

Lohrenz, L. J., & Gardner, R. W. (1973). Cognitive control in recall of similar visual designs versus nonsimilar thematic material. *Perceptual and Motor Skills, 36*, 627-631.

Ludwig, R., & Lazarus, P. J. (1983). Relationship between shyness in children and constricted cognitive control as measured by the Stroop Color-Word Test. *Journal of Consulting and Clinical Psychology, 51(3)*, 386-89.

Pritchard, D. A. (1975). Leveling/sharpening revisited. *Perceptual and Motor Skills, 40* (1), 111-117.

Sampsel, B. D. (1981). Relation in children of psychological differentiation and reasoning by class inclusion. *Perceptual and Motor Skills, 53,* 439-446.

Santostefano, S. (1964). Developmental study of the cognitive control "leveling - sharpening." *Merrill-Palmer Quarterly, 10,* 343-360.

Santostefano, S. (1978). *A biodevelopmental approach to clinical child psychology.* New York: Wiley.

Santostefano, S. (1985). *Cognitive control therapy with children and adolescents.* New York: Permagon.

Satterly, D. J. (1979). Covariation of cognitive styles, intelligence and achievement. *British Journal of Educational Psychology, 49* (2), 179-181.

17

SERIALIST/HOLIST

Description of Serialist/Holist

The serialist/holist cognitive style is a measure of a bipolar information-processing strategy that describes the way that learners select and represent information (Pask, 1976; Pask & Scott, 1972). Pask found that the learning of complex subject matter involves: (a) building descriptions, or an overview of the topic and how topics interrelate, or (b) building operations such as the detailed, underlying interrelationship of concept elements.

Holists use a global, thematic approach to learning by concentrating first on building broad descriptions. The holistic learner typically focuses on several aspects of the subject at the same time and has many goals and working topics that span various levels of the hierarchical structure. The holist then uses complex links to relate multileveled information. Higher ordered relationships are established, essentially using a top-down approach (Tillema, 1982). Interconnections between theoretical, practical, and personal aspects of a topic are made through the use of analogies, illustrations, and anecdotes (Entwistle, 1979; Ford, 1985). Pask (1976) described a holist's learning deficiency as not focusing on enough detail, or "globetrotting."

Serialists use an "operations" approach to learning, concentrating more narrowly on details and procedures before conceptualizing an overall picture (Pask, 1976). They typically combine information in a linear sequence, focusing on small chunks of information that are low in the hierarchical structure, and working from the bottom up. The serialists work step-by-step within this narrow framework, concentrating on well- defined and sequentially ordered chunks that can be related using simple links (Tillema, 1982). Typically, serialists examine links between concepts to develop an objective, logical argument. Pask identified the serialist learning deficiency as ignoring important connections or "improvidence."

Pask (1984) described the *versatile* learners as students who employ both holist and serialist learning strategies and engage in the "creation of valid analogies by juxtaposing and resolving the conflict among several, at the outset conflicting, perspectives or bodies of hypotheses" (p. 16). In doing so, they are able to engage in both global and detailed, local approaches. They succeed in achieving a full or deep understanding that is comprised of both descriptions and procedures. Versatiles are proficient at learning from most or all modes of instruction.

Characteristic Differences in Serialist/Holist

Holist	Serialist
global approach to learning	local approach to learning
conceptually oriented	detail oriented
low-discrimination skills	high-discrimination skills
simultaneous processor	linear processor
broad description building	narrow procedure building
wide range in hierarchy	low in hierarchy structure
top-down processor	bottom-up processor
spans various levels at once	works step-by-step
interconnects theoretical and practical aspects	theoretical/practical aspects learned separately
broad relations	narrow relations
comprehension learning style	operation learning style
forms generalized hypotheses	forms specific hypotheses
relates concepts to prior experience	relates characteristics within concept
personalizes concepts	remains objective
globetrotting--inappropriate connections	improvidence--ignores important connections

Individual Differences Related to Serialist/Holist

Ambiguity tolerance--This describes a readiness to accept perceptions in opposition to convention or those deviating from the ordinary (see chapter 26). Rowland and Stuessy (1987) found a correlation between Study Preference Questionnaire - Holist/Serialist (SPQ) and MacDonald's AT-20 - Ambiguity Tolerance (MAT) which suggests a relationship between high-ambiguity tolerance and the holist style.

Based on stylistic parallels, rather than empirical verification, Entwistle (1979) suggested the following related characteristics:

Field Dependence/Independence--This cognitive control describes the ability to articulate or disambiguate stimuli in an information field (see chapter 7). Because of their global perspective, holists have been related to field dependents, whereas serialists have been related to field independents.

Cognitive tempo--This is a measure of a person's tendency to inhibit initial responses and to reflect on the accuracy of an answer rather than responding impulsively (see chapter 9). Serialists have been related to impulsive learning, and versatile learners have been related to reflectivity.

Convergence/Divergence--This learning style describes differences in information-processing strategies that denote an ability to provide different solutions or perspectives (see chapter 20). Serialists are like convergers, and holists are more related to divergent thinkers.

Hemisphericity--This is a measure of differences in the dominance of the right or left portions of brain functioning. Serialists tend to exhibit right-brain characteristics, whereas holists exhibit characteristics of the left brain.

Instruments for Measuring Serialist/Holist

Spy Ring History Test (Pask, 1973)

Pask developed this test as a convenient method for estimating an individual's bias toward operational (serialist), comprehension (holist), or versatile (both) thinking. A thematic method was used to avoid any reference to school topics and activities that students already knew (Pask, 1973). The students are required to learn and recall the growth of an "International Spy Ring" over three historical epochs and predict/create spy activities for year 4. Connectivity is noted through complex communication patterns among the spies. This is a paper-and-pencil test that is complex and requires considerable time and effort to complete. The scoring scheme, although not standardized, consists of five results: versatility (analogy creation), comprehension (description building), operational learning (procedure building), rote recall, and a neutral score for calibration. A similar test was also developed entitled the *Smuggler's Test*. In this test, connectivity is measured though complex transactions between the smugglers. No reliability data were available for this test.

Clobbits Test (Pask, 1975)

This learning task was constructed by Pask (1975) to distinguish between serialist and holist learners. It consists of cards that present information about a taxonomy of Martian animals. The cards are divided into five categories differing in the number of hypotheses that can be tested about the complexity of information that is presented on the cards. Pupils are unconstrained in the selection of cards. Scoring is based on the number of simple propositions and complex propositions.

Caste and Intuition (Pask, 1976)

These two tests entail the use of a sophisticated computer-monitored apparatus to identify the students' learning strategy as holistic or serialistic.

Study Preference Questionnaire (SPQ) (Ford, 1985)

This five-item self-report questionnaire developed by Ford in 1985 assesses preferences for holistic or serialistic learning strategies. Students are provided two statements, one on the right and one on the left. Using a 5-point scale, they are asked to indicate their degree of agreement with either statement, or to indicate no preference. An example of one of the questions is, on the left, "Generally, I prefer to concentrate on one (or very few) aspect(s) of a subject at a time when I'm learning about it," and on the right, "Generally, I prefer to be learning about a number of different aspects of a subject at the same time." This instrument classifies subjects as holist or serialist based on the majority of their responses. The SPQ can be administered to a group of students and scored by them in less than 15 minutes. If a student scores equally high in both areas, then he or she is said to be a versatile learner. When compared with the Short Inventory of Approaches to Studying, four individual items, as well as the group of questions taken as a whole distinguished holist versus serialist learners.

Short Inventory of Approaches to Studying (Entwistle, 1981)

Entwistle developed a 30-item inventory designed to tap into a number of dimensions of study attitudes and behavior (Entwistle, 1979). Students are asked to rate their agreement on a scale of 0-4. Sample questions include, "I find it easy to organize my study time effectively; When I'm doing a piece of work, I try to bear in mind exactly what that particular teacher/lecturer seems to want; Although I generally remember facts and details, I find it difficult to fit them together into an overall picture." By examining each score separately and in combination, this scale yields eight scores: achieving, reproducing, meaning, comprehension learning, operations learning, versatile approach, learning pathologies, and prediction of success. Entwistle (1981) then published a shortened version that measures comprehension and operation learning, *deep* and *surface* approaches, a *deep versatile* approach, and learning pathologies. No reliability data were available for this test.

Other Measures (Pask, 1973)

Pask also developed several other measures including patterns of word association, codebreaking and imaginative essaywriting.

Theoretical Background

In their development of conversation theory, Pask (1972, 1976) and Pask and Scott (1972) studied patterns of conversations between individuals to identify various styles of learning and thinking. They used entailment meshes, evolutionary graphical frameworks of concepts, to represent how consciousness forms among individuals about concepts. Through these representations of shared agreements, differing patterns for designing, planning, and organizing of thought were studied for different individuals.

They developed the Course Assembly and Tutorial Environment (CASTE), a computer-based tutorial, to help form and interpret these patterns of knowing. Data were collected on the sequence, content, and demonstration items that were selected by students. From these data, models were constructed to represent the different learning and thinking strategies. Three strategies emerged from this research: descriptive, operational/procedural, and analogical, or versatile. Observed patterns were verified through teachback techniques.

Entwistle (1979), synthesizing the research of Pask (1976), Marton (1976), and Biggs (1979), created an integrated perception of this construct. This model is shown in Table 17.1. Marton defined the relationship of intention (shown in column 2), process (shown in columns 4, 5, & 6), and outcome to deep and surface approaches to learning (shown in column 7). Learners using a deep or holist approach consciously pursue and reach deep understanding. Those using a surface or serialist approach seek out facts for memorization (Entwistle, 1979, p. 4). Biggs (1979) then discovered three-second-order motivation factors to add to this understanding. These motivation factors included intrinsic, those related to deep processing and descriptive/holist learning, extrinsic, those related to surface processing and operations/serialist learning, and achievement, those related to versatile learning. Entwistle (1979), using principle component analysis on the results of a students' general study questionnaire, found four common factors: orientation/approach, motivation, process, and outcome. This analysis verified the previous research. The results led to the development of an empirical model of the processes underlying serialist/holist/versatile learning.

Serialist/Holist and Learning

Research

- The achievement of full understanding required both learning approaches, a holistlike global approach and a serialist-like local approach (Pask & Scott, 1972).

- In an examination of learning from holist and serialist materials, 2 out of 26 students performed equally well on both holist and serialist competence tests (Ford, 1985).

Fac-tor	Orientation/ Intention	Motivation	Approach/ Style	Process Stage 1	Process Stage 2	Outcome
I	Understanding	Intrinsic	Deep	All four used	All four used	Deep level of understanding
			Compre-hension learning	Build overall description of content area previous know-ledge or experience and establishing personal meaning	Reorganizing incominginfor-tion to relate	Incomplete understanding attributable to globetrotting
			Operation learning	Detailed atten-tion to evidence to steps in the argument	Relating evi denceto con-lusion and maintaining a critical, objec-tive stance	Incomplete understanding attributable to improvidence
II	Reproducing	Extrinsic	Surface ap-proach	Memorization	Overlearning	Surface level understanding
III	Achieving	Hope for	Organized/ achievement	Any combina-tion	Any combina-tion	High grades with or with-out understanding

Table 17.1. Model of learning processes (Entwistle, 1979).

• Experienced and successful learners, like postgraduate students, tended to learn equally well from materials designed to suit both holist and serialist learning strategies (Ford, 1985).

• In a study of the effect of computer-aided instruction (CAI) modes (simulations and tutorials) and differences in undergraduates' concept learning, holist learning strategies were shown to be superior to serialist on the application test (Rowland & Stuessy, 1987).

Implications of the Characteristics and Research

Implications which are drawn from research are noted with a •; those drawn logically from descriptive information regarding the trait are noted by an *. Based on a limited amount of research and the defining character-istics of serialist/holist learners, we conclude that holists are more likely to excel at learning tasks such as:

* summarizing

* conceptual overviews
* transfer tasks
* elaborations
* synthesizing many topics

and acquire and use effectively learning strategies such as:

* paraphrasing/summarizing
* comparing new knowledge with existing knowledge
* concept mapping/semantic networks
* inferring causes
* predicting outcomes

Based on a limited amount of background research and the defining characteristics of holist/serialist learners, we conclude that serialists are more likely to excel at learning tasks such as:

* recalling information
* paying attention to detail
* organizing knowledge
* procedural, sequential tasks

and acquire and use effectively learning strategies such as:

* searching for information
* validating sources or authenticity
* concentrating on information
* evaluating current information
* repeating material to be recalled
* analyzing key ideas
* outlining

Serialist/Holist and Instruction

Research

• Subjects whose holist/serialist orientation was matched to the appropriate mode of instruction scored significantly higher than those who were mismatched. A mismatched condition led to grossly inferior performance and a pronounced failure to comprehend the principles underlying the subject matter (Pask, 1976).

• Leps (1980), on the other hand, found no better learning effectiveness for undergraduates when holist learners were matched with nonlinear instructional materials than when they were matched with linear instruction.

- Tillema (1982) also found no significant interaction with matching learning strategies (web learning vs. linear presentation) and the holist/serialist learning styles of secondary students.

- The rate, quality, and durability of learning was found to be crucially dependent on whether or not the teaching strategy is suited to the individual (Ford, 1985).

- Rowland and Stuessy (1987) found that the development of conceptual relationships increased when holists were matched to CAI simulations and serialists were matched to CAI tutorials, as opposed to the mismatches of holists using tutorials and serialists using simulations.

- Further research revealed that achievement was significantly greater for serialist tutorial users who also fit the following style variables: field independence, external locus of control, high-discrimination skills, high analytic skill, and low-memory skills. Accordingly, these learners had difficulty learning from simulations, unless the simulation was more structured (Rowland & Stuessy, 1987).

Implications of the Characteristics and Research

Implications which are drawn from research are noted with a •; those drawn logically from descriptive information regarding the trait are noted by an *. Instructional conditions that capitalize on the preferences of the holist student and challenge the serialist student include:

- simulations
* asking the learner to relate to familiar content
* providing divergent examples
* asking learners to recall elaborations
* inferring from information
* creating story lines, narrative descriptions of information
* constructing pattern notes and graphic organizers
* using inductive sequence

Instructional conditions that remediate or compensate for the deficiencies of the holist student include:

* highlighting
* providing outlines
* presenting details in small chunks
* underlining relevant details

* analyzing key ideas
* providing analytical, detailed feedback
* embedding questions throughout the lesson

Instructional conditions that capitalize on the preferences of the serialist student and challenge the holist student include:

* providing outlines of content
* providing matched examples/non-examples
* asking the learner to select information sources
* asking the learner to monitor comprehension
* note taking
* analyzing key ideas
* categorizing elements
* providing analytic, detailed feedback
* overlearning
* using deductive sequence

Instructional conditions that remediate or compensate for the deficiencies of the serialist student would include:

* explaining relevance of content
* establishing context for content
* relating to content familiar to learner
* providing graphic organizers/overviews
* paraphrasing definitions
* using prototypical examples
* providing divergent examples
* providing elaborations
* providing enrichment feedback

References

Biggs, J. (1979). Individual differences in study processes and the quality of learning outcomes. *Higher Education, 8,* 381-394.

Entwistle, N. (1979). *Motivation, styles of learning and the academic environment.* Edinburgh, England: University of Edinburgh. (ERIC Document Rwproduction Service No. ED 190 636).

Entwistle, N. (1981). *Styles of Learning and Teaching.* New York: Wiley.

Ford, N. (1985). Learning styles and strategies of postgraduate students. *British Journal of Educational Technology,* 16(1), 65-77.

Leps, A. A. (1980, April). *Visual instructional strategies and cognitive style.* Paper presented at the annual conference of the Association for Educational Communications and Technology, Denver. (ERIC Document Reproduction Service No. ED 194 108)

Marton, F. (1976). What does it take to learn? Some implications on an alternative view of learning. In N. J. Entwistle (Ed.), *Strategies for Research and Development in Higher Education* (pp. 200-222). Amsterdam: Swets and Zeitlinger.

Pask, G. (1972). A fresh look at cognition and the individual. *International Journal of Man Machine Studies, 4,* 211-216.

Pask, G. (1973). CASTE: A system for exhibiting learning strategies and regulating uncertainties. *International Journal for Man-Machine Studies, 5,* 17-52.

Pask, G. (1975). *Conversation Cognition and Learning,* Amsterdam: Elsevier.

Pask, G. (1976). Styles and strategies of learning. *British Journal of Educational Psychology, 46,* 128-148.

Pask, G. (1984). Review of conversation theory and a protologic (or protolanguage), Lp. *Educational Communications and Technology Journal, 32*(1), 3-40.

Pask, G., & Scott, B. C. E. (1972). Learning strategies and individual competence. *International Journal of Man-Machine Studies, 24,* 205-229.

Rowland, P., & Stuessy, C. L. (1987, April). *Effects of modes of computer-assisted instruction on conceptual understanding and achievement of college students exhibiting individual differences in learning: A pilot study.* Paper presented at the annual meeting of the National Association for Research in Science Teaching, Washington, DC. (ERIC Document Reproduction Service No. ED 282 752)

Tillema, H. (1982). Sequencing of text material in relation to information-processing strategies. *British Journal of Educational Psychology, 32,* 170-178.

Bibliography

Daniel, J. S. (1975, February). Conversations, individuals and knowables, toward a theory of learning. *Engineering Education, 65*, 415-420.

Robertson, I. T. (1985). Human information-processing strategies and style. *Behavior and Information Technology, 4*(1), 19-29.

Rowland, P. (1988, April). *The effect of mode of CAI and individual learning differences on the understanding of concept relationships.* Paper presented at the annual meeting of the International Association for Computing in Education, New Orleans. (ERIC Document Reproduction Service No. ED 297 998)

18

CONCEPTUAL STYLE
(Analytical/Relational)

Description of Conceptual Style

Conceptual style is a measure of the categorizing strategy that individuals use to sort objects and form concepts. Two distinct strategies exist: analytical categorization and relational categorization (Ausburn & Ausburn, 1978). Initially, Kagan, Moss, and Sigel (1963) described a third, inferential category. An individual's style is determined by the degree of equivalence or conceptual differentiation of the categories.

Given a group of objects, individuals who use an analytic, conceptual strategy will focus on the components of these objects rather than on the objects themselves. They appear to have the perceptual ability to break the background and foreground apart, enabling them to see the details of the object rather than be distracted by the object as a whole. As a result, these individuals see more differences between objects and, therefore, create many categories with fewer items in each. They have a low range of equivalence and a high conceptual differentiation. At the elemental level, there may be just one attribute in common across objects such as "people with their left arm up." This conceptual style is regarded as the most sophisticated because individuals must actively search *within* the object rather than accepting the object as a whole. The analytic conceptual style has also been termed *descriptive/analytical* (Kagan et al., 1963; Kogan, 1971).

Individuals who use a relational conceptual style place objects into categories based on functional relationships between or among the objects. Relationals tend to use global, or thematic classifications, such as "hunters," rather than categorizing objects by singular aspects or details such as "people with hats." Perceptually, they seek basic attributes that make each object equivalent. They have a high range of equivalence and a low conceptual differentiation. They do not focus on distinguishing great numbers of differences between objects. As a result, they create few categories, each with many items. This style is regarded as least sophisticated because it involves passive acceptance of the object as a whole (Kagan et al., 1963). Other terms for the relational conceptual style are *nonanalytic* and *thematic*.

Characteristic Differences in Conceptual Style

Relational _____ Analytic

functional categorizer_____attribute categorizer
thematic/storylike_____objective/physical attributes
uses subordination_____uses superordination
uses perceptual cues (appearances)_____uses symbolic abstractions
convergent thinking_____divergent thinking
literal, stereotyped responses_____creative responses
few groups, many items_____many groups, few items
focus on differences_____focus on synthesis
low conceptual differentiation_____high conceptual differentiation
high equivalency_____low equivalency
less exploratory _____openly exploratory
less persistent with problem solving_____persistent with problem solving
anxious_____confident
developmentally less sophisticated___developmentally more sophisticated

Individual Differences Related to Conceptual Style

Field Dependence/Independence--This style describes the ability to disambiguate or separate relevant and irrelevant stimuli in an information field (see chapter 7). Analytic conceptual style is similar to field independence in respect to the individual's ability to differentiate small details in complex visual arrays (Denney, 1972). However, Kagan et al. (1963), in agreement with Witkin, contended that although both field independence and analytical conceptualizing belong to the same family, they actually measure different dimensions. Conceptual style is noted as a stylistic preference, whereas field dependence is a characteristic of one's perceptual capability (Kogan, 1971). Stanes and Gordon (1973) found no significant correlation for very young children.

Breadth of Categorization--This style is a measure of inclusiveness of conceptualization (see chapter 11). This characteristic relates to the equivalence range of conceptual style, with analytics being similar to broad conceptualizers, and relational styles related to narrow conceptualizers (Gardner & Schoen, 1962; Tajfel, Richardson, & Everstine, 1964).

Scanning/Focusing--This describes the differences in intensity and extensiveness of attention (see chapter 10). Pendleton (1972) found that although it may appear to the contrary because of the detailed nature of analytic conceptualization, these styles are equally employed by both analytic and relational styles.

Intelligence--Although the analytic conceptual style has been described as the more sophisticated of the two, Wallach and Kogan (1965), in their investigation of the correlation between conceptual style and IQ, found no significant relationship. In a later study, Roach (1979) found significant positive correlation between the analytic conceptual style and intelligence.

Leveling/Sharpening--This cognitive style describes the ability to make distinctions between types of information in memory (see chapter 16). Considering that analytic conceptualizers must attend to detail, whereas relational conceptualizers attend to themes, it is hypothesized that analytical conceptualizers may be sharpeners and relational conceptualizers, levelers.

Instruments for Measuring Conceptual Style

Kagan Conceptual Styles Test (KCST) (Kagan et al., 1963)

Kagan et al. (1963) developed this test to distinguish between analytic and relational categorizing styles. The test's first form was prepared for adults and consisted of 22 human figures. Subjects were asked to "select out groups of figures that [go] together on a common basis." The types of categories revealed three styles: analytic, relational, and inferential-categorical. A child's version was also developed that consisted of 30 triads (15 on each form of the test) of black-and-white drawings of familiar objects. The young subjects were asked to select the two that "were alike or went together in some way" (p. 82). Examples of the triads include "a donkey (side view) with one ear up and one ear down, a rabbit (front view) with two ears up, and a rabbit (side view) with one ear up and one ear down; rabbit with one eye, rabbit with a pair of glasses, and a boy with one eye." The sets are constructed to elicit two major classes of responses: analytic or relational. A version of the figure-sorting test that replaced the nude figures, or references to sexuality, with people with blank faces was also developed for children. Corrected odd-even reliabilities were reported to be .90 for relational, .91 for analytic, and .74 for inferential responses. After one year, girls showed test-retest reliability at .70, and .64, whereas boys' scores for analytic and relational resulted in .43, and .40.

Baird and Bee's Washington Conceptual Styles Test (WCST) (Baird & Bee, 1969)

Baird and Bee developed a longer version of the Kagan Conceptual Styles Test (Kagan, Moss & Sigel, 1963). They used the same format, administrative procedures, and analysis for scoring. The main difference was the inclusion of 26 CST-like items. Correlation between this test and the CST was .73, and an internal consistency for the WCST was reported at .83.

Adaptation of KCST (Denney, 1971)

Denney (1971) combined 9 items from the Kagan Conceptual Styles Test (Kagan et al., 1963), 22 items from Baird and Bee's Washington Conceptual Styles Test (Baird & Bee, 1969), plus 10 additional new items with the same format. The resulting test used 30 items to discriminate high, medium, and low analytics. Each were then divided into two equivalent forms. Subjects were asked to point to two of the three pictures that "were alike or went together in some way" (p. 148) and then explain their responses. Results yielded the number of analytic responses. Correlation between the two forms was .77. Test-retest reliability was .87 for Form A, and .89 for Form B (Denney, 1971).

Sigel Conceptual Style Test (Sigel, Jarman, & Hanesian, 1967)

This instrument was developed as a simpler version of the Kagan Conceptual Styles Test (Kagan et al., 1963) to administer to children at age 4. In this version, children were given one picture and asked to "select one of the others that 'is like or goes with' the fourth item," and explain their responses. There are 20 sets of four common pictures of humans, animals, or objects. Some examples of the sets include: *smiling nurse*--neutral nurse, smiling stewardess, frowning stewardess; *ranch*--stagecoach, horse, cowboy. Three scores are calculated to reflect "descriptive/analytic, relational-contextual, or categorical-inferential" styles (p. 6). No reliability or validity data were reported.

Theoretical Background

Differences between individuals' categorizing styles were originally noted by Gardner in 1953. He developed the term *equivalence range*, the inclination of individuals to create many or few categories. Those individuals who created many categories had low equivalence, whereas those who created few categories had high equivalence. Gardner and Schoen (1962) captured another quality of the categories, and retermed equivalence to *conceptual differentiation*. This term qualifies groupings by their similarities and differences--the more categories, the more differences noted, and the higher the conceptual differentiation. This definition crossed with broad and narrow conceptualization, although there were no direct correlations. It was speculated, therefore, that conceptual differentiation consisted of two phases of mental activity--that of creating categories, then classifying objects--whereas broad and narrow conceptualization only consisted of doing the second. When simply classifying objects, several objects can remain as ungrouped, single items within no other category. They found this result with the conceptual styles tests.

Low conceptual differentiation also posed some problems to researchers who attempted to explain its underlying thinking processes. Two conflicting explanations for the groupings developed. Individuals simply failed to differentiate, or they made use of a very systematic differentiation scheme. Kagan, Moss, and Sigel (1960) then offered a three-dimensional scheme to distinguish between classes of categorizers: descriptive, categorical-inferential, and relational. The descriptive group categorizes based on "some objective, physical attribute that is abstracted from the object as a whole," categorical-inferentials "reflect groupings that treat the objects as whole entities, each object representing an independent instance of the conceptual label," and relationals categorize according to "temporal functional relationships" between and among the objects (Kogan, 1971, p. 262). Categorical-inferential was later dropped, leaving the style two-dimensional. The descriptive term became *analytic-descriptive*, and finally, just *analytic*. Gardner and Schoen (1962) and Glixman (1965) found that this style for grouping generalized over several domains.

Other researchers, such as Denney (1974), found that the style was more complicated than was represented in the two classifications and divided subjects' responses into more subtle categories. Denney's six categories included: perceptual similarity (objects look alike, as tall, white), functional similarity (both objects hold liquid), unusual similarity (parachute and umbrella), complementary (horse pulls wagon), unusual complementary (rabbit wears glasses), and story or fantasy (fireplace and present, present opened by fireplace).

Conceptual Style and Learning

Research

- Boys employed a descriptive-analytic style more frequently than girls, which pointed to the superior analytic functioning of boys (Kagan et al., 1963; Wallach & Kogan, 1965; Witkin, Dyk, Faterson, Goodenough, & Karp, 1962).

- Analytic children were found to have a greater tendency to differentiate visual arrays and to reflect upon alternative solutions. Relational children approached problems in a more global and impulsive fashion (Kagan et al., 1963).

- Analytic children were more impulsive than relational children, contradicting the study by Kagan et al. (1963) (Denney, 1971).

- Denney (1971) found that analytic subjects demonstrated an ability to shift to relational responses when analytic choices were unavailable.

Relational subjects did not show a parallel shift to analytic responses
when their preferred relational responses were exhausted.

- A linear developmental trend from relational to analytic conceptual
  styles was found in children ages 6 to 12 (Denney, 1971; Kagan, Rosman,
  Day, Albert, & Phillips, 1964; Sigel, 1965).

- Students with a high-science orientation were characterized by a high
  preference for analytic/descriptive concepts (Field, 1972).

- Attentional style measures distinguished poor and good readers better
  than did conceptual style preferences (Denney, 1974).

- College students tended to use more categorical/analytic responses than
  did elderly adults. Elderly adults tended to use more
  relational/thematic responses than did college students (Kogan, 1974).

- The complementary responses of older adults were no more creative
  than were the complementary responses of young children (Denney,
  1974).

- Roach (1979) found that sixth-grade children had a significant positive
  correlation between the analytic conceptual style and both mathematics
  achievement and intelligence.

- Age differences in classification were more a result of differences in preference than of differences in ability (Baird & Bee, 1969; Denney, 1972;
  Denney & Acito, 1974; Kagan et al., 1964; Smiley & Brown, 1979).

- Elderly adults reverted to using more complementary criteria in classification than did younger adults (Annett, 1959; Circirelli, 1976; Denney,
  1974; Denney & Lennon, 1972; Riegel & Riegel, 1964; Smiley & Brown,
  1979).

Implications of the Characteristics and Research

Implications which are drawn from research are noted with a •; those
drawn logically from descriptive information regarding the trait are noted
by an *. Based on the research and the descriptions of conceptual style, we
conclude that *analytical* conceptualizers are more likely to excel at learning
tasks such as:

- * mathematical concept tasks
- • reflective problem solving
- • differentiating visual arrays

• science tasks
* recalling the components of a list

and acquire and use effectively learning strategies such as:

• discrimination
* evaluation
* concentration
* synthesis
* outlining
* analysis

Based on the research and the descriptions of conceptual style, we conclude that *relational* conceptualizers are more likely to excel at learning tasks such as:

• global problem solving
* telling stories
* selecting main ideas

and acquire and use effectively learning strategies such as:

* generating metaphors
* generating analogies
* illustrating or imaging
* creating examples

Conceptual Style and Instruction

Research

• Children who were instructed to delay their responses not only had longer response latencies but also produced more analytic conceptual responses than did children instructed to hasten their responses (Kagan et al., 1964).

• Conceptual styles, either analytic or relational, were altered through the use of reinforcement. Lasting changes in the direction of the developmentally more sophisticated analytic conceptual style appeared to be easier to produce (Baird & Bee, 1969; Ostfeld & Neimark, 1967).

• No relationship was found between latency of responses and the frequency of analytic responses (Denney, 1972).

- When conceptual style was modeled for the subjects and then tested on unrelated tasks, relational models produced more absolute change on an immediate posttest, whereas analytic models produced more permanent change as revealed through a delayed follow-up test (Denney, 1972).

- Onyejiaku (1982) investigated the interaction of discovery versus expository mathematics instruction with conceptual style. No significant effect for teaching method was found.

Implications of the Characteristics and Research

Implications which are drawn from research are noted with a •; those drawn logically from descriptive information regarding the trait are noted by an *. Instructional conditions that capitalize on the preferences of the relational student and challenge the analytic student include:

* establishing context for content
* providing graphic organizers/overviews
* asking learners to recall elaborations
* using summaries
* presenting principles
* using story lines
* applying practice to a real-world situation

      Instructional conditions that remediate or compensate for the deficiencies of the relational student include:

* presenting attributes of rule definition, concepts
* modeling analytical categorization
* providing graphic cues
* creating a content outline
* sequencing instruction according to a story structure
* giving analytical feedback
* providing embedded questions throughout instruction

      Instructional conditions that capitalize on the preferences of the analytic student and challenge the relational student include:

* asking learners to select their own goals
* presenting attributes of rule definition, concepts
* asking learners to create divergent examples
* asking learners to analyze key ideas
* categorizing activities

Instructional conditions that remediate or compensate for the deficiencies of the analytic student include:
* establishing context for content
* showing maps, globes, pictures, tables
* providing graphic organizers/overviews
* providing summaries
* providing paraphrased content
* providing incidental information, with an explanation of relevance
* providing narrative sequences

References

Annett, M. (1959). The classification of instances of four common class concepts by children and adults. *British Journal of Educational Psychology, 59*, (29), 223-226.

Ausburn, L., & Ausburn F. (1978). Cognitive styles: Some information and implications for instructional design. *Educational Communications and Technology Journal, 26*(4), 337-354.

Baird, R., & Bee, H. (1969). Modification of conceptual style preference by differential reinforcement. *Child Development, 40*, 903-910.

Cicirelli, V. G. (1976). Categorization behavior in aging subjects. *Journal of Gerontology, 31*, 676-680.

Denney, D. (1971). The assessment of difference in conceptual style. *Child Study Journal, 1*, 142-155.

Denney, D. (1972). Modeling effects upon conceptual style and cognitive tempo. *Child Development, 43*, 105-119.

Denney, D. (1974). Relationship of three cognitive style dimensions to elementary reading abilities. *Journal of Educational Psychology, 66*(5), 702-709.

Denney, N., & Acito, M. (1974). Classification training in two- and three-year-old children. *Journal of Experimental Child Psychology, 17*, 37-48.

Denney, N., & Lennon, M. (1972). A comparison of middle and old age. *Developmental Psychology, 7*, 210-213.

Field, T. (1972). Cognitive style in science. *Australian Science Teachers Journal, 18*(1), 27-35.

Gardner, R. W. (1953). Cognitive styles in categorizing behavior. *Journal of Personality, 22*, 214-233.

Gardner, R. W., & Schoen, R. A. (1962). Differentiation and abstraction in concept formation. *Psychological Monographs. 76* (41, Whole No. 560).

Glixman, A. F. (1965). Categorizing behavior as a function of meaning domain. *Journal of Personality and Social Psychology, 2*, 370-377.

Kagan, J., Moss, H. A., & Sigel, I. E. (1960). Conceptual style and the use of affect labels. *Merrill-Palmer Quarterly. 6*, 261-278.

Kagan, J., Moss, H. A., & Sigel, I. E. (1963). Psychological significance of styles of conceptualization. In J. C. Wright and J. Kagan (Eds.), *Basic Cognitive Processes in Children* (pp. 73-124). *Monographs of the Society for Research in Child Development.* 28, 2.

Kagan, J., Rosman, R., Day, D., Albert, J., & Phillips, W. (1964). Information processing in the child: Significance of analytic and reflective attitudes. *Psychology Monographs, 78,* 1-36.

Kogan, N. (1971). Educational Implications of cognitive styles. In G. S. Lesser (Ed.), *Psychology and Educational Practice* (pp. 242-292). Glenview, IL: Scott Foresman.

Kogan, N. (1974). Categorizing and conceptualizing styles in younger and older adults. *Human Development, 17,* 218-230.

Onyejiaku, F. O. (1982). Cognitive styles, instructional strategies, and academic performance. *Journal of Experimental Education.* 51(1), 31-37.

Ostfeld, B. M., & Neimark, E. D. (1967). Effect of response-time restrictions upon cognitive style scores. *Proceedings of the 75th Annual Convention of the American Psychological Association,* 169-170.

Pendelton, J. (1972). *Mathematical concept attainment of sixth grade students in relation to their cognitive styles.* Unpublished doctoral dissertation, The University of Texas at Austin.

Riegel, K., & Riegel, R. (1964). Changes in associative behavior during later years of life: A cross-sectional analysis. *Vita Humana, 7,* 1-32.

Roach, D. A. (1979). The effects of conceptual style preference, related cognitive variables and sex on achievement in mathematics. *British Journal of Educational Psychology, 49*(1), 79-82.

Sigel, I. (1965, March). *Styles of categorization in elementary school children: The role of sex differences and anxiety level.* Paper presented at the meeting of the Society for Research in Child Development, Minneapolis.

Sigel, I. E., Jarman, P., & Hanesian, H. (1967). Styles of categorization and their intellectual and personality correlates in young children. *Human Development, 10,* 30-61.

Smiley, S. S., & Brown, A. L. (1979). Conceptual preference for thematic or taxonomic relations: A nonmontonic age trend from preschool to old age. *Journal of Experimental Child Psychology, 28,* 249-257.

Stanes, D., & Gordon, A. (1973). Relationships between Conceptual Styles Test and children's Embedded Figures Test. *Journal of Personality, 41*(2), 185-191.

Tajfel, H., Richardson, A., & Everstine, I. (1964). Individual consistencies in categorizing: A study of judgmental behavior. *Journal of Personality, 32,* 90-108.

Wallach, M. A., & Kogan, N. (1965). *Modes of Thinking in Young Children.* New York: Holt, Rinehart & Winston.

Witkin, H., Dyk, R., Faterson, H., Goodenough, D., & Karp, S. (1962). *Psychological Differentiation.* New York: Wiley.

Bibliography

Denney, D. (1970). *The effect of style and tempo of an adult model upon conceptualization in young children.* Unpublished doctoral dissertation, University of Washington.

Denney, N. (1974a). Evidence for developmental changes in categorization criteria for children and adults. *Human Development, 17,* 41-53.

Denney, N. (1974b). Classification abilities in the elderly. *Journal of Gerontology, 29,* 309-314.

Denney, N. (1974c). Classification criteria in middle and old age. *Developmental Psychology, 10,* 901-906.

Flavall, J. (1970). Cognitive changes in adulthood. In L. R. Goulet & P. B Baltes (Eds.), *Life-Span developmental psychology: Theory and research* (pp. 247-253). New York: Academic.

Frayer, D. A. (1973). *Implications of the model for instructional design.* Paper presented at the annual meeting of the American Psychological Association Montreal, Quebec.

Kagan, J. (1966). Reflection-impulsivity: The generality and dynamics of conceptual tempo. *Journal of Abnormal Psychology, 71,* 17-24.

PART V

LEARNING STYLES

Introduction

Most cognitive controls (see Part III) and, to a lesser extent, cognitive styles (see Part IV) define processing characteristics that are based on task-relevant measures, that is, tests that measure the actual skill or tendency. An outgrowth of the interest in cognitive styles has been the evolution of learning styles, which are general tendencies to prefer to process information in different ways. A number of educators began in the 1960s and 1970s to develop instruments to measure these learner preferences. Learning styles, in effect, are applied cognitive styles, removed one more level from pure processing ability. As evidence of this removal, all of the learning styles reported in this part of the book are based on self-reported learner preferences. That is, the tests ask individual learners about their preferences for, and perceptions of, how they process information. They do not test the actual ability, skill, or processing tendency as do cognitive controls and some cognitive styles. They are less specific than cognitive styles, which are less specific than cognitive controls and abilities.

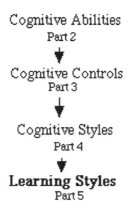

Cognitive Abilities
Part 2

Cognitive Controls
Part 3

Cognitive Styles
Part 4

Learning Styles
Part 5

The validity of learning styles as a construct is based on the assumption that learners' cognitive styles are accurately reflected in their own perceptions. This assumes that learners are aware of how they process information and have developed some internally consistent constructs of themselves as learners. Because learning styles are based on self-report measures, rather than ability tests, validity is one of their most significant problems. There is nothing to prevent learners from answering learning style questions felicitously or according to some construct that implies how they believe that others want them to answer. Self-report data are always suspect in many psychometric circles. However, the learning styles theories and instruments reported in this part of the book (we have not attempted to report all learning style constructs in this book) are based on relevant pedagogical and psychological theory, and their instruments have been validated using tests of cognitive ability and styles as benchmarks. There is some inherent validity in these learning styles.

Probably the primary use of learning styles is as a metaphor for thinking about individual differences. We have used these instruments many times with learners of all ages as introductions to the domain of individual differences. Because they use self-report instruments, they tend to be nonthreatening to learners. They are typically short (except for Hill's) and easy to complete. Invariably, they engage learners in self-reflection, making them more aware of themselves as learners and more aware of some of the complexities of the learning process. Although learning styles may not be legitimate research tools (although that is arguable), they are useful methods for eliciting self-reflection and an understanding of the learning process and the role of individual differences in it.

19

Hill's Cognitive Style Mapping

Description of the Cognitive Style Mapping

Cognitive style mapping (CSM), a diagnostic technique for determining an individual's cognitive styles, was developed by Joseph E. Hill, President of Oakland Community College in Bloomfield Hills, Michigan, during the 1960s and 1970s. The term *cognitive style*, according to Hill, refers to the way students receive and process information to derive meaning from their environment and personal experience. Cognitive styles depend on family background, talent, personal goals, and experiences. These factors contribute to each individual's preferred ways of perceiving, organizing, and retaining information.

The purpose for mapping students' cognitive styles was to identify each person's distinct cognitive style and to prescribe a personalized educational program for optimal learning. Hill believed "that 90% of the students with normal ability can learn 90% of the material 90% of the time if the teaching methods and media are adjusted to the student's educational cognitive style" (Hill, 1976, p. 3). Hill developed an extensive program of CSM using a self-report inventory to produce an individual's cognitive style map, which is the product of the dimensions and variables described next.

Characteristic Differences in the Cognitive Style Mapping

Educational cognitive style is the Cartesian product of four sets of variables:

Cognitive = Style	Symbols and their Meanings	X	Cultural Determinants	X	Modalities of Inference	X	Educational Memory

These four dimensions interact to form an individual's cognitive style. Symbols and their meanings refer to individuals' preferences for using different types of symbols.

Theoretical Symbols

Theoretical symbols are those that learners use to encode and interpret information. Learners may prefer visual or auditory, quantitative or linguistic symbols. That is, learners may prefer to interpret quantitative or verbal symbols through written or spoken communications. These types of encoding include:

- *Theoretical Auditory Linguistic T(AL)*--The individual uses the spoken word to find meaning, comprehends through listening.

- *Theoretical Auditory Quantitative T(AQ)*--The individual uses spoken numbers or quantitative symbols to find meaning, listens for patterns.

- *Theoretical Visual Linguistic T(VL)*--The individual uses the written word to find meaning, comprehends through reading.

- *Theoretical Visual Quantitative T(VQ)*--The individual uses written numbers, symbols, and measurement to find meaning, processes through visual patterns.

Qualitative Symbols

Symbol preferences may also be qualitative, referring to preferences for different types of symbols during learning. These symbolic preferences are of three types: sensory-related qualitative codes, programmatic qualitative codes, and cultural qualitative codes.

Sensory-related Qualitative Codes

These codes relate to preferences for interacting with information that stimulates the five senses.

- *Qualitative Auditory (QA)*--The individual perceives meaning through hearing and distinguishing sounds.
- *Qualitative Visual (QV)*--The individual perceives meaning through sight.
- *Qualitative Olfactory (QO)*--The individual perceives meaning through smell.
- *Qualitative Tactile (QT)*--The individual perceives meaning through touch.
- *Qualitative Savory (QS)*--The individual perceives meaning through taste.

Programmatic Qualitative Codes

These codes refer to programmatic effects or objects. These effects or impressions are more automatic; that is, they create a definite set of images or operations.

- *Qualitative Proprioceptive (QP)*--This denotes the ability to perform complex actions using fine and gross muscle systems and muscular coordination. Fine motor coordination is required for typing, playing a musical instrument, or assembling a circuit board. Gross motor coordination is required for sports. There are several types of proprioceptive symbols, although they are not distinguished or measured by the inventory.

Cultural Qualitative Codes

These refer to the roles and games that we play with others.

- *Qualitative Empathetic (QCEM)*--This represents sensitivity to the feelings of others, identifying with others' perspectives.
- *Qualitative Esthetic (QCES)*--This represents seeing and enjoying beauty in objects or ideas.
- *Qualitative Ethic (QCET)*--This represents holding and committing to a set of values, principles, duties, or obligations.
- *Qualitative Histrionic (QCH)*--This represents deliberately playing a role to affect others.
- *Qualitative Kinesic (QCK)*--This represents understanding gestures, motions, and other non-verbal communications.
- *Qualitative Kinesthetic (QCKH)*--This represents the use of motor skills and muscular coordinations according to an accepted form.
- *Qualitative Proxemics (QCP)*--This represents the ability to judge social distances.
- *Qualitative Synnoetics (QCS)*--This represents a personal knowledge of self.
- *Qualitative Transactional (QCT)*--This represents interacting easily with others, maintaining positive communication to affect others' behavior.
- *Qualitative Temporal (QCTM)*--This represents punctuality setting and obeying time limits.

Cultural Determinants

Cultural determinants refer to the influences that affect the types of symbolic codes that a student uses. That is, students have been influenced by themselves or others in the ways that they behave. Cultural determinants describe the primary effects of the student.

- *Individual (I)*--The student is self-influenced and relies more frequently on his or her own judgments.
- *Family (F)*--The student seeks advice and counsel from his or her family. The student also interprets and understands in ways that his or her family would interpret.
- *Associate (A)*--The student seeks advice from associates and peers, and interprets and explains the world in ways that his or her associates would use.

Modalities of Inference

Modalities of inference refer to the learner's reasoning and inferencing patterns or styles. Having obtained information through various symbol systems, which are influenced by others, individuals must then reason with that information. These modalities describe the forms of inference that individuals use.

- *Magnitude (M)*--The learner uses categorical reasoning, classifies ideas in order to accept or reject them, and defines things to understand them.
- *Difference (D)*--The learner compares and contrasts ideas based on selected characteristics.
- *Relationship (R)*--The learner considers the relationship between characteristics, identifies underlying dimensions and rearranges to form meaning, and analyzes situations to understand parts.
- *Appraisal (L)*--The learner uses all three of these modalities without apparent preference.
- *Deductive (K)*--The learner uses deductive reasoning, forms hypotheses and seeks logical proof, that is, uses general to specific reasoning.

Educational Memory

The ways in which individuals encode information into memory affect the ways that they retrieve the information. Memory processing is an important determinant of how individuals learn. Memory, according to Hill, is affected by memory functions, the components that are being memorized, and the conditions that affect memory. Those conditions include assimilation, accommodation, attendance, and repression. Unfortunately, Hill died before he was able to implement educational memory into CSM.

Individual Differences Related to Cognitive Style Mapping

Hill's Cognitive Style Map is a comprehensive approach to identifying an individual's learning preferences and it attempts to encompass all other cognitive styles and controls into its design. Typically, the other learning styles and characteristics mentioned in the literature concerning Cognitive Style Mapping are used for comparison purposes.

Claxton and Ralston (1978) compared each of Hill's element sets with other characteristics and personality styles:

Field dependence/independence--This describes the how much a learner's perception or comprehension of information is affected by the surrounding perceptual or contextual field. The "Cultural Determinants" set contained aspects relating to the test for this cognitive control (see Chapter 7).

Myers-Briggs Type Indicator--Based on a Jungian personality typology, the Myers-Briggs defines personality type in a way that is similar to the first set, Symbols and Their Meaning.

Perceptive/Receptive--The inclination to assimilate data into concepts or precepts previously held (perceptivity) versus the tendency to take in data in raw form (receptivity) is similar to the Modalities of Inference set (Claxton & Ralston, 1978).

Instruments for Cognitive Style Mapping

Cognitive Style Interest Inventory (Valler & Springhorn, 1978)

Cognitive Style Interest Inventory is Joseph Hill's instrument for the evaluation of an individual's learning preferences. It contains 224 items, eight forced-choice items for each of his 28 variables, presented in a random order. For example: "I would give up an immediate objective rather than sacrifice a principle; I can recognize who is on the phone just by listening to the voice for a few minutes; I understand a lecturer better if I can look at him as he talks." Individuals respond to each statement by deciding whether it describes them "usually, sometimes, or rarely." Each response is weighted (Usually = 5, Sometimes = 3, Rarely = 1), and the scores for each variable are tallied and summed with a minimum score of 8 and a maximum of 40. The higher the score, the more important is that orientation. A major orientation, according to Hill, is any score greater than 28. A minor orientation is indicated by a score of 20-28. The cognitive style map is formed by listing the major and minor orientations in a set of map brackets. The map below is an example of an individualistic categorical type who reads alone frequently. The uppercase letters represent a major orientation for the trait, while the lowercase letters represent a minor orientation.

$$\left\{ \begin{array}{c} T(VL) \\ q(v) \\ Q(ES) \end{array} \right\} \quad X \quad \left\{ \begin{array}{c} I \end{array} \right\} \quad X \quad \left\{ \begin{array}{c} M \end{array} \right\}$$

The Albany Instrument (Fourier, 1983)

The Center for Curriculum and Instruction at the State University of New York at Albany researched and modified the Cognitive Style Interest Inventory instrument. The Albany Instrument is a forced-choice questionnaire, using the same three responses per item as in Hill's inventory and consisting of 125 items with 25 subscales. The data from each questionnaire are entered and scored by a computer, resulting in a computer-generated cognitive style map.

Theoretical Background

In 1976, Dr. Joseph Hill published *The Educational Sciences* at Oakland Community College. This paper was the conceptual foundation for CSM. Hill believed that education is an applied science, and so it ought to have its scientific language, just as other derivative sciences, like law, medicine, and engineering. The language that applies to the field of education is based on four assumptions: (a) education is the process of searching for meaning; thought is different from language, (b) the human creature is a social one with a unique capacity for deriving meaning from the environment and personal experience through the creation and use of symbols, and (c) being discontent with biological satisfaction alone, humankind continually seeks meaning.

The educational sciences, according to Hill, include four variables and the products of their interactions. *Symbols and their meanings* refer to the symbols that individuals use in the perception of information. *Cultural determinants* of the meaning of symbols describe the individual's social perception as a means for interpreting and evaluating previously gathered information. *Modalities of inference* refer to the learner's preferred style of reasoning. *Educational memory* involves a combination of memory function, components, and conditions. These four variables interact to shape educational cognitive style. This cartesian product of the four sets provides a picture or profile of how the individual employs those variables in the search for meaning.

Hill felt that counseling styles and decision making contributed to the educational sciences as well. The Cartesian product of the demeanor, emphasis, and symbolic modes of presenting information and communicating with the learner denotes teaching styles, administrative styles, and counseling styles. Teachers have one of three demeanors: predominant, adjustive, or flexible. Administrators can be dominant, adjustive, cooperative, or passive custodial. Counselors may be directive, situational, or nondirective. Decision making about which teaching, administration and counseling styles to use with different students is based on a systemic analysis of these variables. Hill described a five-step process that consists of stating a mission, setting design criteria, setting performance goals, identifying inputs and outputs, and measuring outputs to feed back to inputs. This process was never fully implemented in the model.

Cognitive Style Mapping and Learning

Research

Numerous studies, especially dissertation research studies, were conducted in the 1970s and early 1980s on CSM. Much of this research suffered methodological problems, so little can be inferred from it.

- CSM can be used to select leaders (Sigren, 1973). The most effective leaders have more qualitative symbolic orientations, are more influenced by family, and use difference and appraisal modalities of inference.

- Ogden and Brewster (1977) found the following unique elements with major orientation in the composite cognitive style map for successful secondary science students: Qualitative Auditory (Q[A]), Qualitative Code Aesthetic (Q[CES]), Qualitative Code Ethic (Q[CET]), Family (F), and Appraisal (L). However, the unsuccessful secondary science students had in their composite cognitive style map minor orientation for the following elements: Theoretical Auditory Quantitative (T[AQ]), Theoretical Visual Linguistics (T[VL]), and Deductive (K).

- Subjects with four major modalities achieved higher standardized spelling scores (Schwendinger, 1976).

- When the cognitive styles of the teacher and the student matched, the student received higher grades (Boozer & Anderson, 1977).

- A major study did not find relationships between cognitive style measures and educational outcomes (American College Testing Program, 1977).

- Sixth graders in a multicultural setting in Hawaii demonstrated different cognitive styles because of their dominant family culture (Harvey, 1981).

- Fourier (1983) found that disclosing cognitive style map information to students resulted in increased academic achievement.

- Pittman (1983) found that the failure-withdrawal rate of the matched groups was significantly different from the nonmatched, and the more elements present on a student's cognitive map predicted a greater chance of success in nursing education.

• The strongest predictors of high versus low achievers were family influence and deductive reasoning variables from Hill's CSM test (Wiggin, 1985).

• Eight studies revealed that when youngsters were taught with instructional resources that matched their preferred modalities, they achieved statistically higher test scores (Dunn, 1988). When children were taught with multisensory resources, initially through their most preferred modality and then reinforced through their secondary or tertiary modality, their scores increased even more (Dunn, Beaudry, & Klavas, 1989).

Implications of the Characteristics and Research

Based on the limited research and the description of *CSM*, we conclude that achievement in different subjects can be marginally predicted by CSM. The relationships, however, are not strong or consistent. Among the CSM variables, it appears that the modalities of inference, rather than symbols or cultural determinants, are probably the most predictive of learning:

Implications which are drawn from research are noted with a •; those drawn logically from descriptive information regarding the trait are noted by an *. Learners with a major orientation in Magnitude (M) modality are more likely to excel at learning tasks such as:

* classifying concepts
* generating and organizing lists
* using rules as standards
* describing criteria for standard performance

and acquire and use effectively learning strategies such as:

* preparing environment
* analyzing key ideas
* recalling data by identification of location (loci method)

Learners with a major orientation in Difference (D) modality are more likely to excel at learning tasks such as:

* classifying by characteristic differences
* perceiving different points of view

and acquire and use effectively learning strategies such as:

* repeating and rehearsing material to be recalled
* matching example/nonexample pairs

* comparing new information with existing knowledge

Learners with a major orientation in Relationship (R) modality are more likely to excel at learning tasks such as:

* generating and evaluating examples and nonexamples
* analyzing the whole to discover the parts
* asking "Why" while learning to evaluate meaningfulness

and acquire and use effectively learning strategies, such as:

* generating metaphors and analogies
* predicting outcomes/inferring causes
* evaluating implications

Learners with a major orientation in Appraisal (L) modality are more likely to excel at learning tasks such as:

* problem-solving tasks
* executive control, leadership tasks

and acquire and use effectively learning strategies such as:

* setting learning goals
* estimating difficulty, time, and effort to complete learning
* judging utility or value of knowledge

Learners with a major orientation in Deductive (K) modality are more likely to excel at learning tasks such as:

* determining rules and rule bases for making decisions
* using logic to solve problems

and acquire and use effectively learning strategies such as:

* generating analogies

Cognitive Style Mapping and Instruction

Research

- Students who learned better from an audio-tutorial approach were high in visual quantitative, whereas those who benefited least were high in visual linguistic and histrionic (Hauser, 1975). Those who learned best from print, self-instructional materials were high in synnoetics and the difference and appraisal modalities of inference.

- Text materials worked well for individuals with a major orientation toward Theoretical Visual Linguistic (T[VL]) and Qualitative Code Ethic (QCE). Individuals with a strong affiliation to Qualitative Auditory (QA) preferred traditional lectures and audiotape material (Claxton & Ralston, 1978).

- Cafferty (1980) found that the greater the degree of the match between students' and teachers' cognitive style maps, the higher were the students' grades. Matching based upon symbolic orientations, cultural determinants, and modalities of inference produced the highest grades.

- The use of a simulation-gaming method to teach an economics survey course was superior over the lecture-discussion method for students that had a major orientation toward the following subtraits: Theoretical Auditory Linguists (T[AL]), Theoretical Auditory Quantitative (T[(AQ]), Qualitative Code Empathetic (Q[CEM]) and Associates (A). The traditional lecture-discussion method was more effective for students who had a major orientation for the following subtraits: Theoretical Visual Linguistics (T[VL]), Theoretical Visual Quantitative (T[VQ]), and Individuality (I) (Rafeld & Fraas, 1980).

- Students high in theoretical visual quantitative and qualitative code ethics (obligation), and low in qualitative visual were more likely to complete a telecourse (Rice, 1984).

Implications of the Characteristics and Research

There have been too few aptitude treatment interaction studies using CSM as the aptitude variable, probably because there are 28 variables. However, adaptive instruction was the primary purpose of CSM. Hill's (1976) purpose for developing the Educational Sciences was to personalize the educational programs of individuals. He saw this as a multistage process, beginning with diagnostic testing and the production of a cognitive style map. After an individual's cognitive preferences have been mapped, a personalized educational program can be developed using instructional strategies to capitalize on those preferences. Hill referred to these instructional modes as *burst* activities. Following an initial presentation of concepts, students would burst to prescription centers, including:

- *Individualized Program Learning Laboratory (IPLL)*--This contains programmed instruction texts, slide and tape shows, films, models, and programmed reading machines. Newer technologies might include CBT tutorials, interactive video, and videotapes. All of these instructional tools would encourage self-discovery. They are designed for students who prefer to work alone and in a structured environment (e. g., I--Individual, M--Magnitude).

- *Carrel Arcades (CA)*--These would contain videotapes, films, audiotapes, slide tapes, paraprofessionals, tutors, tests, and small group discussions. These activities would be assigned to those learners who prefer to see, hear, and interact (e. g., T[AL] Theoretical Auditory Linguistic, T[AQ]--Theoretical Auditory Quatitative, QV--Visual, and Q[EM]--Empathetic).

- *Youth-Tutor-Youth (YTY)*--This entails cooperative learning in small groups or students tutoring other students. This activity was designed for students who work well in a group (e. g., A--Associates, QCT--Transactional).

- *Seminars (SEM)*--These would include facilitated discussions by faculty members with small groups of students. This activity was designed for students who relate well to an authority figure and are more verbal (e. g., F--Family, T[AL]--Theoretical Auditory Linguistic, T[AQ]--Theoretical Auditory Quantitative).

- *Learning Resources Center (LRC)*--This is a center in the college library, which contains books, periodicals, microfilms, and research materials. This activity is designed for students who prefer to work independently and with textual materials (e. g., I--Individual, T[VL]--Theoretical Visual Linguistic, T[VQ]--Theoretical Visual Quantitative).

Following the personalized education program, learners would be tested on the first ideas and move onto the next. Because of the large number of aptitude, treatment, and outcome variables, quality research focusing on the effectiveness of burst activities has never been done. Research with limited matching, however, especially teacher maps with student maps, has shown a strong potential relationship.

References

American College Testing Program. (1977). *Promoting student learning in college by adapting to individual differences in educational cognitive style.* Final Report. (ERIC Document Reproduction Service No. ED 158 699)

Boozer, B., & Anderson, A. (1977). *Cognitive style mapping: a prescription for accountability.* Final Report. (ERIC Document Reproduction Service No. ED 182 402)

Cafferty, E. L. (1980). An analysis of student performance based on the degree of match between the educational cognitive style of the teacher and the educational cognitive style of the students (Doctoral dissertation, University of Nebraska). *Dissertation Abstracts International, 41,* 2908.

Claxton, C. S., & Ralston, Y. (1978). *Learning styles: Their impact on teaching and administration* (Report No. 10). AAHE-ERIC/Higher Education Research. (ERIC Document Reproduction Service No. ED 167 065)

Dunn, R. (1988). *Learning styles, quiet revolution in American secondary schools.* Reston, VA: National Association of Secondary School Principals.

Dunn, R., Beaudry, J. S., & Klavas, A. (1989, March). Survey of research on learning styles. *Educational Leadership, 46,* 50-58.

Fourier, M. J. (1983). Disclosure of cognitive style information: Effects on achievement of adult learners. *Adult Education Quarterly, 34* (3), 147-154.

Harvey, T. E. (1981). *An investigation of cross-cultural cognitive styles among traditional and assimilated communities of Polynesians and Asian-Americans: A pilot study.* Paper presented at the annual convention of the National Association for Asian and Pacific American Education. (ERIC Document Reproduction Service No. ED 206 785)

Hauser, E. J. (1975). An analysis of learning an environmental education concept from an audio-tutorial method and a print self-instructional package based on the educational science of cognitive style (Doctoral dissertation, Kent State University). *Dissertation Abstracts International, 36,* 4381.

Hill, J. E. (1976). *The educational sciences.* Bloomfield Hills, MI: Oakland Community College Press.

Ogden, W. R., & Brewster, P. M. (1977). *An analysis of cognitive style profiles and related science achievement among secondary school students.* Paper presented at the annual meeting of the National Association for Research in Science Teaching. (ERIC Document Reproduction Service No. ED 139 610)

Pittman, M. (1983). *Teaching/learning styles and preferences: relevance and relatedness to health occupations education.* Paper presented at the Annual American Vocational Association Convention. (ERIC Document Reproduction Service No. ED 237 664).

Rafeld, F. J., & Fraas, J. W. (1980). *The use of a cognitive mapping test to analyze the effectiveness of a college economics survey course.* Paper presented at annual meeting of the Eastern Economics Association. (ERIC Document Reproduction Service No. ED 184 936)

Rice, M. A. (1984). Relationship of cognitive style maps to achievement and completion of educational telecourses in community colleges (Doctoral dissertation, Texas Women's University). *Dissertation Abstracts International, 45,* 3517.

Schwendinger, J. R. (1976). A study of modality of inferences and their relationship to spelling achievement of sixth-grade students. Iowa City, University of Iowa. (ERIC Document Reproduction Service No. ED 141 807)

Sigren, V. G. (1973). An exploratory study employing the educational science of cognitive style as a predictor of group leadership within an orientation program (Doctoral dissertation, Michigan State University). *Dissertation Abstracts International, 34,* 3072.

Valler, T., & Springhorn, R. G. (1978). *Cognitive mapping and assessing the communication student.* (Report, East Texas State University). (ERIC Document Reproduction Service No. ED 177 624).

Wiggin, J. A. (1985). A comparison of the cognitive styles of underachieving and achieving high school students (Doctoral dissertation, University of Connecticut). *Dissertation Abstracts International, 46,* 2230.

Bibliography

Bass, R. K. (1978). Personalization of instruction based on cognitive style mapping: Implications for educational gerontology. *Educational Gerontology, 3* (2), 109-124.

Bass, R. K., & Hand, J. D. (1978). Cognitive style mapping: its place in instructional development. In R. K. Bass & C. Dills (Eds.), *Instructional development: The state of the art* (I, pp. 99-110). Columbus: Collegiate.

Hampton, W. (1972). Audiovisual technology: Students find their way to learning with cognitive style mapping. *College and University Business, 52,* 10-16.

Hill, J. E., & Nunney, D. N. (1974). *Personalizing education programs utilizing cognitive style mapping.* Bloomfield Hills, MI: Oakland Community College Press.

Keyser, J. S. (1980). Cognitive style mapping at Mt. Hood Community College. *Community College Review, 8* (30), 19-23.

Munroe, M. J. (1981). *Linking teacher behavior with learning style: Tucson model for effective staff development.* Paper presented to the National Council of States on Inservice Education. (ERIC Document Reproduction Service No. ED 209 235)

Nunney, D. N. (1978). Cognitive style mapping. *Training and Development Journal, 32* (9), 50-57.

Nunney, D. N., & Hill, J. E. (1972). Personalized educational programs. *Audiovisual Instruction, 17* (2), 10-15.

Whitley, J. B. (1982). Cognitive style mapping: Rationale for merging the "old" and "new" technologies. *Educational Technology, 22*(5), 25-26.

20

KOLB'S LEARNING STYLES

Description of Kolb's Learning Styles

Kolb defines learning styles as one's preferred methods for perceiving and processing information. This definition evolved through his four-stage experiential learning cycle, from which he identified four adaptive learning modes: concrete experience (CE), reflective observation (RO), abstract conceptualization (AC), and active experimentation (AE). Concrete experience and AC position themselves at the extreme ends of one continuum that represents how one prefers to perceive the environment or grasp experiences in the world. The second continuum, comprised of RO and AE, represents how one prefers to process or transform incoming information.

Each of these four learning modes has unique characteristics. *Abstract* individuals comprehend information conceptually and symbolically. *Concrete* individuals rely on or apprehend by the tangible, felt qualities of immediate experience. *Active* individuals extend the environment by external manipulation. *Reflective* individuals exhibit intention by internal reflection on the external world.

By crossing the two perception and processing continua, Kolb differentiated four basic ways of relating to the world as four types of learning styles: divergers, assimilators, convergers, and accommodators (Veres, Sims, & Locklear, 1991)(see Table 20.1). For *divergers*, experience is grasped concretely through feelings (apprehension) and transformed through thought (intention). This learning style combines concrete experience with reflective observation. For *assimilators*, experience is grasped through abstract comprehension (conceptualizing) and transformed through thought (intention), combining the characteristics of abstract conceptualization and reflective observation. Experience, for *convergers*, is grasped through abstract comprehension (conceptualizing) and transformed through action (extension), which combines abstract conceptualization and active experimentation. Finally, for *accommodators*, experience is grasped concretely through feelings (apprehension) and transformed by action (extension), which combines concrete experience and active experimentation (Kolb, Rubin, & McIntyre, 1971).

Differences in learning styles are a result of heredity, past life experiences, and the demands of the present environment. Additionally, through socialization experiences in family, school, and work, learners tend to emphasize some learning abilities over others. Each of us has, in a unique way, developed a learning style that has some weak and strong points (Kolb & Fry, 1975).

	Processing/Transformation		Perception	
	Active	Passive	Concrete	Abstract
	AE Action/ Extension	RO Thought/ Intention	CE Feeling/ Apprehension	AC Comprehension/ Conceptualizing
Diverger		X	X	
Assimilator		X		X
Converger	X			X
Accommodator	X		X	

Table 20.1. Perception and processing by Kolb's learning styles

Characteristic Differences in Kolb's Learning Styles

Because these learning styles represent a cross between two dimensions, the strengths and weaknesses of each of the four styles are listed rather than contrasted against the other styles.

Divergent Learners-Concrete Experience/Reflective Observation

Strengths	Weaknesses
ability to assimilate disparateless observations into an integrated explanation	less able to make decisions
oriented toward feelings	less oriented toward thinking
imaginative, intuitive	less concern for theories or generalizations
ability to see many perspectives	less systematic or scientific
ability to generate many ideas	
broad cultural interests	
ability to relate to others	
open-minded	
focus is on thoughtful understanding	less able to apply ideas
ability to gather wide-ranging information	

Assimilative Learners-Abstract Conceptualization/Reflective Observation

Strengths	Weaknesses
sound logic and precision	less focus on people or feelings
theoretical model building	less personal involvement
inductive reasoning	less ability to influence others
ability to assimilate wide-ranging ideas	less able to apply theories/models
	and integrate them
	into a logical explanation
focus on thoughtful understanding	not action oriented
ability to create multiple perspectives	less ability to make decisions
takes a systematic and scientific approach	less artistic
analytic, abstract and quantitative tasks	qualitative or concrete tasks
good organizer of information	
good at designing experiments	

Convergent Learners-Abstract Conceptualization/Active Experimentation

Strengths	Weaknesses
ability to problem solve	have narrow interests
ability to make decisions	relatively unemotional
unemotional	less focus on people or feelings
hypothetico-deductive reasoning	close-minded
focused	unimaginative
ability to apply ideas practically	
ability to select single best or correct answer	
sound logic and precisionless	focus on people or feelings
focus on thoughtful understanding	less intuitive understanding
systematic and scientific approach	less artistic
analytic, abstract and quantitative tasks	qualitative or concrete tasks
ability to influence others and situations	
pragmatic	less concerned with absolute"truth"
ability to get things done	less emphasis on observing
technical tasks or problems	social or interpersonal issues
ability to create new ways of thinking and doing	
experimentally oriented	

Accommodative Learners-Concrete Experience/Active Experimentation

Strengths	Weaknesses
action, results oriented	relies on other people for information
carrying out plans	no reliance of own analytic ability
enjoys and seeks new experiences	sometimes impatient
opportunity seeking	less scientific or systematic
risk taking	
adapts to new situations well	perceived as controlling

relies on facts and "present reality"   disregards theory
intuitive, artistic   trial-and-error mode of solving problems
people oriented
open-minded
ability to influence and lead others and situations
pragmatic   less concerned with absolute "truth"
ability to get things done
personal involvement

Individual Differences Related to Kolb's Learning Styles

Several studies were conducted to establish a correlation between Learning Style Inventory (LSI) and other cognitive, learning, or vocational indicators. No correlations were found for other cognitive styles. Highhouse and Doverspike (1987) found no significant correlation with field dependence/independence, but they found that some subscales of the Vocational Preference Inventory did correlate: Artistic Interest and Concrete Experience, Enterprising and Active Experimentation and Reflective Observation, and Realistic with Active Experimentation and Reflective Observation.

Myers-Briggs Type Indicator (MBTI)--Margerison and Lewis (1979) correlated MBTI with Kolb's LSI general characteristics and learning styles. They found the following relationships of the general characteristics: Concrete related to feeling, abstract to thinking, active to extroverts, reflective to introverts, abstract conceptualization to judgment, and concrete experience related to perception. Of the learning styles, accommodators were associated with extroverted sensing, and assimilative with introversion and intuitive; divergers were associated with introversion and feelings; and convergers were associated with extroversion and thinking (Myers, 1962).

Instruments for Measuring Kolb's Learning Styles

Learning Style Inventory

The LSI measures a person's relative preference for each of the four modes of learning--CE, RO, AC, and AE. The LSI is a nine-item self-report questionnaire. The respondent is asked to rank four words in such a way that best describes the preference. Two scores are computed from these four rankings: AC-CE indicates how much the learning style is biased toward abstraction (positive value) or concreteness (negative value), and RO-AE reflects a possible bias toward reflection (positive number) or activity (negative number). Examples of these items are: "discriminating, tentative, involved, practical; receptive, relevant, analytical, impartial; intense, reserved, rational, responsible."

To improve reliability and construct validity, the LSI was revised in 1984. On this form respondents are asked to rank sentence endings that describe how they learn best. There are twelve items to rank and the sentences contextualize the choices available. Examples of these sentences are: When I learn: I like to deal with my feelings; I like to watch and listen; I like to think about ideas; I like to be doing things. I learn best when: I trust my hunches and feelings; I listen and watch carefully; I rely on logical thinking; I work hard to get things done. I learn best from: personal relationships, observation, rational theories, a chance to try out and practice. Veres et al. (1991) found increased stability in the modified version of the LSI and argued against dismissal of the LSI as an instrument for the study of learning style.

Reliability was questioned by many researchers (Certo & Lamb, 1980; Freedman & Stumpf, 1978, 1979, 1981), who concluded that the instrument is better for learning about one's learning style rather than for making prescriptions. Sewell (1986) summarized the reliability statistics from a series of studies that were .54 to .83 using Spearman Brown, and alpha from .29 to .71. Test-retest reliabilities were .34 to .73.

Theoretical Background

The experiential learning modes reflect a process of conflict, confrontation, and resolution among four basic ways of relating to the world: CE vs. AC and AE versus RO. When responding to a learning situation, the learner is forced to select a mode of dealing with the incoming information.

These two dimensions of learning correspond directly to Piaget's figurative and operative aspects of thought: (a) the figurative aspects, perception and imitation correspond to the comprehension process; and (b) the operative aspect, action, corresponds roughly to the intention process (Kolb, 1984).

Kolb's experiential learning theory is the product of the integration of three models of the experiential learning process: the Lewinian model of action research and laboratory training, Dewey's model of learning, and Piaget's model of learning and cognitive development. Each of these three models describes conflicts between opposing ways of dealing with the world, and suggests that learning results from resolution of these conflicts. The Lewinian model emphasizes the conflicts between concrete experience and abstract concepts and between observation and action. The major dialectic for Dewey's model occurs between the impulse that gives ideas their "moving force" and the reason that gives desire its direction. For Piaget, the processes of accommodating ideas to the external world and assimilating experience into existing conceptual structures are the moving forces of cognitive development (Kolb, 1984).

Therapeutic psychology brings two important dimensions to experiential learning: the concept of adaptation, which gives a central role to affective experience, and the concept of socio-emotional development throughout the life cycle. Brain research is relevant to experiential learning in that it seeks to identify and describe differences in cognitive functioning associated with the left and right hemispheres of the brain (Levy, 1980). The modes of knowing associated with the left and right hemispheres correspond directly with the distinction between abstract cognitive approaches to learning and concrete experiential approaches, respectively. The implication is that these two modes of knowing or grasping the world are equal and complementary processes.

Together, the three models of experiential learning form a unique perspective on learning and development that is characterized by the following propositions.

1. Learning is best conceived as a process, rather than in terms of outcomes. Ideas are not fixed and immutable elements of thought, but are formed and re-formed through experience. Learning is described as a process whereby concepts are derived from, and continuously modified by, experience. From the perspective of experiential learning, the tendency to define learning in terms of outcomes can become a definition of nonlearning; the failure to modify ideas and habits as a result of experience is maladaptive.

2. Learning is a continuous process grounded in experience; "the principles of continuity of experience means that every experience both takes up something from those [experiences] which have gone before and modifies in some way the quality of those which come after" (Dewey, 1938, pp. 35, 44).

3. The process of learning requires the resolution of conflicts between dialectically opposed modes of adaptation to the world. The term *dialectically opposed* refers to mutually opposed and conflicting processes whose results cannot be explained by each other, but whose merger, through the confrontation of the conflicting elements between them, results in a higher order that transcends and encompasses them both.

4. Learning is a holistic process of adaptation to the world.

5. Learning involves transactions between the individual and the environment.

6. Learning is the process of creating knowledge (Kolb, 1984).

The summative conclusion of these propositions is a working definition of experiential learning: "Learning is the process whereby knowledge is created through the transformation of experience" (Kolb, 1984, p. 38).

Kolb's Learning Styles and Learning

Research

Several investigators have criticized the original LSI for having weak stability coefficients. The literature indicates that the revisions made to strengthen the psychometric properties have not improved the LSI and may have weakened the instrument's test-retest reliability (Atkinson, 1988). We summerize research on this learning style with these cautions in mind.

- Kolb and Goldman (1973) found that students who planned graduate study in their major field had learning styles that matched those of their respective field; those whose learning styles were not matched tended to choose careers outside of their field of study. Matched students indicated greater commitment to their chosen career than did mismatched students.

- Plovnick (1974) found significant relationships between the LSI scores and the specialty choices of medical students--accommodators chose family medicine and family care; assimilators chose academic medicine; divergers chose psychiatry; and convergers chose medical specialties. Plovnick also found that LSI scores were related to the process of choosing. Students who thought in concrete terms tended to base their choices on those of role models and acquaintances. Abstract thinkers relied on theoretical material and interest in subject matter.

- Kolb and Fry (1975) found that in an experiential learning environment, accommodators valued a lack of structure, a high amount of peer interaction, and a lack of authority figures in the classroom. Assimilators valued conforming to directions or rules, assigned readings, theory inputs, role playing, and lectures. Divergers valued self-diagnostic activities, open-ended unstructured homework papers, no course requirements (deadlines, number of required papers, etc.) lectures, and little or no peer interaction. Convergers valued instructor/expert inputs, reading, and discussions that link the classroom to the real world. Convergers least preferred open-ended peer discussions and group autonomy.

- Kolb (1981) found that undergraduate business majors tended to have accommodative learning styles, engineering majors tended to have convergent styles, and history, English, political science, psychology, economics, and sociology majors tended to have assimilative styles. Physics majors were very abstract and tended to have either convergent or assimilative styles.

- Carrier, Williams, and Dalgaard (1988) found that students with different learning styles showed distinctly different preferences for note taking. Students who were more concrete (accommodators and divergers) did not practice note taking seriously; however, their counterparts (assimilators and convergers) copied verbatim information from the lecturer.

- Carrier (1987) found that differences in learning styles have been associated with preferences for type, frequency, and intensity of instructional feedback. Computer-based instruction (CBI) was most effective when these different styles and preferences of learners were accommodated.

- Magolda (1989) found that women's cognitive development did not represent a qualitatively different pattern of development from that of men. Men and women did not differ in their views of knowledge and approaches to learning (learning styles).

- Titus (1990) found that adolescents were not nearly as abstract in their learning style as adults; that movement toward greater abstraction is made with maturity; that age, gender, and aptitude are involved in the maturation of learning style; that gender and aptitude have an impact on the development of abstract thought (females tended to be more concrete than males); and that a 4-year span can make a difference in learning style (effects because of age were seen mostly in males, females were homogeneously concrete).

- Brudnell and Carpenter (1990) found that learning style information may be useful in identifying those students who may have a less favorable attitude toward Computer-aided instruction (CAI).

Implications of the Characteristics and Research

Implications which are drawn from research are noted with a •; those drawn logically from descriptive information regarding the trait are noted by an *. Based upon the research and the descriptions of Kolb's learning styles, we conclude that divergers are more likely to excel at learning tasks such as:

- gathering information in novel ways
- self-diagnostic activities
- open-ended assignments
- individualized learning
* imagining implications
* making sense of ambiguity
* open-minded listening
* sensitivity to values and feelings

and acquire and use effectively learning strategies such as:

* searching for information
* evaluating current information
* generating metaphors
* generating examples
* imaging or illustrating knowledge
* inferring causes
* evaluating implications

Based on the research and the descriptions of Kolb's learning styles, we conclude that assimilators are more likely to excel at learning tasks such as:

* organizing information
* building conceptual models
• testing theories and ideas
* designing experiments
* analyzing quantitative data

and acquire and use effectively learning strategies such as:

* selecting information sources
* validating source or authority
* analyzing key ideas
* predicting outcomes
* inferring causes
* evaluating implications

Based on the research and the descriptions of Kolb's learning styles, we conclude that convergers are more likely to excel at learning tasks such as:

* creating new ways of thinking and doing
* experimenting with new ideas
* choosing the best solution
* setting goals
* making decisions

and acquire and use effectively learning strategies such as:

* setting learning goals
* validating sources or authenticity
* repeating material to be recalled
* outlining
* predicting outcomes

Based on the research and the descriptions of Kolb's learning styles, we conclude that accommodators are more likely to excel at learning tasks such as:

• those that lack structure
* committing to objectives
• seeking and exploiting opportunities
• influencing and leading others
* being personally involved and dealing with people

and acquire and use effectively learning strategies such as:

* no specific learning strategies are evident from the characteristics of this type of learner

Kolb's Learning Styles and Instruction

Research

• Dixon (1982) believed that by understanding the differences in learning styles and taking them into account in designing training programs, greater gains can be made in learning, participants' reactions to the program will be more positive, and training time can be reduced.

• Sugarman (1985) recommended that trainers recognize their own preferred learning style and consider how much these preferences are reflected in their course design. And, although people may prefer to learn through particular processes, they can develop their capacities in other fields.

• Svinicki and Dixon (1987) used the experiential learning model as a framework for selecting and sequencing a broader range of classroom activities than was in current use. By constructing learning sequences that lead students through the full experiential cycle, an instructor should be able to foster a more complete learning than can be gained from a single perspective.

• Ellsworth (1991) found that concrete experience and active experimentation learners are more likely to select electronically mediated learning strategies (electronic bulletin boards) to assist them in learning.

• The majority of pre-service education students were concrete experiential and active experiential with role-play being their preferred instructional strategy and lecture, independent study, and computer assisted instruction being their least preferred strategies (Reiff & Powell, 1992). The reflective observation subjects had a negative relationship to computer attitude, and there were no significant differences in the results of the survey after the students had completed five computer based lessons.

Implications of the Characteristics and Research

Implications which are drawn from research are noted with a •; those drawn logically from descriptive information regarding the trait are noted by an *. Instructional conditions that capitalize on the preferences of the diverger, and may challenge the converger, assimilator, and accommodator include:

* providing divergent examples
* using mnemonic strategies
* facilitating learner elaborations through the generation of analogies
* generating examples
* providing practice for far transfer

Instructional conditions that remediate or compensate for the deficiencies of the diverger include:

* providing theoretical background
* presenting theoretical models to explain phenomenon
* providing practice for near transfer
* applying ideas to real-world contexts

Instructional conditions that capitalize on the preferences of the converger, and may challenge the diverger, assimilator, and accommodator include:

* using a deductive sequence for presenting instruction
* asking the learner to select information sources
* creating outlines
* applying real-world or simulated situations (near transfer)

Instructional conditions that remediate or compensate for the deficiencies of the converger include:

* using an inductive sequence that overtly demonstrates the thinking processes
* providing divergent examples, and asking the learner to set each in the context of the instruction
* facilitating elaborations through generating and explaining the relevance of analogies
* providing practice through varied contexts and circumstances (far transfer)

Instructional conditions that capitalize on the preferences of the assimilator, and may challenge the converger, diverger, and accommodator include:

* using inductive sequence for presenting instruction
* providing opportunities to integrate instruction by paraphrasing, or generating analogies or metaphors
* facilitating elaboration though inferences from information
* providing opportunities for the learner to organize information through the use of mind maps, concept maps, pattern notes, or categorization

Instructional conditions that remediate or compensate for the deficiencies of the assimilator include:

* applying real-world or simulated situations (near transfer)
* providing images to facilitate elaboration

Instructional conditions that capitalize on the preferences of the accommodator, and may challenge the converger, diverger, and assimilator would include:

* providing many concrete examples to apply information
* focusing on doing, rather than reflection
* relating information to personal experiences
* using narrative sequence
* using a concrete to abstract sequence
* generating personal examples

Instructional conditions that remediate or compensate for the deficiencies of the accommodator include:

* presenting abstract ideas with explanations
* providing analysis of key ideas
* selecting information sources and learning activities for the learner

References

Atkinson, G. (1988). Reliability of the LSI. *Psychological Reports, 62,* 755-758.

Brudnell, I., & Carpenter, C. S. (1990). Adult learning styles and attitudes toward computer assisted instruction. *Journal of Nursing Education, 29,* 79-83.

Carrier, C. A. (1987). A taxonomy for the design of computer-based instruction. *Educational Technology, 27(10),* 15-17.

Carrier, C. A., Williams, M. D., & Dalgaard, B. R. (1988). College student's perceptions of notetaking and their relationship to selected learner characteristics and course achievement. *Research in Higher Education, 28,* 223-239.

Certo, S. C., & Lamb, S. W. (1980). An investigation of bias within the Learning Styles Inventory through factor analysis. *Journal of Experiential Learning and Simulation, 2,* 1-7.

Dewey, J. (1938). *Logic, the theory of inquiry.* New York: Holt, Rinehart & Winston.

Dixon, N. (1982). Incorporating learning style into training design. *Training Development Journal, 36,* 62-64.

Freedman, R. D., & Stumpf, S. A. (1978). Student Evaluations of courses and faculty based on a perceived learning criterion: Scale construction, validation, and comparison of results. *Applied Psychological Measurement, 2(2),* 189-202.

Freedman, R. D., & Stumpf, S. A. (1979). Expected grade covariation with student ratings of instruction: Individual versus class effects. *Journal of Educational Psychology, 71,* 293-302.

Freedman, R. D., & Stumpf, S. A. (1981). Learning style inventory: Still less than meets the eye. *Academy of Management Review, 6,* 297-299.

Highhouse, S., & Doverspike, D. (1987). The validity of the Learning Style Inventory 1985 as a predictor of cognitive style and occupational preference. *Educational and Psychological Measurement, 47,* 749-53.

Kolb, D. A. (1981). Learning styles and disciplinary differences. In A. W. Chickering (Ed.), *The modern college* (pp. 232-255). San Francisco: Jossey-Bass.

Kolb, D. A. (1984). *Experiential Learning: Experience as a source of learning and development.* Englewood Cliffs, NJ: Prentice-Hall.

Kolb, D. A., & Fry, R. (1975). Toward an applied theory of experiential learning. In C. Cooper (Ed.), *Theories of Group Process* (pp. 33-58). New York: Wiley.

Kolb, D. A., & Goldman, M. (1973). *Toward a typology of learning styles and learning environments: An investigation of the impact of learning styles and discipline demands on the academic performance, social adaptation and career choices of M.I.T Seniors* (M.I.T. Sloan School Working Paper No. 688-73).

Kolb, D. A., Rubin, I. M., & McIntyre, J. M. (1971). *Organizational psychology.* Englewood Cliffs, NJ: Prentice-Hall.

Levy, J. (1980). Cerebral asymmetry and the psychology of man. In M. Wittrock (Ed.), *The Brain and Psychology* (pp. 27-43). New York: Academic.

Magolda, M. B. B. (1989). Gender differences in cognitive development: an analysis of cognitive complexity and learning styles. *Journal of College Student Development, 30,* 213-220.

Margerison, C. J., & Lewis. (1979). Training implications of work preferences. *Journal of European Industrial Training, 2,* 3-5.

Myers, I. B. (1962). *The Myers-Briggs Type Indicator.* Palo Alto, CA: Consulting Psychologists Press.

Plovnick, M. (1974). *Individual learning styles and the process of career choice in medical students.* Unpublished doctoral dissertation, Sloan School of Management, Massachusetts Institute of Technology.

Sewell, T. J. (1986). *The measurement of learning style: A critique of four assessment tools.* (Research Report). Green Bay: Wisconsin University Assessment Center. (ERIC Document Reproduction Service No. ED 267 247)

Sugarman, L. (1985). Kolb's model of experiential learning: touchstone for trainers, students, counselors and clients. *Journal of Counseling and . Development, 64,* 264-268.

Svinicki, M., & Dixon, N. (1987). The Kolb Model modified for classroom activities. *College Teaching, 35,* 141-146.

Titus, T. G. (1990). Adolescent learning styles. *Journal of Research and Development in Education, 23,* 165-171.

Veres, J. C., Sims, R. R., & Locklear, T. S. (1991). Improving the reliability of Kolb's revised Learning Style Inventory. *Educational and Psychological Measurement, 51,* 143-150.

Bibliography

Debello, T. C. (1989, March 10-13). *Comparison of eleven major learning styles models: Appropriate populations; validity of instrumentation; and the research behind them.* Paper presented at the National Conference of the Association for Supervision and Curriculum Development, Orlando, FL.

Sales, G. C., & Carrier, C. A. (1987). The effect of learning style and the type of feedback on achievement in a computer-based lesson. *International Journal of Instructional Media, 14,* 171-185.

21

Dunn & Dunn Learning Styles

Description of Dunn and Dunn Learning Styles

Learning styles as originally conceived by Dunn and Dunn (1974), and refined later with Price, measure a learner's preferred modes for concentration and learning difficult information. Their conception takes into account multiple interacting elements including environmental, sociological, emotional, and physical variables, each with its own sub-factors. Although the number of subfactors has varied from 20 to 24 over the refinement of the sociological and physical elements, the number of variables has remained the same. The *environmental* variable includes four factors: sound, temperature, light, and seating/furniture design. The *sociological* variable includes three general factors for adults and four factors for children consisting of learning groups, presence of authority figures, learning in several ways; and for children, motivation from adults. The *emotional* variable consists of four factors including motivation, responsibility, persistence, and need for structure. Finally, the *physical* variable is comprised of four overall factors: modality preferences, intake, time of day, and mobility.

Because 22 factors are measured in the most current instrument for children and 20 factors for adults, their differences are more easily perceived by outlining them in the next section, rather than providing narrative description here.

Characteristic Differences in Dunn and Dunn Learning Styles

Each preference factor in the following list (in bold) represents an *independent* continuum and is not necessarily related to those on the right or left side of other factors.

Environmental:
Noise Level
prefers quiet   prefers sound

Lighting
prefers low light   prefers bright light

Temperature
prefers cool temperature   prefers warm temperature

Design
prefers formal design   prefers informal design
prefers wooden, steel, or plastic chairs   prefers lounge chair, bed,
                                                                    floor, pillow, or carpeting
prefers conventional classroom   prefers unconventional classroom
or library   kitchen, living room

Sociological:
Learning Groups:
learn alone   peer oriented
covert thinking   discussion and interactions

Presence of Authority Figures
no one of authority   recognized authority

Learning in Several Ways
routine   variety of social groups

Motivation from Adults* (for the Learning Styles Inventory only)
need to please parents or parent figures   no need for parental approval
need to please teachers   no need to please teachers

Emotional:
Motivation
motivated   unmotivated
needs to achieve academically   no need to achieve academically

Responsibility
responsible   irresponsible
conforming   nonconforming
does what he or she thinks ought to be done   does what he or she wants
follows through on what is asked   does not like to do something
                                                                because someone asks

Persistence
persistent   not persistent
inclination to complete tasks   need for intermittent breaks

Need for Structure
wants structure   does not want structure
prefers specific directions   prefers to do it his or her way

Physical:
Modality Preferences

Auditory	Visual	Tactile	Kinesthetic
listening	reading	use their hands	whole body movements
lecture	print	underline	real life experiences
discussion	diagrams	take notes	total involvement
recording	close eyes to recall		acting
			puppetry
			drama
			building
			designing
			visiting
			interviewing
			playing

Intake
eat, drink, chew, or bite while concentrating   no intake while studying

Time of Day
morning energy   evening energy
late morning energy   afternoon energy

Mobility
needs to move   able to sit
still

These differences were described by Dunn, Dunn, and Price (1982, 1989b).

Individual Differences
Related to Dunn and Dunn Learning Styles

Although they are not measured directly with the instruments, several factors have also been related to the processing inclinations of *analytic/global* and *hemispheric preferences* through experimental research (Bruno, 1988; Dunn, Cavanaugh, Eberle, & Zenhausern, 1982). Global, right-brained, holistic individuals appear to prefer low light, informal designs, high sound, high intake, and low persistence. Analytic, left-brained individuals appear to prefer a high amount of light, formal designs, no sound, low intake, and high persistence.

Instruments for Measuring Dunn and Dunn Learning Styles

Learning Styles Questionnaire (LSQ) (Dunn & Dunn, 1978)

This questionnaire is the first in a series of revisions of instruments to measure the Dunn and Dunn factors for learning. This 228-item version was developed for children from grades 3 to 12.

Learning Styles Inventory (LSI) (Dunn, Dunn, & Price, 1979, 1984, 1989a)

Based on content and factor analysis, the LSI represents a major rework of the LSQ and has evolved from a 100-item survey to its current 104-item version for use with students in grades 3 through 12. The instrument uses self-reporting items that employ a 3-choice Likert scale of true, false, and undecided responses for grades 3 and 4 and a 5-choice Likert scale for grades 5 through 12. Twenty-two factors, representing the four variables, are assessed by this instrument. Sample items include: "I study best when it is quiet; I like to study with one or two friends; I study best when the lights are dim; When I do well in school, grown-ups in my family are proud of me; or, I learn better by reading than by talking." A consistency score is also calculated to determine the degree of haphazardness of the learner's responses. Results with consistency scores less than 70% may not be meaningful and are not recommended for use.

 The instrument can be administered in a paper-pencil format, orally, by tape, or by computer, and takes approximately 30 to 40 minutes. Individual profiles, group summaries, and/or subscale summaries are available for analysis with the computer version. The manual that accompanies this instrument provides advice on strategies for instructing to the differences in styles.

 Reliability results reported by the authors indicated that 95% of the test-retest reliabilities for the 22 factors were greater than .60, with only "late morning" preferences at .55. They also reported results of discriminative validity studies, which "successfully discriminated between high and low math achievers, gifted and nongifted, learning disabled and non-learning disabled, and males and females" (Dunn, Dunn, & Price, 1989a, p. 42).

Productivity Environmental Preference Survey (PEPS) (Dunn, Dunn, & Price, 1982, 1989b)

The PEPS, which uses self-report methods to measure preferences for "function[ing], learn[ing], concentrat[ing] and perform[ing] in their occupational or educational activities," is an adult version of the LSI. Like the LSI, it can be administered in a pencil-paper format, orally, by tape, or by computer. This 100-item test measures 20 factors using a Likert scale and takes approximately 30 to 40 minutes to administer. From a norm group of 589 adults, Dunn, Dunn, and Price (1982) reported that "68% of the test-retest reliabilities for the 24 factors were greater than .60."

Learning Style Inventory: Primary Version (Perrin, 1982)

A modified version of the LSI, this instrument is appropriate for children in kindergarten through grade 2.

Theoretical Background

Dunn observed differences in the preferences and learning outcomes of various students and believed that those differences were the result of factors other than ability. She identified approximately 32 areas that consistently showed differences in learning and developed an instrument with 223 items (Dunn & Dunn, 1974). Joined by Price, they began a systematic factor analysis to distill those factors into the independent effects that accounted for the largest proportion of variance in learning. Four major variables (emotional, physical, environmental, and sociological) emerged, each with its own subfactors. Continued refinement resulted in the identification of factors within the learning groups and environmental variables that could be combined.

Both biological and developmental factors were noted (Dunn, 1990). Those that are biological include preferences for sound, light, temperature, seating arrangements, modality strengths, intake, time of day, and mobility. Those that are developmental include sociological preferences, motivation, responsibility, and structure. Persistence remains unclassified.

These factors are identified by a self-report instrument that, therefore, does not attempt to measure "underlying psychological factors, value systems, or the quality of attitudes" (Dunn, Dunn, & Price, 1989b, p. 5), or why the student preferences exist. It also does not assess whether or not learners possess the skills that enable them to use their preferred mode of learning. For example, the skills that are specific to successful learning by oneself or in groups are not indicated by this instrument. These factors denote learner preferences for various external learning conditions, rather than specific cognitive abilities for perceiving and internally manipulating information.

The concept has continued to develop through 20 years of research, mostly through doctoral dissertations investigating the effectiveness of matching versus mismatching learning preferences on learning outcomes, the identification of developmental patterns, establishing relationships between variables, and discriminating preferences between specific subpopulations. Researchers found a developmental pattern for modality preferences, food intake for girls, and a need for teacher motivation (Price, Dunn, & Dunn, 1976, 1977). Style distinctions were found between boys and girls, high and low reading achievement groups, high and low math ability (Dunn, Dunn, & Price, 1981), gifted and nongifted (Price, Dunn, Dunn, & Griggs, 1981), and those with a high and low self-concept (Griggs & Price, 1980).

Dunn and Dunn Learning Styles and Learning

Given that the factors identified by Dunn and Dunn are conditions external to the learner, rather than factors that affect one's ability to internally manipulate incoming information, they affect the external instructional conditions rather than learning strategies internal to the learner. Therefore, this research is reported and implications are drawn in the next section through the interactions of the LSI with instructional techniques.

Dunn and Dunn Learning Styles and Instruction

Research

Dunn (1990) reported that research with their model of learning styles has been extensive, reaching more than 60 colleges and universities, using students from kindergarten through college, and "with every level of academic proficiency, including gifted, average, underachieving, at risk, dropout, special eduction, and vocational/industrial arts populations" (p. 223). Most of this research has investigated the effects of matching and mismatching the Dunn and Dunn learning style factors with learning strategies on learning. A sampling of this literature is presented here and is organized by the four variables.

Environmental Factors

• When examining reading achievement in terms of reading speed and accuracy, Krimsky (1982) found significant positive effects for matching bright- and low-light preferences with bright- and low-light conditions.

• Murrain (1983) found no differences on word recognition when seventh graders were matched with their temperature preferences.

• Two studies demonstrated significant positive effects for matching formal/informal furniture with design preferences in ninth-grade reading students, and seventh- and eighth-grade math students. The latter study also resulted in more significant positive attitudes (Hodges, 1985; Shea, 1983). No effects, however, were found by Stiles (1985) with fifth-grade math students.

- Music without lyrics was more conducive to learning for students with a noise preference (DeGregoris, 1986).

- Pizzo, Dunn, and Dunn (1990) found that sixth graders who studied in a learning environment that matched their noise preference performed significantly better and had better attitudes than did those in a mismatched environment.

Emotionality Factors

- Griggs, Price, Kopal, and Swaine (1984) investigated motivation and the need for structure with sixth-grade suburban students in three types of counseling groups. Matching styles with strategies produced significantly higher career awareness scores than did mismatching styles and strategies.

Sociological Factors

- Even with first and second graders, Perrin (1984) found that matching preferred individual or peer learning preferences with individual or peer learning groups resulted in significantly greater problem solving and word recognition activity.

- DeBello (1985) investigated the effect on writing social studies compositions by matching and mismatching a variety of sociological preferences of suburban eighth graders. Significant positive effects were found when authority-oriented learners revised their compositions with the teacher, and when those who preferred to learn alone used self-review. More positive attitudes were also found with matching.

- Miles (1987) found that matching preferences for learning alone or learning with peers with lone or group learning significantly and positively affected achievement when fifth- and sixth-grade inner-city students studied career awareness and career decision making.

- Dunn, Giannitti, Murray, Rossi, and Quinn (1990) found that middle school children performed equally well when instructional grouping strategies (learning alone, learning with peers, no preference) matched preferred learning styles. No-preference students also performed better in the learning-alone condition. Attitudes were also more positive in the matched conditions.

Physical Factors

- Carruthers and Young (1979) found statistically significant increases in math achievement by junior high school math underachievers when the time of their class was changed to match their time preferences.

- When in-service sessions were matched with high-energy times for teachers, Freeley (1984) found that significantly more innovative ideas were implemented.

- When mobility/passivity preferences were matched with moving opportunities in second-grade reading classes, a positive significant increase in achievement resulted (Miller, 1985).

- MacMurren (1985) found that a match between food-intake preferences and eating opportunities significantly affected the reading speeds and attitudes of sixth graders.

- Seventh-grade students with active/passive learning styles performed best on a verbal learning task when the environment matched their preferences. The two groups did not differ significantly in the passive environment, but the passive preference subjects did significantly worse than those with active preferences in the active environment (Della-Valle, Dunn, Dunn, Geisert, Sinatra, & Zenhausern, 1986).

- When studying adult continuing education, Buell and Buell (1987) found that matching with auditory, visual, and tactile perceptual preferences resulted in significant positive gains in achievement.

- These same results were found in studies of children's vocabulary learning--kindergartners (Carbo, 1980), mathematics of fourth-grade and third-grade underachievers (Jarsonbeck, 1984; Weinberg, 1983), trigram recall of first and third graders (Urbschat, 1977), second-grade learning-disabled students (Wheeler, 1980, 1983), seventh-grade science (Martini, 1986), 9th- and 10th-grade industrial arts (Kroon, 1985), and adult driver's safety (Ingham, 1989).

- Dunn, Dunn, Primavera, Sinatra, and Virostko (1987) found significant achievement gains in reading and math elementary students when schedules and time preferences matched.

- Dunn (1988) provided a research basis for introducing elementary students to new information through their strongest modality, reinforcing through secondary and tertiary strengths and internalizing through a creative activity.

General Factors

• Eight learning style variables were found to significantly correlate with high and low self-concept in third, sixth, and seventh graders (Dunn, Price, Dunn, & Saunders, 1979).

• A review of correlational and experimental studies found that students' achievement increases when teaching methods match their learning styles (Dunn, Beaudry, & Klavas, 1989).

• Children in different American subcultures, in fourth through sixth grades, exhibited significantly different patterns of preferred learning strategies (Dunn et al., 1990).

• Clear differences in patterns of learning strategies of children were reported among different cultural groups, but people within each culture can differ dramatically as well. The researchers concluded that individual rather than group characteristics should be addressed when providing instruction (Dunn & Griggs, 1990).

Implications of the Characteristics and Research

The recommended instructional conditions for each factor of the LSI are drawn from extensive research based on a capitalization model of adaptation, which indicates that matching individuals' styles and preferred strategies results in significant gains in achievement. These recommendations were summarized by Dunn, Dunn, and Price (1989b, 1982) in the LSI manual and in the Interpretative Booklet for the PEPS. Therefore, the instructional conditions that should capitalize on the following preferences include:

Noise level
• providing soft, baroque music on earphones for those who prefer noise
• providing conversation areas for those who prefer noise
• providing quiet, separate areas for those who need quiet

Light
• seating students near windows or providing lamps for those who need light
• using indirect or subdued lighting for those who prefer low light
• using dividers to diffuse light for those who prefer low light

Temperature
• providing supplemental heating, seating in the middle of the room, and allowing sweaters for those who prefer warmth

- providing air-conditioning and ventilation for those who prefer cool temperatures

Design
- providing wooden, plastic, or steel straight-backed chairs with tables for those preferring formal settings
- providing soft chairs, couches, pillows, lounge chairs, carpet, and floor seating areas for those preferring an informal setting

Motivation
- using contract activity packages, self-regulated learning and evaluation strategies, and self-defined objectives for highly motivated students
- providing shorter tasks, frequent supervision, "experiment with short-range motivators and reinforcers", encourage self-developed goals, keep records of progress, and "provide positive immediate, but genuine feedback at frequent intervals" (p. 3) for unmotivated students

Persistence
- using contract activity packages, long-term assignments, little supervision, and praise at the completion of the task for those high in persistence
- using short-term assignments with interim due dates, praise during the process of completing tasks, and providing periodic breaks for those of low persistence

Responsibility
- increasing responsibility as they demonstrate their ability to perform and asking learners to set their including setting own goals for those high in responsibility
- using short-term assignments, supervision and frequent checking, simple directions and procedures, interim rewards, and speaking as a "colleague" rather than as a subordinate for those low in responsibility

Structure
- using contract activity packages, permitting choices in resources, procedures, timelines, reporting, and checking for those preferring little or no structure
- using programmed learning sequences, precise instructions for each assignment, clearly stated objectives, and lists for those preferring high structure

Learning groups
- using contract activity packages, self-selected objectives, and self-evaluation for those who prefer to learn alone
- using techniques such as circle of knowledge, team learning, brainstorming, and case studies for those who are peer-oriented learners

Presence of authority figures
- locating those who prefer to work with authority figures near the teacher or supervisor, scheduling periodic meetings, providing authoritative feedback
- locating those who do not prefer the presence of authority figures away from the supervisor, scheduling infrequent meetings, and allowing self-checking

Learning in several ways
- providing many different options for learning groups for those who prefer variety in learning
- providing more routine and structured activities and avoiding frequent or dramatic change for those not preferring variety

Auditory
- using "tapes, videos, lectures, discussions, records, radio, stereo, oral directions and explanations" (p. 6). Reinforcing through visual, tactile, and kinesthetic resources.

Visual
- using "pictures, filmstrips, films, graphs, single concept loops, transparencies, computers, diagrams, drawings, books, magazines, programmed learning sequences" (p. 6). Reinforcing through auditory, tactile, and kinesthetic resources

Tactile
- using "manipulative and three-dimensional materials, resources that are touchable, movable and readable" (p. 6). Reinforcing through auditory, visual and kinesthetic resources

Kinesthetic
- using multisensory instructional packages, "provide opportunities for real and active experiences in planning and carrying out objectives; visits, projects, acting, floor games, walking" (p. 6), reinforcing through the auditory, visual, and tactile resources

Intake
- providing frequent opportunities for snacking or drinking while working or learning for those who prefer intake
- for those who do not prefer intake, no provision is needed

Evening-Morning
- scheduling difficult tasks in the evening and encouraging homework completion in the evening for those who prefer the evening
- scheduling difficult tasks in the morning and encouraging homework completion before coming to school for those who prefer morning

Late Morning
- scheduling difficult tasks in late morning for those who prefer late morning

Afternoon
- scheduling difficult tasks in the afternoon for those who prefer afternoon

Mobility
- designing activities that allow students who prefer to move about to stand, walk, manipulate objects, and move to different locations
- providing stationary activities for those who prefer not to move about, and allow learners to remain in one place

Parent Figure Motivated*
- providing opportunities for those who are motivated by a parent figure to work near the parent, sending frequent notes home to parents, including parents in student activities, and providing praise in front of the parent
- allowing the learners who are not motivated by a parent figure to work alone, not requiring input from the parent

Teacher Motivated*
- providing opportunities for those motivated by the teacher to work directly with the teacher individually and in small groups and using teacher praise
- allowing the individuals who are not motivated by teacher input to work by themselves or with their peers, and using intrinsic motivation

*   Represents implications for children only

References

Bruno, J. (1988). An experimental investigation of the relationships between ad among hemispheric processing, learning style preferences, instructional strategies, academic achievement, and attitudes of developmental mathematics students in an urban technical college (Doctoral dissertation, St. John's University). *Dissertation Abstracts International, 49*, 1066A.

Buell, B. G., & Buell, N. A. (1987). Perceptual modality preference as a variable in the effectiveness of continuing education for professionals. (Doctoral dissertation, University of Southern California). *Dissertation Abstracts International, 48*, 283A.

Carbo, M. (1980). An analysis of the relationship between the modality preferences of kindergartners and selected reading treatments as they affect the learning of a basic sight-word vocabulary (Doctoral dissertation, St. John's University). *Dissertation Abstracts International, 41,* 1389A.

Carruthers, S. A., & Young, A. (1979, July). *Preference of condition concerning time in learning environments of rural versus inner-city eighth-grade students.* Paper presented at the First Annual Conference on Teaching Students Through Their Individual Learning Styles, New York.

DeBello, T. (1985). A critical analysis of the achievement and attitude effects of administrative assignments to social studies writing instruction based on identified, eighth-grade students' learning style preferences for learning alone, with peers, or with teachers. (Doctoral dissertation, St. John's University). *Dissertation Abstracts International, 47,* 68A.

DeGregoris, C. N. (1986). Reading comprehension and the word recognition scores of seventh-grade students to provide supervisory and administrative guidelines for the organization of effective instructional environments (Doctoral dissertation, St. John's University). *Dissertation Abstracts International, 47,* 3380A.

Della-Valle, J., Dunn, K., Dunn, R., Geisert, G., Sinatra, R., & Zenhausern, R. (1986). The effects of matching and mismatching student's mobility preferences on recognition and memory tasks. *Journal of Educational Research, 79*(5), 267-272.

Dunn, R. (1988). Capitalizing on student's perceptual strengths to ensure literacy while engaging in conventional lecture/discussion. *Reading Psychology: An International Quarterly, 9,* 431-453.

Dunn, R. (1990). Understanding the Dunn and Dunn Learning Styles Model and the need for individual diagnosis and prescription. *Reading, Writing, and Learning Disabilities, 6,* 223-247.

Dunn, R., Beaudry, J. S., & Klavas, A. (1989, March). Survey of research on learning styles. *Educational Leadership, 46,* pp. 50-58.

Dunn, R., Cavanaugh, D., Eberle, B., & Zenhausern, R. (1982). Hemispheric preference: The newest element of learning style. *The American Biology Teacher, 44*(5), 291-294.

Dunn, R., & Dunn, K. (1974, December). Learning style as a criterion for placement in alternative programs. *Phi Delta Kappan, 36,* 275-279.

Dunn, R., & Dunn, K. (1978). *Teaching students through their individual learning styles.* Englewood Cliffs, NJ: Prentice-Hall.

Dunn, R., Dunn, K., & Price, G. E. (1979). *Learning Styles Inventory.* Lawrence, KS: Price Systems.

Dunn, R., Dunn, K., & Price, G. E. (1981). *Productivity, Environmental Preference Survey.* Lawrence, KS: Price Systems.

Dunn, R., Dunn, K., & Price, G. E. (1982). *Productivity, Environmental Preference Survey.* Lawrence, KS: Price Systems.

Dunn, R., Dunn, K., & Price, G. E. (1984). *Learning Styles Inventory.* Lawrence, KS: Price Systems.

Dunn, R., Dunn, K., & Price, G. E. (1989a). *Learning Styles Inventory.* Lawrence, KS: Price Systems.

Dunn, R., Dunn, K., & Price, G. E. (1989b). *Productivity, Environmental Preference Survey.* Lawrence, KS: Price Systems.

Dunn, R., Dunn, K., Primavera, L., Sinatra R., & Virostko J. (1987). A timely solution: A review of research on the effects of chronobiology on children's achievement and behavior. *The Clearing House, 61*(1), 5-8.

Dunn, R., Gemake, J., Jalali, F., Zenhausern, R., Quinn, P., & Spiridakis, J. (1990). Cross-cultural differences in the learning styles of fourth-fifth- and sixth-grade students of Afro, Chinese, Greek, and Mexican heritage. *Journal of Multicultural Counseling and Development, 18*(2), 68-93.

Dunn, R., Giannitti, M. C., Murray, J. B., Rossi, I., & Quinn, P. (1990). Grouping students for instruction: Effects of learning style on achievement and atttitudes. *Journal of Social Psychology, 130*(4), 485-494.

Dunn, R., & Griggs, S. A. (1990). Research on the learning style characteristics of selected racial and ethnic groups. *Journal of Reading, Writing, and Learning Disabilities International, 6*(3), 261-280.

Dunn, R., Price, G. E., Dunn, K., & Saunders, W. (1979). Relationship of learning style to self-concept. *The Clearing House, 53*(3), 155-158.

Freeley, M. E. (1984). An experimental investigation of the relationships among teachers' individual time preferences, in service workshop schedules, and instructional techniques and the subsequent implementation of learning style strategies in participants' classrooms (Doctoral dissertation, St. John's University). *Dissertation Abstracts International, 46,* 403A.

Griggs, S. A., & Price, G. E. (1980, January). Learning styles of gifted versus average junior high school students. *Phi Delta Kappan, 61,* p. 361.

Griggs, S. A., Price, G. E., Kopal, S., & Swaine, W. (1984). The effects of group counseling with sixth-grade students using approaches that are compatible versus incompatible with selected learning style elements. *California Personnel and Guidance Journal, 5*(1), 28-35.

Hodges, H. (1985). An analysis of the relationships among preferences for a formal/informal design, one element of learning style, academic achievement and attitudes of seventh- and eighth- grade students in remedial mathematics classes in a New York City junior high school (Doctoral dissertation, St. John's University). *Dissertation Abstracts International, 45,* 2791A.

Ingham, J. (1989). *An experimental investigation of the relationships among learning style perceptual preference, instructional strategies, training achievement, and attitudes of corporate employees.* Unpublished doctoral dissertation, St. John's University, New York.

Jarsonbeck, S. (1984). The effects of a right-brain and mathematics curriculum on low-achieving fourth-grade students (Doctoral dissertation,
University of South Florida). *Dissertation Abstracts International,
45,* 2397A.

Krimsky, J. (1982). A comparative analysis of the effects of matching and
mismatching fourth-grade students with their learning style preference for the environmental element of light and their subsequent
reading speed and accuracy scores (Doctoral dissertation, St. John's
University). *Dissertation Abstracts International, 43,* 66A.

Kroon, D. (1985). An experimental investigation of the effects on academic
achievement and the resultant administrative implications of instruction congruent and incongruent with secondary industrial arts
students' learning style perceptual preference (Doctoral dissertation,
St. John's University). *Dissertation Abstracts International, 46,* 11A.

MacMurren, H. (1985). A comparative study of the effects of matching and
mismatching sixth-grade students with their learning style preferences for the physical element of intake and their subsequent reading speed and accuracy scores and attitudes (Doctoral dissertation, St.
John's University). *Dissertation Abstracts International, 46,* 3247A.

Martini, M. (1986). An analysis of the relationships between and among
computer-assisted instruction, learning style perceptual preferences,
attitudes and the science achievement of seventh-grade students in
a suburban, New York school district (Doctoral dissertation, St.
John's University). *Dissertation Abstracts International, 47,* 87A.

Miles, B. (1987). An investigation of the relationships among the learning
style sociological preferences of fifth- and sixth-grade students, selected interactive classroom patterns and achievement in career
awareness and career decision-making concepts (Doctoral dissertation, St. John's University). *Dissertation Abstracts International, 48,*
2527A.

Miller, L. M. (1985). *Mobility as an element of learning style: The effect its
inclusion or exclusion has on student performance in the standardized testing environment.* Unpublished master's dissertation,
University of North Florida, Jacksonville.

Murrain, P. (1983). Administrative determinations concerning facilities
utilization and instructional grouping: An analysis of the relationships between selected thermal environments and preferences for
temperature, an element of learning style, as they affect word recognition scores of secondary students (Doctoral dissertation, St. John's
University). *Dissertation Abstracts International, 44,* 1749A.

Perrin, J. (1982). *Learning Styles Inventory: Primary Version.* Jamaica, NY:
Learning Styles Network, St. John's University.

Perrin, J. (1984). An experimental investigation of the relationships among
the learning style sociological preferences of gifted and nongifted
primary children, selected instructional strategies, attitudes, and
achievement in problem solving and rote memorization (Doctoral

dissertation, St. John's University). *Dissertation Abstracts International, 44,* 342A.

Pizzo, J., Dunn, R., & Dunn, K. (1990). A sound approach to improving reading: Responding to students' learning styles. *Journal of Reading, Writing, and Learning Disabilities International. 6*(3), 249-260.

Price, G. E., Dunn, R., & Dunn, K. (1976, 1977). *Learning Style Inventory: Research Report.* Lawrence, KS: Price Systems.

Price, G. E., Dunn, K., Dunn, R., & Griggs, S. A. (1981). Studies in students' learning styles. *Roeper Review, 4*(2), 223-226.

Shea, T. C. (1983). An investigation of the relationship among preferences for the learning style element of design, selected instructional environments, and reading achievement with ninth-grade students to improve administrative determinations concerning effective educational facilities. (Doctoral dissertation, St. John's University). *Dissertation Abstracts International, 44,* 2004A.

Stiles, R. (1985). Learning style preferences for design and their relationship to standardized test results (Doctoral dissertation, University of Tennessee). *Dissertation Abstracts International, 46,* 2551A.

Urbschat, K. S. (1977). A study of preferred learning modes and their relationship to the amount of recall of CVC trigrams (Doctoral dissertation, Wayne State University). *Dissertation Abstracts International, 38,* 2536-5A.

Weinberg, F. (1983). An experimental investigation of the interaction between sensory modality preference and mode of presentation in the instruction of arithmetic concepts to third-grade underachievers (Doctoral dissertation, St. John's University). *Dissertation Abstracts International, 44,* 1740A.

Wheeler, R. (1980). An alternative to failure: Teaching reading according to students' perceptual strengths. *Kappa Delta Pi Record, 17*(2), 59-63.

Wheeler, R. (1983). An investigation of the degree of academic achievement evidenced when second-grade learning-disabled students' perceptual preferences are matched and mismatched with complementary sensory approaches to beginning reading instruction (Doctoral dissertation, St. John's University). *Dissertation Abstracts International, 44,* 2039A.

Bibliography

Dunn, R. (1987). Research on instructional environments: Implications for student achievement and attitudes. *Professional School Psychology, 2(1),* 43-52.

Dunn, R., & Dunn, K. (1979). Learning styles/teaching styles: Should they...can they...be matched? *Educational Leadership, 36*(4), 238-244.

Witkin, H., Oltman, P., Raskin, E., & Karp, S. (1971). *A manual for the Embedded Figures Test.* Palo Alto, CA: Consulting Psychologists Press.

22

GRASHA-RIECHMANN LEARNING STYLES

Description of Grasha-Riechmann Learning Styles

Grasha and Riechmann examined and assessed the learning styles of college students through a social, affective perspective on the different ways individuals approach the classroom environment (Karrer, 1988; Keefe, 1979). This measure can be classified as a social interaction scale because it deals with patterns of preferred styles for interacting with teachers and fellow students in a learning environment rather than how information is perceived or organized (Grasha, 1984; Riechmann, 1980). Although these categories do not translate as readily into instructional strategies, they are "defined around three classroom dimensions: student attitudes toward learning, view of teachers and/or peers, and reactions to classroom procedures" (Riechmann & Grasha, 1974, p. 214). From their initial research, they identified three bipolar dimensions that describe this approach: avoidant/participant, competitive/collaborative, and dependent/independent. Further research into these styles revealed that subjects consistently receive opposite scores only for the participant/avoidant dimension (Andrews, 1981; Riechmann & Grasha, 1974). In fact, they found that most individuals do not score on polar extremes, but rather indicate some degree of preference for each of these categories (Riechmann & Grasha, 1974). Because these classroom dimensions are present in almost all instructional strategies, the six styles identified by the questionnaire are meaningful for understanding student behaviors. Another important distinction to bring out is that the styles for each of the learners are expected to change from class to class. As such, they have designed two different forms of the scale--one that assesses a general class, and the second that relates to a specific course.

The participant/avoidant scale measures how much an individual wishes to become involved in the classroom environment, reactions to classroom procedures, and attitudes toward learning. The collaborative/competitive dimensions measures the motivations behind an individual's interactions with others (i.e., whether or not fellow students are viewed as competitors or colleagues). The third, independent/dependent scale measures attitudes toward teachers and how much the learner desires freedom and control in the learning environment.

Characteristic Differences in Grasha-Riechmann Learning Styles

These characteristics were suggested by Riechmann and Grasha (1974).

Participant	Avoidant
desires to learn course content	no desire to learn course content
enjoys attending class	no enjoyment attending class
assumes responsibility for classroom learning	assumes no responsibility
participates with others when told to do so	does not participate
does what is required	does what they want

Collaborative	Competitive
sharing	competitive
cooperative	has motivation to do better than others
enjoys working with others	enjoys competing
classroom is place for learning and	classroom is win-lose situation
interacting with others	in which they must win

Independent	Dependent
thinks for his or herself	teacher is source of information and structure
works on his or her own	needs authorities to tell them what to do
will learn what is needed	learns only what is required
will listen to others	little intellectual curiosity
confident	

Individual Differences
Related to Grasha-Riechmann Learning Styles

The Grasha-Riechmann learning styles is closely associated with other cognitive styles and controls such as:

Locus of Control--This is a measure of one's feelings about the placement of control in life events and who is responsible for those events (see Chapter 28). Externals were more avoidant and nonparticipant.

Kolb Learning Styles--This is a measure of one's preferred style of perceiving and processing information (see chapter 20). Subjects who preferred avoidance to classroom interactions scored high in regard to concrete experiential learning style.

Instruments for Measuring Grasha-Riechmann Learning Styles

Student Learning Styles Scale (SLSS) (Grasha & Riechmann, 1975)

This is a 90-item self-report inventory that measures the preferences of college and high school students regarding the six dimensions of classroom interaction. It consists of six subscales of 15 items each for each of the six dimensions. Students are asked to rate their agreement or disagreement on a 5-point Likert scale. Sample questions include: "To get ahead in class, I think sometimes you have to step on the toes of the other students; I think an important part of classes is to learn to get along with other people; I accept the structure a teacher sets for a course; I study what is important to me and not necessarily what the instructor says is important; I am eager to learn about areas covered in class; I try to spend as little time as possible on a course outside of class." A composite score is averaged for each of the six styles.

Ferrell (1983) reported test-retest reliability range at .79 to .83 and construct validity through definitional methods used to develop the test. If the constructs are polar opposites, then each should be negatively correlated. Thompson, Finkler, and Walker (1979) found that only half (3/6) of the groups were between independence and dependence, 4/6 for avoidance/ participatory, and only 2/6 for avoidance/collaborative. The 4/6 collaborative/participatory results were positively correlated. They concluded that the inconsistent subscale relationships are problematic and will yield different internal and external validities.

The aforementioned instrument is not without faults. Grasha (1984) brought up two potential problems with any instruments that rely on "ranking and rating things important to learners" (p. 50). One problem revolves around the issue of frames of reference. When students are asked to rank the various activities they enjoy or attitudes they have about classroom procedures, they may be using different classes or an amalgamation of classes as a basis to form their judgments. Hence, a student might rank class discussion very low because he or she dislikes the content of a course which uses discussion as a major instructional strategy. Conversely, a student might rank a lecture class very high because the content appeals to him/her.

Data collection can also be problematic. When people answer questionnaires, they may not want to admit to behaviors which they believe to be socially undesirable. As Grasha (1984) stated, "No one knows the role that social desirability plays in responses to learning style instruments" (p. 50). Similarly, people may believe many things about themselves and use those beliefs as reference points when answering questionnaires, but they may act differently when actually involved in a learning situation.

Theoretical Background

Analysis of learning styles grew out of a desire to understand why individuals performed differently at the same tasks. One of the precursors of this analysis was the examination of personality attributes. These attributes were measured through various kinds of tests, including those that tried to relate various physical characteristics to personality. More recently, hundreds of personality tests have been developed that measure many different types of variables. Grasha (1984) distilled these variables into five categories: cognitive, sensory, interpersonal, intrapersonal, and environmental. Most theorists used a combination of these factors in designing the constructs their tests will measure. Grasha and Riechmann developed this inventory from two years of interviews with college age students at the University of Cincinnati. They used a "rational approach to scale construction" which used students to sort out the attributes into the three dimensions/six characteristics that were exhibited in classroom environments (Riechmann & Grasha, 1974). It was important to develop the instrument and the ideas behind this style based on theory rather than empirical development. As such, through several iterations, successful college undergraduates selected items that best represented classroom behaviors and preferences. Items were retained when there was a 70% agreement among the students.

The resultant instrument is recommended for gaining some insight into class preferences so that the learning environment might be tailored or remediated.

Grasha-Riechmann Learning Styles and Learning

Research

- Thompson et al. (1979) found no correlation of any of the subscales with field dependence/independence, in spite of the similarities in the name.

- Thompson et al. (1979) found that "males were more avoidant, competitive, and less collaborative and participatory than females" (p. 12).

Implications of the Characteristics and Research

The type of styles measured by this instrument deal with students' reactions to external events in the classroom rather than with thinking or learning patterns. Therefore, we are unable to draw implications from their social preferences for identifying strengths or weaknesses about learning strategies.

Grasha-Riechmann Learning Styles and Instruction

Research

- Sapp, Elliott, and Bounds (1983), using the Grasha-Riechmann Learning Styles Inventory Scale, identified the predominant styles of undergraduates as participant, collaborative, and dependent. They suggested that teaching strategies incorporating collaborative and participative factors should be used in college.

- Mucowksi and Hayden (1988), in an assessment of the learning styles of adult children of alcoholics, were able to identify the avoidant and dependent learners and correlate these dysfunctional styles with two role types of placator and action out. They suggested that early identification might facilitate change.

- Zelazek (1986) found that graduate students use different learning styles. Although no significant differences were found, the following trends were noted: men were more avoidant and women more participatory, and individuals were more independent, less avoidant, and more participatory, the greater the life stage.

Implications of the Characteristics and Research

Implications which are drawn from research are noted with a •; those drawn logically from descriptive information regarding the trait are noted by an *. Instructional conditions that capitalize on the preferences of the *competitive* student and challenge the *collaborative* student include:

* a variety of teaching methods
* teacher centered, not student centered focus
* leadership tasks
* opportunities to ask questions in class
* opportunities for recognition

Instructional conditions that remediate or compensate for the deficiencies of the competitive student include:

* providing a small group learning situation in which the learner can lead but is required to bring the group to consensus

Instructional conditions that capitalize on the preferences of the collaborative student and challenge the competitive student include:

* class discussions in small groups
* student designed and taught courses and classes

* group rather than individual projects
* peer-determined grades
* instructor-group interaction
* talking with others outside class about issues of course content

Instructional conditions that remediate or compensate for the deficiencies of the collaborative student include:

* providing opportunities for the learner to make sole decisions with the support of a group

Instructional conditions that capitalize on the preferences of the avoidant student and challenge the participant student include:

* no classroom activity
* no required readings or assignments
* unenthusiastic teachers
* no organized lectures
* no instructor-individual interactions
* self-evaluation
* no tests
* blanket grades with everyone passing

Instructional conditions that remediate or compensate for the deficiencies of the avoidant student include:

* identifying meaningful reinforcements in the learner's life, and drawing the relevance of the instruction to those

Instructional conditions that capitalize on the preferences of the participant student and challenge the avoidant student include:

* lectures and discussions
* opportunities for discussion
* both objective and essay tests
* class reading assignments
* teachers who can analyze and synthesize material well
* enthusiastic presentation of information

Instructional conditions that remediate or compensate for the deficiencies of the participant student include:

* this learner is very versatile and does not appear to have any particular deficiencies dealing with the classroom environment

Instructional conditions that capitalize on the preferences of the dependent student and challenge the independent student include:

* teacher-outlined assignments
* teacher-centered methods
* clear deadlines

Instructional conditions that remediate or compensate for the deficiencies of the dependent student include:

* providing opportunities for the learner to identify own tasks and standards but under the guidance of the instructor

Instructional conditions that capitalize on the preferences of the independent student and challenge the dependent student include:

* independent study
* self-paced assignments
* student designed projects
* student-centered versus teacher-centered methods

Instructional conditions that remediate or compensate for the deficiencies of the independent student include:

* providing opportunities for learning cooperation among groups within the context of leadership opportunities

References

Andrews, J. (1981). Teaching format and student style: Their interactive effects on learning. *Research in Higher Education, 14,* 161-178.

Ferrell, B. G. (1983). A factor-analytic comparison of four learning styles instruments. *Journal of Educational Psychology, 78*(1), 33-39.

Grasha, A. F. (1984). Learning styles: the journey from Greenwich Observatory (1796) to Dalhousie University (1984): An analysis and synthesis. *Improving College and University Teaching Journal, 32*(1), 46-53.

Grasha, A. F., & Riechmann, S. W. (1975). *Student Learning Styles Questionaire.* Cincinatti, OH: University of Cincinatti Faculty Resource Center.

Karrer, U. (1988). *Comparison of learning style inventories (LSI).* Research Report. (ERIC Document Reproduction Service No. ED 296 713)

Keefe, J. W. (1979). *Student learning styles: Diagnosing and prescribing programs.* Reston, VA: National Association of Secondary School Principals.

Mucowksi, R., & Hayden, R. R. (1988, February). *Adult children of alcoholic parents: Their roles and learning styles.* Paper presented at the Eastern Educational Research Association, Miami Beach. (ERIC Document Reproduction Service No. ED 305 527)

Riechmann, S. W. (1980). Learning styles: their role in teaching evaluation and course design. *Resources in Education, 15,* 133-142.

Riechmann, S. W., & Grasha, A. F. (1974). A rational approach to developing and assessing the validity of a student learning styles instrument. *Journal of Psychology, 87,* 213-223.

Sapp, G. L., Elliott, G. R., & Bounds, S. (1983). Dealing with diversity among college students. *Journal of Humanistic Education and Development, 22*(2), 80-85.

Thompson, R., Finkler, D., & Walker, S. (1979, April 8-12). *Interrelationships among five cognitive style tests, student characteristics, and achievement.* Paper presented at the annual meeting of the American Educational Research Association, San Francisco. (ERIC Document Reproduction Service No. ED 174 678)

Zelazek, J. R. (1986). *Learning styles, gender, and life change cycle stage: Relationships with respect to graduate students.* (ERIC Document Reproduction Service No. ED 276 371)

Bibliography

Hruska, S., & Grasha, A. F. (1982). *Student Learning Styles and Brain Behavior.* Alexandria, VA: National Association of Secondary School Principals.

23

GREGORC LEARNING STYLES

Description of Gregorc Learning Styles

The Gregorc Learning Style Delineator measures bidimensional patterns of learning preferences for making sense of the world through the perception and ordering of incoming information. Perceptual preference refers to acquisition in either an abstract or concrete manner, or in some combination. Abstract perception refers to the ability to process information through reason and intuition, often invisible to our physical senses. Concrete perception refers to the ability to process the physical aspects of information through the senses. Ordering preference refers to the way one arranges, prioritizes, and uses information in either a sequential or random order, or in some combination. A sequential style pertains to using a linear, step-by-step organizational scheme. Using a random order style involves organizing data in a networklike format relating data to each other in a variety of ways. Perception and ordering patterns combine into four basic mediation channels: the concrete sequential, the abstract sequential, the concrete random, and the concrete sequential. "These channels help people relate to the world by (style)." Gregorc believes that everyone can process information in any of these four manners. Beyond basic skill, however, individuals are predisposed to one or two of these channels. These predispositions, then, provide "psychological points of view, thinking patterns, mind sets, values and ways of expressing ourselves" (Gregorc, 1984).

Differences between the four types of learners have been delineated across 12 variables of perceiving and organizing: world of reality, ordering ability, view of time, thinking processes, validation process, focus of attention, creativity, approach to change, approach to life, environmental preference, use of language, and primary evaluative words (Gregorc, 1982b).

The *concrete sequential* learner is characterized by the preference for extracting information through hands-on experiences. These learners are orderly, logical, and sequential. The five senses are highly developed and used frequently. Mentally, the concrete sequential learners use if-then and premise-conclusions thought processes. They appreciate and need logic, are well organized, and strive for perfection. Learning is enhanced through hands-on experience. These learners will look for authority and guidance in the learning environment and will often have photographic memories.

The *concrete random* learner is characterized by the need to experiment with ideas and concepts and will employ trial and error in learning. These learners like to explore in a stimulus-rich environment and do not like "cut-and-dry" approaches. Especially in unstructured problem-solving experiences, they grasp information quickly and make broad intuitive judgments in an attempt to detect a unifying idea that relates a concept to the real world. This can result, however, in a tendency to jump to conclusions. These learners are insightful and can easily move from fact to theory. Unlike the concrete sequential learner, they do not like authoritative intervention.

The *abstract sequential* learner is characterized by strengths in the area of decoding written, verbal, and image symbols. This learner stores a wealth of conceptual mental pictures, against which he or she matches information read, heard, or seen in graphic or pictorial form. Preferences include presentations that have substance, are rational, and are sequential. They thrive on theories and making mental constructs. Even dull information will not detract this learner if it is well organized and meaningful. The abstract sequential learner synthesizes ideas and produces new concepts or comes to new conclusions. This learner will defer to authority and has a low tolerance for distractions.

The *abstract random* learner is characterized by a keen awareness of human behavior and an ability to evaluate and interpret atmosphere and mood. This learner associates the "medium with the message" and globalizes the learning experience. He or she learns best in an unstructured atmosphere conducive to group discussions, multisensory activities, and busy environments. These learners perceive and absorb information holistically and evaluate through personal and emotional experiences. They see relationships between people, ideas, places, and things. These learners are reflective and need time to process data before reacting to it.

Characteristic Differences in Gregorc Learning Styles

The styles developed by Gregorc are not described by polar extremes. Rather, individuals fall within ranges on both channels. Therefore, the range of characteristics are listed instead of presented on a bipolar continuum. These characteristics were suggested by Gregorc (1982a,b).

Concrete Sequential
derives information through direct hands-on experience
appreciates order
appreciates logical sequence in presentation
high sensory sensitivity
views time in discrete units
instinctive, methodical, deliberate, and structured
personalizes information

slightly adverse to change
realistic, patient, conservative, perfection-oriented
quiet, stable
succinct, logical use of language
literal

Concrete Random
experimental
trial and error
flashes of insight
intuitive, instinctive, impulsive
practical, applied
independent
doubts authority
three-dimensional thinking
inventive, original, futuristic
open to change
nonliteral

Abstract Sequential
highly verbal, precise, rational
hierarchical, two-dimensional abstract thinking
logical, analytical, synthesizing
uses conceptual pictures in learning
groups concepts and ideas vicariously
appreciates order
indecisive, deliberative
ordered, quiet
nonauthoritative

Abstract Random
feeling, emotional
random, nonlinear, multidimensional ordering
psychic, perceptive, critical
inner guided
focus on relationships
imaginative
impressionable
idealistic, exuberant, intense, active
tuned to nuances of mood and atmosphere
relates medium with message
global evaluation of the learning experience

Individual Differences Related to Gregorc Learning Styles

The Gregorc learning style is closely associated with other cognitive styles such as:

Kirton's Adaptive/Innovative (KAI)--This is a measure of whether or not the learner will use a conventional or innovative procedure for solving problems. Joniak and Isaksen (1988) found that in most cases Gregorc's sequentials were adapters and his random's were innovators, regardless of levels of concreteness or abstractness.

Instruments for Measuring Gregorc Learning Styles

Gregorc's Learning Style Delineator

The Gregorc Style Delineator is a self-report instrument that consists of 40 words arranged in 10 columns of four items each. Examples of these word groups are: "objective, evaluative, sensitive, intuitive; solid, quality, non-judgmental, insightful; persistent, analytical, aesthetic, experimenting." The subject is asked to rank the four words relative to who they are "deep down" with 4 being most , and 1 being least like themselves. Scores for each of the four types can range from 10 to 40. A score of 27 to 40 is considered high, 16 to 26, medium, and 10 to 15, low preference.

Gregorc (1984) reported internal consistency from .89 to .93, and test-retest reliability at .85 to .88. To test construct validity, he used a definitional strategy. After administering the instrument to 475 subjects, he distributed a list of characteristics and asked them to check those which related to their preferred mode of learning. He found 89% agreement with the categories and assessed style. Using confirmatory factor analysis, O'Brien (1990) also tested the construct validity of Gregorc's four channels. Because the Gregorc instrument is not structured to directly contrast abstract with concreteness and randomness with sequential, he constructed approximations of relationships in the model using path analysis (a multiple regression model) (Joreskog & Sorbom, 1989). This program composed matrices that could be analyzed. The results showed that although the correlations were within an acceptable range, they were much lower than the internal consistency estimates Gregorc found.

Joniak and Isaksen (1988) examined the relationship between the Gregorc Style Delineator and Kirton's Adaptive Innovative Distinction (KAI) to investigate the construct validity of the Style Delineator. Using Cronbach's alpha coefficient, they found the KAI to be reliable; however, the alphas showed internal inconsistencies within the subscales of the Gregorc delineator, with no clear polar dimensions. Cronbach's alpha ranged from .23 to .66 on the four scales.

Sewell (1986) severely criticized the results reported by Gregorc: "A review of psychometric information provided in the manual provides little information to support the reliability or validity of the instrument. Normative data is nonexistent. The validity and reliability information provided is so limited and methodologically flawed that no firm conclusions can be drawn" (p. 53).

Theoretical Background

The development of the Gregorc Learning Style evolved from phenomenological research in the classroom using "extensive observations, in-depth interviews, and subsequent analysis of data from students and teachers who are involved in learning and teaching style activities" to study diagnostic/prescriptive instruction and its implications for individual learners (Keefe, 1987). Fundamental to the development of the characteristics of this style is the belief that individuals possess internal, subjective patterns of learning that include general qualities held in common by others, as well as specific physical, emotional and mental qualities that are unique. Gregorc and Ward (1977) developed the idea of mind styles to understand those common and unique patterns of learning and, with that understanding, to help individuals interact more successfully with the outside world. Their notion of styles is based on the Mediation Ability Theory, which states: "The human mind has channels through which it receives and expresses information most efficiently and effectively." They studied the concept of duality in perception and ordering, and identified the bipolar styles of abstract/concrete and sequential/random. They found that these sets of dualities joined together to form the four learner preferences or modes: abstract sequential, abstract random, concrete sequential, and concrete random.

Through interviews, Gregorc and Ward (1977) ascertained that the instructional materials and teaching techniques used by teachers have a direct effect on students. When there is a fit between teachers and learner preferences, the learner usually reacts favorably.

Gregorc Learning Styles and Learning

Research

- In a study of the relationship of learning style to gender and age, Davenport (1986) found that, in general, males preferred the abstract sequential learning style and women preferred abstract random. No age relationships were found.

- Physicians were studied to determine any prevalent learning styles and 63% preferred a concrete sequential style (Van Voorhees, Wolf, Gruppen, & Stross, 1988).

- Walton (1988) investigated the interaction between communication styles and personality types in single mother-son relationships. The concrete abstract and random sequential styles were found to affect this relationship.

- Kreuze and Payne (1989) investigated the relationship of style to learning style preferences of Hispanic and Anglo college students and found no significant patterns.

- Abel, Herbster, and Prince (1989) found no significant relationship between stress level and learning style in elementary or secondary teachers.

Implications of the Characteristics and Research

Other than the practical research conducted by the authors, little research has investigated the relationship of this construct to learning. Therefore, it is with this caveat that we include this section. The conclusions we draw are based on theoretical descriptions rather than empirical findings regarding the various types of styles.

Implications which are drawn from research are noted with a •; those drawn logically from descriptive information regarding the trait are noted by an *. Based on the very limited amount of research and descriptions of the Gregorc Learning Style, we conclude that concrete sequential learners are more likely to excel at learning tasks such as:

* physical manipulations and model building
* planning and conducting lab experiments
* problem solving that involves synthesizing data that can be manipulated concretely
* recognition of cause-and-effect relationships
* conducting task analyses
* writing and following procedural directions
* planning and budgeting time for self and group learning
* flowcharting
* developing logical arguments

and acquire and use effectively learning strategies such as:

* setting learning goals
* selecting information sources

* gauging learning difficulty
* estimating time and effort
* generating examples
* analyzing key ideas
* outlining
* imaging

Based on the limited amount of research and descriptions of the Gregorc Learning Style, we conclude that concrete random learners are more likely to excel at learning tasks such as:

* physical manipulations and model building
* conducting lab experiments
* exploration
* problem solving that involves synthesizing data that can be manipulated concretely
* applying theory and creation of practical examples
* independent thinking
* self-proofs
* intuitive thinking such as troubleshooting
* creating hypotheses
* three dimensional thinking
* questioning authority
• competition

and acquire and use effectively learning strategies such as:

* searching for information
* paraphrasing, summarizing
* generating metaphors and examples
* concept mapping/semantic networking
* inferring causes
* evaluating implications
* judging utility or value of knowledge

Based on the limited amount of research and descriptions of the Gregorc Learning Style, we conclude that abstract sequential learners are more likely to excel at learning tasks such as:

* interpreting textual, and auditory material
* vocabulary building
* verbal learning
* conceptual, hierarchical model building
* abstracting
* logically analyzing problems
* integrating disparate information

* creating matrices
* deliberation and debate
* recognizing main ideas, summarizing and allowing for drawing logical conclusions
* hypothesizing

and acquire and use effectively learning strategies such as:

* evaluating current information
* outlining
* repeating material to be recalled
* comparing new knowledge with existing knowledge
* analyzing key ideas
* synthesizing
* evaluating implications

Based on the very limited amount of research and descriptions of the Gregorc Learning Style, we conclude that abstract random learners are more likely to excel at learning tasks such as:

* global evaluation
* organizing unstructured tasks
* interpersonal encounters and discussions
* affective analysis
* multidimensional analysis
* creative, imaginative tasks
* using symbolic representation

and acquire and use effectively learning strategies such as:

* generating metaphors an analogies
* imaging or illustrating knowledge
* concept mapping/semantic networking

Gregorc Learning Style and Instruction

Research

• Gregorc and Ward (1977) correlated study strategies and styles and found that concrete sequential learners preferred workbooks, ditto sheets, computer-assisted instruction, and kits. Abstract random learners preferred television, movies, and group discussion. Abstract sequential learners preferred lectures, audio tapes, and extensive reading. Concrete random learners preferred independent study, games, and simulations.

- Student teachers were found to be concrete sequential or abstract random learners. There was consistency in the ratings of those who were concrete sequential, indicating a commonality of thought for these types (Walker & Kleine, 1985).

- Lundstrom and Martin (1986) studied the relationship between the learning styles of undergraduates and students involved in a self-study or group interaction method of instruction. They found no achievement or attitude interactions on any of the styles.

- Herbster, Abel, Hargrove, and Weems (1987) found a significant interrelationship between learning style and Joyce and Weil's models of teaching. Conceptual sequential learners preferred information processing; abstract random learners preferred personal/family; abstract sequential learners preferred information processing; and concrete random learners had no consistently identifiable preferred model. No significant relationship was found between learning style and critical thinking modes (risk taking , assumption analysis, or openness).

- No relationship was found between Gregorc learning styles and the reading achievement of sixth-grade students (Atchison & Brown, 1988).

Implications of the Characteristics and Research

Implications which are drawn from research are noted with a •; those drawn logically from descriptive information regarding the trait are noted by an *. Instructional conditions that capitalize on the preferences of the concrete sequential student and may challenge the concrete random, abstract sequential, or abstract random student include:

- workbooks
- ditto sheets
- computer-assisted instruction
- kits
* highly structured and organized information
* hands-on manipulation
* explaining purpose and relevance of content
* describing required performance and standard performance
* pictorial presentation: show maps, globes, pictures, tables
* providing prototypical examples and close-in nonexamples
* advising learner of instructional support needed
* asking the learner to select task difficulty and time
* creating summaries: hierarchical titles
* note taking
* creating content outline
* providing feedback after practice

* providing massed practice sessions
* sequencing instruction in a logical, hierarchical order
* sequencing instruction from concrete to abstract
* providing structured questioning and answering sessions (questions from students, answers from the authority--the teacher, professor, or trainer)
* presenting advance organizers
* presenting structured outlines and organizers

Instructional conditions that remediate or compensate for the deficiencies of the concrete sequential student include:

* using verbal comparatives, relating content familiar to learner
* providing graphic organizers/overviews

Instructional conditions that capitalize on the preferences of the concrete random student and challenge the concrete sequential, abstract sequential, or abstract random student include:

* asking the learner to pose questions to be answered by lesson
* asking the learner to select own goals
* asking the learner to establish criteria for standard performance
* varying lesson unit size
* using divergent, concrete examples
* asking the learner to evaluate meaningfulness of information
* inferring from information
* providing informative, analytical, and enrichment feedback
* using an inductive sequence
* using conceptual elaboration
• using games, simulations
* problem-solving activities
• independent study projects
* using minilectures as triggers for exploration
* optional reading assignments
* open-ended assignments

Instructional conditions that remediate or compensate for the deficiencies of the concrete random student include:

* providing lists of steps in sequences to fill in intuitive leaps
* providing abstract examples
* creating summaries with hierarchical titles

Instructional conditions that capitalize on the preferences of the abstract sequential student and challenge the concrete sequential, concrete random, or abstract random student include:

* gaining the learner's attention by posing questions
* explaining the purpose or relevance of content
* asking the learner to establish criteria for standard performance
* presenting verbal expository advance organizers
* presenting written or verbal structured overviews and organizers
* providing opportunities for the analysis of key ideas
* creating content outlines, or hierarchical concept maps
* categorizing elements
* sequencing instruction according to content organization
* mentally stimulating activities that are ordered, environmentally quiet, and nonauthoritative
• reading, lectures, audiotapes
* orderly, rational presentations by authorities

Instructional conditions that remediate or compensate for the deficiencies of the abstract sequential student include:

* facilitating learner elaborations by first providing images, analogies, and then requesting them of the learner
* facilitating organization through pattern notes or graphic organizers by first providing them and then having them generated by the learner

Instructional conditions that capitalize on the preferences of the abstract random student and challenge the concrete sequential, concrete random, or abstract sequential student include:

* arousing the learner with novelty, uncertainty and surprise
* posing questions to the learner
* facilitating learner elaborations through imaging, analogies, creating story lines
* providing opportunities to integrate new knowledge
* using inductive sequencing of instructional events
* unstructured learning environments
• group discussion, or teamwork
* multisensory experiences free from rules or guidelines
* reflective exercises
* short reading assignments
• using movies and television
* group discussion
* providing question and answer sessions

Instructional conditions that remediate or compensate for the deficiencies of the abstract random student include:

* providing content outlines or hierarchical organizers and then asking
  the to learner generate them
* providing lectures in small chunks, followed by group discussion

References

Abel, F. J., Herbster, D. L., & Prince, R. H. (1989, February 22). *Learning style and in-service teacher stress: Is there a relationship and what can be done about it?* Paper presented at the annual meeting of the Association of Teacher Educators, St. Louis, MO. (ERIC Document Reproduction Service No. ED 304 419)

Atchison, M. K., & Brown, D. M. (1988, November 9-11). *The relationship between the learning styles and reading achievement of sixth-grade students in the state of Alabama.* Paper presented at the annual meeting of the Mid-South Educational Research Association, Louisville, KY. (ERIC Document Reproduction Service No. ED 300 772)

Davenport, J. A. (1986). Learning style and its relationship to gender and age among Elderhostel participants. *Educational Gerontology, 12*(3), 205-217.

Gregorc, A. F. (1982a). *An adult's guide to style.* Maynard, MA: Gabriel Systems, Inc.

Gregorc, A. F. (1982b). *Gregorc style delineator.* Maynard, MA: Gabriel Systems, Inc.

Gregorc, A. F. (1984). Style as a symptom: A phenomenological perspective. *Theory into practice, 23*(1), 51-55.

Gregorc, A. F., & Ward, H. B. (1977). A new definition for individual. *NASSP Bulletin, 61,* 20-26.

Herbster, D. L., Abel, F. J., Hargrove, J. A., & Weems, D. (1987). *Integrating learning styles, critical thinking and models of teaching in the student teaching experience* (Research Report). (ERIC Document Reproduction Service No. ED 303 462)

Joniak, A. J., & Isaksen, S. G. (1988). The Gregorc Style Delineator: Internal consistency and its relationship to Kirton's adaptive-innovative distinction. *Educational and Psychological Measurement, 48*(4),1043-1049.

Joreskog, K. G., & Sorbom, D. (1989). *LISREL 7: A guide to the program and applications* (2nd ed.). Chicago: SPSS.

Keefe, J. (1987). *Learning style: Theory and practice.* Reston, VA: National Association of Secondary School Principals.

Kreuze, J. G., & Payne, D. D. (1989). The learning style preferences of Hispanic and Anglo college students: A comparison. *Reading Improvement, 26*(2), 166-169.

Lundstrom, K. V., & Martin, R. E. (1986). Matching college instruction to student learning style. *College Student Journal, 20*(3), 270-274.

O'Brien, T. P. (1990). Construct validation of the Gregorc Style Delineator: An application of LISREL 7. *Educational and Psychological Measurement, 50,* 631-636.

Sewell, T. J. (1986). *The Measurement of learning style: A critique of four assessment tools* (Research Report). Green Bay: Wisconsin University Assessment Center. (ERIC Document Reproduction Service No. ED 267 247)

Van Voorhees, C., Wolf, F. M., Gruppen, L. D., & Stross, J. K. (1988). Learning styles and continuing medical education. *Journal of Continuing Education in the Health Professions, 8*(4), 257-265.

Walker, R. M., & Kleine, P. F. (1985, October 23-25). *Constructs and style preferences of student teachers.* Paper presented at the meeting of the Rocky Mountain Educational Research Association, Las Cruces, NM. (ERIC Document Reproduction Service No. ED 264 229)

Walton, W. T. (1988). The effects of personality types and communication/behavior styles of single parent mothers on their male children. *International Journal for the Advancement of Counselling, 11*(4), 283-291.

Bibliography

Cronbach, L. J. (1951). Coefficient alpha and the internal structure of tests. *Psychometrika, 16,* 297-334.

Gregorc, A. F. (1979). Learning/teaching styles: Potent forces behind them. *Educational Leadership, 36,* 234-36.

Gregorc, A. F. (1985). *Inside styles: Beyond the basics.* Maynard, MA: Gabriel Systems.

Kirton, M. J. (1976). Adapters and innovators: A description and measure. *Journal of Applied Psychology, 61,* 622-629.

PART VI

PERSONALITY TYPES AND LEARNING

Introduction

Personality is perhaps the broadest dimension of individual differences, subsuming to a large degree, most of the other dimensions. Its essence, the crux of human differences, has occupied philosophers and psychologists for centuries. Personality has often been defined in terms of the characteristics of human behavior or in terms of the sum of our inherited and learned mental qualities. Some theorists have defined personality as the organization and integration of components or attributes of personality, such as Freud's ego, id, and super ego. Other definitions are sociocultural, descriptive of our ability to adapt and adjust to our social and cultural environment.

    Perhaps the oldest approach to the study of personality (one that is consistent with the theme of this book) is the identification of personality types based on individual traits. Aristotle and his contemporaries studied the "humors," bodily substances that supposedly produced different temperaments. These humors have given rise to four temperaments: sanguine (enthusiastic, sociable, contented), melancholic (sad, anxious, worried, serious), choleric (irritable, hot-headed, histrionic), and phlegmatic (passive, controlled, calm) (Eysenck & Eysenck, 1985). These temperaments, according to the Greeks, result from an overabundance of different bodily fluids. Since the Greeks, personality researchers have focused on defining personality types through different classification schemes based on shared human characteristics.

    Twentieth century research has featured personality assessment by researchers such as Cattell, Eysenck, and a host of people studying Jungian types who have used factor analysis to isolate personality types, much the same as intelligence researchers used it to isolate mental abilities (see Part II). Most of this research has produced a consistent set of factors, often referred to as the "Big 5" (McCrae, 1989). These five most robust major personality types describe dimensions of personality (Digman, 1989; Digman & Inouye, 1986), including:

- surgency
  talkative-silent
  social-reclusive
  adventurous-cautious

- agreeableness
  good natured-irritable
  mild-headstrong
  cooperative-negativistic

- conscientiousness
  responsible-undependable
  persevering-quitting
  tidy-carelessness

- emotional stability
  calm-anxious
  composed-excitable
  poised-nervous

- intellect
  intellectual-nonreflective
  imaginative-simple
  artistic-insensitive

Clearly, individuals exhibit many intellective, emotional, and motivational traits that describe how they interact with their sociocultural environment. Researchers have debated for years about just how many personality types there are. What is important to this book is not the specific number of traits but rather how those traits that do exist interact with learning and instruction.

The model of personality that we use to organize this part of the book and relate it to other parts was developed by Miller (1988, 1991), whose typology consists of three personality dimensions: cognitive, affective, and conative. These types describe three dimensions of characteristics that interact with each other, as illustrated in Fig. 24.1. Miller and his model have strong associations to learning and education, which makes this an appropriate structure for the following discussion.

Cognitive Dimension. The cognitive dimension in Miller's model is consistent with other theories that stress the importance of intellective functions to the personality. Miller's conception of the cognitive dimension, however, relates to cognitive style rather than cognitive ability or content. The ability descriptions were summarized in Part II of the book. Cognitive style relates to *how*, rather than *what*, an individual cognizes or thinks and was described in Parts III and IV of this volume. The most pervasive style or cognitive trait in Miller's model is an analytic-holistic dimension, which describes a tendency to focus on parts as opposed to wholes.

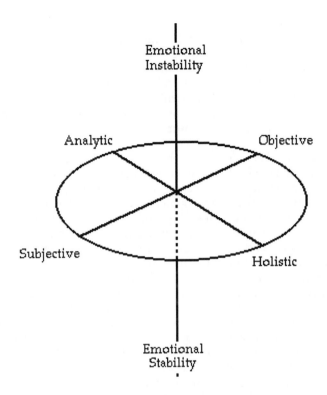

Fig. 24.1. Miller's Personality Typology.

Analytic individuals have a tendency to break down objects into parts and study each part as a discrete entity in isolation from its context. Holistic thinkers perceive objects as wholes, including the context in which they occur. This analytic-holistic dimension is an underlying principle of many cognitive controls and styles such as field independence, cognitive flexibility, cognitive complexity, serialist/holist, and conceptual style. Miller has described what is perhaps the most pervasive style dimension in the cognitive domain.

Affective Dimension. The affective dimension combines the pervasive personality traits, extroversion and neuroticism (see chapter 29), into a dimension, labeled emotional stability-instability, which refers to the intensity of emotional reactions to life. At one end of the dimension (see Fig. VI.1) are individuals who react to all events with such strength that their lives and those around them are made difficult. At the other extreme of the affective personality dimension is the placid individual, slow to anger or excite and emotionally stable. Emotions are most often expressed in arousal-behavioral, neurological/physiological, and cognitive terms. Emotionally unstable individuals are easily aroused and tend to react more negatively when aroused. Chapters 24 through 27 describe this affective personality dimension. Anxiety, tolerance for unrealistic experiences, ambiguity tolerance, and frustration tolerance are affective traits that have been shown to affect learning and instruction. Many other traits could be used to instantiate this affective dimension; however, these are the ones related to the learning process, the primary focus of this book.

Conative Dimension. Conative behavior, according to Miller, refers to the effortful, striving, self-willing, volitional behavior of individuals. He uses conation to describe the conscious motivational aspects of personality rather than unconscious drive states or behavioral response tendencies that are popular in social learning and personality theory. This "will" component is extremely important to learning and instructional outcomes because it determines an individual's predilection to perform. The conative dimension (objective-subjective) refers to motivational content, those things for which people strive. The objective-subjective dimension (see Fig. VI.1) refers to an intrapsychic conflict between the need for individuality (autonomy, independence...objective experiences) and interdependence (cooperation, collaboration, intimacy...subjective experiences). Individuals at the objective end of the dimension seek power and emotional detachment, whereas those at the subjective end seek love and empathy. Chapters 28 through 31 describe those conative dimensions of personality that have been shown to affect learning and instruction. These dimensions include locus of control, extroversion, achievement motivation, and risk taking. Many other personality characteristics may be used to instantiate the conative dimension, but these are the best known and most related to the learning process.

Personality Types. Combining the cognitive and conative dimensions, Miller identified four distinct personality types.

* *Reductionist* (objective-analytic): scientific, impersonal, precise, value-free, realistic, controlled, impersonal, skeptical

* *Schematist* (objective-holist): conceptual, theorist, value-free, imaginative, ambiguous, speculative
* *Gnostic* (subjective-analytic): artistic, personal, value-based, non-rational, personal knowledge, involved, biased

* *Romantic* (subjective-holistic): political, personal, value-based, uncertain causes, imaginative, speculative

These personality types are merely indicators that are descriptive of different types of individuals. Those differences affect how individuals perceive themselves and the world. Different personality types react variably to different types of learning and to different instructional techniques.

References

Digman, J. (1989). Five robust trait dimensions: Development, stability, and utility. *Journal of Personality, 57*, 195-214.

Digman, J., & Inouye, J. (1986). Further specification of the five robust factors of personality. *Journal of Personality and Social Psychology, 50*, 116-123.

Eysenck, H., & Eysenck, M. (1985). *Personality and individual differences.* New York: Plenum.

McCrae, R. R. (1989). Why I advocate the five-factor model: Joint factor analysis of the NEO-PI with other instruments. In D. M. Buss & N. Cantor (Eds.), *Personality psychology: Recent trends and emerging directions* (pp. 237-245). New York: Springer-Verlag.

Miller, A. (1988). Toward a typology of personality types. *Canadian Psychology, 29*, 263-283.

Miller, A. (1991). *Personality types: A modern synthesis.* Calgary, AL, Canada: University of Calgary Press.

24

ANXIETY

Description of Anxiety

Anxiety, part of an individual's emotional structure, is most commonly used in modern psychology to denote a "transitory emotional state or condition characterized by feelings of tension and apprehension and heightened autonomic nervous system activity" (Spielberger, 1972, p. 24). This emotional state has been attributed to causing both negative and positive effects--effects which motivate and facilitate as well as disrupt and inhibit cognitive actions such as learning. Although many feel that anxiety is synonymous with fear, this is an incomplete perception. Izard (1972) defined anxiety as being comprised of a combination of interacting fundamental effects: neurophysiological (such as tremors, sweating hands, flushing, increased heart rate, high blood pressure) behavioral-expressive, and phenomenological or subjective. He proposed, therefore, that anxiety includes fear reactions plus two or more basic emotions: distress, anger, shame (including shyness and guilt), on the negative side, and interest and excitement representing the positive side. Individuals differ in the intensity of their reactions to anxiety depending on their predisposition to experiencing anxiety and the level of anxiety-causing stimuli. Three types of anxiety were defined:

- *Trait Anxiety*--This denotes an anxiety that is a general personality trait, a semipermanent predisposition to experience a similar level of anxiety across a number of situations. The more trait anxiety individuals possess, the more likely they are to become anxious in many different situations.

- *State Anxiety*--This relates to anxiety that varies depending on an event or combination of events experienced at the time. It represents a transient emotional mood or condition. State anxiety is determined by the interaction of trait anxiety and the situational threat perceived, and so is responsive to situational factors. An individual who generally responds to any number of situations with low anxiety may react with high anxiety if there are multiple anxiety-causing conditions present.

• *Situation-Specific Anxiety*--This describes anxiety that occurs consistently over time in a given situation. Taking tests might cause situation-specific anxiety in some students, whereas for others, it may be giving an oral report that causes the anxiety.

Liebert and Morris (1967) made an important distinction between the cognitive and motivational-arousal components of anxiety. They describe these two aspects of anxiety as worry and emotionality. Worry is the cognitive component of anxiety. It involves concern about how one is performing and is associated with negative task expectations and negative self-evaluations. Emotionality involves fluctuation in the level of physiological functioning and the feelings of uneasiness, tension, and nervousness that it creates.

Finally, Yerkes, and Dodson (1908) found a curvilinear relationship between the levels of anxiety and task difficulty. A certain level of arousal is needed for the performance of any task. This is represented by the Zone of Comfort. Too little arousal results in boredom, whereas too much arousal results in debilitating distraction. This comfort zone varies depending on the level of cognitive processing required of the task. A high level of arousal enhances the performance of low-level tasks, whereas it will impair performance of high-level tasks requiring deeper processing.

Characteristic Differences in Anxiety

High Anxiety   **Low Anxiety**

Physiological:

high physiological response_____low or no physiological response

Behavioral:

restlessness_____calmness
tenseness of posture_____relaxed posture
increased rate of speech_____normal rate of speech
general distractibility_____focused attention
more frequent experiences of anxiety (trait)_____infrequent experiences of
                                                                                                       anxiety
wide range of situations perceived   narrow range of situations perceived
as dangerous or threatening (trait)_____as dangerous or threatening
high state anxiety response_____lower state anxiety response
self-esteem threatened_____confident
shallow processing facilitated_____deeper processing facilitated
better performance on simple tasks___better performance on complex tasks
difficulty in communicating_____good communication skills

<u>**High Anxiety**</u>   <u>**Low Anxiety**</u>

Psychological:

shy_____adventuresome
negative attitudes_____positive attitudes
negative self-image_____positive self-image
insecure, cautious_____secure
less task or academically oriented_____task or academically oriented
submissive_____independent
lack of ambition, responsibility_____ambitious, responsible
underactivity, underachievement_____active, achieving
hides emotions_____shows emotions

These characteristics were identified by Tucker, Hamayan, and Genessee (1976); Trylong (1987); Lipsitt (1958); Rosenberg (1953); Suinn and Hill (1964); Sarason, Davidson, Lighthall, Waite, and Ruebush (1960); Sarason (1975); and Davidson (1959).

Individual Differences Related to Anxiety

Anxiety is closely associated with other cognitive styles and controls:

Ambiguity Tolerance--This attentional-engagement style refers to the willingness to accommodate or adapt to ambiguity in various situations (see chapter 26). Intolerance of ambiguity was found to be positively associated with the level of anxiety in an interview situation (Keenan, 1978). Less tolerant individuals tend to be more anxious.

Frustration Tolerance--This attentional-engagement style describes and predicts the quality of a person's performance in a task after frustration occurs (see chapter 27). Low-frustration tolerance individuals were more anxious, worried a great deal, were troubled with thoughts of hell, had more severe headaches, and more often than not had an unhappy childhood (Watson, 1934).

Locus of Control--This expectency-incentive style is a measure of one's feelings about placement of control in his or her life events and who is responsible for those events (see chapter 28). Kennedy-Liaing (1980) found considerable overlap between locus of control and state anxiety. Externals are more likely to be anxious in general (Joe, 1971). They are also the least anxious in traditional, teacher-centered, lecture, highly structured learning environments. Biaggio (1985) found a significant positive correlation between externality and trait anxiety in undergraduate females.

Achievement and Attitudes--Anxiety was negatively correlated with achievement in foreign language classes, whereas favorable attitudes were positively related to achievement. There was also a negative relationship between anxiety and attitudes, such that anxious students tended to have less positive attitudes (Trylong, 1987). Whereas some studies reported a significant relationship between test anxiety and course grades, others found no relationship. The general belief of educators, however, is that such a relationship exists (Hunsley, 1985).

Intelligence--Early in learning, high-anxiety levels help the performances of subjects with high IQs and impair function for those with low IQs (as compared to those with low anxiety) (Gaudry & Spielberger, 1971).

Instruments for Measuring Anxiety

The Test Anxiety Questionnaire (TAQ) (Mandler & Sarason, 1952)

Mandler and Sarason (1952) designed the TAQ to measure the anxiety reactions of adults taking course examinations or intelligence tests. This test was revised by Mandler and Cowen (1958) for high school students (The Test Anxiety Scale) and again by Sarason and his colleagues in 1960 for children (Test Anxiety Scale for Children or TASC). The TASC has 30 questions about test situations to which the respondent answers yes or no. The following are representative examples from the questionnaires: "Do you think you worry more about school than do other children?" and "Do you worry a lot before you take a test?" No reliability data were available for this instrument.

The Manifest Anxiety Scale (MAS) (Taylor, 1953)

The MAS was the first anxiety questionnaire to be developed and used extensively for research. Using a true and false format, the subject is asked 50 questions similar to the Minnesota Multiphasic Personality Inventory (MMPI). Examples include: "I blush easily" and "I worry more than other people." The score is based on the total number of items marked positively as indicative of the presence of anxiety. Compared to the State-Trait Anxiety Style Inventory (STAI), it lacks a similar reliability and validity and takes considerably more time to administer because of the greater number of items.

The Achievement Anxiety Test (AAT) (Alpert & Haber, 1960)

Because both the TASC and TAQ were based on the assumption that there is a high negative correlation between debilitating and facilitating anxiety, Alpert and Haber (1960) constructed the AAT to differentiate among individuals whose academic performance is facilitated or impaired by the stress of the testing situation. They felt that it is possible to have both debilitating and facilitative effects, neither, or one or the other. Therefore, two scales comprise this test: a 9-item "facilitating anxiety scale," and a 10-item "debilitating anxiety scale." The items on the test were chosen from a larger pool of test items based on their ability to predict the grade point average of college students. The facilitating anxiety scale asks such questions as: "Nervousness while taking a test helps me to do better" and "I look forward to exams." Samples of items on the debilitating anxiety scale are: "In a course where I have been doing poorly, my fear of a bad grade cuts down my efficiency" and "I find myself reading exam questions without understanding them, and I must go back over them so that they will make sense." No reliability or validity data were available for this test.

State-Trait Anxiety Inventory (STAI) (Spielberger, 1983)

The STAI is currently the most widely used and most theoretically and methodologically sound instrument for measuring both trait and state anxiety in a variety of contexts. There are two scales, one each for trait and state anxiety. Each scale contains 20 items; 10 items are keyed positively and 10 are keyed negatively for anxiety. Both scales use self-report questions with a 4-point Likert scale. The trait scale assesses the subjects' feelings *in general*, by asking questions such as: "I feel pleasant" and "I become tense and upset when I think about my present concern." The state anxiety scale asks questions about how the subject feels *at the particular moment* they are taking the test, such as: "I feel upset" and "I feel calm." Alpha reliability coefficients are consistently reported to be above .90.

Theoretical Background

Arousal and performance were related as early as 1908. The Yerkes-Dodson Law assumed a curvilinear relationship between arousal and performance, with the optimal level of *performance* resulting from moderate levels of arousal. The optimal level of arousal for maximum performance was found to vary inversely with the difficulty of the task (Yerkes & Dodson, 1908).

Spence and Spence (1966) investigated this relationship by teaching laboratory animals to learn simple tasks. They found that performance was a function of habit-strength and drive [P=f(H*D)]. In this case, *habit-strength* is defined as the existing tendency to make a response (determined by the frequency and complexity of the response), and drive, which energizes or activates the behavior of the learner. He hypothesized that the effect of drive on performance will depend on the level of difficulty of the task for the learner. In other words, in a simple task in which the correct response is dominant, high drive will facilitate performance, but in a more complex task, in which incorrect responses are stronger, high drive will impair performance.

Gaudry and Spielberger (1971) extended Spence's work, using the Manifest Anxiety Scale (Taylor, 1953) to measure drive in humans. They found that high-anxious subjects performed better than low-anxious subjects on simple tasks but performed more poorly than the low-anxious subjects on complex tasks.

Sarason's conception of test anxiety was influenced by psychoanalytic theory. He believed that anxiety is environmentally developed through the constant evaluation of the individual in the family setting, in the earliest years, and then continually throughout life. When negative evaluation occurs, feelings of hostility can result. Because of their dependent role, children are unable to express negative feelings. This may result in an elevated level of guilt and anxiety. These children then appear "dependent, unaggressive, and self-derogatory in test-like situations" (Sarason et al., 1960, p. 15) because they are more attentive to their own anxiety responses than to the task. Performance may be impaired, if they realize that they are being evaluated, because of the resulting elevated level of anxiety. This conception of anxiety influenced his development of the TAQ with Mandler in 1952.

The distinction of state and trait anxiety was promoted by Cattell and Scheier (1961) and Spielberger (1966) with the premise that state anxiety should be more predictive of task performance than trait anxiety. The trait-state anxiety theory states that stress in a situation will be perceived as threatening, which, in turn, will elevate state anxiety. The perception of threat is largely dependent on past experience. Individuals with high trait anxiety will be more prone to feeling threatened and experiencing elevated state anxiety.

The next important distinction to be made was between the cognitive and motivational components of anxiety (Liebert & Morris, 1967). Eysenck (1979) argued that anxiety caused by the inclusion of task-irrelevant *cognitive* activities, or those activities that result when someone is anxious, will impair the quality of performance. Because working memory is theorized to have limited capacity, task-irrelevant information competes with the task-relevant information for processing. However, the *motivational* component of anxiety, the positive emotionality portion, should enhance the quality of performance by inducing increased effort and attention. High-anxiety subjects who are more motivated than low-anxiety subjects should exert more effort. An additional factor, however, is that motivation is directly related to the probability of success, (high probability of success, high motivation). This complicates the motivation/anxiety/performance relationship because high-anxiety individuals tend to set difficult goals, which have a lower probability of success, and thus tend to lessen motivation.

The progression of research over the past 40 plus years has made significant contributions to linking anxiety to learning and instruction. The next two sections summarize those links.

Anxiety and Learning

Research

• French class anxiety was more evident as students progressed to higher grades. By grade 11, anxiety in French class was one of the best predictors of language proficiency (Gardner, Smythe, Clement, & Gliksman, 1976).

• High anxiety impaired the rehearsal and storage of task-relevant information in demanding and complex tasks. Access and transformation times remained the same for both high- and low-anxiety subjects (Eysenck, 1985).

• In a moderately difficult problem-solving task involving ego stress, high anxiety reduced the performances of high-IQ subjects compared to low-anxiety subjects. Reassurance was debilitating to low anxiety subjects but was beneficial to high-IQ boys (Gupta & Sharma, 1986).

• Sharma and Gupta (1988) found that high-intelligence subjects showed the debilitating effects of high anxiety and ego-stress in an anagram task. Those with low anxiety also showed debilitated performance from reassurance.

• Language classes were more anxiety provoking than other courses such as math or English. In studies by both Horwitz, Horwitz, and Cope (1986) and MacIntyre and Gardner (1989), French classes were found to produce more anxiety.

• Chapin (1989) found that anxiety facilitated the academic performance of high anxiety, high performers but debilitated high anxiety, low performers.

• Low trait anxiety subjects under stress and high trait anxiety subjects not under stress set more narrow boundaries to categories, created more categories, and rejected more nonprototype members than low trait anxiety subjects not under stress or high trait anxiety subjects under stress. High trait anxiety subjects under stress had more difficulty perceiving similarities (Mikulincer, Kedem, & Paz, 1990).

• High trait anxiety undergraduates did not demonstrate higher state anxiety than low trait anxiety subjects on immediate recall but did on long-term retention, suggesting possible habituation to threatening stimuli that is associated with the task (Johnsen, Hohn, & Dunbar, 1973). They also found that high trait anxiety undergraduates experienced higher state anxiety regardless of test difficulty. Perceptual differences of test difficulty was significant for high and low trait anxiety groups but not for the medium trait anxiety group (Johnsen, Hohn, & Dunbar, 1991).

Implications of the Characteristics and Research

Although the amount of research on the construct of anxiety itself is extensive, the breadth of evidence is limited, yet fairly conclusive, concerning its affects on learning. Implications which are drawn from research are noted with a •; those drawn logically from descriptive information regarding the trait are noted by an *. We conclude that *high-anxiety* learners are more likely to excel at learning tasks such as:

* simple, noncomplex tasks
* mechanical tasks
* repetitive tasks
* those which require reassurance
* those which require visual discrimination
* those which require heightened awareness
* those which require shallow processing
* those which do not require effective communication

and acquire and use effectively learning strategies such as:
* repetition
* rehearsal strategies
* using/creating mnemonics
* searching for information

We conclude that *low-anxiety* learners are more likely to excel at learning tasks such as:

• language learning
• rehearsal and storage of task-relevant information
• problem solving
* complex tasks
• those which require deep processing
• those which require concentration
• those which require analysis
• those which require transfer
• those which require effective communication
• those which require comprehension

and acquire and use effectively learning strategies such as:

* paraphrasing
* analyzing key ideas
* prediction
* inferencing
* evaluation

Anxiety and Instruction

Research

* Highly anxious children looked for "safe" ways to express their anxiety and hostility; therefore, they were less likely to explore unknown and unfamiliar situations (Penney, 1965).

* Programmed instruction facilitated the performance of anxious students (Kight & Sassenrath, 1966).

* College students with high state anxiety made more errors using computer-based instruction on the more difficult materials and fewer errors on the easier materials than low state anxiety students (O'Neil, Spielberger, & Hansen, 1969).

* Testing procedures that provided memory support, such as open book tests, aid the highly anxious learner (Sieber & Kameya, 1967).

* State anxiety was found to be higher in undergraduates when overt responses were required (Tobias, 1973).

* Feedback under learner control affected state anxiety more. High state anxiety subjects made more errors under feedback than without any (Hansen, 1974).

* Sarason (1975) found a significant interaction between instruction type and anxiety. He also found that when low and high anxiety undergraduates received either achievement-oriented or neutral instructions, the low anxiety groups generally performed better than the high.

* Fowle and Merrill (1975) found no effect of sequencing different item-difficulty test forms on performance for different levels of anxiety in undergraduates.

* When instructions included "ego" elements, the anxiety state of highly anxious (trait) students increases (Waid et al., 1978).

- Waid et al. (1978) found that students with low-anxiety traits and states demonstrated superior reading comprehension.

- Distributed practice has been found to lower anxiety state levels (Waid, Kanoy, Blick, & Walker, 1978).

- Subjects who practiced physical exercise as a way to self-regulate anxiety reported less somatic, but more cognitive, anxiety than those who used meditation (Schwartz, Davidson, & Goleman, 1978). This suggested that different types of relaxation techniques were needed for anxiety caused by different sources.

- High anxiety greatly reduced the recall of information given with weak cues but had little effect on recall of information given with strong cues (Eysenck & Eysenck, 1979).

- Callis and Dickey (1980) found that for students with low initial achievement and high anxiety, the television lecture-supervised laboratory mode was the most efficient learning environment.

- Highly anxious undergraduates had lower achievement on humorous tests, whereas low-anxiety students had higher achievement, indicating that humor is not a positive factor in reducing test anxiety (Townsend & Mahoney, 1981).

- Szafran (1981) found that study guides of sample questions, used before an exam, reduced test anxiety.

- Geen (1983) found that providing evaluation with the promise of future help on a paired-associates task did not affect performance, but not providing the promise produced a higher level of state anxiety than in those who were not evaluated at all.

- A negative relationship was found between anxiety and time-on-task; however, a positive relationship was found between time-on-task and achievement (Guida, Ludlow, & Wilson, 1985).

- Monetary incentives improved the performances of low-anxious subjects but not the performances of high-anxious subjects (Eysenck, 1985). The thought was that high-anxiety subjects are already close to their maximum resource allocation and benefit less from added motivation.

- In a moderately difficult problem-solving task involving ego stress, high anxiety reduced the performances of high-IQ subjects compared to low-anxiety subjects. Reassurance was debilitating to low-anxiety subjects but was beneficial to high-IQ boys (Gupta & Sharma, 1986).

- Newhouse (1986) found that highly anxious subjects performed well in both visual-based and audio tutorial instruction, whereas low-anxiety undergraduates performed best in the visual-based instruction.

- Gupta and Sharma (1987) also found that high anxiety was debilitating to high-intelligence ninth-grade girls in a paired-associates task. Reassurance was most beneficial to high-intelligence, highly anxious subjects. Low-intelligence subjects performed poorly regardless of the degree of anxiety or stress.

- When more positive, supportive, and interpersonal type comments were added to a social studies text, high-anxiety students did better and low-anxiety students did more poorly. Evaluative comments and probability statements interfered with the performance of high-anxiety students but helped the low-anxious students (Crismore & Hill, 1988).

- Calvo, Alamo, and Ramos (1990) found that when undergraduates were allowed to perform motor tasks with no time limitations, trait anxiety and state anxiety were associated with slight performance impairments only in the highly demanding tasks.

Implications of the Characteristics and Research

Implications which are drawn from research are noted with a •; those drawn logically from descriptive information regarding the trait are noted by an *. Instructional conditions that capitalize on the preferences of the high-anxiety student and challenge the low-anxiety student include:

* setting goals for the learner
* providing a structured routine
• using visual-based exercises
• using audio-based exercises
• using programmed instruction
• providing supervised labs
• using television lectures
• using supportive rather than evaluative feedback systems
* using structured overviews and organizers
* instructing in a less formal, narrative format
* using role-playing to express emotions
* providing opportunities for plenty of practice to develop confidence before testing
• providing opportunities for covert practice
• using open-book evaluation techniques, or those that provide memory support
• providing positive feedback, praise, and support for performance

Instructional conditions that remediate or compensate for the deficiencies of the high-anxiety student include anxiety-reducing conditions such as:

* using few stimulating colors and little novelty or surprise
• reducing motivation rather than increasing it
• using meditative relaxation techniques
* establishing a verbal, expository context familiar to the learner
* using content adapted to learner preference and prior knowledge
* providing instruction in small chunks
• embedding cuing systems in the instruction
• using structured materials such as programmed instruction
* using sequenced materials (easy to difficult)
* providing gradual transitions
* providing alternatives to oral reporting such as written reports
* providing increased time for rehearsal
* providing opportunities for overlearning/automatization
* providing study guides with sample questions
• providing reassurance
• providing opportunities for distributed practice
* providing plenty of opportunities for success
* embedding questions throughout the instruction
* reducing the importance of test taking

Instructional conditions that capitalize on the preferences of the low-anxiety student and challenge the high-anxiety student include:

* using an objective, formal evaluation style
* providing changes in routine
* using self-management/regulation tasks
• using visually-based instruction
• using evaluative comments and probability statements
• providing opportunities for overt practice
• providing feedback
• using achievement oriented instruction
• using humorous testing

Instructional conditions that remediate or compensate for the deficiencies of the low-anxiety student include:

* increasing motivation and stimuli for repetitive tasks
* arousing the learner with stimulating colors, novelty, or surprise
• using monetary incentive
• adding ego-stress

References

Alpert, R., & Haber, R. N. (1960). Anxiety in academic achievement situations. *Journal of Abnormal and Social Psychology, 61*, 207-215.

Biaggio, A. M. (1985). Relationships between state-trait anxiety and locus of control: Experimental studies with adults and children. *International Journal of Behavioral Development, 8*(2), 153-166.

Callis, C., & Dickey, L. E. (1980). Interactive effects of achievement anxiety, academic achievement and instructional mode on performance and course attitudes. *Home Economics Research Journal, 8*(3), 216-227.

Calvo, M., Alamo, L., & Ramos, P. (1990). Test anxiety, motor performance and learning: Attentional and somatic interference. *Personality and Individual Differences, 11*, 29-38.

Cattell, R. B., & Scheier, I. H. (1961). *The meaning of measurement and neuroticism and anxiety.* New York: Ronald Press.

Chapin, T. J. (1989). The relationship of trait anxiety and academic performance to achievement anxiety: Students at risk. *Journal of College Student Development, 30*(3), 229-236.

Crismore, A., & Hill, K. (1988). The interaction of metadiscourse and anxiety in determining children's learning of social studies textbook materials. *Journal of Reading Behavior, 20*, 249-267.

Davidson, K. (1959). Interviews of parents of high-anxious and low-anxious children. *Child Development, 31*, 307-311.

Eysenck, M. C., & Eysenck, M. W. (1979). Effects of anxiety on the depth and elaboration of processing. *British Journal of Psychology, 70*, 114-132.

Eysenck, M. W. (1979). Anxiety, learning, and memory: a reconceptualization. *Journal of Research in Personality, 13*, 363-385.

Eysenck, M. W. (1985). Anxiety and cognitive-task performance. *Personality and Individual Differences, 6*, 579-586.

Fowle, N. J., & Merrill, P. F. (1975). Effects of anxiety type and item-difficulty sequencing on mathematics test performance. *Journal of Educational Measurement, 12*(4), 241-249.

Gardner, R. C., Smythe, P. C., Clement, R., & Gliksman, L. (1976). Second language acquisition: A social psychological perspective. *The Canadian Modern Language Review, 32*, 198-213.

Gaudry, E., & Spielberger, C. (1971). *Anxiety and educational achievement.* New York: Wiley.

Geen, R. G. (1983). Evaluation apprehension and the social facilitation/inhibition of learning. *Motivation and Emotion, 7*(2), 203-212.

Guida, F. V., Ludlow, L. H., & Wilson, M. (1985). The mediating effect of time-on-task on the academic anxiety/achievement interaction: A structural model. *Journal of Research and Development in Education, 19*(1), 21-26.

Gupta, A., & Sharma, S. (1986). The effect of trait anxiety, intelligence and psychological stress on problem solving. *Personality Study and Group Behavior, 6*(2), 9-22.

Gupta, A., & Sharma, S. (1987). The effects of trait anxiety, intelligence and ego-stress on paired-associates learning. *Journal of Personality and Clinical Studies, 3*(1), 55-61.

Hansen, J. B. (1974). Effects of feedback. learner control, and cognitive abilities on state anxiety and performance in a computer-assisted instructional task. *Journal of Educational Psychology, 66*(2), 247-254.

Horwitz, E. K., Horwitz, M. B., & Cope, J. (1986). Foreign language classroom anxiety. *The Modern Language Journal, 70,* 125-132.

Hunsley, J. (1985). Test anxiety, academic performance, and cognitive appraisals. *Journal of Educational Psychology, 77,* 678-682.

Izard, C. (1972). Anxiety: a variable combination of interacting fundamental emotions. In C. D. Spielberger (Ed.), *Anxiety: Current trends in theory and research* (pp. 51-106). New York: Academic Press.

Joe, V. C. (1971). Review of the internal-external control construct as a personality variable. *Psychological Reports, 28,* 619-640.

Johnsen, E. P., Hohn, R. L., & Dunbar, K. R. (1973). The relationship of state-trait anxiety and task difficulty to learning from written discourse. *Bulletin of the Psychonomics Society, 2*(2), 89-90.

Johnsen, E. P., Hohn, R. L., & Dunbar, K. R. (1991). The effects of trait anxiety on state anxiety and perception of test difficulty for undergraduates administered high- and low-difficulty tests. *Journal of Instructional Psychology, 18*(1), 65-68.

Keenan, A. (1978). Selection interview performance and intolerance of ambiguity. *Psychological Reports, 42,* 353-354.

Kennedy-Liaing, E. (1980). A study of the relationships among state-trait anxiety, locus of control, and mastery learning in associate degree nursing students in a community college (Doctoral dissertation, University of San Francisco). *Dissertation Abstracts International, 41,* 46-52.

Kight, H. R., & Sassenrath, J. M. (1966). Relation of achievement motivation and test anxiety to performance in programmed instruction. *Journal of Educational Psychology, 57,* 14-17.

Liebert, R. M., & Morris, L. W. (1967). Cognitive and emotional components of test anxiety: A distinction and some initial data. *Psychological Reports, 20,* 975-978.

Lipsitt, L. P. (1958). A self-concept scale for children and its relationship to the children's form of the MAS. *Child Development, 29,* 463-472.

MacIntyre, P. D., & Gardner, R. S. (1991). Methods and results in the study of anxiety and language learning: A review of the literature. *Language Learning, 41,* 85-117.

Mandler, G., & Cowen, J. (1958). Test anxiety questionnaires. *Journal of Consultative Psychology, 22,* 228-229.

Mandler, G., & Sarason, S. B. (1952). A study of anxiety and learning. *Journal of Abnormal and Social Psychology, 50,* 93-98.

Mikulincer, M., Kedem, P., & Paz, D. (1990). The impact of trait anxiety and situational stress on the categorization of natural objects. *Anxiety Research, 2*(2), 85-101.

Newhouse, R. C. (1986). Trait anxiety as related to two types of mediated teaching procedures. *Psychological Reports. 59*(1), 229-230.

O'Neil, H. F., Spielberger, C. D., & Hansen, D. N. (1969). The effects of state-anxiety and task difficulty on computer-assisted learning. *Journal of Educational Psychology, 60*, 343-350.

Penney, R. (1965). Reactive curiosity and manifest anxiety in children. *Child Development, 36*, 697-702.

Rosenberg, M. (1953). The association between self-esteem and anxiety. *Journal of Psychology, 48*, 285-290.

Sarason, I. G. (1975). Test anxiety and the self-disclosing coping model. *Journal of Consulting and Clinical Psychology, 43*(2), 148.

Sarason, S. B., Davidson, K. S., Lighthall, F. F., Waite, R. R., & Ruebush, B. K. (1960). *Anxiety in elementary school children.* New York: Wiley.

Schwartz, G., Davidson, R., & Goleman, D. (1978). Patterning of cognitive and somatic processes in the self-regulation of anxiety: Effects of meditation versus exercise. *Psychosomatic Medicine, 40*, 321-328.

Sharma, S., & Gupta, A. (1988). Interactive effects of trait anxiety and intelligence on anagram performance. *Psychological Studies, 33*(2), 99-104.

Sieber, J. E., & Kameya, L. (1967). *The Relationship between anxiety and children's need for memory support in problem solving* (Revised Research Memorandum No. 11), Stanford, CA: Stanford Center for Research and Development in Teaching.

Spence, J. T., & Spence, K. W. (1966). The motivational components of manifest anxiety: Drive and drive stimuli. In C. D. Spielberger (Ed.), *Anxiety and behavior* (pp. 291-326). London: Academic Press.

Spielberger, C. D. (1966). The effects of anxiety on complex learning and academic achievement. In C. D. Spielberger (Ed.), *Anxiety and behavior* (pp. 361-398). London: Academic Press.

Spielberger, C. D. (1972). Anxiety as an emotional state. In C. D. Spielberger (Ed.), *Anxiety: Current trends in theory and research.* New York: Academic Press, pp. 23-49.

Spielberger, C. D. (1983). *Manual for the State-Trait Anxiety Inventory (Form Y).* Palo Alto, CA: Consulting Psychologists Press.

Suinn, R. M., & Hill, H. (1964). Influence of anxiety on the relationship between self-acceptances of others. *Journal of Consultative Psychology, 28*, 116-119.

Szafran, R. F. (1981). Question-pool study guides: Effect on test anxiety and learning retention. *Teaching Sociology, 9*(1), 31-43.

Taylor, J. A. (1953). A personality scale of manifest anxiety. *Journal of Abnormal and Social Psychology, 48*, 285-290.

Tobias, S. (1973). Distraction, response mode, anxiety, and achievement in computer assisted instruction. *Journal of Educational Psychology, 65*(2), 233-237.

Townsend, M. A. R., & Mahoney, P. (1981). Humor and anxiety: Effects on class test performance. *Psychology in the Schools, 18*(2), 228-234.

Trylong, V. L. (1987). *Aptitude, attitudes, and anxiety: A study of their relationships to achievement in the foreign language classroom.* Unpublished doctoral dissertation, Purdue University, West Lafayette, IN.

Tucker, R., Hamayan, E., & Genessee, F. H. (1976). Affective, cognitive and social factors in second language acquisition. *The Canadian Modern Language Review, 32*, 214-226.

Waid, L. R., Kanoy, R. C., Blick, K. A., & Walker, W. E. (1978). Relationship of state-trait anxiety and type of practice to reading comprehension. *Journal of Psychology, 98*, 27-36.

Watson, G. (1934). A comparison of the effects of lax versus strict home training. *Journal of Social Psychology, 5*, 102-105.

Yerkes, R. M., & Dodson, J. D. (1908). The relation of strength of stimulus to rapidity of habit-formation. *Journal of Comparative Neurology of Psychology, 18*, 459-482.

25

TOLERANCE FOR UNREALISTIC EXPERIENCES

Description of Tolerance for Unrealistic Experiences

Tolerance for unrealistic experience was originally defined as a perceptual cognitive control that refers to how much an individual will accept cognitive experiences that do not agree with what an individual already knows to be "true" (Klein, 1962; Koff, 1967). This style has also been described as tolerance for incongruous experiences. Tolerants appear to be in touch with external reality but are much more relaxed in their acceptance of ideas and perceptual organizations that vary from the ordinary. They consider many organizational possibilities before drawing any conclusions. Intolerants appear to make a continual effort to alter their experience to conform to ideas and perceptions from the external world. They try to quickly place new ideas and perceptions into the cognitive organizations they already possess. If no organization exists, they seek to clarify or break down the new idea or perception into manageable categories that are often unqualified or oversimplified. The intolerant individual may seek to avoid unrealistic situations because they can evoke unpleasant emotional reactions ranging from uneasiness to anxiety. Although there are clearly cognitive components to this characteristic, the emotional aspects cause us to characterize it more as a personality variable.

The difference between tolerant and intolerant individuals is best exemplified by their acceptance of facts in stories that are incongruent with prior knowledge. When asked to recount the events of the story, intolerants will organize the events around what they previously knew and ignore the inconsistencies, whereas tolerants will recount the events as they were told. An intolerant individual will also have a difficult time seeing beyond the inkblot in the Rorschach test to imagine other representations. In this test, an individual must be able to go beyond reality. How far one will venture into fantasy is a good measure of tolerance.

Characteristic Differences
in Tolerance for Unrealistic Experiences

Tolerant   Intolerant

Tolerant	Intolerant
flexible thinker	inflexible thinker
form openness	form boundedness
accepts uncertainty	reduces uncertainty
slower closure	quicker closure
accepts new reality	forces new reality into existing mind-set
creates depth in constructions	creates constructions close to reality
identifies constructions quickly	identifies constructions slowly
identifies more constructions	identifies fewer constructions
not overly concerned with reasonableness	concern for reasonable responses
approximate, figurative	literal
elaborative	avoidance of associative elaboration

These characteristics were described by Klein (1962) and Koff (1967).

Individual Differences
Related to Tolerance for Unrealistic Experiences

Field Dependence/Independence--This is a measure of the how much the surrounding perceptual or contextual field affects the perception or comprehension of information (see chapter 7). High dependence-prone subjects showed less tolerance for unrealistic experience and more readily perceived apparent movement than low dependence-prone subjects (Tiwari, 1985).

Tolerance for Ambiguity--This cognitive control refers to an individual's willingness to accommodate or adapt to encounters with ambiguity (see chapter 26). Klein suggests that the two are related and that the research references overlap each other. This relationship requires further exploration.

Constricted/Flexible Control--This cognitive control is a measure of the ability to ignore distractions to focus on relevant stimuli (see chapter 8). Loomis and Moskowitz (1958) found that rigid subjects tended to perseverate, whereas flexible control subjects tended to report more overlapping cues on the slides; however, other processes may be present simultaneously.

Instruments for Measuring Tolerance for Unrealistic Experiences

Rorschach Test

Subjects are shown inkblot pictures and are asked open-ended questions about what they see. The test administrator offers no rules to aid response formulation. The test measures how far the subjects will depart from the most certain or least controversial explanation of the stimulus and allows them to conceptualize how the inkblots are organized. Tolerants and intolerants differ in the "freedom the subject permits themselves in tampering with the reality of the card" by the number of responses given (Koff, 1967; Kogan, 1971). A positive correlation was found between the Rorschach, used in this way, and the range of apparent movement. No other reliability or validity data were available for the use of the Rorschach to test this style, in part because it is an interpreted test that has no standard answers.

Range Of Apparent Movement

Images that the subjects accept as real are made increasingly ambiguous by varying the configuration of the stimulation. During the test, the subject is aware that the stimuli-producing movement is illusionary. The test measures how much visual perceptions must be maintained as they are known to be, or to what extent reality demands the stability and immobility of known stationary forms. The sooner one accepts the change, the more tolerant of unrealistic experiences he or she is said to be (Koff, 1967). No other reliability or validity data were available.

Reversible Figures Test

The subjects are shown pictures in which two possible perceptual organizations are inherent. The test measures the number of reversals under normal conditions and the ability to resist reversal when told to do so. The fewer the reversals and the greater the ability to resist, the more intolerant of unrealistic experience one is said to be (Koff, 1967; Ragan, 1979). Klein (1962) found a positive correlation between this test and the range of apparent movement. No other reliability or validity data were available.

Aniseikonia Lenses

These lenses are used to measure an individual's willingness to perceive distortion. The subject looks through a lens that induces a decided tilt or distortion in the vertical frontal plane. Those who recognize the tilt sooner are determined to be more tolerant of unrealistic experiences (Koff, 1967). Klein (1962) also found a significant positive correlation of this test and the range of apparent movement. No other reliability or validity data were available.

Theoretical Background

The cognitive control, tolerance for unrealistic experience, was first noted by Klein and Schlessinger in their 1951 research. They noted differences in responses on tests of apparent motion and on the Rorschach test. These differences related to people's willingness to accept visual perceptions contrary to what they know or have been told. The studies that followed used several different instruments to measure this phenomenon. For example, Klein and Schlesinger (1951) found that the range of apparent movement was successfully predicted from ratings of Rorschach protocols. The range of apparent movement test was then further correlated by Klein in 1962 to the reversible figures test and aniseikonia lenses. His conclusion was, however, that the most important predictor of tolerance for unrealistic experiences was the apparent movement test. The results from these tests verified the existence of differences in tolerance for perceptual illusions.

Several researchers have created convincing, logical arguments of the similarity of tolerance for unrealistic experience to other cognitive controls such as ambiguity tolerance (Martin, 1953-54; Loomis & Moskowitz, 1958), constricted and flexible control, and rigidity (Frenkel-Brunswick, 1949-50). Although investigating different phenomenon, these researchers used the same tests (Rorschach, apparent movement), and from this, concluded similarities. Koff (1967) cautioned against generalizing these to other style dimensions because of the possible dilutory effect of the construct, and suggested that tolerance for unrealistic experiences may be only one factor of many underlying the other more complex constructs. The direct extrapolation of variables characteristic of the other two would then be unwarranted.

Except for research on similarities between this construct and others, little evidence exists that establishes any verifiable relationship between tolerance for unrealistic experience and learning or instruction. Any associations generated are based on linking the known characteristics of tolerant/intolerant behaviors with theoretical reactions in various learning or instructional environments. This, one might add, denotes the debilitating effects of the low, unrealistic, experiential tolerance that is inherent in our own scientific method.

Tolerance for Unrealistic Experiences and Learning

Research

- Kaplan (1952) found that tolerant subjects recalled more contradictory elements of a story than those intolerant of unrealistic experiences.

Tolerance may impact on an individual's ability to recall instructional content that deals with unrealistic or illogical elements (Koff, 1967).

• Frenkel-Brunswick (1949-50) investigated the relationship of emotional ambiguity to experiments on perceptual ambiguity. Using a research group of ethnically prejudiced individuals, she conducted three tests. She found prejudiced individuals prematurely reduced ambiguous cognitive patterns to certainty, often on an unfounded or oversimplified basis.

• Using aniseikonia lenses, Martin (1953-54) found that individual differences in responses to ambiguous social situations were related to tolerance of unrealistic experiences. He suggested that the person intolerant in the aniseikonia lens test sought to reduce social ambiguity and maintain predictability or social constancy.

Implications of the Characteristics and Research

Implications which are drawn from research are noted with a •; those drawn logically from descriptive information regarding the trait are noted by an *. Based on the very limited amount of research and descriptions of *Tolerance for Unrealistic Experiences*, we conclude that *intolerant* learners are more likely to excel at learning tasks such as:

* tasks that require close transfer
* tasks that have right and wrong answers
* literal tasks
* mathematics
• those that closely match existing understanding

and acquire and use effectively learning strategies such as:

* concentrating on information
* memorization
* repeating material to be recalled
* rehearsal

Based on the very limited amount of research on and descriptions of Tolerance for Unrealistic Experiences, we conclude that *tolerant* learners are more likely to excel at learning tasks such as:

* using concrete and abstract stimuli
* broad elaborations
* far transfer
* transforming complex elements
* generating creative constructions

• justifying contradictory elements of a story

and acquire and use effectively learning strategies such as:

* evaluating current information
* generating metaphors, analogies
* illustrating knowledge
* inferring causes
* predicting outcomes

Tolerance for Unrealistic Experiences and Instruction

Research

Although many studies exist on the effects of realism and instruction, none were found that related those to tolerance. Those implications, drawn in the next section are based on extrapolated relationships between validated characteristics of tolerance and cognitive requirements underlying the instructional tasks.

Implications of the Characteristics and Research

Implications which are drawn from research are noted with a •; those drawn logically from descriptive information regarding the trait are noted by an *. Instructional conditions that capitalize on the preferences of the intolerant student include:

* presenting material in a realistic or concrete manner
* providing perceptual organizational structure when presenting material
* using matched example/nonexamples
* adapting content to prior knowledge
* providing corrective and remedial feedback

    Instructional conditions that remediate or compensate for the deficiencies of the intolerant student include:

* explaining the relationships between analogies and situation
* using prototypical examples and gradually selecting divergent ones
* asking the student to evaluate paraphrased material

    Instructional conditions that capitalize on the preferences of the tolerant and challenge the intolerant student include:

* arousing the learner with novelty, uncertainty, surprise
* using fantasy

* using analogies and metaphors
* presenting the material and asking the learner to provide organization
* using graphic organizers
* providing enrichment feedback

There do not appear to be any learning deficiencies in the tolerant students because they demonstrate an ability to accept a variety of perceptual messages presented to them.

References

Frenkel-Brunswick, E. (1949-1950). Intolerance of ambiguity as an emotional and perceptual personality variable. *Journal of Personality, 18,* 108-143.

Kaplan, J. (1952). Predicting memory behavior from cognitive attitudes toward instability. *American Psychologist, 7,* 322 .

Klein, G. (1962). Tolerance for unrealistic experience: A study of the generality of a cognitive control. *British Journal of Psychology,* 41-55.

Klein, G., & Schlesinger, H. (1951). Perceptual attitudes toward instability: 1. prediction of apparent movement experiences from Rorschach responses. *Journal of Personality, 19,* 289-302.

Koff, R. (1967). *The definition of a cognitive control principle: A case of diminishing returns.* Washington DC: Office of Education, Bureau of Research.

Kogan, N. (1971). Educational implications of cognitive styles. In G. S. Lesser (Ed.), *Cognition, Learning, and Educational Practice* (pp. 242-292). Glenview, IL: Scott Foresman.

Loomis, N., & Moskowitz, S. (1958). Cognitive style and stimulus ambiguity. *Journal of Personality, 26,* 349-364.

Martin, B. (1953-54). Intolerance of ambiguity in interpersonal and perceptual behavior. *Journal of Personality,* 494-503.

Ragan, T. (1979). *Cognitive Styles: A Review of the Literature--Interim Report for Period January 1977--January 1978.* Brooks AFB, TX: Air Force Resource Lab. (ERIC Document Reproduction Service No. ED 174 655)

Tiwari, B. (1985, January). Effect of dependence proneness, distance, and size on perception of apparent movement. *Psychological Studies,* 39-42.

26

AMBIGUITY TOLERANCE

Description of Ambiguity Tolerance

Ambiguity tolerance refers to an individual's willingness to accommodate or adapt to encounters with ambiguous situations or ideas (Ausburn & Ausburn, 1978). Ambiguous situations develop from novel circumstances that have no familiar cues, complex situations with many cues to be considered, contradictory situations where different elements or cues suggest different structures (Budner, 1962), or unstructured situations containing cues that cannot be interpreted (Norton, 1975). For instance, travel to a foreign country produces many ambiguous situations that are novel, confusing, and demanding. Individuals differ in their their abilities to adapt to these strange situations.

Ambiguity may result from three clusters of behavioral situations: multiple interpretation situations, situations difficult to categorize, and situations including contradictions (Kreitler, Maguen, & Kreitler, 1975). In each case, the individual's affective perception of that situation determines his or her negative or positive reaction. Tolerance for ambiguity is "the tendency to perceive ambiguous situations as desirable" (Budner, 1962, p. 29).

Tolerant individuals accept or invite new situations in which the rules or procedures are not known. They also like complex problem situations where the answers are uncertain. We expect tolerant individuals to perform well when faced with a learning situation containing a great deal of novelty, complexity, contradiction and/or lack of structure (MacDonald, 1970). Tolerant individuals are more likely to be risk takers and persistent processors. They can also hypothesize well and provide their own structures for learning.

Intolerance for ambiguity is "the tendency to perceive ambiguous situations as sources of threat" (Budner, 1962, p. 29). Learners who are intolerant of ambiguity are expected to avoid learning situations that possess unknown goals or expectations, unstated criteria for success, or unclear procedures on how to perform. Intolerant learners have difficulty providing structure to learning situations that they perceive to be ambiguous in nature. We might expect that such learners are detail-oriented and unable or unwilling to view situations in global terms. Birckbichler and Omaggio (1978) suggested that such learners are unable to hypothesize well and do not enjoy taking risks. In addition, students who are intolerant of ambiguity tend to give up quickly when faced with an ambiguous learning task.

Ambiguity tolerance has frequently been confused with rigidity, the belief being that rigidity means an inability to tolerate multiple interpretations or contradictions. However, a rigid person is one who will overrely on a single response despite empirical evidence to the contrary, whereas an intolerant person will more likely substitute a bad response (MacDonald, 1970). One may be intolerant of ambiguity and yet be flexible or, of course, rigid. Ambiguity tolerance and rigidity/flexibility are independent constructs.

Characteristic Differences in Ambiguity Tolerance

Tolerant	Intolerant
global	detail oriented
risk taking	cautious
flexible	inflexible
tolerates range of answers	looks for right-wrong answers
simultaneous	linear (sequential)

Individual Differences Related to Ambiguity Tolerance

Intelligence--Budner (1978) claimed that implicit in the definition of ambiguity tolerance is a correlation with intelligence.

Cognitive complexity--Cognitive complexity/simplicity describes an individual's discriminating perception of his or her environment or social behavior (see chapter 12). Cognitive complexity is negatively correlated with intolerance of ambiguity (Peters & Amburgey, 1982; Rotter & O'Connell, 1982). As tolerance for ambiguity decreases, cognitive complexity (abstractness) increases. College students who are tolerant of ambiguity have high SAT verbal scores.

Anxiety--This emotional state, characterized by feelings of tension and apprehension, has been attributed to causing both negative and positive effects--effects that motivate and facilitate, as well as disrupt and inhibit, actions and/or learning (see chapter 24). Intolerance of ambiguity was found to be positively associated with level of anxiety in an interview situation (Keenan, 1978). Less tolerant individuals tend to be more anxious.

Dogmatism--Low dogmatic persons have greater tolerance for ambiguity and a more flexible view of themselves (Goldsmith, 1984; Lee, 1987; MacDonald, 1970).

Self-esteem--Ambiguity tolerance, or open processing, is positively related to empathy and self-esteem (Goldsmith, 1984).

Instruments for Measuring Ambiguity Tolerance

The majority of tests that measure tolerance/intolerance of ambiguity come from the area of clinical psychology. Chapelle and Roberts (1986) and others used these tests to identify tolerance/intolerance of ambiguity as a cognitive learning style, even though these tests are concerned, for the most part, with tolerance/intolerance for ambiguity as a personality variable. Only one scale measuring tolerance/intolerance for ambiguity as a cognitive variable was found in the literature (Ely, 1989).

Scale of Tolerance/Intolerance of Ambiguity (Budner, 1962)

This scale was developed as part of the Budner's dissertation. It contains 16 items, 8 of which are positive, and 8 of which are negative. The test uses a 7-point Likert scale ranging from 1-7 (strong disagreement to strong agreement) for positively worded items and the reverse for negative items. Following are examples, positive and negative respectively, of items used in the scale: "The sooner we all acquire similar values and ideals, the better" and "I would like to live in a foreign country for a while." The possible scores for the scale extend from 1-16 for strong disagreement to 96-112 for strong agreement, with varying ranges in between. Based on this scoring scheme, the higher the score obtained, the more intolerant the person.

Measurement of Ambiguity Tolerance (MAT-50) (Norton, 1975)

In 1975, Norton developed the Measurement of Ambiguity Tolerance. This is a 7-point Likert scale (YES! to NO!) containing 61 items that correspond to eight different categories (philosophy, interpersonal communication, public image, anything that is job-related, problem solving, social, habit, and art forms). One sample item from each of these categories is presented:
- Personally, I tend to think that there is a right way and a wrong way to do almost everything.
- It really disturbs me when I am unable to follow another person's train of thought.
- If I were a scientist, I might become frustrated because my work would *never* be completed (science will always make new discoveries).
- Complex problems appeal to me only if I have a clear idea of the total scope of the problem.
- I get pretty anxious when I'm in a social situation I have little control of.

• It matters to me to know what day it is.
• If I miss the beginning of a good movie, I like to stay to see the start of it.

The possible scores for the scale extend from 1 - 61, for very strong disagreement, to 367 - 427, for very strong agreement, with varying ranges in between. Like the Budner scale, the higher the score obtained, the more intolerant the person is. The test has an internal reliability (K-R 20) of .88 and high internal and test-retest reliability when compared with other scales. Results of validity studies on the scale indicate that it has high content, criterion, and construct validity (Norton, 1975).

Tolerance Ambiguity Scale (Ely, 1989)

In 1989, Ely reported on a study in which he developed a second language-specific scale of ambiguity. The purpose of the scale was to explore tolerance of ambiguity as a possible predictor of strategy use. The 12-item scale has a Cronbach alpha reliability of .82.

Developed to assess language students' tolerance of ambiguity under task specific situations in the learning of Spanish, this scale contains 12 self-report items, presented in a 6-point Likert scale, with possible responses of "strongly disagree," "moderately disagree," "slightly disagree," "slightly agree," "moderately agree," or "strongly agree." The possible scores for the scale extend from 1 - 12, for strong disagreement, to 61 - 72 for strong agreement, with varying ranges in between. Like the two previous scales, the higher the score obtained, the more intolerant the person. These single sample items represent a "tolerant" and "intolerant" question, respectively: "I enjoy reading something in Spanish that takes a while to figure out completely" and "I don't like the fact that it's often impossible to find Spanish words that mean exactly the same as some English words."

Rydell-Rosen Tolerance of Ambiguity Scale (MacDonald, 1970; Rydell & Rosen, 1966)

This scale consists of 20 true-false items that assess ambiguity tolerance such as: "I would rather bet 1 to 6 on a long shot than 3 to 1 on a probable winner" (T) and "I don't like to work on a problem unless there is a possibility of coming out with a clear-cut and unambiguous answer." The test has a spilt-half reliability of .86 and a retest reliability of .63. Construct validity tests show that it assesses the same dimension as rigidity and dogmatism.

Open Processing Scale, Form B (Leavitt & Walton, 1975, 1983)

The open-processing scale measures ambiguity tolerance (Goldsmith, 1984). The scale consists of 24 items (12 positive and 12 negative) and has a reliability coefficient of .72.

Omnibus Personality Test, CO Subscale (Psychological Corporation, 1962)

The CO subscale of the Omnibus Personality Inventory assesses tolerance for ambiguity and cognitive complexity (Peters & Ambergey, 1982). Tolerance and complexity are related to an open, creative approach to phenomena. They are related to creativity, need for autonomy, and need for change. Internal reliability estimates range from .67-.89.

Theoretical Background

The term *tolerance of ambiguity* has been used since 1949 when Frenkel-Brunswik used the term to define a person's emotional and cognitive orientation toward life. According to Frenkel-Brunswik (1949), a person intolerant of ambiguity tends to seek black-and-white solutions, to arrive at premature closure, and to think concretely.

Budner (1962) later attempted to define the variable in terms of its component dimensions, to develop an adequate measure of it, and also to determine under what situations tolerance of ambiguity may be a significant variable.

In the subsequent decade, Norton (1975) improved the operational definition of ambiguity tolerance as a construct and developed the MAT-50, which proved to have a much higher reliability and validity than previously developed scales.

Ambiguity Tolerance and Learning

Research

Very little research relating ambiguity tolerance to learning outcomes has been completed.

- Ebeling and Spear (1980) found that tolerants outperformed intolerants on both an ambiguous task and an unambiguous task.

- Art students were significantly more tolerant than business students in the university (Tatzel, 1980).

- Peters and Amburgey (1982) found that high-tolerance teachers used higher cognitive levels of verbal responses when teaching.

- Comadena (1984) found that subjects high in ambiguity tolerance produced more ideas in a brainstorming session, which is more affected by social characteristics like ambiguity tolerance than by cognitive requirements.

• Brice (1985) found that hearing students were less tolerant of ambiguity than deaf children. Among deaf children, less tolerant subjects were more advanced in social cognition.

• Chappelle and Roberts (1986) found that ambiguity tolerance was a significant predictor of English as a second language proficiency for foreign students in the United States.

• In a study on the relationship between tolerance of ambiguity and second language strategy use, Ely (1989) developed a situation-specific scale to measure tolerance of ambiguity within a language learning environment. Results of his study were inconclusive; that is, tolerance of ambiguity was found to be a predictor of some, but not all, of the strategies.

Implications of the Characteristics and Research

Implications which are drawn from research are noted with a •; those drawn logically from descriptive information regarding the trait are noted by an *. Based on the little bit of research and the descriptions of *ambiguity tolerance,* we conclude that *tolerant* learners are more likely to excel at learning tasks such as:

* complex problem-solving situations
* novel transfer problems using new examples or embedded in new cultures, contexts, or scenarios
* divergent learning tasks where the outcomes are not clear
• brainstorming
• language learning

and acquire and use effectively learning strategies such as:

* selecting information sources
* searching for information
* generating metaphors
* inferring causes, evaluating implications

Based on the little bit of research and the descriptions of ambiguity tolerance, we conclude that intolerant learners are more likely to excel at learning tasks such as:

* reliable but repetitive tasks
* tasks requiring application of well-defined rules

and acquire and use effectively learning strategies such as:

* concentrating on information
* reviewing material
* outlining
* regulating environment

Ambiguity Tolerance and Instruction

Even fewer studies have related ambiguity tolerance to different forms of instruction.

Research

• Significant increases in intolerance for ambiguity resulted from a cross-cultural simulation (Glover, Romero, Romero, & Peterson, 1978).

• Domangue (1978), in a study on the effects of inconsistency between the verbal and nonverbal components of a message, found that ambiguity tolerance affects the use of inconsistent nonverbal cues. Low-tolerance subjects were less influenced by nonverbal cues when verbal cues were positive and nonverbal were negative.

• Nursing students who experienced less stress were more tolerant of ambiguity and tended to choose psychiatric nursing more often (Williams, 1980).

• Ream (1984) found that group discussion of ambiguous situations or characterizations using personal experience examples increased students' tolerance of ambiguity.

• When presented options differing in ambiguity, most people selected the less ambiguous one. Curly, Yates, and Abrams (1986) believed that decision makers selected choices with the smallest degree of ambiguity because they appear most justifiable to others.

Implications of the Characteristics and Research

Implications which are drawn from research are noted with a •; those drawn logically from descriptive information regarding the trait are noted by an *. Instructional conditions that capitalize on the preferences of the intolerant student and challenge the tolerant student include:

• allowing group discussion

* using personal examples
* single interpretations activities
* easy classifications
* presenting goals for the learner to select
* describing criteria for standard performance
* adapting content to prior knowledge
* providing oral cues or directions

Instructional conditions that remediate or compensate for the deficiencies of the intolerant student include:

* posing questions to the learner
* providing verbal outlines of content
* providing matched example/nonexample pairs when teaching concepts

Instructional conditions that capitalize on the preferences of the tolerant student and challenge the intolerant student include:

* asking learners to select their own goals
* providing situations with novelty, complexity, or lack of structure
* providing students with general guidelines of the type of information being requested and asking them to identify the information without providing them with specific questions
* providing constructivistic learning experiences
* providing problem-solving situations
* providing situations with multiple correct answers

Instructional conditions that remediate or compensate for the deficiencies of the tolerant student include:

* presenting information in small chunks

References

Ausburn, L. J., & Ausburn, F. B. (1978). Cognitive styles: Some information and impications for instructional design. *Educational Communications and Technology Journal, 26,* 337-354.
Birckbichler, D. W., & Omaggio, A. C. (1978). Diagnosing and responding to individual learner needs. *Modern Language Journal, 62,* 336-345.
Brice, P. J. (1985). A comparison of levels of ambiguity in deaf and hearing children. *American Annals of the Deaf, 130*(3), 226-230.
Budner, S. (1962). Intolerance of ambiguity as a personality variable. *Journal of Personality, 30,* 29-50.
Budner, S. (1978). Intolerance of ambiguity and need for closure. *Psychological Reports, 43,* 628.

Chapelle, C., & Roberts, C. (1986). Ambiguity tolerance and field independence as predictors of proficiency in english as a second language.
Language Learning, 41, 287-303.

Comadena, M. E. (1984). Brainstorming groups: Ambiguity tolerance
communication apprehension, task attraction, and individual productivity. *Small Group Behavior, 15*, 251-264.

Curley, S. P., Yates, J. F., & Abrams, R. A. (1986). Psychological sources of
ambiguity avoidance. *Organizational Behavior and Human
Decision Processes, 38*(2), 230-256.

Domangue, B. B. (1978). Decoding effects of cognitive complexity, tolerance
of ambiguity, and verbal-nonverbal inconsistency. *Journal of
Personality, 46*, 519-535.

Ebeling, K. S., & Spear, P. S. (1980). Preference and performance on two
tasks of varying ambiguity as a function of ambiguity tolerance.
Australian Journal of Psychology, 32, 127-133.

Ely, C. M. (1989). Tolerance of ambiguity and use of second language
strategies. *Foreign Language Annals, 22*(5), 437-445.

Frenkel-Brunswik, E. (1949). Intolerance of ambiguity as an emotional and
perceptual personality variable. *Journal of Personality, 18*, 108-143.

Glover, J. A., Romero, D., Romero, P., & Peterson, C. (1978). Effects of a
simulation game upon tolerance of ambiguity, dogmatism, and risk
taking. *Journal of Social Psychology, 105*, 291-296.

Goldsmith, R. E. (1984). Some personality correlates of open processing.
Journal of Psychology, 116, 59-66.

Keenan, A. (1978). Selection interview performance and intolerance of
ambiguity. *Psychological Reports, 42*, 353-354.

Kreitler, S., Maguen, T., & Kreitler, H. (1975). The three faces of intolerance
of ambiguity. *Archiv fur Psychologie, 127*(3), 238-250.

Leavitt, C., & Walton, J. (1975). Development of a scale for innovativeness.
In M. J. Schlinger (Ed.), *Advances in consumer research* (Vol. 2, pp.
545-554). Chicago: Association for Consumer Research.

Leavitt, C., & Walton, J. (1983). *The open processing scale: A predictor of
innovative cognitive style.* Columbus, OH: College of
Administrative Sciences, Ohio State University.

Lee, C. K. (1987). Dogmatism and authoritarianism in the transformation
of intercultural. (Doctoral Dissertation, Michigan State University).
Dissertation Abstracts International, 49(3A), 394.

MacDonald, A. P. (1970), Revised scale for ambiguity tolerance: Reliability
and validity. *Psychological Reports, 26*, 791-798.

Norton, R. (1975). Measurement of ambiguity tolerance. *Journal of
Personality Assessment, 39*, 607-619.

Peters, W. H., & Amburgey, B. S. (1982). Teacher intellectual disposition
and cognitive classroom verbal interactions. *Journal of Educational
Research, 76*, 94-99.

Psychological Corporation. (1962). *Omnibus personality inventory manual.* New York: Psychological Corporation.

Ream, M. N. (1984). Effects of teaching strategies in increasing tolerance of ambiguity among middle school students (Doctoral Dissertation, West Virginia University). *Dissertation Abstracts International, 45*(5A), 1289.

Rotter, N. G., & O'Connell, A. N. (1982). The relationships between sex-role orientation, cognitive complexity, and tolerance for ambiguity. *Sex Roles, 8*(12), 1209-1220.

Rydell, S. T., & Rosen, E. (1966). Measurement and some correlates of need cognition. *Psychological Reports, 19*, 139-165.

Tatzel, M. (1980). Tolerance for ambiguity in adult students. *Psychological Reports, 47*, 377-378.

Williams, R. A. (1980). The relationship of field independence, tolerance of ambiguity and stress in undergraduate nursing students (Doctoral Dissertation, University of Washington). *Dissertation Abstracts International, 41*(7A), 3021.

Bibliography

Endler, N. S. (1973). The Person versus the situation--a pseudo issue? A response to Alker. *Journal of Personality, 30*, 29-50.

Mischel, W. (1977). The Interaction of person and situation. In D. M. Magnusson & N. Endler, (Eds.), *Personality at the crossroads: Current issues in interactional psychology* (pp. 333-352). Hillsdale, NJ: Lawrence Erlbaum Associates.

27

FRUSTRATION TOLERANCE

Description of Frustration Tolerance

Frustration tolerance describes and predicts the quality of a person's performance in a task after frustration occurs. Frustration results from something observable and external to the individual. Frustration, as an objective event, occurs when a person encounters: an obstacle large enough to require special effort en route to satisfying a need (Rosenzweig, 1978), something that prevents or interferes with direct progress toward a goal (Waterhouse & Child, 1953), an object that interferes with the goal of moving in a certain direction (Minsky, 1986) or, something blocking the individual's route, alternate paths to choose from, or a new and dominant stimulus for which he or she has no learned response (Maier, 1961).

The effects of frustration on information processing, such as its effects on the performance of a subsequent task, are internal to the individual. For instance, we know that: frustration deprives a person of a tensionless state or peace of mind (Rosenzweig, 1978); all frustration has inherent motivational properties (Reber, 1985); low tolerance for frustration is related to deficient self-reinforcement (Scorzelli & Reinke-Scorzelli, 1976); and frustration behavior is determined by forces other than the individual's goals; therefore, it is demotivating (Maier, 1961). It is this internal state, a person's internal reaction to something frustrating, that accounts for individual differences in the effects of frustration. Researchers have tended to ascribe all such differences to the unipolar trait of frustration tolerance.

Tolerance of frustration denotes the ability to resist or endure its effects. Individuals are characterized as having a high tolerance or a low tolerance of frustration. High-tolerance people are not as easily frustrated as low-tolerance people. High tolerance may also indicate a weak frustration reaction to potentially frustrating events, whereas low tolerance indicates a strong frustration reaction. Tolerance also refers to a person's innate susceptibility or threshold for frustration, that is, how easily he or she is frustrated. That is, a given frustrating event may or may not frustrate an individual, and if it does, the reaction may be strong or weak. An individual's tolerance level is assessed, most commonly, by noting the external effect--the quality of performance that follows the frustrating event. If performance quality remains the same, tolerance is high. If performance drops, tolerance is low. Researchers generally agree that once a frustrating event affects a person, that is, when a person becomes frustrated, frustration-based behavior follows, and that behavior then interferes with the original performance of the task. Most researchers agree that performance suffers from experiences of frustration. The greater the strength of reaction or interference, the lower the performance (Waterhouse & Child, 1952). This chapter assumes that there are degrees of frustration tolerance.

Characteristic Differences in Frustration Tolerance

Level of frustration is essentially a unipolar range of responses based on the strength of the frustration reaction. We describe high-frustration behavior at one end of the scale and low-frustration behavior (sometimes referred to a motivation-based behavior) at the other (Maier, 1961).

Low-Frustration Behavior	High-Frustration Behavior
need or goal driven	defensive or reactive
trial and error learning	fixated
flexible	rigid, resistant to change
goal-oriented	frustration- or relief-oriented
constructive	destructive
influenced by goals or anticipated results	influenced by availability
active/positive	resigned
fight/confront/focus/persist	fight/avoid/digress/resist
variable responses	rigid, fixed responses
affected by reward/punishment	unaffected by reward/punishment
responses are means to ends	responses are ends in themselves
unaltered by guidance	altered by guidance
selected responses	impulsive/compulsive responses
responses satisfy only if adaptive	relieve frustration, adaptive or not
mature	childish
adaptive	stubborn

Individual Differences Related to Frustration Tolerance

Prior knowledge--Prior knowledge and achievement are the knowledge, skills, or abilities that the student brings to the learning environment prior to instruction (see chapter 33). The higher the level of prior knowledge or skill, the lower the level of frustration tolerance (DeJoy, 1985).

Extroversion/Introversion--Thinking and behavior that are directed inward, or to oneself, is known as introversion; and the thinking and behavior that is directed outward, or to the surrounding environment, is extroversion (see chapter 29). Introverts are more likely to have low tolerance for frustration, although no research supports this hypothesis.

Anxiety--This emotional state, characterized by feelings of tension and apprehension, has been attributed to causing both negative and positive effects--effects that motivate and facilitate, as well as disrupt and inhibit, actions and/or learning (see chapter 24). Low-frustration tolerance people are more anxious, worry a great deal, are more troubled by thoughts of hell, have more severe headaches, and more often have had an unhappy childhood (Watson, 1934).

Instruments for Measuring Frustration Tolerance

Picture-Frustration Study (Rosenzweig, 1978)

This test measures aggression in personality by assessing patterns of response to everyday frustrations. Twenty-four cartoons of frustrating situations involving two people, where one is the frustrator, are presented. The participant writes a reply for the frustrated cartoon character. Results indicate types of aggression. Based on his analysis of aggression, Rosenzweig found that certain types of aggressiveness in response to frustration are destructive, others are constructive.

Interference Questionnaire/Tests (Waterhouse & Child, 1953)

Designed for college-age individuals, this test consists of a 150-item questionnaire that indicates individual tendencies to respond to frustration in six different ways along three dimensions: Preoccupation-Pessimism, Defendance-Self-aggression, and Aggression-Distractibility. Following the questionnaire, individual testing sessions are administered by an examiner, including a battery of 12 psychological fitness tests (motor and intellectual tasks). The examiner frequently interrupts half of the subjects to make comments about their poor performances in the tasks. The idea is to frustrate the subject's desire to feel that he or she is doing well. The examiner leads the other half of the subjects to believe that they are doing as well as expected (neutral messages). Subjects who rated themselves in the initial questionnaire as strongly frustrated and prone to interfering responses had an overall lower quality of performance in the subsequent psychological fitness tests than subjects who rated themselves as weakly frustrated. They also found that subjects who rated themselves as strongly frustrated tended to do better than the others in the test sessions that did not impose examiner frustrations.

Lax versus Strict Home Training Questionnaires (Watson, 1934)

This is a group-administered questionnaire consisting of 17 home environment questions, for example: "Required to attend Sunday school and church whether the child wished to do so or not." Scores categorize subjects into four levels of restrictiveness or confinement during upbringing. The highest and lowest rated subjects were then given questions regarding four types of behavior associated with frustration response: aggression, regression, fixation, and anxiety. Watson found that these four categories of behavior covered the range of frustration responses and that constricted subjects indicated behavior in these four categories much more frequently than the other subjects.

Theoretical Background

Given an objective frustrating event, theory will predict a wide variety of effects. For example, philosophers such as Dewey have said that human nature depends on problems or difficulties as occasions for creative intellectual activity, and perhaps even thought itself. Some psychologists have observed that unreduced tension gives rise to adjustment, including adjustments of the very highest intellectual quality. Most psychologists, however, have found that frustration has a disorganizing effect because of emotional arousal or other interference. Some have found that frustration is an alternate source of motivation that, however, still reduces the quality of the individual's performance on a task (Maier, 1961). What accounts for one person stubbing a toe and swearing or hitting something with a fist, but another person planning and carrying out an intricate and ingenious escape from prison (Waterhouse & Child, 1953)? The study of frustration tolerance has broad interest. It is viewed both as a major stimulus to human progress and as a major obstacle to individual learning. It is an ingredient of a great deal of behavior (Rosenzweig, 1978).

Frustration Tolerance and Learning

Research

The research into frustration tolerance provides very little evidence for how different learning outcomes might be facilitated or impeded depending on the learner's level of tolerance (high to low). It is assumed that most learning outcomes are impeded by low-frustration tolerance and most outcomes are facilitated by high-frustration tolerance.

- Greater practice actually led to superior performance once the interfering responses were not evoked by failure or frustration (McClelland & Apicella, 1947).

- The most constricted subjects never showed superiority in adaptive or rational choice responses (Maier, 1961).

- Scorzelli and Reinke-Scorzelli (1976) suggested a relationship between self-reinforcement and low-frustration tolerance. Response latencies occurred on an identification task after frustration was introduced. This study was done with Skid Row alcoholics, so the results may not be generalizable.

Implications of the Characteristics and Research

Implications which are drawn from research are noted with a •; those drawn logically from descriptive information regarding the trait are noted by an *. Based on the very little bit of research and the descriptions of *frustration tolerance*, we conclude that *high-tolerance/low-frustration* learners are more likely to excel at learning tasks such as:

* timed, complex tasks that impose pressure
* divergent or uncertain tasks that possess a higher risk of failure and/or frustration
* tasks that require response construction

and acquire and use effectively learning strategies such as:

* setting own learning goals and treating personal skills
* gaging task difficulty
* judging the utility or value of knowledge

Based on the very little bit of research and the descriptions of frustration tolerance, we conclude that *low-tolerance/high-frustration* learners are more likely to excel at learning tasks such as:

* untimed tasks that impose no performance pressure
* tasks with clearly stated expectations and outcomes

and acquire and use effectively learning strategies such as:

* repeating and rehearsing material to be recalled

Frustration Tolerance and Instruction

Research

Very little research with frustration tolerance as an instructional variable has been conducted. Obviously, instructional strategies that reduce frustration will support low-tolerant learners, whereas high-tolerant learners can withstand higher levels of frustration.

- Prior experience on an externally paced coding task with distractions reduced frustration tolerance, indicating that control over the effects of stressors is important in a learning situation (DeJoy, 1985).

- Heavy video game users have a lower frustration tolerance, indicating the need for mastery over experiences (Kestenbaum & Weinstein, 1985).

Implications of the Characteristics and Research

Implications which are drawn from research are noted with a •; those drawn logically from descriptive information regarding the trait are noted by an *. Instructional conditions that capitalize on the preferences of the high-tolerance/low-frustration student and challenge the low-tolerance/high-frustration student include:

* asking learners to select their own goals or posing questions to be answered
* using large instructional chunks
* changing the contexts or circumstances of practice items
• using trial and error strategies

   Instructional conditions that remediate or compensate for the deficiencies of the high-tolerance/low-frustration student include:

• making punishment only severe enough to produce avoidance, not frustration

   Instructional conditions that capitalize on the preferences of the low-tolerance/high-frustration student and challenge the high-tolerance/low-frustration student include:

* making consistent use of positive reinforcement and avoiding punishment
* designing instruction to the lowest frustration tolerance level, such as linear programmed instruction
* providing guidance and instruction, previous to the learning task, that encourages flexibility and creativity in problem solving

* describing the required performance and criteria or standards for performance
* using small instructional chunks

   Instructional conditions that remediate or compensate for the deficiencies of the low-tolerance/high-frustration student include:

* providing for individual paths, pace, help, and feedback in the instruction (both instruction that is too fast or difficult, and instruction that is too slow or easy can frustrate learners.)
* channeling frustration into harmless direction (dissipate tension)
* using oral or verbal comparative organizers to relate content to ideas familiar to the learner
* using cueing systems such as oral directions
* advising the learner about instructional support such as a number of examples or practice items
* overlearning
* using easy-to-difficult instructional sequence

References

DeJoy, D. M. (1985). Information input rate, control over task pacing, and performance during and after noise exposure. *Journal of General Psychology, 112,* 229-242.

Kestenbaum, G. I., & Weinstein, L. (1985). Personality, psychopathology, and developmental issues in male adolescent video game use. *Journal of the American Academy of Child Psychiatry, 24,* 329-333.

Maier, N. R. F. (1961). *Frustration: The study of behavior without a goal.* Ann Arbor: University of Michigan Press.

McClelland, D. C., & Apicella, F. S. (1947). Reminiscence following experimentally induced failure. *Journal of Experimental Psychology, 37,* 159-169.

Minsky, M. (1986). *The society of mind.* New York: Simon & Schuster.

Reber, A. S. (1985). *The Penguin Dictionary of Psychology.* London: Penguin Books.

Rosenzweig, S. (1978). *Aggressive behavior and the Rosenzweig Picture-Frustration Study.* New York: Praeger.

Scorzelli, J. F., & Reinke-Scorzelli, M. (1976). Effects of frustration on the response rate of skid row alcoholics on a performance task. *Rehabilitation Counseling Bulletin, 20*(2), 137-140.

Waterhouse, I. K., & Child, I. L. (1952). Frustration and the quality of performance: 1. A critique of the Barker, Dembo, and Lewin experiment. *Psychological Review, 59,* 351-362.

Waterhouse, I. K., & Child, I. L. (1953). Frustration and the quality of performance: 2. A theoretical statement. *Psychological Review, 60*(2), 127-139.

Watson, G. (1934). A comparison of the effects of lax versus strict home training. *Journal Social Psychology, 5,* 102-105.

Bibliography

Barker, R. G., Dembo, T., & Lewin, K. (1941). Frustration and regression: an experiment with young children. *University of Iowa Studies in Child Welfare, 18,* 1-314.

Waterhouse, I. K., & Child, I. L. (1953). Frustration and the quality of performance: 3. An experimental study. *Journal of Personality, 21*(3), 298-311.

28

LOCUS OF CONTROL

Description of Locus of Control

The word *locus* comes from the Latin word for *place*. *Locus of control*, therefore, refers to an individual's feelings about the *placement* of control over his or her life events, and who is *responsible* for those events. Locus of control describes an individual's belief regarding the causes of his or her experiences (causal attributions), those factors to which an individual attributes his or her successes and failures. These attributions may include mood, knowledge, effort, help, task requirements, luck, skill, chance, competence, ability, and biases. "With the locus of control construct, we are dealing with a person as he or she views him or herself in conjunction with things that befall him or her and the meaning that he or she makes of those interactions between his or her self and his or her experiences" (Lefcourt, 1982, p. 35). Locus of control in relation to learning and instruction is an affective learning style, specifically an expectancy or incentive style (Keefe, 1987). That is, locus of control does not mediate learning directly, but it affects learning outcomes through the learner's expectations of success and the resulting motivation to perform. Many factors, such as ethnic group, gender, education, and socio-economic status interact with internality/externality to produce various effects.

Internals tend to attribute causes of success and failure to themselves. Success is the result of effort, ability, or competence, and failure results from the lack of those. Internals have a sense of personal efficacy that tends to increase with age.

Externals, on the other hand, tend to attribute their successes and failures to external forces that control an individual's performance such as ability or likelihood to perform acceptably. Externals attribute success to the availability of help, easy tasks, luck, chance, or preferential biases and failure to bad luck, a lack of help, or unnecessarily difficult tasks. One of the most external groups of people tend to be college students.

Characteristic Differences in Locus of Control

Locus of control, like most learner characteristics, is best represented as a continuum: external to internal. Individual beliefs along this continuum are often described in the research in terms of undesirable and desirable (i.e., a univariate dimension), with *external* being the undesirable characteristic and *internal* being the desirable. Lefcourt (1982) attributed this perception to the measuring instruments. He believed that measurement tools and criterion situations focused on subject-controllable events (p. 183). Perceptions of control by powerful others that are realistic because of the nature of specific situations or cultural sanctions (e.g., prisoners) may actually allow for more effective and innovative behaviors (Levenson, 1982, p. 54). With those cautions, here is a range of reported research differences.

Internal	External
self	other
open-minded	dogmatic
higher achievers	lower achievers
goal-driven	fear of failure
self-assured	anxious
persistent	frustrated
reflective	impulsive
risk takers	cautious
organized	distracted
verbal	visual/kinesthetic
analytic	global

Individual Differences Related to Locus of Control

Locus of control is closely associated with other cognitive styles and controls:

Anxiety--This emotional state, characterized by feelings of tension and apprehension, has been attributed to causing both negative and positive effects--effects that motivate and facilitate, as well as disrupt and inhibit, actions and/or learning (see chapter 24). Kennedy-Liang (1980) found considerable overlap between locus of control and state anxiety. Externals are more likely to be anxious in general (Joe, 1971). They are also the least anxious in traditional, teacher-centered, lecture, highly structured learning environments. Thus, it seems likely that remedial treatments work best with externals in that kind of environment.

Academic performance/field independence--Many researchers have suggested a strong relationship between field independence and academic performance and internality. Both internality and field independence predict better academic performance (Kletzing, 1982).

Instruments for Measuring Locus of Control

Internal-External Locus of Control Scale (Rotter, 1966)

Rotter constructed the first test for locus of control in 1966, The Rotter Internal-External Locus of Control Scale (Rotter, 1966). His scale was intended to assess an individual's widespread beliefs concerning reinforcement control potential, but it was generalized by subsequent researchers to other behaviors. It consisted of 29 items (six fillers) measuring seven general areas:

- the average citizen's belief that he or she can have an influence in government decisions: "With enough effort we can wipe out political corruption."
- that when one makes plans he or she can make them work: "What happens to me is my own doing."
- success in the job: "Getting a good job depends mainly on being in the right place at the right time."
- belief in fate: "Many times I feel that I have little influence over the things that happen to me."
- friendship: "People are lonely because they don't try to be friendly."
- respect: "In the long run, people get the respect they deserve in this world."
- and academic achievement: "There is a direct connection between how hard I study and the grade I get."

   Higher scores indicate externality (0-23). Daniels and Stevens (1976) considered subjects scoring in the upper 27% (17-23 as high externals, and those scoring in the lower 27% (2-8) as high internals. Reliability varies with the population; however, most ratings are in the .6 to .9 range.

Intellectual Achievement Responsibility Scale (IAR) (Crandall, Katkovsky, & Crandall, 1965)

The Crandalls developed the IAR to assess children's acceptance of responsibility for their successes (I+) and failures (I-) within an academic setting. It differs from other scales because it limits sources of external control to persons the children are most likely to encounter (teachers, parents, peers). The IAR consists of 34 forced-choice items such as: "When you have trouble understanding something in school, it is usually (a) because the teacher didn't explain it clearly, or (b) because the teacher explained it clearly?" Scores can range from 0 to 34, with higher scores indicating greater internality. With reliabilities of .69-.74, the validation showed slight increases in internality with age (grades 3-5 vs. grades 6-12).

Stanford Preschool Internal-External Scale (SPIES) (Mischel, Zeiss, & Zeiss, 1974)

Based on the Crandalls' earlier work, Mischel, Zeiss, and Zeiss developed the SPIES to assess perceived control of potentially positive or potentially negative outcomes, but not in an academic setting. A sample question is: "When somebody brings you a present, is that (a) because you are a good boy (girl), or (b) because they like to give people presents?" (Gregory, 1981 p. 71-73).

IPC Scales (Levenson, 1982)

Levenson later developed three scales that represent a more differentiated reconceptualization of Rotter's original scale. The scales consist of three 8-item, Likert-type subscales: the I Scale (Internal), which measures beliefs in personal control over one's own life; the P Scale (Powerful Others), which measures beliefs in powerful others; and the C Scale (Chance), which measures beliefs in chance or fate. Three questions from the IPC Scales are:
• I Scale, "When I make plans, I am almost certain to make them work."
• P Scale, "In order to have my plans work, I make sure that they fit in with the desires of people who have power over me."
• C Scale, "It's not wise for me to plan too far ahead because many things turn out to be a matter of good or bad luck."
Reliability estimates for the three scales are in the .6 to .8 range. The three scales were found to be significantly related to Rotter's scale.

Nowicki-Strickland Internal-External Control Scale **(NSIE)** (Nowicki & Duke, 1974; Nowicki & Strickland, 1973)

The Nowicki-Strickland I-E Scale is a paper-and-pencil measure with 40 yes/no items. Based on Rotter's definition, the items on the Children's NSIE (Nowicki & Strickland, 1973) was written on a fifth-grade level to describe reinforcement situations in areas such as affiliation, achievement, and dependency, such as:
• Do you believe that most problems will solve themselves if you just don't fool with them? (negative)
• Do you feel that when good things happen they happen because of hard work? (positive)
Validity was moderately high (.61, .38) when compared with Rotter's scale. Reliability was reported from .62 - .81 depending on the age of the test takers. The Adult NSIE (Nowicki & Duke, 1974) was a more advanced version of the childrens' scale with acceptable reliability with noncollege populations.

Trent Attribution Profile (TAP) (Wong, Watters, & Sproule, 1978)

The TAP presents three simulated achievement-oriented common life situations (academic, social, and financial) to measure locus of control and stability, including ability, effort, task difficulty, and luck. In each item, success and failure outcomes are presented in two different orientations (self and other). The test consists of 12 items that represent each possible condition for each situation. For example:
• When people fail school, it is due to (a) a lack of academic skills, (b) bad breaks, (c) a lack of effort, (d) harsh judgments by the teachers (academic failure for others item).
Respondents rate the importance of each option on a 5-point scale. The test was found to be valid ($r=.51$) when compared with Rotter's I-E Scale. Test-retest reliability coefficients were high.

James I-E Scale (James, 1957; MacDonald, 1973)

This test is a 30-item Likert scale in which respondents agree or disagree with externally oriented statements. Reliability coefficients of .76 to .89 were generated in two different studies.

Multidimensional-Multiattributional Causality Scale (Lefcourt, VonBaeyer, Ware, & Cox, 1979)

This test measures locus of control for achievement and affiliation. Each subscale consists of 24 Likert-type items, half concerning success and half concerning failure. The items are divided equally between four attributions, ability or skill, effort and motivation, task difficulty, and luck or fate. Scores range from 0 to 96 with higher scores indicating a more external orientation. Reliability ratings range from .61 to .77.

Other Scales

A number of other general purpose locus of control scales have been developed such as The Attributional Style Scale, (Seligman, 1975), Desirable-Undesirable Events Locus of Control Scale (Gregory, 1981), and Locus of Desired Control and Psychological Adjustment (Ziegler & Reid, 1979). Other content or context-specific locus of control scales have been developed, such as the Multidimensional Health Locus of Control Scale (Wallston, Wallston, Kaplan, & Maides, 1976). These scales have been infrequently used for research with learning or instruction and so are beyond the scope of this book.

Theoretical Background

Locus of control has its roots in Rotter's social learning theory (Rotter, 1954), specifically in the area known as *human expectancies*. Rotter believed that human behavior is a function of the expectancies for reinforcement. His model integrated ideas from both the stimulus-response psychology and the more contemporary cognitive (field theory) tradition associated with Lewin. He originally conceived of locus of control as a generalized expectancy to perceive reinforcement either as contingent on one's own behaviors (internal) or as the result of forces beyond one's control (external).

Locus of control has also been explained in terms of attribution theory. To whom or what does the individual attribute success or failure? Is it attributed internally or externally? Weiner (1971) added a second dimension of causality in a person's beliefs and behaviors. Causality, he argued, differs--some are constant or stable, whereas others fluctuate. For example, ability is usually perceived as a relatively stable trait, whereas effort and mode tend to fluctuate.

Attribution Theory:
Causes of Success and Failure

		Locus of Control	
		Internal	External
Causes	Unstable	Effort	Luck
	Stable	Ability	Task Difficulty

Locus and control are, in fact, independent dimensions. Some internal factors, mood for example, may be perceived as uncontrollable whereas others, such as effort, may be controllable. Factors (effort, persistence) may be subject to volitional control or may be uncontrollable, (fatigue, ability). This dimension became known as controllability.

A number of factor analyses of locus of control instruments have been conducted, many of which indicate that the internal-external concept is multidimensional. Duffy, Shiflett, and Downey (1977) isolated five separate factors, including the easiness, justness, predictability, political responsiveness, and friendliness of the world.

Locus of Control and Learning

Research

Because locus of control emerges from clinical psychology, most of the research does not concern learning or instructional effects. However, locus of control has become such a popular personality construct that it has been featured in a great deal of learning research.

- Seeman and Evans (1962) found that internals avail themselves of information more than externals because they believe that they can act on their own behalf and therefore need more information.

- Significant relationships were found between internal locus of control and higher grade point averages but not intelligence (Nowicki & Roundtree, 1971).

- Internals had better study habits and more positive academic attitudes (Ramanaiah, Ribich, & Schmeck, 1975).

- Externals who expected a poor course grade showed poorer attitudes toward the course and the examinations than did internals, or both internals and externals expecting a good grade (Page & Roy, 1975).

- In a review of 36 studies on locus of control and academic achievement (Bar-Tal & Bar-Zahor, 1977), 31 showed that internals achieved more because of internals' greater persistence, effort, and better use of task-relevant information.

- Internals had a better attitude toward math with better performance (Brown, 1980).

- Internals performed better in biology courses than extroverts (Cuomo-Miller, 1982).

- Externals tended to encode material in more superficial ways than internals when required to encode word lists semantically, othographically, and acoustically (Thal & Harris, 1983).

- Although locus of control predicted achievement on immediate and delayed posttests (internals better), it did not predict the number or type of options selected (Carrier, Davidson, & Williams, 1985).

- No differences in recall from cued and uncued, relevant and irrelevant passages questioned the contentions of social learning theory that internals would be superior only on relevant passages (Beaule & McKelvie, 1986; Brooks & McKelvie, 1986).

Implications of the Characteristics and Research

Implications which are drawn from research are noted with a •; those drawn logically from descriptive information regarding the trait are noted by an *. Based on a sizable body of research and the descriptions of *locus of control*, we conclude that *internal* learners are more likely to excel at learning tasks such as:

* conceptual tasks that require learners to integrate a lot of information
* problem-solving and higher order thinking tasks that require more intense involvement with the learning situation
• seeking out one's own information
• using persistent effort
• using task-relevant information
• mathematics
• biology

and acquire and use effectively learning strategies such as:

* concentrating on information
* predicting outcomes or inferring causes
* testing personal skills
* judging utility or value of knowledge

Based on a sizable body of research and the descriptions of locus of control, we conclude that external learners are more likely to excel at learning tasks such as:

* social interaction tasks
* tasks requiring empathy and understanding

and acquire and use effectively learning strategies such as:

* repeating or rehearsing material
* imaging or illustrating knowledge
* regulating mood

Locus of Control and Instruction

Research

- External males were more responsive to praise on an ambiguous coding task than internals, females, or for a reading task (Lintner & Ducette, 1974).

- Internals performed better under a contract-for-grade plan, whereas externals performed better under teacher control in an introductory psychology course (Daniels & Stevens, 1976).

- Internals benefitted more from instruction in which some of the structuring of course content is left to the learner (Hickey, 1980), whereas externals benefitted more from teacher-structured instruction.

- Conceptual cueing and mapping helped externals retain more information on a retention test than externals without help, whereas internals were unaffected (Sherris, 1980).

- Internals performed better in a small-group variation of direct instruction, probably because they had some control over their learning (Janicki & Peterson, 1981).

- Students in individualized, computer-based learning became more internal because they could relate success to their own efforts, whereas non-computer-based students became more dependent on the teacher (Warner, 1981).

- Internals achieved more when taught with the inductive method, whereas externals achieved more from deductive instruction (Horak & Horak, 1982).

- Internals benefitted more from instruction in which they determined response correctness, whereas externals benefitted more from instruction in which teachers determined response correctness (Pascarella, 1983).

- With abstract content, internals performed better with individualized instruction than externals, whereas externals performed better using traditional methods (Anderson, 1983).

- Elementary students in a mastery learning situation became more internal as a result of the method (Dertinger, 1984).

- Adult students who persisted longer were more internal (Vockroth, 1984).

- Instruction emphasizing self-management, goal clarification, and individualized course expectations increased science locus of control (Haurey, 1985).

- When given control of instruction on videocassette, internals made greater use of the controls than externals because internals will search harder for information; however, there were no performance differences or interactions (Fischler, 1986).

- Locus of control influenced both performance and confidence of learners, whereas learner control of instructional treatments had no affect (Klein & Keller, 1990).

- Perceived control influenced academic performance by promoting or impeding active engagement in learning activities (Skinner, Welbourn, & Connell, 1990).

- Internality affected achievement, time on instruction, attitude toward content, and task interaction frequency in a computer-based instruction lesson (Dalton, 1990).

Implications of the Characteristics and Research

Implications which are drawn from research are noted with a •; those drawn logically from descriptive information regarding the trait are noted by an *. Instructional conditions that capitalize on the preferences of the external student and challenge the internal student include:

- deductive activities
- highly structured instruction that is controlled by the teacher or the lesson
* instruction that provides much reinforcement
- elaborately cued instruction in which important information or tasks are signalled to the learner
* kinesthetic or visual, rather than verbal, material
* instruction that incorporates movement and avoids long periods of immobility
- instruction that provides praise and rewards after learner responses

Instructional conditions that remediate or compensate for the deficiencies of the external student include:

* gradually reducing cueing and reinforcements that challenge but do not prove too anxiety provoking for internals, thereby encouraging them to persist with difficult tasks

* using the contract-for-grade plan, although preferred by internals, could be used to challenge externals if it were highly structured and positive teacher feedback were provided
* providing more individual attention to learning about behavior consequences and more consistency in the environment
* providing achievement-motivation courses
* learning to learn skills, helps increase internality
* personal causation training to increase initiative (internality) such as determining realistic goals for themselves, knowing their own strengths and weaknesses, concretizing action to achieve goals, and determining when they approached their goals (Lefcourt, 1982)
* offering challenge and reinforcement based on accomplishment
* providing high structure, clear directions, specific choices, work being checked immediately, and imposed time limits
* using increased class meetings, more frequent and more heavily weighted examinations, more explicit knowledge of grade results and absence of open-ended projects (Strom & However, 1982)
* providing clear task instructions to moderate the effects of external locus of control on conceptual insight and ideational fluency
* providing analytic feedback that relates performance to effort

Instructional conditions that capitalize on the preferences of the internal student and challenge the external student include:

• asking students to evaluate their own success
• providing inductive experiences
• providing individualized instruction for abstract content
• asking students to provide their own structure
• providing tasks that require persistent attention
* providing tasks that require analytical thinking
• asking students to regulate their own learning rate, style, pace, or or mode of delivery (i.e., independent study and contract-for-grade)
• presenting many instructional options
• problem-solving situations, especially where learners must select and apply relevant information
• involved and complex tasks that require persistence

Instructional conditions that remediate or compensate for the deficiencies of the internal student include:

• work under observation, rather than in isolation, in a typical workplace (Lefcourt, 1982)
• directed attention to cues that doesn't seem to interfere with internals
• small group situations where high-ability students teach the low-ability students

References

Anderson, A. (1983). A comparison of two methods of teaching the calculation of medications to associate nursing freshmen and differing effects of locus of control (Doctoral dissertation, Boston University). *Dissertation Abstracts International, 44,* 317.

Bar-Tal, D., & Bar-Zahor, Y. (1977). The relationship between perception of locus of control and academic achievement. *Contemporary Educational Psychology, 2,* 181-199.

Beaule, B., & McKelvie, S. J. (1986). Effects of locus of control and relevance on intentional and incidental memory for passages. *Perceptual and Motor Skills, 63* (Pt. 2), 855-862.

Brooks, R. E., & McKelvie, S. J. (1986). Effects of locus of control, cueing and relevance on memory for passages. *Canadian Journal of Behavioural Sciences, 18,* 278-286.

Brown, C. D. (1980). The effect of individualized instruction, locus of control, and sex on student achievement and attitude (Doctoral dissertation, Boston University). *Dissertation Abstracts International, 41,* 590.

Carrier, C., Davidson, G., & Williams, M. (1985). The selection of instructional options in a computer-based coordinate concept lesson. *Educational Communications and Technology Journal, 33,* 199-212.

Crandall, V. C., Katkovsky, W., & Crandall, V. J. (1965). Children's beliefs in their own control of reinforcements in intellectual-academic situations and their embedded figures test performance. *Child Development, 43,* 1123-1134.

Cuomo-Miller, R. A. (1982). Relationship between learning styles and academic achievement of freshman baccalaureate nursing students (Doctoral dissertation, University of Pittsburgh). *Dissertation Abstracts International, 44,* 2664

Dalton, D. (1990). The effects of cooperative learning strategies on achievement and` attitudes during interactive video. *Journal of Computer-Based Instruction, 17,* 8-16.

Daniels, R. L., & Stevens, J.P. (1976). The interaction between the internal-locus of control and two methods of college instruction. *American Education Research Journal, 13(2),* 103-113.

Dertinger, T. D. (1984). An experimental study of the effects of mastery learning on the locus of control of sixth-grade science students (Doctoral dissertation, SUNY-Albany). *Dissertation Abstracts International, 45,* 107.

Duffy, P. J., Shiflet, S., & Downey, R. G. (1977). Locus of control: Dimensionality and predictability using Likert scales. *Journal of Applied Psychology, 62,* 214-219.

Fischler, H. A. (1986). Locus of control and two types of instructional television: An aptitude treatment interaction (Doctoral dissertation, New York University). *Dissertation Abstracts International, 48,* 635.

Gregory, W. L. (1981). Controllability, attributions, and behavior. In H. M. Lefcourt (Ed.), *Research with the locus of control construct. Volume 1: Assessment methods*, (pp. 67-124). New York: Academic Press.

Haurey, D. L. (1985, April 15-18). *Evidence that science locus of control orientation can be modified through instruction*. Paper presented at the annual meeting of the National Association for Research in Science Teaching, French Lick, IN. (ERIC Document Reproduction Service No. ED 255 375)

Hickey, P. S. (1980). A long-range test of the aptitude treatment interaction hypothesis in college-level mathematics (Doctoral dissertation, University of Texas). *Dissertation Abstracts International, 41*, 1452.

Horak, V. M., & Horak, W. J. (1982). The influence of student locus of control and teaching methods on mathematics achievement. *Journal of Experimental Education, 51*, 18-21.

James, W. H. (1957). Internal versus external control of reinforcement as a basis variable in learning theory (Doctoral dissertation, Ohio State University). *Dissertation Abstracts International, 17*, 2314.

Janicki, T. C., & Peterson, P. L. (1981). Aptitude-treatment interaction effects of variations of indirect instruction. *American Educational Research Journal, 18*, 63-82.

Joe, V. C. (1971). Review of the internal-external control construct as a personality variable. *Psychological Reports, 28*, 619-640.

Keefe, J. (1987). *Learning style: Theory and practice*. Reston, VA: National Association of Secondary School Principals.

Kennedy-Liaing, E. (1980). A study of the relationships among state-trait anxiety, locus of control, and mastery learning in associate degree nursing students in a community college (Doctoral dissertation, University of San Francisco). *Dissertation Abstracts International, 41*, 4652.

Klein, J. D., & Keller, J. (1990). Influence of student ability, locus of control, and type of instructional control on performance and confidence. *Journal of Educational Research, 83*, 140-146.

Kletzing, D. (1982). Congruence between field independence and locus of control as a predictor of student performance (Doctoral dissertation, Indiana University). *Dissertation Abstracts International, 43*, 2534.

Lefcourt, H. M. (1982). *Locus of control: Current trends in theory and research* (2nd ed.). Hillsdale, NJ: Lawrence Erlbaum Associates.

Lefcourt, H. M., VonBaeyer, C. L., Ware, E. E., & Cox, D. J. (1979). The multidimensional-multiattributional scale: The development of goals specific locus of control. *Canadian Journal of Behavioral Science, 11*, 286-304.

Levenson, H. (1982). Differentiating among internality, powerful others, and chance. In H. M. Lefcourt (Ed.), *Research with the locus of control construct: Vol. 1. Assessment methods* (pp. 15-63). New York: Academic Press.

Lintner, A. C., & Ducette, J. (1974). The effects of locus of control, academic failure, and task dimensions on a students' responsiveness to praise. *American Educational Research Journal, 11*, 231-239.

MacDonald, A. P. (1973). Measures of internal-external locus of control. In J. P. Robinson & P. R. Shaver (Eds.), *Measures of social psychological attitudes* (pp. 67-84). Ann Arbor: Institute for Social Research, University of Michigan.

Mischel, K. W., Zeiss, R., & Zeiss, A. (1974). Internal-external control and persistence: Validation and implications of the Stanford preschool internal-external scale. *Journal of Personality and Social Psychology, 29*, 265-278.

Nowicki, S., & Duke, M. P. (1974). A locus of control scale for college as well as noncollege adults. *Journal of Personality Assessment, 38*, 136-137.

Nowicki, S., & Roundtree, J. (1971). Correlates of locus of control in a secondary school population. *Developmental Psychology, 4*, 477-488.

Nowicki, S., & Strickland, B. R. (1973). A locus of control scale for children. *Journal of Consulting and Clinical Psycology, 40*, 148-154.

Page, M. M., & Roy, R. E. (1975). Internal-external control and independence of judgment in course evaluation among college students. *Personality and Social Psychology Bulletin, 1*, 509-512.

Pascarella, E. T. (1983). Interaction of internal attribution for effort and teacher response mode in reading instruction: A replication note. *American Educational Research Journal, 20*, 269-276.

Ramanaiah, N. V., Ribich, F. D., & Schmeck, R. R. (1975). Internal-external control of reinforcement as a determinant of study habits and academic attitudes. *Journal of Research in Personality, 9*, 375-384.

Rotter, J. B. (1954). *Social Learning and clinical psychology.* Englewood Cliffs, NJ: Prentice-Hall.

Rotter, J. B. (1966). Generalized expectancies for internal versus external control of reinforcement. *Psychological Monographs: General and Applied. 80* (1), 1-28.

Seeman, M., & Evans, J. (1963). Alienation and learning in a hospital setting. *American Sociological Review, 69*, 270-284.

Seligman, M. E. P. (1975). *Helplessness: On depression, development, and death.* San Fransisco: Freeman.

Sherris, J. D. (1980). The effects of instructional organization and selected individual difference variables on the meaningful learning of high school biology students (Doctoral dissertation, Purdue University). *Dissertation Abstracts International, 42*, 1088.

Skinner, E. A., Wellborn, J. G., & Connell, J. P. (1990). What it takes to do well in school and whether I've got it: A process model of perceived control and children's engagement and achievement in schools. *Journal of Educational Psychology, 82*, 22-30.

Strom, B., & However, D. (1982). Course structure and student satisfaction: An attribute-treatment interaction analysis. *Educational Research Quarterly, 7* (1), 21-30.

Thal, J. S., & Harris, J. D. (1983). Locus of control and depth of processing in children. *Journal of General Psychology, 109*, 31-42.

Vockroth, R. W. (1984). A study of selected factors relating to to persistence of adult learners in the two year college (Doctoral dissertation, Cornell University). *Dissertation Abstracts International, 45*, 1271.

Wallston, B. S., Wallston, K. A., Kaplan, G. D., & Maides, S. A. (1976). Development and validation of the health locus of control (HLC) scale. *Journal of Consulting and Clinical Psychology, 44*, 580-585.

Warner, T. D. (1981). The effects of computer-based education on sixth-grade students' self-concept, locus of control, and mathematics achievement (Doctoral dissertation, University of Akron). *Dissertation Abstracts International, 42*, 1040.

Weiner, B. (1971). *Perceiving the causes of success and failure.* Morristown, NJ: General Learning Press.

Wong, P. T., Waters, D. A., & Sproule, C. F. (1978). Initial validity and reliability of the Trent Attribution Profile (TAP) as a measure of attribution schema and locus of control. *Educational and Psychological Measurement, 38*, 1129-1134.

Ziegler, M., & Reid, D. W. (1979). Correlates of locus of control in two samples of elderly persons: Community residents and hospitalized patients. *Journal of Consulting and Clinical Psychology, 47*, 977-979.

Bibliography

Corno, L., & Snow, R. E. (1985) Adapting teaching to individual differences among learners. In M. C. Wittrock (Ed.), *Handbook of research on teaching* (3rd ed. pp. 605-629). New York: MacMillan.

Dillashaw, F. G. (1980). The effects of a modified mastery learning strategy on achievement, attitudes, and time on task of high school chemistry students (Doctoral dissertation, University of Georgia). *Dissertation Abstracts International, 41*, 1519.

Grabinger, R. S., & Jonassen, D. W. (1988). *Independent study: Personality, cognitive, and descriptive predictors.* Proceedings of Selected Research Papers presented at the Annual Meeting of the Association for Educational communication and Technology. (ERIC Document Reproduction Service No. ED 295 641)

Jonassen, D. H. (1985). Relating cognitive styles to independent study. *International Journal of Instructional Media, 12*(4), 271-281.

Lefcourt, H. M. (1981). *Research with the locus of control construct: Vol. 1. Assessment methods.* New York: Academic.

Lefcourt, H. M. (1983). *Research with the locus of control construct. Vol. 2. Developments and social problems.* New York: Academic.

Rotter, J. B. (1975). Some problems and misconceptions related to the construct of internal versus external control of reinforcement. *Journal of Consulting and Clinical Psychology, 43,* 56-67.

Strickland, B. (1977). Internal-external locus of control. In T. Blass (Ed.), *Personality variables in social behavior* (pp. 219-280). Hillsdale, NJ: Lawrence Erlbaum Associates.

Weiner, B. (1985). An attributional theory of achievement motivation and emotion. *Psychological Review, 92,* 548-573.

Wesley, B. E., Krockover, G. H., & Hicks, C. R. (1985). Locus of control and acquisition of computer literacy. *Journal of Computer-Based Instruction, 12,* 12-16.

29

EXTROVERSION AND INTROVERSION

Description of Extroversion/Introversion

The personality traits, extroversion (E)/introversion (I), are among the few that researchers agree provide consistent and valid information. In addition to describing and predicting social behavior, they also have been shown to predict learning and the ways that individuals process information. As the words imply, thinking and behavior that are directed inward or to oneself is known as introversion; the thinking and behavior that is directed outward, or to the surrounding environment, is extroversion. Some researchers and educators use the terms *action-oriented* for extroverts and *reflective-oriented* for introverts because the terms *extroversion* and *introversion* have negative connotations in some circles. Henjum (1982) described two types of introverts: Type-A introverts who are self-sufficient, hardworking, confident, and successful; and Type-B introverts who are shy, uncommunicative, withdrawn, and self-conscious.

As a personality trait, level of introversion and extroversion is relatively constant, although some studies have indicated that environment may influence thinking and behavior. As people mature they tend to become more introverted.

Extroverts exhibit the following characteristics:
- are continuously alert to events outside themselves
- turn outward to pick up cues, ideas, expectation, values, and interest
- have a variety of interests
- take an active approach to life
- use trial-and-error approach to learning
- are practical, active, vocal, and enjoy being with people

On the other hand, introverts:
- naturally look inward for resources and cues
- pursue fewer interests more deeply and intensely
- attend more to their inner perceptions and judgments
- are reflective, prefer being by themselves or with a few friends

The differences in thinking and learning between extroverts and introverts is attributable largely to the ways in which they respond to stimuli. Introverts are easily stimulated. As a result they prefer environments with less stimuli. Extroverts are the opposite; they require more stimuli to generate a response.

It is important to remember that a pure personality trait does not exist. An individual may be extremely introverted, but in an exceptional case, show extroverted behavior. However, there are certain characteristics that are prevalent. The extreme extrovert values the outer world much more than his or her own inner world of ideas and directs his or her energies outward. The individual is active and sociable, seeking excitement, enjoying change, and acting on impulse. In addition, they like practical jokes, enjoy a good laugh, tend to lose their temper very easily, but will not hold a grudge for a long period of time. Introverts, on the other hand, although not losing their temper easily, will build up dislikes over a long time. The friendships that are established are deeper and tend to be more constant. Also the introvert is more introspective, needs less stimulation from the outside world, is less ambitious, less worldly, plans ahead, prefers an ordered life, is serious-minded, and less aggressive.

Characteristic Differences in Extroversion and Introversion

Extroverts	Introverts
look to outside world	look inward
adept at complex motor sequences	read more
conditioned by positive reinforcement	conditioned by negative reinforcement
skilled at short-term retention	long-term memory retention
seek affiliation	seek academic achievement
tolerant of frustration	intolerant of frustration
sociable, friendly	quiet, retiring, introspective
desire excitement, take chances	contemplative and reflective
impulsive	plan ahead, nonimpulsive
tolerant of cognitive dissonance/inconsistency	intolerant of cognitive dissonance/inconsistency
energetic/enthusiastic	prone to fatigue
respond quickly	reflect prior to response
easily distracted	academically superior, less distracted
dislike complicated procedures	concentrate longer on tasks
task-oriented, seek closure	conceptually oriented
less sensitive to noise, stimuli	dislike interruptions and intrusions
influenced by public opinion and events	influenced by personal values

Individual Differences Related to Extroversion/Introversion

Field dependence/independence--FD/I describes how much a learner's perception or comprehension of information is affected by the surrounding perceptual or contextual field (see chapter 7). It appears that field dependent individuals would be more extroverted, that is, oriented toward environmental clues in social settings, and that introverted people should be more field independent. However, numerous studies have indicated no relationship between the two variables. Fine (1972) indicated no relationship between field dependence and extroversion/introversion, but he found that in 85% of his sample, those individuals who were scoring high in neuroticism were overrepresented in the areas that embody field dependence and introversion.

Verbalizer/Visualizer--The visual/verbal cognitive style describes individual preferences for attending to and processing visual versus verbal information (see chapter 15). Extroverts are better verbalizers, whereas introverts are better imagers (Riding & Burt, 1982).

Kolb's Learning Styles--Kolb defines learning styles as one's preferred methods for perceiving and processing information. Extroversion is related to the concrete experience and active experimentation learning styles from Kolb's Learning Styles Inventory (see chapter 20), whereas introversion is related to the reflective observation learning style (Hinkle, 1986).

Tolerance for ambiguity--Ambiguity tolerance refers to an individual's willingness to accommodate or adapt to encounters with ambiguity. Norman and Watson (1976) found that because extroverts are less aroused than introverts, they had greater tolerance for inconsistency. Introverts, on the other hand, viewed the imbalance as aversive and unpleasant. Such findings likely generalize ambiguity tolerance (see chapter 26).

Cognitive Tempo--Impulsivity/reflectivity, also referred to as *cognitive tempo* or *conceptual tempo*, measures a person's tendency to inhibit initial responses and to reflect on the accuracy of an answer rather than responding impulsively (see chapter 9). Extroverts are frequently characterized as active-oriented, whereas introverts are reflective-oriented. Research showed that many of the effects attributable to extroversion/introversion are in reality impulsivity effects (Humphreys & Revelle, 1984). Extroversion/introversion also describes impulsive or reflective processing styles.

Instruments for Measuring Extroversion/Introversion

Eysenck Personality Inventory **(EPI)** (Eysenck & Eysenck, 1968)

The EPI is probably the most widely test used to measure extroversion/introversion. The form consists of 57 items, including 24 questions assessing neuroticism/stability, 24 yes-no questions assessing extroversion/introversion that were selected on the basis of factor analysis, and nine-response distortion items. The test, which replaces the earlier, more complicated Maudsley Personality Inventory (Eysenck, 1962), takes about 10 minutes to complete. Over several months, the reliability of the EPI exceeds .85. Concurrent validity has been established by comparing the EPI to the Maudsley Personality Inventory, the Psychoticism-Extroversion-Neuroticism Scale, and the Eysenck Personality Questionnaire. Eysenck's contributions to personality theory make this one of the most prevalent tests used to measure this aspect of personality.

Singer Loomis Inventory of Personality **(SLIP)** (Singer & Loomis, 1984)

This inventory measures several personality traits including introversion and extroversion. The SLIP is based on Jung's theory of psychological types, which identifies attitude types and functions. Extroversion/introversion is one of the most important attitude types. These are described in terms of the attitude functions, sensation/intuition (perceiving functions) and thinking/feeling(judging functions). This test generates scores for each of the eight cognitive modes that result. It consists of 15 situations with eight possible responses for each situation. Participants are asked to check each response on a scale from never to always. Reliability coefficients for the eight modes average .64. and .85 for extroversion/introversion.

Myers Briggs Type Indicator **(MBTI)** (Myers, 1962)

Based on Jung's theory of psychological types, this instrument assesses four dimensions of personality, including extroversion/introversion, sensing/intuition, thinking/feeling, and judgment/perception. It is among the most frequently used personality instruments. There are several versions of this test available, including self-scoring tests. Questions are presented and participants must choose between answers provided. This test is highly reliable and is one of the most frequently used personality measures available.

NEO Personality Inventory **(NEOPI)** (McCrae & Costa, 1987)

The NEOPI generates 23 personality scores in five dimensions: neuroticism, extroversion, openness, agreeableness, and conscientiousness. The extroversion dimension consists of subscales: warmth, gregariousness, assertiveness, activity, excitement seeking, and positive emotions. It is self-administered in print or on computer.

Omnibus Personality Inventory **(OPI)** (Psychological Corporation, 1962)

The OPI generates 15 scores including thinking, introversion, and social extroversion. It is most suitable for use in a college context. It has been criticized for the methods used in scale development.

Willingness to Communicate **(WTC)** (McCroskey & Richmond, 1990)

This brief test measures an individual's willingness to communicate with friends, acquaintances, and strangers and indicates introversion tendencies. Respondents are asked to indicate the percent of time they would choose to communicate with a list of people they may encounter.

Keegan Type Indicator (Keegan, 1984)

Also based on Jung's theory of types, this test takes 20 minutes and produces three scores, extroversion/introversion, sensing/intuition, and thinking/feeling. No reliability and validity data are available.

Theoretical Background

According to Eysenck (1960, 1962, 1983) the terms *extroversion* and *introversion* were in use in Europe for several hundred years prior to their use in the vernacular of psychology as we know it today. The theoretical background of these traits has been explored by many people, but probably the individual most noted for his work in this area is H. J. Eysenck. Eysenck, born in Berlin in 1916, studied at the University of London and developed an appreciation for the analysis of human behavior through experimentation. Eysenck felt that, to advance our understanding of problem-solving behavior we need to assume scientific research methods and totally reevaluate psychoanalytic theory. During World War II, Eysenck was responsible for a hospital outside London in which research was conducted on patients who had become incapacitated because of the war.

Eysenck attempted to classify human behavior rather than trying to understand the individual. He believed that specific measurement was necessary for scientific advancement. He attempted to classify human behavior using the concepts of trait and type. A trait is identified by observing consistencies in behavior. Type is a more inclusive factor that refers to a group of traits which have been correlated with each other. For example, an introvert would show such traits as shyness, persistence, and rigidity.

Eysenck stressed the importance of heredity in his research. According to his theory, genetics plays an important role in the formation of personality. The autonomic nervous system determines how an individual will react emotionally. The reasons for this, according to Eysenck, are because of the ascending reticular formation of the brain stem. The brain stem will either excite or inhibit the activity of the cortex when dealing with incoming sensory impulses. When the level is depressed, the individual will seek more stimulation from the outside world. Consequently the behavior will be more extroverted. If the cortex is over-bombarded, the introverted behavior patterns will emerge to suppress the cortex.

The conclusions that Eysenck reached were the culmination of extensive research using factor analysis on a battery of tests with many subjects. He discovered a general factor that appeared to be neurotic tendencies or neuroticism (N). The term *neurotic* refers to a general tendency to respond excessively with emotion and a liability to neurotic disturbances such as anxiety reactions under stress. This tendency appeared to be a bipolar dimension that contrasted anxiety and depression on one end with hysteria at the other. He established this as a continuum that had very stable nonemotional individuals at one end, and highly unstable individuals at the other. A person high in neuroticism possesses the following traits: moodiness, relentlessness, high anxiety, touchiness, and aggressiveness. The individual at the other end of the continuum is calm, even tempered, carefree, and reliable.

Eysenck continued to analyze his findings by testing those people in the unstable half of the dimension. He found that one half of that group, which he termed *dysthymic*, was characterized by excessive tiredness, constant introspection, feelings of guilt, and an overconcern for religious and ethical matters. The second group, which he termed *hysteric*, was found to be impulsive, changeable, irresponsible, and lacking in moral fiber. His next step was to examine the stable half of the dimension. Applying factor analysis, Eysenck was able to determine that they did not form a homogeneous group. Because the dysthymics resembled the introvert described by Jung and the hysterics the extrovert, Eysenck adopted these terms for the second dimension. Later in his research, Eysenck added a third dimension, psychoticism, and accepted the dimension of general intelligence as presented by Charles Spearman. This completed a four-dimensional structure that Eysenck developed to describe human personality.

With the addition of Eysenck's contribution of introversion and extroversion, the study of personality traits has been greatly enhanced. As Eysenck's theories grew in popularity and Jung's theories came into prominence, Eysenck became increasingly critical of Jung's contributions, stating that the clear-cut descriptive patterns were complicated by Jung's descriptions of the thinking, feeling, sensing, and intuitive types.

Extroversion/Introversion and Learning

Research

- Lynn and Gordon (1961) found a relationship between introversion and academic success. Because there was no significant correlation between introversion and the level of intelligence, the relationship was predicted to have resulted from the introvert's ability to apply him or herself.

- Kline (1966) determined that introversion was strongly related to academic success even in other cultures.

- Farley (1967) explored the speed of performance and personality type using problems found in intelligence tests. Extroverts were faster than introverts and ambiverts.

- Savage (1966) revealed that children high in extroversion had higher academic attainment scores than others.

- Entwistle and Cunningham (1968) found no significant correlation between extroversion and scholastic achievement. Extroverted females and introverted males did better than introverted females and extroverted males.

- When retrieving information from memory, introverts and extroverts scanned for physical features at an equal rate; however, introverts were not as quick as extroverts in scanning for semantic features (Eysenck & Eysenck, 1979).

- Art education and music education majors tend to be more extroverted (Todd, 1980).

- Low-IQ introverts outperformed low-IQ extroverts, whereas high-IQ introverts and extroverts performed the same on a mathematical task (Bhartiya, 1981).

- Creativity in the arts was positively related to introversion (Eysenck, 1983).

- Nurmi and von Wright (1983) found that introverts recalled more items than extroverts in an immediate recall task.

- Extroverts are differentially effective on addition, subtraction, multiplication, and division when compared with introverts (Riding & Borg, 1987).

- Introverts attempted more problems and committed fewer errors on an anagram task and outperformed extroverts on a maze task (Malhotra, Malhotra, & Jerath, 1989).

Implications of the Characteristics and Research

Implications which are drawn from research are noted with a •; those drawn logically from descriptive information regarding the trait are noted by an *. Based on the sometimes conflicting research and the descriptions of extroversion/introversion, we conclude that extroverted learners are more likely to excel at learning tasks such as:

- tasks that require rapid processing of information
- multimodal, multi-image tasks that present large amounts of stimuli
- social and behavioral assessment and interaction tasks
- those involving art and music

and acquire and use effectively learning strategies such as:

- searching for information
- generating examples

Based on the sometimes conflicting research and the descriptions of extroversion/introversion, we conclude that introverted learners are more likely to excel at learning tasks such as:

- visual, imaginal, or spatial manipulation tasks
- organizing and structuring information for recall
- analysis required for problem solving

and acquire and use effectively learning strategies such as:

- preparing environment
- concentrating on information
- evaluating information
- rehearsing and reviewing material
- paraphrasing and summarizing
- imagining or illustrating knowledge

Extroversion/Introversion and Instruction

Research

- Eysenck (1959) found that although extroverts were faster on the first part of an exam and then slowed down, the introverts started slow and built up speed, so although the extroverts began with a quick start, they tended to give up quicker when faced with difficulty.

- Entwistle and Entwistle (1970) found that introverts had better study habits than extroverts.

- When rules were presented before examples, the introverts' performance was superior. When rules were presented after examples, the extroverts were superior (Trown, 1970).

- Farley (1977) found that extroverted college males seek more stimulation, but no relationship was found for ninth graders.

- Extroverts selected study locations that provided greater external stimulation (Campbell & Hawley, 1983).

- Learning environments stimulating enough for extroverts were too stimulating for introverts (and for the teacher) (Schmeck & Lockhart, 1983).

- In an operant conditioning task, extroverts were better conditioned by positive reinforcement, whereas introverts responded better to punishment (Gupta & Shukla, 1989).

- Hecht, Boster, and LaMer (1989) revealed that extroverts were more self-monitoring, using external cues to control and adjust their communication. Extroverts were more aware of people and events and attempted to match their communication styles to their surroundings. Introverts were low self-monitors, less aware of others, and did not adjust their communication styles.

- McCroskey and Richmond (1990) showed that extroverts were more willing to communicate but less so than indicated in the listener adapted communication study. Because introverts placed less value on communication, they were less willing to communicate given the choice.

Implications of the Characteristics and Research

Implications which are drawn from research are noted with a •; those drawn logically from descriptive information regarding the trait are noted by an *. Instructional conditions that capitalize on the preferences of the extroverted student and challenge the introverted student include:

• providing positive reinforcement frequently and consistently
• group-oriented, collaborative activities with much interactivity
• experiences requiring higher level of activity
• using multimedia, audio-visual presentations and other high-stimulus environments
* open-spaced classroom with discovery
* presenting material that is not structured, where the learners can proceed at their own pace
* using inductive instructional sequence
• providing opportunities to monitor progress

Instructional conditions that remediate or compensate for the deficiencies of the extroverted student include:

• presenting instruction that is not long in duration
* using vocabulary preteaching activities
* presenting information in small chunks
* posing questions to the learner
* asking the learner to select personal goals or establish criteria for performing
* providing verbal outlines and structured overviews of material
* providing divergent, example/nonexample pairs of concepts
* providing graphic cues: lines, colors, arrows, and so forth
* advising learners of instructional support needed: number of examples or practice items
* analyzing key ideas, constructing concept maps, or graphic organizers

Instructional conditions that capitalize on the preferences of the introverted student and challenge the extroverted student include:

• providing negative reinforcement through verbal communication
* silent, solitary reading
* presenting very structured material that involves a large degree of conditioned learning
• providing a quiet and less stimulating atmosphere
• providing a structured learning environment
• presenting a deductive sequence of instruction

Instructional conditions that remediate or compensate for the deficiencies of the introverted student include:

* presenting simultaneous instruction using both physical, visual, and semantic approaches
* insuring that feedback is provided in a consistent and even manner
* arousing learner with novelty, uncertainty, or surprise

* presenting pictorial organizers, structured overviews, graphic organizers, or concept maps
* providing enrichment feedback or having the learner self-generate feedback
* ordering instruction according to narrative sequence

References

Bhartiya, A. (1981). The effectiveness of mathetics in mathematics in relation to certain student characteristics (Doctoral dissertation, Meerut University). *Dissertation Abstracts International, 43,* 2263.

Campbell, J. B., & Hawley, C. W. (1983). Study habits and Eysenck's theory of extroversion-introversion. *Journal of Research in Personality, 16,* 139-146.

Entwistle, N. J., & Cunningham, S. (1968). Neuroticism and school attainment--a linear relationship? *British Journal of Educational Psychology, 38,* 137-51.

Entwistle, N. J., & Entwistle, D. (1970). The relationship between personality, study methods, and academic performance. *British Journal of Educational Psychology, 40,* 132-141.

Eysenck, H. J. (1959). *Manual of the Maudsley Personality Inventory.* London: University of London Press.

Eysenck, H. J. (1960). *The structure of human personality.* London: Methuen.

Eysenck, H. J. (1962). *The Maudsley Personality Inventory.* San Diego: Educational and Industrial Testing Service.

Eysenck, H. J. (1983). The roots of creativity: Cognitive ability or personality trait? *Roeper Review, 5*(4), 10-12.

Eysenck, H. J., & Eysenck, S. B. G. (1968). *Manual: Eysenck Personality Inventory.* San Diego: Educational and Industrial Testing Service.

Eysenck, M. W., & Eysenck, M. C. (1979). Memory scanning, introversion-extroversion, and levels of processing. *Journal of Research in Personality, 13,* 305-315.

Farley, F. H. (1967). Extroversion and stimulus-seeking motivation. *Journal of Consulting Psychology, 31,* 215-225.

Farley, F. H. (1977). The stimulation-seeking motive and extroversion in adolescents and adults. *Adolescence, 12,* 65-71.

Fine, B. J. (1972). Intrinsic motivation, intelligence, and personality as related to cognitive and motor performance. *Perceptual and Motor Skills, 34*(1), 319-29.

Gupta, S., & Shukla, A. P. (1989). Verbal operant conditioning as a function of extroversion and reinforcement. *British Journal of Psychology, 80,* 39-44.

Hecht, M. L., Boster, F. J., & LaMer, S. (1989). The effect of extroversion and differentiation on listener-adapted communication. *Communication Reports, 2*(1), 1-12.

Henjum, A. (1982). Introversion: A misunderstood "individual difference" among students. *Education, 103*(1), 39-43.

Hinkle, K. S. (1986). An investigation of the relationships among learning style preferences, personality types, and mathematics anxiety of college students (Doctoral dissertation, University of Maryland). *Dissertation Abstracts International, 47,* 2437.

Humphreys, M. S., & Revelle, W. (1984). Personality, motivation, and performance: A theory of the relationship between individual differences and information processing. *Psychological Review, 91,* 153-184.

Keegan, W. (1984). *Judgments, choices, and decisions: Effective management through self-knowledge.* New York: Wiley.

Kline, P. (1966). Extroversion, neuroticism, and academic performance among Ghanaian university students. *British Journal of Educational Psychology, 36,* 92-94.

Lynn, R., & Gordon, I. E. (1961). The relation of neuroticism and extroversion to intelligence and educational attainment. *British Journal of Educational Psychology, 31,* 194-203.

Malhotra, L., Malhotra, L., & Jerath, J. (1989). Speed and accuracy in learning as a function of personality. *Journal of Personality and Clinical Studies, 5,* 5-8.

McCrae, R. R., & Costa, P. T. (1987). Validation of the five-factor model of personality across instruments and observers. *Journal of Personality and Social Psychology, 52,* 81-90.

McCroskey, J. C., & Richmond, V. P. (1990). Willingness to communicate. *Journal of Social Behavior and Personality, 5* (2), 19.

Morris, L. W. (1979). *Extroversion and introversion: An interactional perspective.* New York: Hemisphere.

Myers, I. B. (1962). *The Myers-Briggs Type Indicator.* Palo Alto, CA: Consulting Psychologists Press.

Norman, M. G., & Watson, L. D. (1976). Extroversion and reactions to cognitive inconsistency, *Journal of Research in Personality, 10*(4), 446.

Nurmi, J. E., & vonWright, J. (1983). Interactive effects of noise, neuroticism, and state anxiety in the learning and recall of a textbook passage. *Human Learning: Journal of Practical Research and Applications, 2,* 119-125.

Psychological Corporation. (1962). *Omnibus personality inventory manual.* New York: Psychological Corporation.

Riding, R. J., & Borg, M. G. (1987). Sex and personality differences in performance on number computation in 11-year-old children. *Educational Review, 39,* 41-46.

Riding, R. J., & Burt, J. M. (1982). Reading vs. listening in children: The effects of extroversion and coding complexity. *Educational Psychology, 2,* 47-58.

Savage, R. D. (1966). Personality factors and academic attainment in junior school children. *British Journal of Educational Psychology, 36,* 91-92.

Schmeck, R. R., & Lockhart, D. (1983). Introverts and extroverts require different learning environments. *Educational Leader, 40*(5), 54.

Singer, J., & Loomis, M. (1984). *The Singer-Loomis Inventory of Personality.* Palo Alto, CA: Consulting Psychologists Press.

Todd, M. E. (1980). A comparative study of art education and music education majors at Texas Technical University (Doctoral dissertation, Texas Technical University). *Dissertation Abstracts International, 41,* 1353.

Trown, E. A. (1970). Some evidence on the interaction between teaching strategy and personality. *British Journal of Educational Psychology, 40,* 209-211.

Bibliography

Bischof, L. J. (1964). Symbolical, mathematical learning. In G. Murphy (Ed.), *Interpreting personality theories* (pp. 604-613). New York: Harper & Row.

Boddy, J., Carver, A., & Rowley, K. (1986). Effects of positive and negative verbal reinforcement on performance as a function of extraversion-introversion: Some tests of Gray's theory. *Personality and Individual Differences, 7*(1), 81.

Handky, G. D. (1979). Eysenck's functional theory of personality structure and causal dynamics. In D. S. Cartwright (Ed.), *Theories and models of personality* (pp. 422-445). Dubuque, IA: Brown.

Kawash, G. F. (1982). Anxiety and extroversion. *Journal of Clinical Psychology, 2,* 301-311.

Richardson, J. T. (1982). Introversion-extroversion and experimenter effect in memory tasks. *Personality and Individual Differences, 3*(3), 327.

30

ACHIEVEMENT MOTIVATION

Description of Achievement Motivation

Achievement motivation is a personality measure that describes an individual's willingness to achieve. Motivation, more broadly described, is what energizes us to action (Gage & Berliner, 1984) and includes needs, values, attitudes, interests, aspirations, and incentives. Achievement motivation has been described by many terms; however, in this chapter, achievement motivation is constrained to the type most relevant to learning and instruction, that is, need for achievement. *Need* is defined as "a lack of something that a given outcome can provide" (p. 338). The urge to satisfy those needs translates into one's motivation. Murray (1938) described achievement motivation as the need to:

> accomplish something difficult. To master, manipulate or organize physical objects, human beings or ideas. To do this as rapidly, and as independently as possible. To overcome obstacles and attain a high standard. To excel one's self. To rival and surpass others. To increase self-regard by the successful exercise of talent....[manifested by actions which] make intense, prolonged and repeated efforts to accomplish something difficult...[and] work with singleness of purpose towards a high and distant goal. To have the determination to win. To try to do everything well. To be stimulated to excel by the presence of others, to enjoy competition. To exert will power; to overcome boredom and fatigue. (p. 164.)

Some theorists contrast this personality measure with other personality variables such as need for affiliation, abasement, inferiority avoidance, blame avoidance, play, exhibition (Murray, 1938).

More recently, two types of individuals have been designated under the rubric of achievement motivation that capture the essence of these two contrasting personality types: those with a need to succeed, and those who have a need to avoid failure (Atkinson, 1964; McClelland, 1961). The former is associated with a success orientation and the latter with an anxiety about not being able to deal with the negative effects of failure. Two expectancies result from this orientation. Those who have a need to achieve expect to succeed and feel proud, whereas those who fear failure expect to fail and feel shame as a result of it. McClelland (1965) identified several characteristics of high achievers: "personal responsibility for actions, willingness to take moderate risks, and the desire for knowledge of results of actions" (Biehler & Snowman, 1986, p. 516).

The effect of this construct on achievement can be explained through an interactive person/situation paradigm much like the state/trait dimensions of anxiety. One's motive (trait) is a "predisposition" to one's motivation (state), which results from a merger of motives and situations. Several variables combine to comprise a "situation." Atkinson (1964) postulated the multiplicative effect of *probability of success (failure), perceived difficulty of the task,* and *positive incentive value of success (negative incentive value of failure)* to determine one's tendency to act. Humphreys and Revelle (1984) defined tendency to act in terms of persistence, success on information transfer tasks in long-term memory, or short-term memory tasks such as recall, recognition, or memory scan. Maehr (1982) included attention and activity, intensity, continuing motivation to conduct a task without supervision, and performance as well as persistence and performance.

Humphreys and Revelle (1984) identified feedback type, incentives, threat of punishment, time of day, stimulant drugs (i.e., caffeine), depressant drugs, heat, cold, and noise as situational variables that can affect the state of one's motives. Motivation can be reduced by devaluing the importance of the task, impairing self-esteem, or deliberately making the task unpleasant. Conversely, increasing the incentive or negative consequences of failure can increase motivation and perseverance on a task (Gage & Berliner, 1984). Whereas a high degree of achievement motivation can produce positive results in performance, too much may have a negative effect. Weiner (1978) suggested that a medium degree of motivation as stimulated by the situation is probably the best.

Although achievement motivation has been defined as a stable trait that develops from environmental and familial stimulation while growing up, McClelland (1965) and Kolb (1965) demonstrated that one's orientation can be altered through achievement motivation training.

Characteristic Differences in Achievement Motivation

Motive to Achieve Success	Motive to Avoid Failure
success orientation	failure orientation
pride orientation	shame orientation
prefers medium difficulty tasks	prefers easy or hard tasks
confident	anxious
independent	dependent on feedback and supervision
persistent	reluctant
perceives failure as a lack of effort	perceives failure as a lack of ability
can handle long-term goals	prefers short-term goals
zest, ambition	blandness

These differences were suggested by Stipek (1988), Wendt (1955), French and Thomas (1958), and Murray (1938).

Individual Differences Related to Achievement Motivation

Achievement Motivation is closely associated with other cognitive styles and controls:

Anxiety--This refers to a "transitory emotional state or condition characterized by feelings of tension and apprehension and heightened autonomic nervous system activity" (Spielberger, 1972, p. 24). Anxiety (see chapter 24) is one of the most commonly accepted causes of motivationally induced deficits in performance and has been associated with a motive to avoid failure (Humphreys & Revelle, 1984).

Locus of Control--This describes an individual's belief regarding those factors to which an individual attributes his or her successes and failures (see chapter 28). Stake (1979) found that measures of achievement motivation, other than course grades, were related to locus of control for both sexes of undergraduates. Verma (1986) found the same relationship between internals and high achievement motivation in 15-17 year-old boys. Borges and Laning (1979) found no correlation between the two variables.

Risk Taking/Cautiousness--This personality difference refers to an individual's preference for selecting high-payoff/low-probability or low-payoff/high-probability alternatives (see chapter 31). Those with high-achievement motivation select tasks of moderate risk, whereas those with low-achievement motivation select tasks of either high or low risk (Gage & Berliner, 1984).

Extroversion/Introversion--Thinking and behavior that is directed inward, or to oneself, is termed *introversion* (see chapter 29); and thinking and behavior that is directed outward, to one's surroundings, is termed *extroversion*. De and Jhe (1978) found that extroversion and neuroticism are related to high-achievement motivation in undergraduates.

Intelligence--A .49 correlation was found between achievement motivation and intelligence in undergraduates (De & Jhe, 1978). Obviously, more motivated students perform better on standardized intelligence tests.

Instruments for Measuring Achievement Motivation

Ray (1982) reported the development of over 70 self-reporting instruments that measure achievement motivation, each with varying levels of reliability and validity. Fineman (1977) classified these instruments into projective, comprehensive personality inventories and specific questionnaire measures of need for achievement. Reporting on all of these is beyond the scope of this chapter; however, selected instruments that are representative of the groups, or have higher reliabilities, are reported here.

Murray's Behavioral Questionnaire (Murray, 1938)

From his 2-year study of personality, in which 44 variables emerged, Murray developed the following questions to identify those males with a high need for achievement. These are part of a questionnaire containing three sections of 200 items in each. Subjects use a -3 to a +3 scale to compare themselves with most men of their own age. We include this description to help define the original construct from which many other measures of this variable evolved. Therefore, no reliability or validity data are presented. His questions included:

1. I am driven to ever greater efforts by an unslaked ambition.
2. I feel that nothing else that life can offer is a substitute for great achievement.
3. I feel that my future peace and self-respect depend on my accomplishing some notable piece of work.
4. I set difficult goals for myself, which I attempt to reach.
5. I work with energy at the job that lies before me instead of dreaming about the future.
6. When my own interests are at stake, I become entirely concentrated on my job and forget my obligation to others.
7. I enjoy relaxation wholeheartedly only when it follows the successful completion of a substantial piece of work.
8. I feel the spirit of competition in most of my activities.
9. I work like a slave at everything I undertake until I am satisfied with the result.
10. I enjoy work as much as play.

Thematic Apperception Test (TAT) (McClelland & Atkinson, 1948; McClelland, Atkinson, Clark, & Lowell, 1953; Morgan & Murray, 1935)

Murray (1938) described this test as a projective means "to stimulate literary creativity and thereby evoke fantasies that reveal covert and unconscious complexes" (p. 530). In the TAT, subjects are shown an ambiguous picture and asked a series of questions about the events and the future. Individuals are expected to project their own achievement motivation to the events and outcomes perceived in the picture. There is no standard set of pictures, but researchers have found that it is important to have at least one person in the picture to elicit empathy and identification. Twenty pictures comprised the first set, which were administered to young men between the ages of 20-30. A set of 103 pictures is available for use in this test (Atkinson, 1958). Examples of the type of pictures include a picture of a boy looking up from a book (Gage & Berliner, 1984, p. 338); a huddled form of a boy with his head bowed on his right arm is on the floor leaning against a couch with an object resembling a revolver beside him; or a dim figure of a man clinging to a rope, either climbing up or down (Murray, 1938, p. 536-537).

Atkinson (1958) also found that presenting more than eight pictures incurred a loss of predictive validity; therefore, he recommended the use of six to gain an adequate perception of achievement motivation in most subjects. To administer the test, the examiner shows the picture to the subject and the following directions are read:

> This is a test of your creative imagination. I shall show you a picture and I want you to make up a plot or story for which it might be used as an illustration. What is the relation of the individuals in the picture? What has happened to them? What are their present thoughts and feelings? What will be the outcome? Do your very best. Since I am asking you to indulge your literary imagination you may make your story as long and as detailed as you wish. (Murray, 1938, p. 532)

These directions were modified to include a time limit of 4 minutes, and a question sheet that presents four questions which are essentially the same as those in the aforementioned paragraph.

Points are accumulated in eight categories: achievement imagery, need statement, instrumental activity, anticipatory goal states, obstacles or blocks, nurturant press, affective states, and achievement thema.

Although there is agreement about its validity, the instrument has been strongly criticized in the literature as being very difficult to measure, and as not being highly reliable. Reliability results reported in the literature varied from a low of .37 to most in the 70s. Variations in the reliability were attributed to difference in length, consideration of verbal ability of subjects, and other unexplained causes (Ray, 1974; Vestewig & Paradise, 1977). Another criticism is that the test is culturally biased toward "middle-class whites" (Castenell, 1984, p. 437).

Test of Insight (French, 1958)

This test is a modification of the TAT using projective, verbal stimuli instead of visual ones to test both need for achievement and need for affiliation. Two forms of 10 items each form a pool of 20 statements that make up this instrument. It can be administered in about 30 minutes. Test directions include:

> This is a test of your understanding of the reasons why people behave as they do. You will be given a characteristic behavior of each of a number of men. Your task is to explain why each man behaves as he does. Read each description and then decide what you think would usually be the reason why a man does what this man does. Decide what this man is like, what he wants to have or do, and what the results of his behavior are apt to be. If you think of more than one explanation give only the one you think is most likely. Write your answers in the space provided. (French, 1958, p. 244)

Sample items include: "Bill always lets the other fellow win; John's friends can always depend on him for a loan; Pete said, 'I'm pretty sure I can do it'; Dave likes a good argument" (p. 245).

The responses are scored for evidence of 13 different categories of information: desire for goal, goal-directed activity, personal qualifications for goal attainment, expectation of goal attainment, goal attainment, positive affect to goal attainment, desire to avoid failure, activity directed toward avoiding failure, lack of qualification for, or possession of, qualifications preventing goal attainment, expectation of failure, defensive statements or rationalization, failure to attain goal, and negative affect to failure (p. 246).

Establishing validity for this instrument were attempted by comparing scores on this instrument with observed judgments of motivation and goal attainment. Correlations of .82 was obtained for need for achievement (Ray, 1974).

Graphic Expression Measurement (Aronson, 1958).

To reduce the verbal nature of the TAT and avoid anxiety, Aronson devised an alternative measure for need for achievement using an individual's graphic expression. Scribble patterns for an item are projected for 1.8 seconds. Given 2 minutes, subjects are asked to reproduce the pattern. In a test of 196 males, differences were found in five qualities of the reproductions, which led to the development of five subscales: discreteness versus fuzziness, unused space, diagonal configurations, S-shaped lines, and multiwave lines. Those with a high need for achievement tended to use single, unattached, discrete lines, leave a smaller margin at the bottom, use diagonal configurations, two-directional, nonrepetitive S-shaped lines, and fewer "lines consisting of two or more crests in the same direction" (p. 252).

Scoring reliability was established at .89. Correlations with the TAT were .09-.51 and were relatively unstable between subgroups.

Nach-Naff Scale (Lingren, 1976)

This scale was developed based on Lingren's (1976) notion that need for achievement and need for affiliation are inversely proportional. It consists of 30 pairs of adjectives that are diametrically opposed--half representative of need for achievement, the other half representative of need for affiliation. Examples include, "aggressive, alert ambitious, dominant" for need for achievement and "warm, trusting, sociable, and talkative" for need for affiliation. Subjects are forced to one of those that best fits their perception of themselves. It is short, easy to administer, and free of sexual bias. Sid and Lindgren (1982) report split half reliabilities at .80, test-retest at .88. They also reported a modest degree of concurrent validity with measures of academic achievement.

Adjective Check List (ACL) (Gough & Heilbrun, 1980)

This 300-adjective instrument measures self-reported achievement motivation. Subjects are asked to circle those adjectives that are most self-descriptive. Construct validity was established by Fowler (1973), Gough and Hall (1975), and Heilbrun (1959). Peidmont, Diplacido, and Keller (1989) found that this instrument was a relevant predictor for measuring internal orientation of females.

Theoretical Background

Achievement is most directly related to the cognitive dimension of personality described in the introduction to this section. That is, it describes drive-states that impel learners to achieve. The cause of these drive-states may be intrinsic to the learner or extrinsic, that is, elicited by some reward outside the learner. Biehler and Snowman (1986) identified two basic approaches to the study of achievement motivation: the broad societal theory of David McClelland (1961), and the formal theory of risk preference by John Atkinson (1957, 1964, 1974) that built on McClelland's work. McClelland defined a *motive to achieve success* (M_s), while Atkinson added the second dimension, a *motive to avoid failure* (M_f). M_s represents a positive effect in situations representing a moderate challenge to the individual. M_f implies an anticipation of negative effect under the same circumstances. Others would include Weiner's attribution theory as part of achievement motivation; however, because his theory deals with an individual's perception of why particular outcomes were achieved, rather than the motive to achieve, it is not included in the discussion of achievement motivation in this chapter (see chapter 28).

Verifying Atkinson's attributes in a factorial study of achievement-related motives of undergraduates, Yamauchi and Doi (1977) also found three underlying aspects: the motive to achieve, the motive to avoid failure, and a personality component of the achievement tendency. The multidimensionality of achievement motivation was also supported in another factorial analytic study of 17- and 18-year-old military training women (Erwee & Boshoff, 1982).

The most interesting development of this phenomenon has been on the selection of tasks and performance based on one's level of achievement motive. Atkinson created a mathematical formula to predict one's *tendency* (T) to act based on *task difficulty* (P), *incentive* (I), *motive* (M), and one's *orientation toward achieving success* (S) or *avoiding failure* (F) ($T_S=M_S*P_S*I_S$; and $T_f=M_f*P_f*I_f$). From this formula, he predicts that those with a high need for achievement would be more comfortable with tasks that have about a 50/50 probability of success. These individuals have a realistic estimation of their ability and, therefore, would not select a task that had too high a probability for failure and, at the same time, are not motivated with tasks that are deemed too easy. Those with a need to avoid failure would be more comfortable with tasks at either extreme and would avoid those tasks in the 50% probability range. Tasks with a high probability of success enable the subjects to avoid failure, and for the very risky tasks, the subject is able to justify failure and avoid embarrassment because of the difficult nature of the task. Atkinson also predicts that motive would have no effect on motivation for either the M_S or M_f subjects on either extreme, with the effect evident in the 50% probability range. M_S subjects would increase their motivation, and M_f subjects would decrease their motivation to act. Nygård (1981) provided empirical support that alters the prediction in concert with the theory. He demonstrated that M_S individuals were, in fact, demotivated to act with very easy and very difficult tasks, whereas M_f individuals were energized.

Fear of success has also been studied in women and has been thought to be a part of achievement motivation. This theory postulates that with women who are high achievers, there is a subset who fear success (Horner, 1972). This phenomenon has been explained as a woman's struggle with accepting social rejection or losing her femininity, which may be associated with success. In cases where fear of success has been noted, performance has been impaired when the task has been identified as a male task or when it will be evaluated by men. Although there has been much research on this phenomenon, it has suffered from some serious methodological flaws and must be interpreted with caution. This is especially true where the theory has been extended to men or to all women in general (Piedmont, 1988b).

One final caveat is important with the development of this theory. Most of the research conducted to develop the construct has been conducted using men. Until recently, few women were part of this research. Therefore, it is as yet uncertain if all of the results and predictions can be extended to women.

Achievement Motivation and Learning

Research

• Heckhausen (1967) found that those with a high achievement motivation were able to sustain interest in a task, even when interrupted or extended over a long period.

• Weiner and Kukla (1970) found that high achievers persist longer than low achievers, even when they are failing.

• Women and men responded similarly to projective achievement cues, except for autonomous achievement where men's cues were far lower. Women used more private, intrinsic cues (Depner & Veroff, 1979).

• In a study of grades 1-12, Uguroglu and Walberg (1979) found that 11.4% of the variance in achievement was accounted for by motivation. Motivation and achievement were more highly correlated in the higher grades.

• Christian (1979) found that a need for achievement in females ages 17-28 was unaffected by age, socioeconomic status, rural or urban background, fear of failure, hope for success, or concern.

• High-need-for-achievement undergraduate males were found to be future-oriented and have an extended time perspective. This suggests that high need for achievement affects performance on immediate and long-term achievement-related tasks (Agarwai & Tripathi, 1980).

• No relationship was found between creativity and achievement, affiliation, or power in undergraduates (Gopal, Sharma, & Singh, 1980).

• Edwards and Waters (1981) found that achievement motivation moderated the relationship between academic ability and cumulative grade point average.

• Need for achievement was positively correlated to expectancy of academic achievement but was not significantly related to social desirability in postgraduate students (Parvathi & Rama-Rao, 1982).

• Achievement motivation scores were positively correlated with grade point average for both sexes (Sid & Lindgren, 1982).

• Levine, Gillman, and Reis (1982) found that, for undergraduates, achievement motivation was the most consistent predictor of gender differences and that males attributed their success to ability, whereas females attributed their success to effort and luck.

- Autonomous achievement motivation was similar in both sexes, but social achievement orientation differed. In males, it was associated with social approval and responsiveness concerns, but not so for females (Battistich, Thompson, Mann, & Perlmutter, 1982).

- In a study of unmarried undergraduates, middle-aged married women students, and middle-aged married homemakers, Erdwins, Tyer, and Mellinger (1982) found that older students showed a higher achievement motivation, with homemakers' needs characterized by conformity and cooperation, and mature students' needs by greater independence and self-reliance. Homemakers also showed a higher need for affiliation than did young women.

- Achievement scores related positively to approach motivation exhibited by success-oriented, high-ability sixth-grade girls and moderate ability boys (Gjesme, 1983).

- Gaeddert (1983) surveyed undergraduates and found that males used more extrinsic evaluation standards than females used, whereas femininity is more related to social affiliation achievement attempts. Both sexes agreed on the important domain of accomplishment.

- Self-confidence and need for achievement were positively correlated as well as self-confidence and academic achievement, with a small linear relationship between need for achievement and academic achievement (Reddy, 1983).

- Burger (1985) found that those undergraduates who exhibited a high desire to control also showed patterns of success and failure attributions associated with high-achievement levels.

- Verma (1986) found that achievement motivation was positively affected by ego-strength, internal control, emotional maturity, and intelligence, with significant interaction effects for emotional maturity and internal control.

- Men and women undergraduates' academic achievement arose out of different motivations and were influenced by different factors. Men's achievement was better predicted by prior achievement, mastery-related expectancies, and values. Women's achievement was better predicted from person-related values and evaluations of the academic atmosphere (Inglehart, Nyquist, Brown, & Moore, 1987).

- High-need-for-achievement undergraduates showed a tendency to at-tribute success to effort and failure to a lack of effort and task difficulty. Affective responses correlated with internal causes and expectations with stable causes, especially for high-need-for-achievement subjects in the failure condition (Dalal & Sethi, 1988).

- In a study of undergraduate males, Scapinello (1989) found that subjects high in achievement motivation were less inclined to attribute failure to ability than those low in achievement motivation.

- Biernat (1989) found that with undergraduate males, the achievement motive was a strong predictor of math performance in those who value achievement over affiliation. Nonconscious (motive) and conscious (value) measures are both useful information, but for different purposes--the former for predicting action and the latter for predicting thinking responses.

Implications of the Characteristics and Research

Implications which are drawn from research are noted with a •; those drawn logically from descriptive information regarding the trait are noted by an *. Based on extensive research and the descriptions of *achievement motivation*, we conclude that those learners with a *motive to achieve success* are more likely to excel at learning tasks such as:

* tasks that are very important
• tasks that require attention
• long-term tasks
* tasks that require independence of thought and action
• academic subjects
• leadership roles that capitalize on their desire to control

and acquire and use effectively learning strategies such as:

* setting personal learning goals
* selecting information sources
* gauging difficulty of learning
* estimating time and effort
* preparing environment
* searching for information
* concentrating on information
* regulating environment
* testing personal skills

Based on extensive research and the descriptions of achievement motivation, we conclude that those learners with a motive to avoid fail-

ure are less skilled than those with a high motive to achieve and, therefore, will probably not excel at any tasks. At least, there is no research to
support any learning advantages for those with a motive to avoid failure.

Achievement Motivation and Instruction

Research

- High achievers should do better than low achievers in a nonarousing
  situation or when performing a task that mainly requires SIT resources
  (Humphreys & Revelle, 1984),

- French (1956) found that those students with a high need for achievement selected study partners based on their competency rather than
  their friendliness. Those with a high need for affiliation selected the
  opposite.

- Undergraduates high in achievement motivation and low in test anxiety
  achieved higher grades when they saw the course as important to their
  future (Raynor, 1970).

- Tessler and Schwartz (1972) found that help was sought more by those
  with low achievement motivation rather than with high achievement
  motivation.

- High achievement motivation did not necessarily result in overmotiva-
  tion, but it made the subject very susceptible to arousal-induced deficits
  (Atkinson, 1974).

- Latta (1978) found that for undergraduate males, success feedback had no
  effect on easy tasks, had a positive effect for high-achievement-need subjects on difficult tasks, and had a negative effect for low-achievement-
  need subjects on difficult tasks.

- In undergraduate subjects whose achievement motivation was higher
  than fear of failure, the peak of risk preference was from moderate to
  more difficult tasks if the standard was more difficult, and to easier tasks
  if the standard was easier. In those with higher fear of failure, an
  inverse relationship between standard difficulty and preferred difficulty
  was found (Kuhl, 1978).

- Borges and Laning (1979) found achievement motivation higher for undergraduates under competitive conditions for both sexes but found no
  correlation with assertiveness, feminist attitudes, or locus of control.

- Trope (1980) found that high-achievement-motivated subjects were more interested in obtaining diagnostic information than in succeeding at difficult tasks.

- Instructions were found to interact with a woman's role orientation in determining performance and achievement. Nontraditional women showed achievement motivation under standard conditions, but traditional women showed greater motivation under affiliative conditions (Gralweski & Rodgon, 1980).

- O'Connell (1980) found that undergraduate males set higher goals than undergraduate females. Fear of success was positively correlated with anxiety and negatively correlated with need for achievement and personal goals. This contradicted previous research that demonstrated that fear of success was a phenomenon which occurs only in high-need-for-achievement women (Horner, 1972).

- High-need-for-achievement undergraduate males were found to be future-oriented and to have an extended time perspective. This perspective suggests that high need for achievement affects performance on immediate and long-term achievement-related tasks (Agarwai & Tripathi, 1980).

- Touhey and Villemez (1980) found that high-need-for-achievement undergraduates increased their judgments of their abilities in response to task success with effort, whereas low-need-for-achievement subjects increased their judgments after less effortful success.

- Lens and deVolder (1980) found an inverted U-shaped relationship between strength of motivation and level of performance relative to intelligence in a high ego-involvement condition.

- In undergraduate subjects, Matsui, Okada, and Kakuyama (1982) found that only subjects higher in achievement need performed better after, rather than before, feedback.

- After receiving noncontingent success/failure feedback on a task, no differences were found for the high- and low-achievement motivation high school males on performance, attribution, or expectancy. Feedback did produce significant overall differences for attribution and expectancy, suggesting a situational rather than trait effect (McCaughan, 1983).

- The following relationships were found between need for achievement and undergraduate subjects' distribution of rewards after a task: those high in need for achievement appreciated performance differences and distributed the rewards equitably; those high in need for affiliation divided the rewards according to partner's behavior; and those high in both need for achievement and affiliation exploited a generous partner (O'Malley & Schubarth, 1984).

- Choice of goal was motivating for undergraduates low in need for achievement who selected a difficult goal. Goals imposed by the experimenter motivated low-need-for-achievement subjects with easy goals (Alexander & Schuldt, 1984).

- In an investigation of the process through which competence information affects intrinsic motivation in 15-18-year-old males, high achievers responded positively to competence cues, but low achievers suffered reduced interest from positive feedback. Competence information had a positive impact on high achievers' intrinsic motivation, whereas efficacy information increased intrinsic motivation for low achievers (Harackiewicz, Sansone, & Manderlink, 1985).

- Delay of reward impaired learning by low achievers but had no effect on high-achieving undergraduate males (Srivastava, 1986).

- Achievement motivation scores were found to be positively related to task performance only in an intrinsic task orientation condition (Schroth, 1987).

- Early conditioning and child-rearing practices created perceptions of gender-appropriate activities. Females pursued activities more cautiously, considered social factors, and had lower, more situational expectancy of success. When feedback was provided, females' future predictions of success were similar to those of males (Silvestri, 1987).

- Piedmont (1988a) found that positive effects of achievement motivation in undergraduates were constant regardless of manipulation of success expectancy or presentation rate, but some situations facilitated performance in an additive manner. Anxiety had different effects on performance based on achievement motivation.

- Grabinger and Jonassen (1988), using discriminant analysis, found a significant relationship between those subjects who had a high need for achievement, internal locus of control, and preferred learning via active experimentation, and those who selected independent study over teacher-directed study.

- In an examination of the effects of three components of need for achievement in undergraduates on goal commitment, Johnson and Perlow (1990) found that a need for mastery influenced goal commitment and performance, but a need for work and competitiveness did not.

Implications of the Characteristics and Research

Implications which are drawn from research are noted with a •; those drawn logically from descriptive information regarding the trait are noted by an *. Instructional conditions that capitalize on the preferences of the motive to achieve success student and challenge the motive to avoid failure student include:

• selecting own learning partners
• low-arousal environment
• moderately difficult tasks
• providing for active experimentation
• using independent study
• providing competitive conditions
• providing for a moderate level of ego-involvement
* involving the learners in the development of their own learning goals
* using discovery learning
• using a moderate level of ego-involving instructions
• using feedback as diagnostic information, especially success feedback
* explaining the purpose or relevance of the task
* describing the required performance along with stated standards
* providing lessons in large chunks

The qualities of individuals with a motive to achieve success are positive attributes that have been shown to contribute to learning. Therefore, there is no need for remediational or compensational instructional conditions for this type of individual.

Instructional conditions that capitalize on the preferences of the motive to avoid failure student and challenge the motive to achieve success student include:

* providing confirmatory and corrective feedback
• making extra help available often
• using teacher-provided goals
• providing for immediate feedback
* providing many opportunities for positive feedback

Instructional conditions that remediate or compensate for the deficiencies of the motive to avoid failure student include:

* selecting objectives that are challenging, but achievable

* helping learners to select realistic goals and to establish realistic levels of aspiration
* encouraging an orientation toward achievement and a positive self-concept
* providing opportunities for learners to experience success
* presenting goals and inviting students to select from among them
* inviting students to select activities of their own
* using tests for diagnostics rather than comparison
* encouraging individualized instruction
* dealing with failure privately
* using a mastery approach
* encouraging learners to emulate attributes of a high achiever by using prosocial self-rating scales
* using performance contracts
* using self-competitive games

References

Agarwai, A., & Tripathi, L. B. (1980). Time perspective in achievement motivation. *Psychologia: An International Journal of Psychology in the Orient, 23*(1), 50-62.

Alexander, C. J., & Schuldt, W. J. (1984). Effects of choice, goal difficulty, and need achievement on performance. *Journal of Clinical Psychology, 40*(6), 1354-1361.

Aronson, E. (1958). The need for achievement as measured by graphic expression. In J. W. Atkinson (Ed.), *Motives in fantasy, action, and society* (pp. 249-265). Princeton: Van Nostrand.

Atkinson, J. W. (1957). Motivational determinants of risk-taking behavior. *Psychological Review, 64*, 359-372.

Atkinson, J. W. (1958). *Motives in fantasy, action, and society.* Princeton: Van Nostrand.

Atkinson, J. W. (1964). *An introduction to motivation.* New York: Van Nostrand.

Atkinson, J. W. (1974). Strength of motivation and efficiency of performance. In J. W. Atkinson and J.O. Raynor (Eds.), *Motivation and achievement* (pp. 193-218). Washington, DC: Winston.

Battistich, V. A., Thompson, E. G., Mann, I. T., & Perlmutter, L. (1982). Gender differences in autonomous and social achievement orientations. *Journal of Personality, 50*(1), 98-114.

Biehler, R. F., & Snowman, J. (1986). *Psychology applied to teaching.* Boston: Houghton Mifflin.

Biernat, M. (1989). Motives and values to achieve: Different constructs with different effects. *Journal of Personality, 57*(1), 69-95.

Borges, M. A., & Laning, B. (1979). Relationships between assertiveness, achievement motivation, feminist attitudes, and locus of control in the college population. *Psychological Reports, 44*(2), 545-546.

Burger, J. M. (1985). Desire for control and achievement-related behaviors. *Journal of Personality and Social Psychology, 48*(6), 1520-1533.

Castenell, L. A. (1984). A cross-cultural look at achievement motivation research. *Journal of Negro Education, 53*, 435-443.

Christian, J. A. (1979). A study of achievement motivation and its related variables. *Asian Journal of Psychology and Education, 4*(1), 48-56.

Dalal, A. K., & Sethi, A. (1988). An attributional study of high- and low-need achievers in India. *Journal of Social Psychology, 128*(1), 55-64.

De, B., & Jhe, M. M. (1978). Achievement motivation in relation to personality and intelligence: A study. *Indian Educational Review, 13*(1), 46-51.

Depner, C. E., & Veroff, J. (1979). Varieties of achievement motivation. *Journal of Social Psychology, 107*(2), 283-286.

Edwards, J. E., & Waters, L. K. (1981). Moderating effect of achievement motivation and locus of control on the relationship between academic ability and academic performance. *Educational and Psychological Measurement, 41*(2), 585-597.

Erdwins, C. J., Tyer, Z. E., & Mellinger, J. C. (1982). Achievement and affiliation needs of young adult and middle-aged women. *Journal of Genetic Psychology, 141*(2), 219-224.

Erwee, R., & Boshoff, A. B. (1982). Women's achievement motivation: A multidimensional construct. *South Africa Journal of Psychology, 12*(2), 41-50.

Fowler, M. G. (1973). Relationship of serum uric acid to achievement motivation. *Psychosomatic Medicine, 35*, 13-22.

Fineman, S. (1977). The achievement motive construct and its measurement: Where are we now? *British Journal of Psychology, 68*, 1-22.

French, E. G. (1956). Motivation as a variable in work partner selection. *Journal of Abnormal and Social Psychology, 56*, 45-48.

French, E. G. (1958). Development of a measure of complex motivation. In J. W. Atkinson (Ed.), *Motives in fantasy, action, and society* (pp. 242-248). Princeton: Van Nostrand.

French, E. G., & Thomas, F. (1958). The relation of achievement motivation to problem-solving effectiveness. *Journal of Abnormal and Social Psychology, 56*, 45-48.

Gaeddert, W. P. (1983). *Sex and sex role effects on achievement strivings: An examination of four explanations.* Paper presented at the Eastern Psychological Association, Philadelphia, PA. (ERIC Document Reproduction Service No. ED 248 418)

Gage, N. L., & Berliner, D. C. (1984). *Educational Psychology.* Boston: Houghton Mifflin.

Gjesme, T. (1983). Motivation to approach $T_s$and motivation to avoid failure T_f at school. *Scandinavian Journal of Educational Research,* 27(4), 145-164.

Gopal, A. K., Sharma, V. K., & Singh, A. K. (1980). Motivational difference among high- and low-creative university students. *Psychologia: An International Journal of Psychology in the Orient,* 23(4), 240-246.

Gough, H. G., & Hall, W. B. (1975). An attempt to predict graduation from medical school. *Journal of Medical Education, 30,* 940-950.

Gough, H. G., & Heilbrun, A. B. (1980). *Manual for the Adjective Checklist.* Palo Alto, CA: Consulting Psychologists Press.

Grabinger, R. S., & Jonassen, D. H. (1988). *Independent study: Personality, cognitive and descriptive predictors.* Paper presented at the annual convention of the Association for Educational Communications and Technology, New Orleans, LA. (ERIC Document Reproduction Service No. ED 295 641)

Gralweski, C., & Rodgon, M. M. (1980). Effects of social and intellectual instruction on achievement motivation as a function of role orientation. *Sex Roles, 6*(2), 301-309.

Harackiewicz, J. M., Sansone, C., & Manderlink, G. (1985). Competence, achievement orientation, and intrinsic motivation: A process analysis. *Journal of Personality and Social Psychology, 48*(2), 493-508.

Heckhausen, H. (1967). *The anatomy of achievement motivation.* New York: Academic.

Heilbrun, A. B. (1959). Validation of a need scaling technique for the Adjective Check List. *Journal of Consulting Psychology, 23,* 347-351

Horner, M. S. (1972). Toward an understanding of achievement-related conflicts in women. *Journal of Social Issues, 28,* 157-175.

Humphreys, M. S., & Revelle, W. (1984). Personality, motivation, and performance: A theory of the relationship between individual differences and information processing. *Psychological Review, 91*(2), 153-184.

Inglehart, M. R., Nyquist, L., Brown, D. R., & Moore, W. (1987). *Gender differences in academic achievement--The result of cognitive or affective factors?* Paper presented at the Midwestern Psychologica Association, Chicago. (ERIC Document Reproduction Service No. ED 285 064)

Johnson, D. S., & Perlow, R. (1990). *The impact of need for achievement components on goal commitment.* Paper presented at the American Psychological Association, Boston.

Kolb, D. A. (1965). Achievement motivation training for underachieving boys. *Journal of Personality and Social Psychology, 2,* 783-792.

Kuhl, J. (1978). Standard setting and risk preference: An elaboration of the theory of achievement motivation and an empirical test. *Psychological Review, 85*(3), 239-248.

Latta, R. M. (1978). Interactive effects of initial achievement orientation and prior success feedback on the mastery of subsequent difficult and easy tasks. *American Educational Research Journal, 15*(1), 17-24.

Lens, M., & deVolder, M. (1980). Achievement motivation and intelligence test scores: A test of the Yerkes-Dodson hypothesis. *Psychologica Belgica, 20*(1), 49-59.

Levine, R., Gillman, M. J., & Reis, H. (1982). Individual differences for sex differences in achievement attributions? *Sex Roles, 8*(4), 455-466.

Lingren, H. C. (1976). Measuring need to achieve by Nach-Naff Scale: A forced choice questionnaire. *Psychological Reports, 39*, 907-910.

Maehr, M. (1982). *Motivational factors in school achievement.* Paper commissioned by the National Commission on Excellence in Education. (NIE 400-81-0004, Task 10)

Matsui, T., Okada, A., & Kakuyama, T. (1982). Influence of achievement need on goal setting, performance, and feedback effectiveness. *Journal of Applied Psychology, 67*(5), 645-648.

McCaughan, L. R. (1983). Effects of achievement motivation and success/failure on attributions, expectancies, and performance on a psychomotor task. *Perceptual and Motor Skills, 56*(3), 901-902.

McClelland, D. C. (1961). *The achieving society.* New York: Van Nostrand.

McClelland, D. C. (1965). Toward a theory of motive acquisition. *American Psychologist, 20*, 321-333.

McClelland D. C., & Atkinson, J. W. (1948). The projective expression of needs: Pt. 2. The effects of different intensities of the hunger drive on thematic apperception. *Journal of Experimental Psychology, 38*, 643-658.

McClelland, D. C., Atkinson, J. W., Clark, R. A., & Lowell, E. L. (1953). *The achievement motive.* New York: Appleton-Century-Crofts. Reprint (1958). In J. W. Atkinson (Ed.), *Motives in fantasy, action, and society.* Princeton: Van Nostrand.

Morgan, C. D., & Murray, H. A. (1935). The Thematic Apperception Test. *Archives of Neurology and Psychiatry, 34*, 289-306.

Murray, H. A. (1938). *Explorations in Personality.* New York: Oxford University Press.

Nygård, R. (1981). Toward an interactional psychology: Models from achievement motivation research. *Journal of Personality, 49*(4), 363-387.

O'Connell, A. N. (1980). Effects of manipulated status on performance, goal setting, achievement motivation, anxiety, and fear of success. *Journal of Social Psychology, 112*(1), 75-89.

O'Malley, M. N., & Schubarth, G. (1984). Fairness and appeasement: Achievement and affiliation motives in interpersonal relations. *Social Psychology Quarterly, 47*(4), 364-371.

Parvathi, S., & Rama-Rao, P. (1982). Problem solving, need for achievement, expectancy of academic achievement and social desirability. *Journal of Psychological Research, 26*(2), 88-92.

Piedmont, R. L. (1988a). The relationship between achievement motivation, anxiety and situational characteristics on performance on a cognitive task. *Journal of Research on Personality, 22*(2), 177-187.

Peidmont, R. L. (1988b). An interactional model of achievement motivation and fear of success. *Sex Roles, 19*(7/8), 467-490.

Peidmont, R. L., DiPlacido, J., & Keller, W. (1989). Assessing gender-related differences in achievement orientation using two different achievement scales. *Journal of Personality Assessment, 53*(2), 229-238.

Ray, J. J. (1974). Projective tests can be made reliable: Measuring need for achievement. *Journal of Personality Assessment, 38*(4), 303-307.

Ray, J. J. (1982). *Self-report measures of achievement motivation: A catalog.* Australia: University of South Wales. (ERIC Document Reproduction Service No. ED 237 523)

Raynor, J. O. (1970). Relationships between achievement-related motives, future orientation, and academic performance. *Journal of Personality and Social Psychology, 15*(1), 28-33.

Reddy, M. S. (1983). Study of self-confidence and achievement motivation in relation to academic achievement. *Journal of Psychological Research, 27*(2), 87-91.

Scapinello, K. F. (1989). Enhancing differences in the achievement attributions of high- and low-motivation groups. *Journal of Social Psychology, 129*(3), 357-363.

Schroth, M. L. (1987). Relationships between achievement-related motives, extrinsic conditions, and task performance. *Journal of Social Psychology, 127*(1), 39-48.

Sid, A. K. W., & Lindgren, H. C. (1982). Achievement and affiliation motivation and their correlates. *Educational and Psychological Measurement, 42*(4), 1213-1218.

Silvestri, L. (1987). Achievement: Is it sex or situation specific? *Journal of Instructional Psychology, 14*(2), 74-82.

Spielberger, C. D. (1972). Anxiety as an emotional state. In C. D. Spielberger (Ed.), *Anxiety and current trends in theory and research* (pp. 23-49). New York: Academic.

Srivastava, S. K. (1986). Goal gradient hypothesis and achievement motivation. *Psychological Research Journal, 10*(1-2), 43-47.

Stake, J. E. (1979). The relationship between achievement orientation and locus of control. *Journal of Social Psychology, 109*(1), 149-150.

Stipek, D. J. (1988). *Motivation to learn: From theory to practice.* Englewood Cliffs, NJ: Prentice-Hall.

Tessler, R. C., & Schwartz, S. H. (1972). Help seeking, self-esteem, and achievement motivation: An attributional analysis. *Journal of Personality and Social Psychology, 21*(3), 318-326.

Touhey, J. C., & Villemez, W. J. (1980). Ability attribution as a result of variable effort and achievement motivation. *Journal of Personality and Social Psychology, 38*(2), 211-216.

Trope, Y. (1980). Self-assessment, self-enhancement, and task preference. *Journal of Experimental Social Psychology, 16*(2), 116-129.
Uguroglu, M. E., & Walberg, H. J. (1979). Motivation and achievement: A quantitative synthesis. *American Educational Research Journal, 16*(4), 375-389.
Verma, O. P. (1986). Achievement motivation: A multivariate study. *Indian Psychological Review, 30*(2), 1-3.
Vestewig, R. E., & Paradise, C. A. (1977). Multidimensional scaling of the TAT and the measurement of achievement motivation. *Journal of Personality Assessment, 41*(6), 595-603.
Weiner, B. (1978). Achievement strivings. In H. London & J.E. Exner, Jr. (Eds.), *Dimensions of personality* (pp. 219-230). New York: Wiley.
Weiner, B., & Kukla, A. (1970). An attributional analysis of achievement motivation. *Journal of Personality and Social Psychology, 15*, 1-20.
Wendt, H. W. (1955). Motivation, effort, and performance. In D. C. McClelland (Ed.), *Studies in motivation.* (pp. 448-459). New York: Appleton-Century-Crofts.
Yamauchi, H., & Doi, K. (1977). Factorial study of achievement-related motives. *Psychological Reports, 41*(3, Pt. 1), 796-801.

Bibliography

Alpert, R., & Haber, R. N. (1960). Anxiety in academic achievement situations. *Journal of Abnormal and Social Psychology, 61*, 207-215.
Domino, G. (1971). Interactive effects of achievement orientation and teaching style on academic achievement. *Journal of Educational Psychology, 62*(5), 427-431.
Edwards, A. L. (1959). *Edwards personal preference schedule, manual.* New York: Psychological Corporation.
Harper, F. B. (1975). The validity of some alternative measures of achievement motivation. *Educational and Psychological Measurement, 35*(4), 905-909.
Heckhausen, H. (1968). Achievement motive research: Current problems and some contributions towards a general theory of motivation. In W. J. Arnold (Ed.), *Nebraska Symposium on Motivation, 1968* (pp. 103-174). Lincoln: University of Nebraska Press.
Izard, C. E. (1962). Personality characteristics (EEPS), level of expectation, and performance. *Journal of Consulting Psychology, 26*, 394.
Jackson, D. N. (1967). *Personality research form-manual.* NY: Research Psychologists Press.
Krug, R. E. (1959). Over- and underachievement and the Edwards Personal Preference Schedule. *Journal of Applied Psychology, 43*, 133-136.
Mandler, G., & Sarason, S. B. (1952). A study of anxiety and learning. *Journal of Abnormal and Social Psychology, 47*, 166-173.

Mehrabian, A. (1969). Measures of achieving tendency. *Educational and Psychological Measurement, 29,* 445-451.

Neumann, Y., Finaly, E., & Reichel, A. (1988). Achievement motivation factors and student's college outcomes. *Psychological Reports, 62*(2), 555-560.

Nygård, R., & Gjesme, T. (1973). Assessment of achievement motives: Comments and suggestions. *Scandinavian Journal of Educational Research, 17,* 39-46.

Sarason, S. B., Davidson, K., Lighthall, F., & Waite, R. R. (1958). A test anxiety scale for children. *Child Development, 29,* 105-113.

Weiner, B. (1972). *Theories of motivation.* Chicago: Rand McNally.

Worell, L. (1960). EPPS Achievement and verbal paired-associates learning. *Journal of Abnormal and Social Psychology, 60,* 147-150.

31

RISK TAKING VERSUS CAUTIOUSNESS

Description of Risk/Cautious Behavior

Risk taking/cautiousness is a personality dimension that refers to an individual's preference for selecting high-payoff/low-probability or low-payoff/high-probability alternatives. In educational and training situations, numerous opportunities exist in which the decisions individuals make involve actual or perceived risk to self-esteem, success, or well-being. Examples include responding in class, selecting response strategies for achievement or standardized ability exams, selecting courses that are "known" to be difficult, or even learning new patterns of study (Ely, 1986).

The high risk taker continually faces the probability of failing for the opportunity to succeed under the specified odds. Coupled with high anxiety and defensiveness, high risk takers have been shown to make poor decisions in cases where only partial knowledge exists, especially in standardized exams when a penalty for wrong responses is added. Moderate risk taking, however, has been associated with increased performance, perceived competence, self-knowledge, pride, and satisfaction (Kogan, 1971).

Cautiousness, or fear of risk taking, can also impede learning. Students who fear failure may avoid beneficial learning experiences. Extreme cautiousness has been linked to perfectionism. Such students maintain extremely high standards, most often with impossible goals, and ultimately measure their self-worth entirely in terms of productivity and accomplishment. Perfectionists are very impatient with a trial-and-error style of learning. They can actually paralyze themselves, avoiding new experiences for fear of failure. Perfectionists suffer excessive anxiety and panic attacks about their academic responsibilities (Adderholsdt-Elliot, 1989).

Creativity is strongly tied to the dimension of risk taking. An individual who presents new ideas opens him or herself to the possibility that the ideas may be wrong, inappropriate, or socially unacceptable. The greater the departure from the standard, the greater the risk (Pankove & Kogan, 1968; Wallach & Kogan, 1965).

One basic concern regarding this style is the generalizability of risk/cautious behavior across all situations. Wallach and Kogan (1965) found that the indicators of risk taking were consistent but were not demonstrated across tasks, indicating the presence of a trait-state variant to the dimension. This effect is especially strong as it relates to indicated intention in hypothetical situations versus demonstrating actual behavior.

Characteristic Differences in Risk Taking Vs. Cautiousness

Risk Taking	Cautiousness
adventuresome	circumspect
spontaneous	systematic
socially flexible	socially restrained
focus on positive outcomes	anticipates negative outcomes
process-oriented	product- oriented
internal rewards	external rewards
enjoys competition	fears failure
high tolerance for errors	low tolerance for errors
relaxed about schoolwork	anxious about schoolwork
accepts faults in self	plagued by self-criticism
likes to try out new things	impatient with trial-and-error
internalized locus of control	externalized locus of control

Individual Differences Related to Risk/Cautious Behavior

Risk taking/cautiousness is associated with other personality variables, cognitive styles and controls, such as:

Breadth of Categorizing--This is a measure of the range of instances included in a cognitive category (see chapter 11). There are mixed perceptions regarding the associations between this cognitive control and risk/caution behavior. In cases in which cautiousness has been associated with narrow categorizing, it has been explained that narrow categorizers make finer discriminations before classification, thus acting to reduce uncertainty. However, "inclusion implies greater certainty of class membership than does exclusion," hence, also a lesser degree of risk (Kogan & Wallach, 1964). They suggested that wide categorizing actually represents a reduction in risk taking because reduced judgmental confidence reduces uncertainty, whereas narrow categorizers take greater risks by segmenting. Harris (1970) found that wide categorizers were more cautious in nonpayoff conditions than narrow categorizers.

Locus of Control--Internals have a sense of personal efficacy. In learning situations their expectations of success are based on their view of their effort, ability, and competence (see chapter 28). Thus, internals correlate to risk takers. Externals attribute success or failure partially by how acceptable one's performance is to others and tend to be more anxious in general. This correlates to individuals who are more cautious in a learning situation, wanting to avoid mistakes and failure, and who are thus more nervous and wanting to perform correctly (Gutierrez, 1982). Cohen, Sheposh, and Hillix (1979), however, found that internals took greater risks on skill tasks, whereas externals took greater risk on chance tasks. Similar results were found by Karabenick and Addy (1979) for externals.

Achievement Motivation--This is a measure of level of attribution to a task (see chapter 30). Intermediate risk behavior was found to correlate with achievement motivation and was avoided by those who avoid failure (Hamilton, 1974; Roberts, 1975). Those subjects who avoid failure showed a greater preference for extreme risk choices than for moderate or no risk (Roberts, 1974). Kuhl (1978) found that when a standard for success was added, subjects with a motive to achieve success preferred moderate to more difficult tasks only if the standard was difficult, but preferred easy tasks if the standard is easier. In subjects with a failure orientation, there was an inverse relationship between difficulty of standards and preferred difficulty level.

Conceptual Tempo--Impulsivity/reflectivity measures a person's tendency to inhibit initial responses and to reflect on the accuracy of an answer rather than to respond impulsively (see chapter 9). Kopfstein (1973) found that risk-taking behavior was *not* associated to impulsivity/reflectivity for grade 4 subjects.

Instruments for Measuring Risk/Cautious Behavior

General Instruments (Kogan & Wallach, 1964)

Kogan and Wallach (1964) used a number of diverse tasks to study the generality of the risk-caution dimension across a variety of decision-making situations. These included hypothetical life dilemmas, dice-betting preferences, betting in context of motor skill, information seeking entailing prizes for correct solutions and monetary costs for each item of information, and the acceptance or rejection of a final bet with the experimenter in which the subject's prior winnings constituted the stake.

Willingness to Risk Questionnaire (Wesley, 1967)

The Willingness to Risk Questionnaire is a 55-item, unpublished test that measures five factors of risk: life in general, money, social embarrassment, legal matters, and health. Subjects are asked a question to which they are to respond "never, seldom, or frequently." These are translated into 0, 1, or 2, such that the total possible score for a high risk taker would be 100. Examples of the items include: "Have you ever run a red light? Have you ever left your door unlatched at night? Have you ever played cards for money? Have you ever been purposely late for work or for a class? Did you ever leave home without your raincoat and overshoes when the weather looked threatening?" Ten items are included for each of the five categories. Five additional items, that are termed "lie items," determine the individual's credibility in answering these questions truthfully. An example of this type of item is "Have you ever broken a rule?" Internal consistency for this test was reported at .71.

A second, more complex form of the test has also been developed. Students are asked 100 multiple choice questions to which they must respond with an answer *and* an indication of their degree of certainty. Only 20 items of the 100 have correct items. Example questions include: "How many states border Colorado?   The estimated 1949 population of Afghanistan was...? One of the following was not a product of Burma...?" Reported correlation with Form A of the test was very low, at .30, suggesting that this test measured something other than risk as it was defined.

Measure of Risk Taking for Young Adults (Alexander et al., 1990)

To determine the differences between perceptions of risk taking between young adults and adolescents, Alexander et al. (1990) surveyed young adults as to what constituted "excitement and thrills" for them. As a result of this survey, a six-item questionnaire was developed that was more representative for this age group. Students respond on one of three levels: never, once or twice, or several times. Risk scores range from 6-18. Sample questions include: "Have you ever raced on a bike or boat? Have you ever slipped out at night while your parents thought you were sleeping?" Internal consistency was reported at .78-.80.

Risk-Taking Verbal Observation Scale (Horn, 1973)

Risk taking has been tested under different assumptions with this instrument. Those behaviors that are assessed encompass four academic areas: "willingly subjects himself to possible criticism/failure;   expresses his opinions, feelings, or criticisms regardless of the presence of authority; participates freely in class discussions; and, indicates a willingness to try new approaches" (p. 341). Consistency of categorization was reported as an 84% agreement.

Risk-Taking Inventory (Jackson, Hourany, & Vidmar, 1971)

Jackson, Hourany, and Vidmar (1971) developed a 120-item scale to measure four risk-taking subscales: monetary, physical, ethical, and social. The Social Risk-Taking subscale is a measure of an individual's willingness to risk social embarrassment to attain a goal (Lee & Bednar, 1977).

Melnick and Wicher (1977) reported high convergent and discriminant validity for the Social Risk-Taking scale. No other information was available for this instrument.

Bush-Iannotti Adult Risk-Taking Scale (BIARTS) (Bush & Iannotti, 1987)

A 13-item adult risk-taking scale was created using factor analysis from 25-items administered to 270 urban adults. Five items refer to risk of injury, five to risk of illness, one to gambling, and two to general risk-taking propensity. Subjects rated each question on a 6-point Likert scale. Sample questions include: "I drive over the speed limit or ride with people who do; I check for fire exits when I go to new places; If I won $20 in a game of chance, I would keep the money rather than keep on playing; I am careful to dress so that I won't get wet or cold." Cronbach alpha was 0.77 and was reported as internally reliable.

Pilot Questionnaire (Ely, 1986)

In a study related to risk taking in a language learning classroom, Ely (1986) used a pilot questionnaire before the course began. The questionnaire included items such as: "I don't like trying out a difficult sentence in class; I like to wait until I know exactly how to use a Spanish word before I speak it; In class, I prefer to say a sentence to myself before I speak it." Students responded to each item using a 6-point scale ranging from "strongly disagree" to "strongly agree," and were then categorized according to risk-taking propensity. Observers sat in on the language classes and tracked the number of times students asked or answered questions without being individually nominated to do so. The attribute of "language class risk taking" was a significant positive predictor of classroom participation, thus demonstrating content validity.

Theoretical Background

Research by Kogan and Wallach (1964) and Slovic (1962) addressed the generalizability of risk taking/cautiousness across a variety of decision-making situations. Using diverse tasks such as dice-betting preferences and hypothetical life dilemmas, they concluded that an individual's risk-taking level varies with the particular situation. "Motivational disturbances," such as anxiety and defensiveness, were found to be important mediating variables to this result. Highly consistent behavior was found with a subgroup who rated high on anxiety and defensiveness. Subjects in this group, strongly influenced by a need to conform, may have perceived consistency in decision making as the "correct" behavior. Those with low-motivational disturbance functioned "cognitively," changing their risk-taking behavior based on the actual conditions that exist during the various situations (Kogan, 1971).

Several researchers observed and reported on guessing behavior (Kogan & Morgan, 1969; Quereshi, 1960; Sheriffs & Boomer, 1954). Kogan (1971) related this research to risk taking/cautiousness, and concluded again that "motivational disturbances" affect the outcomes of risk taking or "guessing." Those individuals who experience high anxiety and engage in high-risk behavior perform more poorly on verbal aptitude tests. Those who experience low anxiety but still engage in high-risk behavior perform better. He explains that motivation may affect the ability of high-anxiety individuals to make appropriate decisions based on partial knowledge because their attention is drawn away by their anxiety. Low-anxiety individuals can focus more attention on their knowledge of the question and tend to guess correctly. He also postulated that anxiety level may actually be a confounding variable in verbal ability scores; that is, those who are highly anxious and are high risk takers guess wildly and are penalized.

Academic risk taking is viewed as a key factor in the pursuit of excellence and success in educational endeavors. Included in this definition of risk taking is the willingness to risk social embarrassment in front of one's peers (as is necessary to contribute in class), or the "selection of school subjects varying in difficulty and probability of success" (Clifford, 1990, p. 46). Much documentation exists that encourages moderate risk taking for the empowerment and creative development of the student especially in academic settings.

Risk Taking/Cautiousness and Learning

Research

- Sheriffs and Boomer (1954) observed that highly anxious subjects were less likely to take risks than less anxious subjects and omitted more question items.

- On inductive reasoning tests, Quereshi (1960) found that motivation disturbances affected the number of omitted items.

- For subjects with low anxiety and low defensiveness, greater risk taking was associated with higher verbal aptitude scores. Highly test-anxious subjects taking high risks had lower verbal aptitude scores (Kogan & Wallach, 1964).

- Creative ability was significantly correlated with disposition toward risk taking in a task of motor skill for fifth-grade boys (Wallach & Kogan, 1965).

- Kogan and Morgan (1969) found that highly anxious and defensive boys were most likely to guess wrong than less anxious, less defensive boys.

- Individuals low in test anxiety and defensiveness were task centered and consistently risky or cautious across similar situations. Anxious and defensive individuals had higher motivation (Kogan, 1971).

- Age had a significant effect on expectancy for success and risk-taking behavior. Boys and young adults displayed high expectancies and preferred intermediate risks (Chaubey, 1974).

- In an examination of early group development, high risk takers in a behavioral structure reported higher group cohesion, were more involved in self-disclosure and interpersonal feedback, and reported greater perceived depth of communication (Evensen & Bednar, 1978).

Implications of the Characteristics and Research

Implications which are drawn from research are noted with a •; those drawn logically from descriptive information regarding the trait are noted by an *. Based on the research and descriptions of *risk-taking/cautious behavior*, we conclude that *risk takers* (when they are low anxious and low defensive) are more likely to excel at learning tasks such as:

- inductive reasoning
* making predictions that are not certain
* creative tasks that involve trying out new ideas
* experimentation with new ideas
* competition where there is some element of risk involved
* group learning, where they are socially flexible
- verbal aptitude
* academic exams

and acquire and use effectively learning strategies such as:

* setting learning goals
* self-regulated learning
* generating metaphors and knowledge
* generating examples
* imaging or illustrating knowledge
* predicting outcomes

Based on the research and descriptions of risk/cautious behavior, we conclude that *cautious* learners are more likely to excel at learning tasks such as:

* taking time to reflect before responding to insure being correct
* musing systematic thinking to organize knowledge
* tasks that involve concentration and focused attention
* exercising quality control to insure the elimination of errors
* independent learning tasks where there is no risk of social embarrassment

and acquire and use effectively learning strategies such as:

* searching for information
* concentrating on information
* evaluating current information
* repeating material to be learned
* rehearsing material to be recalled
* practicing covertly
* analyzing key ideas
* outlining
* testing personal skills and knowledge

Risk Taking/Cautiousness and Instruction

Research

* Kogan and Morgan (1969), investigating the effect of evaluation conditions on test-taking risk behavior in fifth-grade children, found that for boys, the evaluation conditions elicited more risk-taking behavior (wild guessing) than a more relaxed atmosphere.

* Modeling risk-taking behavior was not successfully transferred to first or fifth graders (Montgomery & Landers, 1974).

* Touhey and Villemez (1975) found that the risk-taking preferences of low-need-for-achievement undergraduates were moderated by ability instructions. Differences among high-need-for-achievement subjects were moderated by effort instructions.

* In groups with mixed high/low-anxiety and high/low risk-taking subjects, the following perceptions were noted: high risk takers were viewed as more verbally active, self-disclosing, and risk taking but were not seen by others as more valuable group members, even though they viewed themselves so; high-risk/high-anxiety and high-anxiety/low-risk subjects had self-observations different from other group members; and high-anxiety/low-risk subjects had a high dropout potential (Melnick & Wicher, 1977).

- Lee and Bednar (1977) found that structure was effective in eliciting the desired behavior in low risk-taking subjects.

- Coet and McDermott (1979) found that risk-oriented instruction produced significantly greater risk taking than neutral instructions. In this study, males also consistently showed greater risk taking than females.

- Gutierrez (1982) found that risk takers, more than cautious subjects, were willing to risk social embarrassment.

- Support groups were used to help students who were afraid of taking risks (Clabby & Belz, 1985).

- Linn (1985) found gender differences in risk-taking expectations about performance, help seeking, and success and failure attributions in a computer environment.

- People willing to take risks in a language class are more likely to participate in the classroom (Ely, 1986).

- Multimodal intervention helped children become comfortable and gain minimal competence with computers (Crosbie-Burnett & Pulvino, 1990).

- Students chose more difficult problems when the number of points offered increased with the difficulty of the problem and when a risk-taking task was presented within a game or practice situation (Clifford, 1990).

- Students chose risk over certainty when the consequences of risk were more satisfying and informative (Clifford, 1990).

Implications of the Characteristics and Research

Implications which are drawn from research are noted with a •; those drawn logically from descriptive information regarding the trait are noted by an *. Instructional conditions that capitalize on the preferences of a risk taker and challenge the cautious learner include:

- providing opportunities for self-disclosure
- providing opportunities to be verbally active
- providing evaluative conditions
- providing an opportunity to participate in social situations
* presenting goals for the learner to select
* asking the learner to pose questions to be answered
* asking the learner to select study methods

* asking the learner to generate integration activities
* asking the learner to generate an organization for information
* providing risk-oriented instructions
* using ability as a motivator in the instruction for those with low achievement motivation
* using effort as a motivator in the instructions for those with high achievement motivation
* spontaneous classroom participation

Instructional conditions that remediate or compensate for overly *risky* students include:

* providing some structure on tasks, such as due-dates and intermediate goals
* providing guidelines and goals for experimentation
* providing a focus or target for creative projects
* making clear the consequences of losing a risky choice

Instructional conditions that capitalize on the preferences of a cautious learner and challenge the risk taker include:

* explaining the purpose or relevance of content
* describing the criteria for standard performance
* presenting advance organizers
• presenting structured overviews and organizers
• providing instructional support
* providing integrated information
• providing organizational structure for the information
* tasks that require preparation before class
• well-structured practice tasks
* providing feedback on many nonevaluative tasks
* providing short-term goals, with a maximum of explanation and guidance
* embedding questions throughout instruction
* using an easy to difficult sequence
• providing multimodal presentations
• providing opportunities for which the consequence of risk is satisfying and informative

Research trends indicate that moderate risk taking fosters learning. Cautiousness, or fear of risk taking, is viewed as an impediment to learning. Consequently, most literature deals with overcoming the fear of risk taking. Starting with this assumption, the following remedial or compensatory methods and instructional conditions can help students to become less cautious and take more risks:

- using support group techniques to facilitate trust, disclosure, and discussion among group members such as:
  * relaxation techniques (e.g., lowering the lights)
  * guided imagery of past successes and failures to help sharing
  * videotape to see how personal style helps or hinders group interaction

- using strategies (Adderholdt-Elliot, 1989) to eliminate the fear of being imperfect such as:
  * setting more reasonable goals
  * dividing large tasks into smaller ones
  * developing support systems to handle stress
  * giving rewards for small accomplishments

- using multimodal counseling as suggested by Crosbie-Burnett and Pulvino (1990) which includes:
  * practice tasks
  * risk-taking imagery
  * helping students organize and plan activities
  * tactile exploration (e.g., let the student play with parts of the computer)
  * talking about fears and feelings
  * helping students make decisions and develop problem-solving skills
  * using other students as models, sharing their experiences

- challenging and encouraging risk taking (Clifford, 1990):
  * making the success probability for each alternative clear
  * minimizing the imposed external constraints
  * providing greater payoff for greater risks
  * providing a relaxing and nonthreatening environment
  * providing an environment that is tolerant of error-making and supportive of error correction
  * making a clear distinction between formative evaluation activities (such as practice exercises and skill-building activities) and providing summative evaluation activities that are used to determine grades
  * making formative activities far more plentiful than summative activities; making these formative activities optional, relevant, varied, and of a playful nature
  * allowing "retake exams" for summative evaluations

- encouraging creativity

References

Adderholdt-Elliot, M. (1989). Perfectionism and underachievement. *The Gifted Child Today, 12,* 19-21.

Alexander, C., Jim, Y. J., Ensminger, M., Johnson, K. E., Smith, B. J., & Dolan, L. J. (1990). A measure of risk taking for young adolescents: Reliability and validity assessments. *Journal of Youth and Adolescence, 19*(6), 559-569.

Bush, P. J., & Iannotti, R. J. (1987). *Development of an adult risk-taking scale.* Rockville, MD: National Institute on Drug Abuse. (ERIC Document Reproduction Service No. ED 290 779)

Chaubey, N. P. (1974). Effect of age on expectancy of success and on risk-taking behavior. *Journal of Personality and Social Psychology, 29*(6), 774-778.

Clabby, J. F., & Belz, E. J. (1985). Psychological barriers to learning: Approach using group treatment. *Small Group Behavior, 16,* 525-533.

Clifford, M. M. (1990). Students need challenge, not easy success. *Educational Leadership, 48,* 22-26.

Coet, L. J., & McDermott, P. J. (1979). Sex, instructional set, and group make-up: Organismic and situational factors influencing risk-taking. *Psychological Reports, 44*(3, Pt.2), 1283-1294.

Cohen, P. A., Sheposh, J. P., & Hillix, W. A. (1979). Situational and personality influences on risk-taking behavior: Effects of task, sex, and locus of control. *Academic Psychology Bulletin, 19*(1), 63-67.

Crosbie-Burnett, M., & Pulvino, C. J. (1990). PRO-TECH: A multimodal group intervention for children with reluctance to use computers. *Elementary School Guidance and Counseling, 24,* 272-280.

Ely, C. M. (1986). An analysis of discomfort, risk taking, sociability, and motivation in the L2 classroom. *Language Learning, 36,* 1-25.

Evensen, E. P., & Bednar, R. L. (1978). Effects of specific cognitive and behavioral structure on early group behavior and atmosphere. *Journal of Counseling Psychology, 25*(1), 66-75.

Gutierrez, R. J. (1982). *A study of the relation between locus of control and risk taking for graduate students in education.* (master's thesis, California State University, Northridge). (ERIC Document Reproduction Service No. ED 233 246)

Hamilton, J. O. (1974). Motivation and risk-taking behavior: A test of Atkinson's theory. *Journal of Personality and Social Psychology, 29*(6), 856-864.

Horn, J. G. (1973). Risk taking in explanation of biological events. *Journal of Research in Science Teaching 10*(4), 341-346.

Jackson, D. W., Hourany, L., & Vidmar, N. J. (1971). *A four-dimensional interpretation of risk taking* (Research Bulletin #185). London, Canada: University of Western Ontario.

Karabenick, S. A., & Addy, M. M. (1979). Locus of control and sex differences in skill and chance risk-taking conditions. *Journal of General Psychology, 100*(2), 215-228.

Kogan, N. (1971). Educational implications of cognitive styles. In G. Lesser (Ed.), *Psychology and educational practice.* (pp. 242-292). Glenview, IL: Scott, Foresman.

Kogan, N., & Morgan, F. T. (1969). Task and motivational influences on the assessment of creative and intellectual ability in children. *Genetic Psychology Monographs, 80,* 92-127.

Kogan, N., & Wallach, M. A. (1964). *Risk taking: A study in cognition and personality.* New York: Holt, Rinehart & Winston.

Kopfstein, D. (1973). Risk-taking behavior and cognitive style. *Child Development, 44*(1), 190-192.

Kuhl, J. (1978). Standard setting and risk preference: An elaboration of the theory of achievement motivation and an empirical test. *Psychological Review, 85*(3), 239-248.

Lee, F., & Bednar, R. L. (1977). Effects of group structure and risk-taking disposition on group behavior, attitudes and atmosphere. *Journal of Counseling Psychology, 24*(3), 191-199.

Linn, M. C. (1985). Gender equity in computer-learning environments. *Computers in Social Sciences, 1*(1), 19-27.

Melnick, J., & Wicher, D. (1977). Social risk-taking propensity and anxiety as predictors of group performance. *Journal of Counseling Psychology, 24*(5), 415-419.

Montgomery, G. T., & Landers, W. F. (1974). Transmission of risk taking through modeling at two age levels. *Psychological Reports, 34*(3, pt. 2), 1187-1196.

Pankove, E., & Kogan, N. (1968). Creative ability and risk taking in elementary school children. *Journal of Personality, 36,* 420-439.

Quereshi, M. Y. (1960). Mental test performance as a function of payoff conditions, item difficulty, and degree of speeding. *Journal of Applied Psychology, 44,* 65-77.

Roberts, G. C. (1974). Effect of achievement motivation and social environment of risk taking. *Research Quarterly, 45*(1), 42-55.

Roberts, G. C. (1975). Sex and achievement motivation effects on risk taking. *Research Quarterly, 46*(1), 58-70.

Sheriffs, A. C., & Boomer, D. S. (1954). Who is penalized by the penalty for guessing? *Journal of Education Psychology, 45,* 81-90.

Slovic, P. (1962). Convergent validation of risk taking measures. *Journal of Abnormal and Social Psychology, 65,* 68-71.

Touhey, J. C., & Villemez, W. J. (1975). Need achievement and risk-taking preference: A clarification. *Journal of Personality and Social Psychology, 32*(4), 713-719.

Wallach, M. A., & Kogan, N. (1965). *Modes of thinking in young children.* New York: Holt, Rinehart & Winston.

Wesley, R. (1967). *Willingness to risk questionnaire.* Princeton: Educational Testing Service. (University Microforms 005353)

Bibliography

Adderholdt-Elliot, M. (1990). A comparison of the "stress seeker" and the "perfectionist." *Gifted Child Today, 13,* 50-51.

Burns, D. D. (1980, November). The perfectionist's script for self defeat. *Psychology Today,* 34-52.

Johnson, M. M., Schmitt, F. A., & Pietrukowicz, M. (1989). The memory advantages of the generation effect: Age and process differences. *Journal of Gerontology, 44*(3), 91-94.

Lesser, G. S. (Ed.). (1971). *Psychology and educational practice.* Glenview, IL: Scott, Foresman.

Lynch, J. (1988). *Living Beyond Limits.* Walpole, NH: Stillpoint.

PART VII

PRIOR KNOWLEDGE

Introduction

In other parts of the book, we reviewed general learning abilities and personality characteristics and their relationship to the ability to learn different skills from different forms of instruction. These are generalized learning tendencies that are, to some degree, related to the content or skill being learned. They affect an individual's general ability to learn.

In this final part of the book, we discuss specific knowledge of content and how it affects an individual's ability to learn specific content. That is, we are discussing the effects of what an individual knows on his or her ability to learn. It seems intuitive to suggest that the more one knows about a domain of content, the more that one can learn; however, the premise extends beyond this somewhat simplistic view. In this part of the book, we describe how to assess what learners already know and the theoretical rationale for its relationship to the potential for learning new knowledge, as well as the implications for developing instructional intervention to increase the learning of those with low prior knowledge.

As described in the next chapter, *prior knowledge* is the knowledge, skills, or ability that students bring to the learning process. That prior knowledge may also constitute prerequisite knowledge that is required to learn a new skill or information. It may also constitute the general knowledge that the learner brings to the learning environment that can and will be used to acquire new knowledge.

Prior knowledge is a complex and ill-structured concept. We describe prior knowledge and ability in terms of two constructs: prior knowledge/achievement and structural knowledge. The former generally refers to the use of content tests to assess an individual's entry level knowledge or skills related to specific content domain. Structural knowledge is a relatively new construct that describes a learner's understanding of the constituent concepts and the relationships between them in a given content domain.

Prior knowledge, regarded in terms of both quantity and type of knowledge, as well as the structure of that knowledge, is among the strongest predictors of learning. As the level of prior knowledge increases, the need for instruction decreases, and learning increases. Conversely, as the level of prior knowledge decreases, the need for instructional support increases. A book on learner characteristics is incomplete without addressing prior knowledge. Learners are characterized as much by what they know as by how they think and behave. It is important to consider the interactive role of prior knowledge in the design of instructional methods.

32

PRIOR KNOWLEDGE AND ACHIEVEMENT

Description of Prior Knowledge and Achievement

Prior knowledge and achievement are the knowledge, skills, or abilities that the student brings to the learning environment prior to instruction. In the context of instruction, two common conceptions are held. The first, prerequisite knowledge, is knowledge that is necessary to understand the new information. Students lacking this information would not significantly profit from instruction at all (Tobias, 1981). An assessment of this type of prior knowledge can point to where the learner should begin in the instructional sequence.

The second conception is defined by the total existence of knowledge and prior achievement that the learner brings to the learning environment which can and will be activated by the instruction--in other words, what the learner already knows both directly germane and remotely related to the content. Research on the impact of this more broadly defined conception of prior knowledge is voluminous and has demonstrated its effect on comprehension, reconstructive recall, and retrieval of information. In some cases it has been shown to prevent the acquisition of new knowledge by forming a barrier of preconceived ideas, which must be overcome before learning can take place. In addition, research confirms the existence of an achievement/treatment interaction, or an inverse relationship between level of prior knowledge and instructional support (Tobias, 1976). As level of prior knowledge rises, the need for instructional support decreases; conversely, as level of prior knowledge decreases, the need for instructional support rises.

Instructors can accept a level of prior knowledge and plan instruction accordingly, or use a prefamiliarization strategy, such as that employed by Abramson and Kagen (1975), to increase prior knowledge. In the latter case, background information is provided prior to the instructional lesson.

Characteristic Differences in Prior Knowledge

Individuals differ in the amount and type of prior knowledge they bring to the learning environment. The amount of knowledge simply refers to the quantitative aspects or how much information an individual possesses about a topic. The type of prior knowledge refers to more qualitative aspects. This includes level of overall versus detailed knowledge about the topic, level of confidence they have about the accuracy of their prior knowledge, and what other information the learner will consider to be related to the topic.

Individual Differences Related to Prior Knowledge

Structural Knowledge--Structural knowledge (see chapter 33) is closely related to achievement because it describes the knowledge (ideas and relationships) that an individual has available to use in trying to achieve some goal. Structural knowledge is the basis for achievement (Jonassen, Beissner, & Yacci, 1993).

Instruments for Measuring Prior Knowledge

Tobias (1982) stated that prior knowledge is simply tested via a pretest developed specifically for a content domain. On the whole, studies have measured the existence or nonexistence, degree or amount, and accuracy of prior knowledge (Maria & MacGintie, 1987). Tests have used multiple choice (in which learners use recognition memory for selecting from a list), free recall (in which learners recall information and construct their own response), true/false, matching, structured probe, (in which learners are given related questions when they answer a question correctly), or discussion in a small or large group to measure comprehension, recall, or recognition. Some pretests also include a scale for learners to indicate their degree of confidence with their answer. This provides an opportunity for the instructor to determine whether the learner is simply guessing, has tentative knowledge, or truly understands. A 5-point scale is typically used to indicate assessment. Related domains of knowledge can be assessed using word association tests in which the learners are given a word and either respond with their first thought or brainstorm all related topics.

Theoretical Background

One of the strongest and most consistent individual difference predictors of achievement is prior knowledge. Research on the effect of this difference is vast, consistent, and significant. Depending on the match between type of information presented and level of prior knowledge, achievement has been both enhanced and obstructed. The results of this research can be categorized and explained from the perspective of learning and instruction.

From a learning perspective, some explanations of the importance of prior knowledge can be offered. The first is transfer of learning. Prior skills and knowledge transfer directly to new learning. That is, they directly affect learning. Skills already possessed directly transfer to the acquisition of expanded skills. For example, an individual who has learned to program in a procedural computer language will find the acquisition of a new procedural language much easier. The prior programming skill directly transfers to the acquisition of new programming skills.

Other theoretical explanations for the importance of prior knowledge are schema theory, information-processing theory, and memory research. Schema theory, traced back to Bartlett (1932), and explicated by Rumelhart and Ortony (1977) more recently, explains the acquisition of new information through a learner's active, constructive integration of new information into existing networks of knowledge (see chapter 33). Learners use the networks as scaffolding to help them remember and comprehend new information (Anderson, 1977; Rumelhart & Ortony, 1977; Spiro, 1980). When new knowledge is built on the old, the new information loses its discreteness through the learner's personal interpretation and transformation of it. In other words, distinguishing new from old is no longer possible. This phenomenon was observed in both adults and children (Landis, 1982). Hacker (1980), and Spiro and Tirre (1980) also demonstrated that when prior knowledge exists, the acquisition of new information is facilitated; although, as explained by information-processing theory, the accuracy of that information may be questioned.

From information-processing theory we know that perception and attention play central roles in learning and memory (Atkinson & Shiffrin, 1968; Kulhavy, Peterson, & Schwartz, 1986) through an attentional set or expectation defined by sociocultural factors such as attitudes, beliefs, cultural references, ethnic and religious beliefs and social group affiliations, as well as motivation, intent, and prior experience or knowledge (Ormrod, 1990). This attentional set, in essence, is an internal control for what an individual will perceive and then attend to in any given situation--instructional or otherwise. When individuals come to the instructional situation with preexisting knowledge, their attention, what they actually perceive, and ultimately what they learn, is affected. Often, what learners perceive is what they *feel* they should perceive or *predict* they will perceive (Stein & Glenn, 1979). If the new information is accurate or congruous with preexisting knowledge, learning is facilitated. If the information is incongruous with preexisting knowledge, then one's perception takes precedence and actually interferes with the acquisition of accurate information. In the cognitive domain, this effect was demonstrated across grade level, content areas, and instructional modes (Lipson, 1982; Maria, 1987). As well, in the affective domain, Cooper (1984) demonstrated that when much prior knowledge exists, attitudes are less likely to change if the instruction takes an opposite position.

Tobias (1976, 1981, 1982) speculated that prior knowledge will affect a learner's perception of how difficult it will be to learn the information that is presented in the instruction. The more background one has on a topic, the easier additional information may be to learn, and vice versa. He hypothesized that when information is difficult, there will be a greater need for embedded instructional support than when the information is perceived as easy. High instructional support (i.e., the inclusion of elaborate feedback, visual enhancements, or organized structure) assists the novice through reassurance, correcting misconceptions, and integrating new information to existing knowledge. However, when much prior knowledge exists, the learner may have enough confidence such that high-instructional support may cause the learner to become disinterested. He argued this point from the perspective of mathemagenic/generative (Rothkopf, 1970) learning theory, or how media or methods mentally engage the learner in the instruction. Given that active mental engagement is a necessary condition for learning to occur, the external conditions should not reduce cognitive activity by frustrating a novice learner or boring one with more prior knowledge. The external conditions, media or methods, therefore, need to be regarded "only in terms of the degree to which they influence student's cognitive activities engaged by the instructional content" (p. 6).

Prior Knowledge and Learning

Research

The following sample of research on prior knowledge and learning is intended to demonstrate the types of research findings. Far more studies have assessed the role of prior knowledge in learning than could be represented in this volume.

- When prior knowledge was activated, reading comprehension improved (Bransford & Johnson, 1973; Dooling & Lachman, 1971).

- Royer, Perkins, and Konold (1978) found that false positive information resulted from prior knowledge of famous persons' presentation of prose passages when undergraduate subjects were told the passage would be about a famous or fictitious person.

- Transfer of learning was found to be contingent on congruence of elementary students' prior knowledge and the instruction that follows (Doran & Ngoi, 1979; Wittrock & Cook, 1975).

- Mintzes (1979) found that for undergraduate biology students, learning was affected by prior knowledge more than by locus of control.

- Morris, Stein, and Bransford (1979) found, in a study of undergraduates, that when subjects were given prior knowledge that was consistent with the subject's knowledge, this information enhanced learning of information in prose passages, whereas this effect was not found for the provision of prior knowledge that was inconsistent.

- Anderson (1977), Rumelhart (1980), and Spiro (1980) each found that what students already know about a subject will greatly influence how well they will comprehend what they learn about that subject.

- Stevens (1980) found that background knowledge enhanced comprehension of text for ninth-grade subjects.

- Langer and Nicolich (1981) in a recall task with high school seniors, found that amount of recall of text passages was related to the amount of prior knowledge, even when IQ was partialled out.

- Memory distortion was found in 7- and 10-year-olds who were presented information incongruous to their prior knowledge of familiar TV characters on a 3-week follow-up test (Ceci, Caves, & Howe, 1981).

- Clifton and Slowiaczek (1981) found that "activating old knowledge facilitates integration and that new information is not necessarily integrated with all old knowledge about a given concept but is organized with a subconcept" (p. 142).

- Landis (1982) found that when children are familiar with a topic, they integrate new knowledge with it, such that they are unable to distinguish new information from old 1 week later.

- In addition to disembedding and evolutionary belief, prior knowledge was a significant predictor of achievement of evolution and natural selection concepts in college students. Again, in this study, mental capacity and developmental level did not predict achievement (Lawson, 1983).

- Cooper (1984), in a study of attitudes of six experts in the field of school desegregation and black achievement, found that with a high degree of prior knowledge, subjects reviewing literature are less likely to change their attitudes.

- Finley (1985) found a significant effect of differences in students' prior knowledge on the acquisition of immediate and delayed propositions in physics.

- Prior knowledge is often used as a filter for interpreting new data. Students often resist changing their prior knowledge, so they often maintain the knowledge they bring with them in spite of conflicts with information which is presented to them during the course of instruction (Lipson, 1982; Maria, 1987).

- Chandran, Treagust, and Tobin (1987) studied the relationship of four cognitive styles and achievement on lab application, chemical calculation, and content knowledge exams in secondary education. Prior knowledge and formal reasoning ability emerged as significant factors, whereas field independence/dependence or memory capacity did not.

- In a case study investigation measuring learning of college chemistry in undergraduates, Braathen and Hewson (1988) found qualitative and quantitative differences in learning related to prior knowledge.

- Many subjects are not aware of inconsistencies between their understanding of a subject and information presented in a text (Marshall, 1988). It is hypothesized that perhaps a minimum level of knowledge is necessary before students can effectively self-monitor prior knowledge.

- Difficulty comprehending abstract concepts can often be traced to a lack of prior knowledge. Prior knowledge was a significant predictor of achievement of abstract concepts in molecular genetics and appeared to contribute more than formal reasoning ability (Zeitoun, 1988).

Implications of the Characteristics and Research

Implications which are drawn from research are noted with a •; those drawn logically from descriptive information regarding the trait are noted by an *. Based on the research and the descriptions of prior knowledge, we conclude that the existence of prior knowledge will likely enhance any learning tasks but will be most helpful for:

- problem solving and transfer of learning
- comprehension of material to be learned
- retention and recall of material
- formal reasoning ability

and be prerequisite for using learning strategies such as:

- self-monitoring

* search for information
* integration of knowledge
* paraphrasing/summarizing
* comparing new knowledge with existing knowledge, beliefs
* generating metaphors
* generating examples
* elaboration of knowledge

Prior Knowledge and Instruction

Research

* For a letter-based reasoning task, achievement was facilitated for learners with low prior knowledge when the pretest was identical to the posttest as opposed to being just similar (Skanes, Sullivan, Rowe, & Shannon, 1974).

* Well-organized instruction facilitated learning about heart disease for both college and high school subjects with little familiarity more than randomly organized content. No differences were found for high-familiarity content (Abramson & Kagen, 1975; Dyer & Kulhavy, 1974; Tobias, 1973).

* Tobias (1973) and Tobias and Ingber (1976) found that constructed responses were more effective for learning about heart disease and religious rituals than simply reading when the material was unfamiliar, whereas the superiority of the constructed responses decreased with an increase in prior knowledge.

* Mastery-based instruction for college calculus that used formative evaluation and remedial loops was found to be more effective than regular class instruction without those instructional supports for those with low prior knowledge only (Ott, 1976; Pascarella, 1978).

* Individual viewing of video modules was more effective than group viewing of video modules for individuals with low prior knowledge than for those with high prior knowledge (Deutsch & Tobias, 1980).

* Cohen (1981) found that even with mediated presentations, stereotypic prior knowledge interacted with and, in cases where information was incongruous with known information, it interfered with acquired knowledge regarding two types of occupations.

* Ross and Rakow (1981) and Hansen, Ross, and Rakow (1977) found that adaptive instruction was more effective for teaching algebra and

statistics to subjects with low prior knowledge than nonadaptive instruction, whereas no differences were found with those with high prior knowledge.

- Joseph and Dwyer (1984) investigated the effects of prior knowledge on a student's ability to learn (as demonstrated on the comprehension test) from visualized instruction in an externally or self-paced mode. They found that students who had high prior knowledge scored equally as well or significantly higher than those with low prior knowledge regardless of visualization strategy; and they seemed to be "able to benefit more from realistic visuals, particularly when instruction is self-paced" (p. 117).

- Tobias (1985) found significant interactions between prior knowledge, prior anxiety, and achievement based on different review strategies presented and the presence of adjunct questions.

- Dwyer (1987) found that practice strategies were effective in reducing differences in knowledge by those possessing different levels of prior knowledge.

- Maria and MacGintie (1987) found that with fifth and sixth graders, information that is incongruent with prior knowledge is best taught by contrasting the reader's misconception with actual information, rather than in a pure expository form. They suggested using graphic organizers and probing students to explain relationships.

- The value of written texts directly refuting misconceptions in prior knowledge is in doubt. One study found that such a text improved learning (Maria, 1987), where Alvermann and Hynd (1986) found the opposite to be true.

- Grabinger and Jonassen (1988) found no effect of prior knowledge on selection of independent versus a teacher-directed study with preservice undergraduate education majors.

Implications of the Characteristics and Research

Two important implications can be gleaned from this research. The first relates to achievement/treatment interactions that have been demonstrated:

- The more prior knowledge an individual possesses, the less instructional support is needed; the less prior knowledge an individual possesses, the more instructional support will be needed.

The second relates to the interference potential of prior knowledge:

• The less congruous the new information is with preexisting knowledge, the more important it will be to overtly contrast the reader's conception with the new information, rather than present the information in a purely expository form.

References

Abramson, R., & Kagen, E. (1975). Familiarization of content and different response modes in programmed instruction. *Journal of Educational Psychology, 67,* 83-88.

Anderson, R. C. (1977). The notion of schemata and the educational enterprise. In R. C. Anderson, R. J. Spiro, & W. E. Montague (Eds.), *Schooling and the acquisition of knowledge* (pp. 415-431). Hillsdale, NJ: Lawrence Erlbaum Associates.

Atkinson, J. W., & Shiffrin, R. M. (1968). Human memory: A proposed system and its control processes. In K. W. Spence and J. T. Spence (Eds.), *The psychology of learning and motivation: Vol. 2. Advances in research and theory* (pp. 89-195). New York: Academic.

Bartlett, F. C. (1932). *Remembering.* Cambridge: Cambridge University Press.

Braathen, P. C., & Hewson, P. W. (1988, April 10-13). *A case study of prior knowledge, learning approach, and conceptual change in an introductory college chemistry tutorial program.* Paper presented at the annual meeting of the National Association of Research in Science Teaching, Lake of the Ozarks, MO. (ERIC Document Reproduction Service No. ED 292 687)

Bransford, J. D., & Johnson, M. K. (1973). Consideration of some problems of comprehension. In W. G. Chase (Ed.), *Visual information processing* (pp. 1-31). New York: Academic.

Ceci, S. J., Caves, R. D., & Howe, M. J. (1981). Children's long-term memory for information that is incongruous with their prior knowledge. *British Journal of Psychology, 72(4),* 443-450.

Chandran, S., Treagust, D. F., & Tobin, K. (1987). The role of cognitive factors in chemistry achievement. *Journal of Research in Science Teaching, 24(2),* 145-60.

Clifton, C., & Slowiaczek, M. L. (1981). Integrating new information with old knowledge. *Memory and Cognition, 9(2),* 142-148.

Cohen, C. E. (1981). Person categories and social perception: Testing some boundaries of the processing effects of prior knowledge. *Journal of Personality and Social Psychology, 40(3),* 441-452.

Cooper, H. M. (1984). *On the social psychology of using research: The Case of desegregation and black achievement.* Washington, DC: National

Institute of Education. (ERIC Document Reproduction Service No. ED 252 646)

Deutsch, T., & Tobias, S. (1980, September). *Interaction among prior achievement, anxiety, and instructional method.* Paper presented at the annual convention of the American Psychological Association, Montreal.

Dooling, D. J., & Lachman, R. (1971). Effects of comprehension on retention of words in episodic memory. *Journal of Experimental Psychology, 88,* 216-222.

Doran, R., & Ngoi, M. K. (1979). Retention and transfer of selected science concepts in elementary school students. *Journal of Research in Science Teaching, 16*(3), 211-216.

Dwyer, C. (1987, February). *The effect of varied practice activities in complementing visualized instruction.* Paper presented at the annual convention of the Association for Educational Communications and Technology, Atlanta.

Dyer, J. W., & Kulhavy, R. W. (1974). Sequence effects and reading time in programmed learning. *Journal of Educational Psychology, 43,* 53-70.

Finley, F. N. (1985). Variations in prior knowledge. *Science Education, 69*(5), 697-705.

Grabinger, R. S., & Jonassen, D. H. (1988). Independent study, personality, cognitive, and descriptive predictors. In M. Simonson (Ed.), *Proceedings of Selected Papers presented at the Annual Meeting of the Association for Educational Communications and Technology* (pp. 302-307). Washington DC: Association for Educational Communications and Technology.

Hacker, C. J. (1980). From schema theory to classroom practice. *Language Arts, 57(8),* 866-871.

Hansen, D. N., Ross, S., & Rakow, E. (1977, March). *Adaptive models for computer-based training systems.* Memphis, TN: Memphis State University.

Joseph, J. H., & Dwyer, F. M. (1984). The effects of prior knowledge, presentation mode, and visual realism on student achievement. *Journal of Experimental Education, 52*(2), 110-121.

Jonassen, D. H., Beissner, K. L., & Yacci, M. A. (1993). *Structural knowledge.* Hillsdale, NJ: Lawrence Erlbaum Associates.

Kulhavy, R. W., Peterson, S., & Schwartz, N. H. (1986). Working memory: The encoding process. In G. D. Phye and T. Andre (Eds.), *Cognitive classroom learning: Understanding, thinking, and problem solving* (pp. 67 81). New York: Academic.

Landis, T. (1982). Interaction between text and prior knowledge in children's memory for prose. *Child Development, 53*(3), 811-814.

Langer, J. A., & Nicolich, M. (1981). Prior knowledge and its relationship to comprehension. *Journal of Reading Behavior, 13*(4), 373-379.

Lawson, A. E. (1983). Predicting science achievement: The role of developmental level, disembedding ability, mental capacity, and prior knowledge and beliefs. *Journal of Research in Science Teaching, 20*(2), 117-129.

Lipson, M. Y. (1982). Learning new information from text: The role of prior knowledge and reading ability. *Journal of Reading Behavior, 14,* 243 - 261.

Maria, K. (1987). *Overcoming misconceptions in science, A replication study at the fifth-grade level.* Paper presented at the National Reading Conference, St. Petersburg, FL.

Maria, K., & MacGintie, W. (1987). Learning from texts that refute the reader's prior knowledge. *Reading Research and Instruction, 26*(4), 222-238.

Marshall, N. (1988). Overcoming problems with incorrect prior knowledge: An instructional study. In S. McCormick & J. Zutell (Eds.), *Cognitive and Social Perspectives for Literacy Research and Instruction. Thirty-Eighth Yearbook of the National Reading Conference, Proceedings of the Annual Meeting of the National Reading Conference* (pp. 323-344). Tucson, AZ: National Reading Conference.

Mintzes, J. J. (1979). Prior knowledge and locus of control in cognitive learning among college biology students. *Education, 100*(2), 138-145.

Morris, C. D., Stein, B. S., & Bransford, J. D. (1979). Prerequisites for the utilization of knowledge in the recall of prose passages. *Journal of Experimental Psychology Human Learning and Memory, 5*(3), 253-261.

Ormrod, J. E. (1990). *Human learning: Theories, principles and educational applications.* Columbus, OH: Merrill.

Ott, M. D. (1976). Evaluation of methods of instruction and procedures for assigning students to methods. *American Journal of Physics, 44,* 12-17.

Pascarella, E. T. (1978). Interactive effects of prior mathematics preparation and level of instructional support in college calculus. *American Educational Research Journal, 15,* 275-285.

Ross, S. N., & Rakow, E. A. (1981). Learner control versus program control as adaptive strategies for selection of instructional support on math rules. *Journal of Educational Psychology, 73,* 745-753.

Rothkopf, E. Z. (1970). The concept of mathemagenic activities. *Review of Educational Research, 40,* 325-336.

Royer, J., Perkins, M. R., & Konold, C. E. (1978). Evidence for a selective storage mechanism in prose learning. *Journal of Educational Psychology, 70*(4), 457-462.

Rumelhart, D. E. (1980). Schemata: The building blocks of cognition. In R. J. Spiro, B. C. Bruce, & W. F. Brewer (Eds.), *Theoretical issues in reading comprehension* (pp. 33-58). Hillsdale, NJ: Lawrence Erlbaum Associates.

Rumelhart, D. E., & Ortony, A. (1977). Representation of knowledge. In R. C. Anderson, R. J. Spiro, & W. W. Montague, (Eds.), *Schooling and the Acquisition of Knowledge* (pp. 99-135). Hillsdale, NJ: Lawrence Erlbaum Associates.

Skanes, G. R., Sullivan, A. M., Rowe, E. J., & Shannon, E. (1974). Intelligence and transfer: Aptitude-by-treatment interactions. *Journal of Educational Psychology, 66,* 563-568.

Spiro, R. J. (1980). Construction processes in prose comprehension and recall. In R. J. Spiro, B. C. Bruce & W. F. Brewer (Eds.), *Theoretical Issues in Reading Comprehension* (pp. 342-355). Hillsdale, N.J.: Lawrence Erlbaum Associates.

Spiro, R. J., & Tirre, W. C. (1980). Individual differences in schema utilization during discourse processing. *Journal of Educational Psychology, 72*(2), 204-208.

Stein, N. L., & Glenn, C. G. (1979). An analysis of story comprehension in elementary school children. In R. Freedle, (Ed.), *New directions in discourse processing* (pp. 37-42). Norwood, NJ: Ablex.

Stevens, K. C. (1980). The effect of background knowledge on the reading comprehension of ninth graders. *Journal of Reading Behavior, 12*(2), 151-154.

Tobias, S. (1973). Review of the response mode issues. *Review of Educational Research, 43,* 61-74.

Tobias, S. (1976). Achievement treatment interactions. *Review of Educational Research, 46,* 61-74.

Tobias, S. (1981). Adapting instruction to individual differences among students. *Educational Psychologist, 16,* 11-120.

Tobias, S. (1982). When do instructional methods make a difference? *Educational Researcher, 11*(4), 4-9.

Tobias, S. (1985, March 31-April 4). *Optional and required text review strategies and their interaction with student characteristics (Tech. Report No. 5).* Paper presented at the annual meeting of the American Educational Research Association, Chicago. (ERIC Document Reproduction Service No. ED 261 336)

Tobias, S., & Ingber, T. (1976). Achievement treatment interactions in programmed instruction. *Journal of Educational Psychology, 68,* 43-47.

Wittrock, M. C., & Cook, H. (1975). Transfer of prior learning to verbal instruction. *American Education Research Journal, 12*(2), 147-156.

Zeitoun, H. H. (1988). *The relationship between abstract concept achievement and prior knowledge, formal reasoning ability, and sex among some Egyptian secondary school students.* Paper presented at the annual meeting of the National Association for Research in Science Teaching, Lake of the Ozarks, MO.

Bibliography

Alvermann, D. E., & Hynd, C. R. (1986). *The effects of varying prior knowledge activation modes and text structure on nonscience majors' comprehension of physics text.* Paper presented at the meeting of the National Reading Conference, Austin, TX.

Anderson, J. R. (1981). Effects of prior knowledge on memory for new information. *Memory and Cognition, 9*(3), 237-246.

Marshall, N. (1987). *When tests fail to meet reader expectations.* Paper presented at the National Reading Conference, St. Petersburg, FL.

33

STRUCTURAL KNOWLEDGE

Description of Structural Knowledge

The previous chapter described achievement scores as the primary means by which prior knowledge is normally assessed. That is, prior knowledge is described in terms of performance on achievement tests prior to instruction. This chapter asserts that there is another type of knowledge, *structural knowledge*, that describes and facilitates the application of prior knowledge. Structural knowledge is the knowledge of how ideas within a domain are interrelated (Diekhoff, 1983). Explicit awareness of those interrelationships and the ability to personally describe those relationships is a fundamental component in prior knowledge and an essential component in higher order thinking. It is not enough to *know that* (as measured by recall tests). To *know how* (application of prior knowledge), you must *know why*. Structural knowledge provides the conceptual basis for *why*. It describes how prior knowledge is interconnected. For example, to say that "warm air rises" requires connections between "air" and its modifier, "warm" as opposed to "cold." That this type of air rises is predicated on a causal relationship between "warm" and "rising," which forms the principle of convection. Structural knowledge enables learners to develop the understanding of connections that is required to describe and use prior knowledge.

Structural knowledge is most often depicted in terms of some sort of concept map that visually describes the relationships between the ideas in a knowledge domain. A simple structural knowledge representation of ideas related to lasers that was generated by a beginning engineering student is presented in Fig. 33.1. The blocks (or nodes) identify the important concepts or ideas in this student's knowledge structure. The lines (or links) show relationships between those ideas.

Structural knowledge was also defined as conceptual knowledge. Conceptual knowledge is the "integrated storage of meaningful dimensions...in a given domain of knowledge" (Tennyson & Cocciarella, 1986). More than just the storage of declarative knowledge, it is the "understanding of a concept's operational structure within itself and between associated concepts." Conceptual knowledge is used to develop procedural knowledge for solving domain problems. Structural (conceptual) knowledge involves the integration of declarative knowledge into useful knowledge structures.

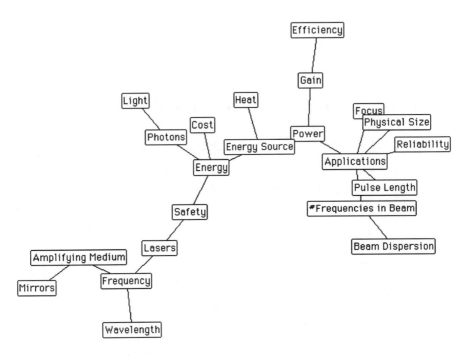

Fig. 33.1. Example of a simple structural knowledge representation.

These knowledge structures were also described as "cognitive structure," the pattern of relationships among concepts in memory (Preece, 1976). Cognitive structure in learners is a reflection of subject matter structure. Structural knowledge can be thought of as the understanding of one's cognitive structure.

Structural knowledge describes an individual's organization of ideas (knowledge structure) about different content domains. This knowledge is essential to understanding the content and the ability to apply it. Requiring learners to reflect on their knowledge using any of these techniques is also a useful learning strategy that will help them to use that knowledge and to acquire more knowledge.

Characteristic Differences in Structural Knowledge

Structural knowledge, like many of the other cognitive variables described in this volume, is not a bipolar construct. Each individual's structural knowledge of any content domain will differ based on the experiences and formal study relating to that content domain. Individual representations, such as that in Fig. 33.1, will differ in some quantifiable ways, such as those described below.

Number of constructs--The number of concepts that an individual generates relative to a topic, idea, or content domain is a reflection of the richness of that knowledge structure. The more concepts that an individual can interrelate, the richer is his or her knowledge structure.

Relatedness--Relatedness is determined by the number and variety of links that an individual uses to connect the concepts. The greater the number of links in a representation, the higher the degree of relatedness. Use of a variety of types of links to interrelate concepts indicates a more meaningful representation.

Semantic Distance--Most of the techniques used to assess structural knowledge (Jonassen, Beissner, & Yacci, 1993) display structural knowledge spatially. These techniques all assume that semantic distance (the degree of semantic relatedness between concepts) can be represented in geometric space. That is, semantic distance between concepts is rerrpresented by spatial distance between those concepts on a map. This is a critical assumption.

Dimensionality--Dimensionality refers to the number of dimensions that an individual uses to describe his or her knowledge domain. Some of the statistically based mapping techniques, those techniques for measuring structural knowledge, can generate maps in several dimensions. These solutions are intellectually correct in that they show the complexity of individual knowledge representations; however, multidimensional representations are difficult for humans to understand or conceptualize.

Coherence--Coherence refers to the interconnectedness of the knowledge representation. This does not simply mean the number and variety of links but also the extent to which each node is connected to all other nodes. Concepts with only a single link to another concept are not well integrated into the knowledge structure. However, if all of the concepts are connected to several other concepts in the representation, then the knowledge representation is more coherent. The concepts with the most links to other, either first-order (direct links) or second-order links (number of direct links plus the number of concepts that those first-order connections are connected to), are the most central (therefore, the most important) concepts in the learner's knowledge representation.

Individual Differences Related to Structural Knowledge

Achievement--Structural knowledge is closely related to achievement because it describes the knowledge (ideas and relationships) that an individual has available to use in trying to achieve a goal. Structural knowledge is the basis for achievement (Jonassen, Beissner, & Yacci, 1993).

Techniques for Measuring Structural Knowledge

The methods for measuring structural knowledge are quite different from traditional tests of knowledge. First, they are not convergent; that is, there are no right answers. They attempt to capture what someone knows, and what each individual knows is different from what all others know. We all share knowledge in common, but exactly what we each know and how we organize it is individualistic.

These methods seek to identify all of the concepts or ideas in one's memory that are related to the topic or ideas that are being assessed. They then try to determine how closely the ideas are related (semantic distance), and in some cases, the nature of the relationships between those ideas. The resulting representation, which is usually in the form of a concept map, describes the knowledge structure that an individual possesses related to a topic. The positions of the ideas in the map relative to each other represent the semantic distances between those ideas. These techniques assume that semantic distance can be represented in terms of geometric space. Most researchers agree that these experimental procedures make it possible to operationally define cognitive structure (structural knowledge) (Jonassen, 1987; Preece, 1976; Shavelson, 1972, 1985).

Similarity Data

The benchmark method for reflecting cognitive structure is the free word association task (Preece, 1976). Subjects are given a set of stimulus words, from which they generate a set of words that come first to mind (e.g., "Think of all of the ideas or terms that are important or related to _____."); that is, they free-associate. The words that come first to mind have the strongest relationship to the stimulus word. In a related set of words that are common to a particular content domain, concepts tend to appear in the associate lists of each other. The degree of overlap (commonality of shared concepts and similarity of their relative position in the lists) between two concepts defines their relatedness. These relatedness coefficients can then be analyzed using statistical methods such as multidimensional scaling, cluster analysis, or principal components analysis, which result in a concept map in which more closely related items appear closer on the map.

Instead of calculating relatedness coefficients for statistical analysis, learners can provide similarity ratings for the terms in the subject area (Diekhoff, 1983; Johnson, Cox, & Curran, 1970; Stanners & Brown, 1982). Each of the terms is paired up with every other word, and learners are asked to rate the degree of similarity between each pair of concepts on a scale of 1 to 9 or 10. The resulting intercorrelation matrix can be scaled to produce a map such as that in Fig. 33.1.

Most of these methods require the use of advanced statistical techniques, like principal components, cluster analysis, or multi-dimensional scaling to discover the dimensional framework underlying the set of concepts. Such tests usually require a familiarity with statistics and computer analysis methods. Some computer programs, such as KNOT (Knowledge Network Orientation Tool) (Interlink, 1990; Schvanenveldt et al., 1985) provide a set of user-friendly programs for performing the type of analysis previously described. That program was used to produce the knowledge representation in Fig. 33.1.

Concept Maps

Another technique for representing an individual's structural knowledge is to generate concept maps in various forms.

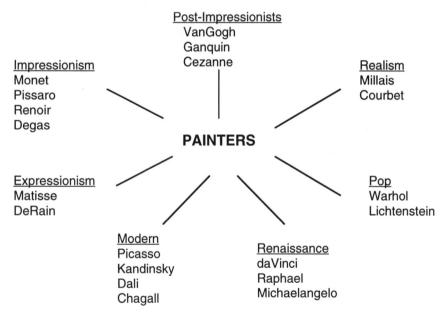

Fig. 33.2. Semantic map of painters.

Semantic mapping. Semantic mapping (Johnson, Pittleman, Toms-Bronowski, & Levin, 1984; Johnson, Toms-Bronowski, & Pittleman, 1982; Pittleman, Levin, & Johnson, 1985) is a learning strategy that uses the categorization of concepts to clarify new vocabulary and convey the structure of reading passages (see Fig. 33.2). In the technique, new vocabulary words are related to students' prior knowledge and experiences to increase their understanding of new concepts. Semantic mapping is a classroom strategy that uses student discussion to generate a map of the relationships between words.

The semantic mapping procedure is relatively simple. A general topic area is defined and written in the center of a piece of paper (or chalkboard). Next, concepts that are related to the main topic are identified, and examples of these secondary concepts are identified and listed beneath these concepts. Thus, a three-tiered hierarchy of concepts is generated and graphically represented.

Spider Maps. Hanf (1971) developed a technique called *spider maps* as an alternative to traditional note taking from text. In spider mapping, the main idea of the text passage is written in the center of a page, and related, subordinate concepts are drawn on lines connected to the central idea (see Fig. 33.3). Additional lines with increasingly detailed content can be added to the drawing so that the end product looks similar to a spider web. Although this mapping strategy was developed as a means of noting the structure of a passage of text (Van Patten, Chao, & Reigeluth, 1986), it can also be used as a general mapping strategy through the inclusion of content from prior knowledge or the use of multiple sources to represent content structure.

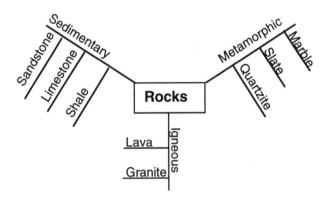

Fig. 33.3. Spider map of rocks.

Pattern Notes. Pattern noting is a note-taking technique that was developed by Buzan (1974) for organizing and displaying information in a relational manner. Buzan referred to these models as "brain patterns," but they are more commonly referred to as pattern notes. The pattern usually starts with a central idea that is blocked in the center of the page. The central idea may be the main topic of a report, lecture, or the subject being analyzed for instruction. The pattern noter then free-associates about the idea, thinking of all of the ideas he or she can, which are related to the idea. These ideas are linked to the central topic. Each idea is also free-associated with ideas linked to it by lines, so that the pattern noter develops an enlarging web of ideas. When the pattern is large enough, the noter then looks at all of the ideas and interconnects related ideas by direct lines.

This pattern note (see Fig. 33.4) illustrates the fundamentals of pattern noting.

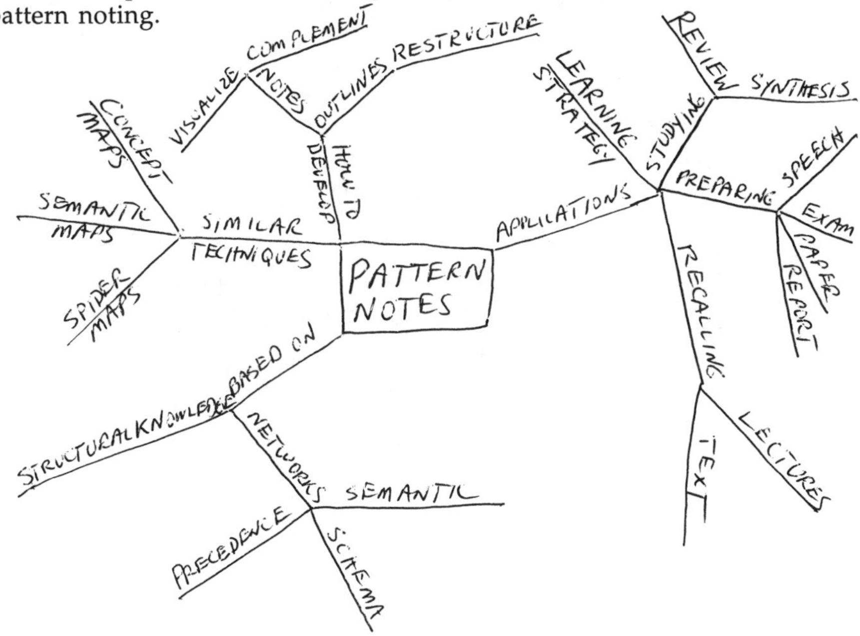

Fig. 33.4. Example of a pattern note.

Concept Maps. Concept maps (Beyerbach, 1986; Novak, 1980; Novak & Gowin, 1984; Stewart, 1984; Stewart, Van Kirk, & Rowell, 1979) consist of concepts or *nodes* linked by labeled lines to show relationships and interrelationships between terms. Concepts are arranged hierarchically so that the most inclusive, subsumptive concepts appear at the top of the map, with less inclusive, subordinate concepts below (see Fig. 33.5). As with note patterns, relationships between concepts are depicted by lines. Here, labels of the relationship type are simply words selected by the map maker rather than symbolic labels representing a fixed set of relationship types. To produce concept maps, students are trained to graphically represent concepts and their interrelationships using any of these techniques.

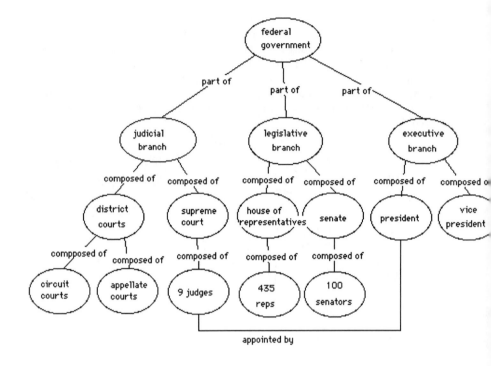

Fig. 33.5. Example of a concept map.

Schematizing

Schematizing (Camstra & van Bruggen, 1984; Mirande, 1984) is another structural knowledge study strategy that uses concepts representing main ideas linked to other concepts via symbolic labels. Rather than specifying precise concept relationships, the labels used in schematizations are: dynamic relationship, static relationship, similarity, interaction, and the negation of these four types of relationships. Schematizations include "specifications lists," which are lists and definitions of each of the concepts used in the schematization graphic (see Fig. 33.6). Like networking and mapping, this technique was developed as a strategy for studying text.

Theoretical Background

There are two related theoretical constructs that underlie structural knowledge: *schema theory* and *semantic networks*. Schema theory

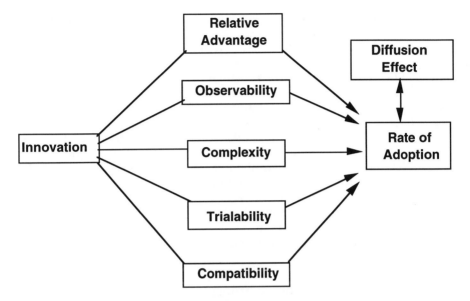

Fig. 33.6. Example of schematizing.

(Rumelhart, 1980; Rumelhart & Ortony, 1977) avers that knowledge is stored in memory in information packets, or schemas. These schemas represent our mental constructs for ideas. A schema for an object, event, or idea is comprised of a set of attributes or slots that describe the object or event. For instance, most of us have a well-developed schema for *automobile* that includes attributes or slots such as body, wheels, engine, steering wheel, radio, and so on. Individual schemas are interconnected to form larger classes, called schemata, such as transportation, travel, status symbol, and so on. Likewise, our automobile schema has specific slots that are filled with more specific examples, such as a Ford or BMW. Each individual possesses a unique schema for objects or events depending on personal life experiences. Each schema that we construct represents a miniframework in which to interpret ideas.

Schemas and schemata vary in complexity. They can resemble concrete or abstract concepts, such as *automobile, ice cream cone, anger,* or *trust,* or they can be complex combinations of events or objects, such as *planning a vacation.* These more complex, *event schemas* involve episodes and all of the related information encoded into the schema's slots. For instance, a schema for driving a car interrelates to schemata for power, acceleration, vector forces, direction, and a host of other physical factors or schemas. We must understand these to reliably drive our cars. We may also encode specific, event-related information to the driving schemata, such as *commuting to work.* The interrelationships between schemata and the formation of more complex schemata describes the process of constructing structural knowledge. That is, structural knowledge is built with schemas and interrelated schemata.

Schemas are all arranged in networks of interrelated concepts known as semantic networks. Perhaps the best known conceptualization of semantic networks are active structural networks (Quillian, 1968): structures that are composed of nodes (the equivalent of schemas) and ordered, typed (e.g., subordinate, disjunctive) relationships or links connecting them (Norman, Gentner, & Stevens, 1976). The nodes are instances of concepts or propositions and the links describe the relationships between them. If memory is organized as a semantic network, then one way to look at learning is as a reorganization of these networks. These networks describe what a learner knows, which provides the foundations for learning new ideas. These semantic networks are a representation of structural knowledge, and structural knowledge is essential for learning. Describing these networks helps us to understand what a learner knows, which enables us to adapt instruction accordingly.

Structural Knowledge and Learning

Research

- Structural knowledge is essential to comprehension (Bruner, 1960). Acquiring knowledge about the structure of a content allowed learners to better comprehend and retain content and apply it to new situations.

- As instruction progressed, the learners' conceptions of content (including structure) became more interrelated and corresponded more closely with the teacher's content structure (Shavelson, 1974).

- Experts represented structural knowledge more efficiently and effectively than novices (Larkin, McDermott, Simon, & Simon, 1980), developing more elaborate structures that enabled them to reason more effectively.

- "Meaning does not exist until some structure, or organization, is achieved" (Mandler, 1983, p. 4) so without structure nothing could be understood.

- Camstra and van Bruggen (1984) concluded that instruction in basic study skills including schematizing has been effective in improving students' academic performances.

- When provided a total of 12 hours of instruction on schematizing, pre- and posttests on a text passage comprehension revealed no differences, thus not supporting the use of schematizing (Camstra & van Bruggen,

1984). In a follow-up study, after lower achieving education majors were instructed in schematizing, they reversed their standings with respect to the rest of the class. Within 6 months, the experimental group that received instruction in schematizing increased their grades above controls not instructed in schematizing. Student response to the technique was positive, and the instruction in schematizing was considered to be a success.

• How much problem-solving protocols contained relevant structural knowledge was the strongest predictor of how well learners solve transfer problems in physics (Robertson, 1990). Domain-specific problem solving relies on adequate and appropriate knowledge structures.

• Structural knowledge is essential to problem solving (Chi & Glaser, 1985).

• Beyerbach (1986) found that in assessing teachers' concept development, the richness and complexity of the cognitive maps produced by teachers expanded over time.

• Jonassen (1987) showed that pattern noting, a concept-mapping technique, accurately reflects cognitive structure when compared with the free word association data.

Implications of the Characteristics and Research

Implications which are drawn from research are noted with a •; those drawn logically from descriptive information regarding the trait are noted by an *. Based on the research and descriptions of *structural knowledge,* we conclude that high levels of structural knowledge will enhance:

• problem solving and transfer of learning
• comprehension or understanding of material to be learned
• retention and memory of material

Those who possess more structural knowledge will be more effective at acquiring these learning strategies:

* evaluating current information
* analyzing of key ideas
* generating metaphors and analogies
* predicting outcomes, inferring causes, and explaining implications

Structural Knowledge and Instruction

Research

- Students who constructed their own structured overviews outperformed both the group that received the advanced structured overviews and those who simply read the passage twice (Barron & Stone, 1974). They concluded that structured overviews provide the greatest benefit when presented (or drawn) after reading from text.

- Students who were provided with the structured overviews outperformed control group students on comprehension of content and production of hierarchies. Not all of the students who drew their own hierarchies were able to do so accurately. Those students who did outperformed the other students in this group as well as the control group (Eggen, Kauchak, & Kirk, 1978)

- Learning vocabulary prior to reading was enhanced by semantic mapping with several populations (low-ability readers and learning-disabled students) (Johnson, Toms-Bronowski, & Pittleman, 1982; Jones, 1984; Pittleman, Levin, & Johnson, 1985; Sinatra, Berg, & Dunn, 1985; Toms-Bronowski, 1982).

- In a study of the networking (concept mapping) strategy, students with high-verbal aptitude were able to use a less structured networking technique with good results, whereas low-verbal aptitude students using a less structured networking method did not perform any better than did the control groups (Holley & Dansereau, 1984).

- Schematizing has been effective in improving students' academic performance (Camstra & van Bruggen, 1984).

- Boothby and Alvermann (1984) found that a class of students who received traditional instruction preceded by structured overviews performed better on tests of recall of main ideas than students who received only traditional instruction.

- Amerine (1986) found that students whose instruction included discussion of a structured overview prior to instruction scored significantly higher on post instructional comprehension tests than students who received only traditional instruction.

Implications of the Characteristics and Research

Because these structural knowledge techniques are examples of learning strategies, the only implications of the research is that they should be integrated into instruction to facilitate learning. Structural knowledge skills represents a unipolar skill, so that the less skilled a learner is, the more instruction he or she needs.

References

Amerine, F. J. (1986). First things first. *Clearing House, 59*, 396-397.

Barron, R. F., & Stone, V. F. (1974). Effect of student-constructed graphic post organizers upon learning vocabulary relationships. In P. L. Nacke (Ed.), *Interaction: Research and practice for college-adult reading.* (pp. 172-175). Twenty-third Yearbook of the National Reading Conference. Clemson, SC: National Reading Conference.

Beyerbach, B. A. (1986). *Concept mapping in assessing prospective teachers' concept development.* (ERIC Document Reproduction Service No. ED 291 800)

Boothby, P. R., & Alvermann, D. E. (1984). A classroom training study: The effects of graphic organizer instruction on fourth graders' comprehension. *Reading World, 23*, 325-339.

Bruner, J. (1960). *The Process of Education.* New York: Random House.

Buzan, T. (1974). *Use Your Head.* London: British Broadcasting Publications.

Camstra, B., & van Bruggen, J. (1984). Schematizing: The empirical evidence. In C. D. Holley & D. F. Dansereau (Eds.), *Spatial learning strategies: Techniques, applications, and related issues* (pp. 45-58). New York: Academic.

Chi, M. T., & Glaser, R. (1985). Problem-solving ability. In R. S. Sternberg (Ed.), *Human abilities: An information-processing approach* (pp. 121-152). San Fransisco: Freeman.

Diekhoff, G. M. (1983). Relationship judgments in the evaluation of structural understanding. *Journal of Educational Psychology, 75*, 227-233.

Eggen, P. D., Kauchak, D. P., & Kirk, S. (1978). The effect of hierarchical cues on the learning of concepts from prose materials. *Journal of Experimental Education, 46*(4), 7-11.

Hanf, M. B. (1971). Mapping: A technique for translating reading into thinking. *Journal of Reading, 14*, 225-230, 270.

Holley, C. D., & Dansereau, D. F. (1984). Networking: The technique and the empirical evidence. In C. D. Holley & D. F. Dansereau (Eds.), *Spatial learning strategies: Techniques, applications and related issues* (pp. 21-44). New York: Academic.

Interlink. (1990). *KNOT: Knowledge network organizing tool.* Las Cruces, NM: Interlink.

Johnson, D. D., Pittleman, S. D., Toms-Bronowski, S., & Levin, K. M. (1984). *An investigation of the effects of prior knowledge and vocabulary acquisition on passage comprehension* (Program Report, 84-85). Madison: Wisconsin Center for Educational Research.

Johnson, D. D., Toms-Bronowski, S., & Pittleman, S. D. (1982). *An investigation of the effectiveness of semantic mapping and semantic features analysis with intermediate grade level children.* (Program Report 83-3). Madison: Wisconsin Center for Educational Research, University of Wisconsin.

Johnson, P. E., Cox, D. L., & Curran, T. E. (1970). Psychological reality of physical concepts. *Psychometric Science, 19,* 245-247.

Jonassen, D. H. (1987). Assessing cognitive structure: Verifying a method using pattern notes. *Journal of Research and Development in Education. 20*(3), 1-14.

Jonassen, D. H., Beissner, K., & Yacci, M. A. (1993). *Structural knowledge: Techniques for representing, conveying, and acquiring structural knowledge.* Hillsdale, NJ: Lawrence Erlbaum Associates.

Jones, S. T. (1984). The effects of semantic mapping on vocabulary acquisition and reading comprehension of black inner-city students (Doctoral dissertation, University of Wisconsin, Madison). *Dissertation Abstracts International, 45,* 3061A.

Larkin, J. H., McDermott, J., Simon, D. P., & Simon, H. A. (1980). Models of competence in solving physics problems. *Cognitive Science, 4,* 317-345.

Mandler, J. (1983, August 26-30). *Stories: The function of structure.* Paper presented at the annual convention of the American Psychological Association, Anaheim, CA. (ERIC Document Reproduction Service No. ED 238 247)

Mirande, M. J. (1984). Schematizing: Techniques and applications. In C. D. Holley & D. F. Dansereau (Eds.). *Spatial learning strategies: Techniques, applications and related issues.* (pp. 233-256). New York: Academic.

Norman, D. A., Gentner, S., & Stevens, A. L. (1976). Comments on learning schemata and memory representation. In D. Klahr (Ed.), *Cognition and instruction* (pp. 137- 149). Hillsdale, NJ: Lawrence Erlbaum Associates.

Novak, J. D. (1980). Learning theory applied to the biology classroom. *The American Biology Teacher, 42,* 280-285.

Novak, J. D., & Gowin, D. B. (1984). *Learning how to learn.* Cambridge: Cambridge University Press.

Pittleman, S. D., Levin, K. M., & Johnson, D. D. (1985). *An investigation of two instructional settings in the use of semantic mapping with poor readers* (Program Report 85-84). Wisconsin Center for Educational Research.

Preece, P. F. W. (1976). Mapping cognitive structure: A comparison of methods. *Journal of Educational Psychology, 68,* 1-9.

Quillian, M. R. (1968). Semantic memory. In M. Minsky (Ed.), *Semantic information processing* (pp. 43 67). Cambridge, MA: MIT Press.

Robertson, W. C. (1990). Detection of cognitive structure with protocol data: Predicting performance on physics transfer problems. *Cognitive Science, 14*, 253-280.

Rumelhart, D. E. (1980). Schemata: The building blocks of cognition. In R. J. Spiro, B. C. Bruce, & W. F. Brewer (Eds.), *Theoretical issues in reading comprehension: Perspectives from cognitive psychology, linguistics, artificial intelligence, and education* (pp. 33-58). Hillsdale, NJ: Lawrence Erlbaum Associates.

Rumelhart, D. E., & Ortony, A. (1977). The representation of knowledge in memory. In R. C. Anderson, R. J. Spiro, & W. E. Montague (Eds.), *Theoretical issues in reading comprehension: Perspectives from cognitive psychology, linguistics, artificial intelligence, and education* (pp. 99-135). Hillsdale, NJ: Lawrence Erlbaum Associates.

Schvanenveldt, R. W., Durso, F. T., Goldsmith, T. E., Breen, T. J., Tucker, R. G., & DeMaio, J. C. (1985). *Measuring the structure of expertise.* Las Cruces: Computing Research Laboratory, New Mexico State University.

Shavelson, R. J. (1972). Some aspects of the correspondence between content structure and cognitive structure in physics instruction. *Journal of Educational Psychology, 63*, 225-234.

Shavelson, R. J. (1974). Methods for examining representations of subject matter structure in students' memory. *Journal of Research in Science Teaching, 11*, 231-249.

Shavelson, R. J. (1985, April 3). *The measurement of cognitive structure.* Paper presented at the annual convention of the American Educational Research Association, Chicago.

Sinatra, R. C., Berg, D., & Dunn, R. (1985). Semantic mapping improves reading comprehension of learning-disabled students. *Teaching Exceptional Children, 17*, 310-314.

Stanners, R. F., & Brown, L. T. (1982). Conceptual interrelationship on learning in introductory psychology. *Teaching of Psychology, 9(2)*, 74-77.

Stewart, J., Van Kirk, J., & Rowell, R. (1979). Concept maps: A tool for use in biology teaching. *The American Biology Teacher, 41*, 171-175.

Stewart, J. H. (1984). The representation of knowledge: Curricular and instructional implications for science teaching. In C. D. Holley & D. F. Dansereau (Eds.), *Spatial learning strategies: Techniques, applications and related issues* (pp. 101-122). New York: Academic.

Tennyson, R. D., & Cocciarella, M. J. (1986). An empirically based instructional design theory for teaching concepts. *Review of Educational Research, 56*, 40-71.

Toms-Bronowski, S. (1983). An investigation of the effectiveness of selected vocabulary teaching strategies with intermediate grade level children (Doctoral dissertation, University of Wisconsin, Madison, 1982). *Dissertation Abstracts International, 44*, 1405A.

Van Patten, J., Chao, C., & Reigeluth, C. M. (1986). A review of strategies for sequencing and synthesizing instruction. *Review of Educational Research, 56*, 437-471.

Bibliography

Alvermann, D. E. (1982). Restructuring text facilitates written recall of main ideas. *Journal of Reading, 25*, 754-758.

Alvermann, D. E., & Boothby, P. R. (1984). *Knowledge of text structure and its influence on a transfer task.* Paper presented at the annual meeting of the American Educational Research Association, New Orleans, LA. (ERIC Document Reproduction Service No. ED 243 081)

Anderson, T. H. (1979). Study skills and learning strategies. In H. F. O'Neil, Jr. & C. D. Spielberger (Eds.), *Cognitive and affective learning strategies* (pp. 77-97). New York: Academic.

Dansereau, D. F., Collins, K. W., McDonald, B. A., Holley, C. D., Garland, J. C., Diekhoff, G. M., & Evans, S. H. (1979). Development and evaluation of a learning strategy training program. *Journal of Educational Psychology, 71*, 64-73.

Holley, C. D., Dansereau, D. F., McDonald, B. A., Garland, J. C., & Collins, K. W. (1979). Evaluation of a hierarchical mapping technique as an aid to text processing. *Contemporary Educational Psychology, 4*, 227-237.

Jonassen, D. H. (1984). Developing a learning strategy using pattern notes: A new technology. *Programmed Learning and Educational Technology, 21*, 163-175.

Moore, D. W., & Readance, J. E. (1984). A quantitative and qualitative review of graphic organizer research. *Journal of Educational Research, 78*, 11-17.

Schvanenveldt, R. W., Durso, F. T., & Dearholt, D. W. (1985). *Pathfinder: Scaling with network structures.* (Memorandum in Computer and Cognitive Science, MCCS-85-9). Las Cruces: Computing Research Laboratory, New Mexico State University.

Author Index

Abel, F.J., 294, 297, *300*
Abrams, R.A., 339, *341*
Abramson, R., 419, 425, *427*
Acito, M., 226, *229*
Adams, V.M., 95, *98*
Adderholdt-Elliot, M., 403, 413, *414, 416*
Addy, M.M., 405, *415*
Agarwai, A., 389, 393, *396*
Akerstrom, S, 119, *121*
Alamo, L., 319, *321*
Albert, J., 113,114,115, *123*, 181, *187*, 226, 227, *230*
Alexander, C., 406, *414*
Alexander, C.J., 394, *396*
Alpert, R., 312, *321, 401*
Alvermann, D.E., 426, *430*, 444, *445, 448*
Amburgey, B.X., 156, 159, *162*, 334, 337, *341*
American College Testing Program, 241, *247*
Amerine, F.J., 444, *445*
Amernico, H.., 159, *160*
Anderson, A., 241, *246*, 359, *362*
Anderson, C., 156, *162*
Anderson, J.R., *430*
Anderson, R.C., 42, 421, 423, *427*
Anderson, T.H., *448*
Andrews, D.H., xiii, *xvii*
Andrews, J., 281, *287*
Annett, M., 226, *229*
Antonovitch, S., 195, *199*
Apicella, F.S., 347, *349*
Appelle, S., 183, *186, 188*
Argyris, C., *124*
Arlin, M., 131, *134*
Aronson, E., 386, *396*
Asch, S.E., 91, *102*
Ash, G., 115, *121*
Aster, D.J., 165, 167, *170*
Atchison, M.K., 297, *300*

Atkinson, G., 255, *260*
Atkinson, J.W., 381, 382, 384, 385, 387, 392, *396*, 399, 421, *427*
Ault, R.L., *124*
Ausburn, F., 221, *229*
Ausburn, F.B., 37, *41*, 173, *175*, 333, *340*
Ausburn, L., 221, *229*
Ausburn, L.J., 37, *41*, 173, *175*, 178, *186*, 333, *340*
Australian Council for Educational Research, 193, *198*
Axelrod, S., 91, *98*
Baehr, M.E., 90, *98*
Baird, R., 223, 224, 226, 227, *229*
Ballinger, F., 94, *100*
Baltes, P.B., 59, *61*
Banister, D., 152, *160*
Banta, T.J., 116, *121*
Bar-Tal, D., 15, *17*, 357, *362*
Bar-Zahor, Y., 5, *17*, 357, *362*
Barbe, W., 193, *199*
Barker, R.G., *350*
Barron, R.F., 444, *445*
Bartlett, F.C., 195, *198*, 421, *427*
Bass, R.K., *247*
Battistich, V.A., 390, *396*
Beaudry, J.S.., 242, *246*, 271, *275*
Beaule, B., 358, *362*
Bednar, R.L., 406, 409, 411, *414, 415*
Bee, H., 223, 224, 226, 227, *229*
Beechy, T.H., 159, *160*
Beissner, K., 420, *428*, 435, 436, *446*
Belz, E.J., 411, *414*
Bennett, G.K., 194, *198*
Berg, D., 444, *447*
Berkowitz, L., 155, *162*
Berliner, D.C., 24, 28, *31*, 381, 382, 383, 385, *397*
Beyerbach, B.A., 439, 443, *445*
Bhartiya, A., 373, *377*
Biaggio, A.M., 311, *321*
Biehler, R.F. , 382, 387, *396*

Subject Index